BRITISH COMIC

British Comics
A CULTURAL HISTORY

James Chapman

REAKTION BOOKS

For my parents

Published by Reaktion Books Ltd
33 Great Sutton Street
London EC1V 0DX, UK
www.reaktionbooks.co.uk

First published 2011

Copyright © James Chapman 2011

All rights reserved
No part of this publication may be reproduced, stored in a retrieval system, or transmitted, in any form or by any means, electronic, mechanical, photocopying, recording or otherwise, without the prior permission of the publishers.

Printed and bound in Great Britain
by CPI/Antony Rowe, Chippenham, Wiltshire

British Library Cataloguing in Publication Data
Chapman, James, 1968–
British comics : a cultural history.
1. Comic books, strips, etc.–Great Britain–History and criticism. 2. Comicbooks, strips, etc.–Social aspects–Great Britain–History. 3. Comic books, strips, etc.–Publishing–Great Britain–History.
I. Title
741.5'941-dc22

ISBN 978 1 86189 855 5

Contents

Introduction 7
1 Comic Cuts and Saucy Strips 16
2 On the Wings of Eagles 45
3 Ripping Yarns 76
4 Girls on Top 108
5 The Violent Years 125
6 I Am the Law! 144
7 The Strange World of the British Superhero 172
8 The Rise and Fall of Alternative Comics 200
9 The Growing Pains of British Comics 223
10 The British Comics Renaissance 242
References 258
Sources 289
Acknowledgements 292
Index 293

Introduction

> Comics have not yet arrived in the way that films and television have, accepted as a rational amusement for adults and a proper subject for academic study. Comics are still liable to be dismissed wholesale as trash, appropriate for weak or under-developed minds, and probably detrimental. Curiously enough much the same was said of the drama in Shakespeare's day and of the novel in Jane Austen's time.
> Paul Dawson.[1]

The comic strip, in Britain at least, has not been afforded even the grudging critical respect extended to other forms of popular visual culture such as films and television. This is not the case elsewhere. In France, for example, comics have long been accepted as a legitimate form of entertainment for children and adults alike, and the *bande dessinée* (literally meaning 'drawn strip') enjoys a degree of cultural legitimacy unprecedented elsewhere in the world: there is even a Centre National de la Bande Dessinée and state subsidy for comics to the tune of €4.5 million a year.[2] And in the United States, despite the onslaught once led upon them by Dr Fredric Wertham, comics are widely regarded as a vibrant form of mass popular culture, comparable to motion pictures as a medium that has provided entertainment for millions and has created a popular mythology attuned to ideological currents in American society.[3]

In Britain, however, comics remain beyond the pale, and scholarly attention has been thin on the ground. The work of Martin Barker and Roger Sabin represents the only sustained academic engagement with comics in Britain. I shall return to the work of these two scholars later. Even in the popular historiography, however, British comics have generally suffered in comparison with their French and American counterparts.[4] A parallel can be made here with the critical status of British cinema, which for many years was regarded as possessing neither the psychological depth of French cinema nor the uninhibited popular appeal of Hollywood. As Lindsay Anderson wrote in 1949:

> As, geographically, Britain is poised between continents, not quite Europe, and very far from America, so from certain points of view the British cinema seems to hover between the opposite poles of France and Hollywood. Our directors and producers never or rarely have the courage to tackle, in an adult manner, the completely adult subject: yet they lack also the flair for popular showmanship that is characteristic of the American cinema.[5]

The British comic, similarly, has never achieved the cultural cachet of the *bande dessinée*, but nor has it found a popular mythology equivalent to the American superhero tradition.

How can we explain the lack of critical interest in British comics? One reason is the view, perhaps more prevalent in Britain than elsewhere, that comics are an ephemeral medium that exist only to satisfy the immediate curiosity of their readers. This is a view that has been perpetuated by many comic creators. For example, Frank S. Pepper, a prolific writer of both prose and picture serials for juvenile periodicals, said: 'As I always saw it, and still do, I was producing something purely ephemeral. It was designed to amuse children and be forgotten when next week's instalment came out. It is disconcerting when grown-ups take it so seriously.'[6] Much the same view has been expressed by artist Phil Elliott, one of the leading proponents of the self-published 'Fast Fiction' comics of the 1980s: 'Comics should be enjoyed, well-thumbed, passed around – thrown away even. I simply can't get my head around this new trend in hermetically sealing comic books.'[7] Even Dez Skinn, the editor of *Warrior*, one of several attempts to create comics for mature readers in the 1980s, responded to one high-minded letter with the rhetorical question: 'Or are we the disposable ephemera we really should be? To be read, hopefully enjoyed, and then discarded.'[8]

Here there is a marked contrast with European comics, where it has been common practice for serials that have appeared originally in newspapers to be collected into hardcover albums for collectors. This trend began with Tintin, by the Belgian artist Hergé (Georges Rémi), who appeared first in a newspaper strip and then in a long series of albums beginning with *The Adventures of Tintin in the Land of the Soviets* in 1930. The Tintin albums became available in Britain from the 1950s, where they were sold in bookshops rather than in newsagents. In this context the Tintin albums may be seen as the first 'graphic novels'.[9]

Another barrier to taking comics seriously has been the perception, still widespread, that comics are only for children. The popular historiography of British comics privileges the 'classic' tradition exemplified by hardy perennial favourites such as *Dandy, Beano, Beezer, Topper, Eagle* and *Bunty*. This popular view maintains that characters like Rupert the Bear, Korky the Cat, Desperate Dan and Dennis the Menace represent an integral part of the British childhood experience. Consider, for example, the catalogue produced for an exhibition of British comics at Bath in 1971, which declared that 'the sense of healthy effervescent delight evoked by the deft pens of the great masters of the British Comic are part of our national heritage and a basic and happily stable part of almost every child's life and memory.'[10] The view that comics rightfully belong to a lost world of childhood innocence has often been invoked when they have come under the scrutiny of the media. In 1976, for example, when the new juvenile boys' comic *Action* came under sustained attack for its violent and anti-authoritarian content, Denis Gifford, the doyen of British comic historians, was called upon to provide a counter view of what comics should be like: 'I look back to the days of my youth when comics were things of joy and pleasure rather than blood and guts. My own favourite was the one called *Happy Days*... Nothing but fun from beginning to end.'[11] As for the notion of adult comics – an idea pursued with varying degrees of success by publishers in the 1980s – this was roundly dismissed by the newspaper columnist Julie Burchill: 'Comic books for adults is a complete contradiction in terms, as anyone who reads comics is *not* an adult and should have their voting rights removed ASAP.'[12]

In Britain, furthermore, the cultural status of comics has undoubtedly suffered from their association with America. A distaste for all things popular and American has long been a characteristic of intellectual culture in Britain, evident on both the intellectual left and the intellectual right, and there is nothing manifestly both more popular and more American than comic books. In *The Uses of Literacy*, for example, Richard Hoggart lamented the Americanization of British culture and pointed the finger at comics in particular:

> At the lowest level this is illustrated in the sales here of the American or American-type serial-books of comics, where for page after page big-thighed and big-bosomed girls from Mars step out of their space-machines, and gangsters' molls scream away in high-powered sedans. Anyone who sees something of Servicemen's reading, of the popularity of American and English comics (with the cruder English boys' comics serving their turn where the supply of hotter material runs out) knows something of this.

> The process continues, for a substantial number of adults especially; a passive taking-on of bad mass art geared to a very low mental age.[13]

The view that American comics were polluting the minds and corrupting the morals of their British readers (including some adults) was a major factor in the campaign in the early 1950s to ban a certain type of publication (so-called 'horror comics') that ultimately resulted in the passing of the Children and Young Persons (Harmful Publications) Act in 1955.[14]

However, there are counter arguments in response to each of these points. Against the low critical status of British comics we can set the fact that Britain can claim talent to match the best in the world. There will never be critical consensus as to the best comic strip artist: individual styles and different national traditions are simply too diverse to allow meaningful comparison. But many (including myself) maintain that Frank Hampson deserves a place in the pantheon: the sheer visual imagination of his strip 'Dan Dare – Pilot of the Future', which he drew for the boys' paper *Eagle* in the 1950s, has rarely been equalled. In comic fandom, moreover, British writer Alan Moore enjoys a particularly privileged reputation. To a greater degree than any other writer, Moore is regarded as having brought a level of psychological complexity and critical respectability to the comic book through an extensive body of work that includes *Miracleman, V for Vendetta, Watchmen* and *From Hell* – all landmarks in the history of the medium. It seems something of a paradox that a nation where comics have been so marginalized has nevertheless produced one of the most acclaimed artists and by common consent the most influential modern comic writer.

Against the supposedly ephemeral nature of the medium we can set the fact that many British comics have enjoyed extraordinary longevity. *Dandy* and *Beano*, which first appeared in 1937 and 1938 respectively, and which are still published today, can lay claim to being the longest running comics in continuous production in the history of the medium. (*Detective Comics* in the United States also began in 1937, but like most American comic books it was published quarterly, whereas *Dandy* and *Beano* have appeared weekly, except during the Second World War when they were fortnightly.) Other enduring titles have included *Topper* (1953–90), *Tiger* (1954–85), *Beezer* (1956–90), *Bunty* (1958–2001), *Judy* (1960–91), *Victor* (1961–92), *Commando* (1961–) and *2000AD* (1977–). Frank S. Pepper may have maintained that his writing was ephemeral, but in 'Roy of the Rovers' he created one of the great icons of British comic history: Roy Race of Melchester Rovers made his First Division debut in 1954 and did not hang up his boots until 1993. His retirement made national headlines.[15]

The view that comics are only for children, moreover, does not stand up to scrutiny. The first comics to appear in Britain in the late nineteenth century were intended primarily as leisure reading for adults; only later, as publishers realized they were also widely read among children, were comics geared specifically towards younger readers. And, even if most comics have been intended for juveniles, the letters pages of boys' papers such as *Eagle* and *Battle* provide anecdotal evidence that they were also read by fathers, uncles and elder brothers. Furthermore, there has been a long tradition of comics for adult readers, from the radical, underground 'comix' of the 1970s to the emergence of more mainstream titles in the 1980s including *Warrior*, *Crisis*, *Deadline* and *Revolver*. The work of contemporary British comic writers such as Pat Mills, Alan Grant, Alan Moore, Steve Moore, Peter Milligan, Grant Morrison, Neil Gaiman, Warren Ellis and Garth Ennis demonstrates a level of emotional maturity and intellectual sophistication that indicates an assumed adult readership.

As for their association with American popular culture, this is to ignore the fact that it was in Britain that the first comics appeared. The consensus among comic historians is that *Ally Sloper's Half-Holiday* (1884–1914) was the first modern comic in that it featured picture strips and a recurring character. The British comic really took shape in the 1890s with Alfred Harmsworth's *Comic Cuts* and *Illustrated Chips*, which established the style and format of the medium for a generation. In America the history of comics took another direction with the advent of newspaper strips such as 'The Yellow Kid' (1896) and 'Krazy Kat' (1913). The first American 'comic books' in the 1930s were reprints of newspaper strips – *Funnies on Parade* and *Famous Funnies* were the first – but it was towards the end of the decade that superheroes and crime-fighters emerged into the popular consciousness through titles such as *Action Comics* (where Superman made his debut in 1938) and *Detective Comics* (which saw the first appearance of Batman in 1939). At this time most British comics were 'funnies' for younger children: adventure comics did not really emerge until after the Second World War. While some American comic books arrived with GIs during the war it was not until the end of the 1950s that they became widely available in Britain. The 'American-type' comics to which Hoggart took such exception were in fact mostly British reprints of US titles.

The premise of this book is that British comics represent a distinct mode of cultural practice in their own right and that they deserve to be afforded the same critical attention as their American and European counterparts. But why should historians be concerned with the comic antics of Ally Sloper or the extraordinary adventures of Dan Dare? It is my contention that comics, like other popular media including cinema, television and popular literature, are a valuable but neglected source of social history that provide insights into the societies and cultures in which they were produced and consumed. The 'historical turn' in cultural studies has focused attention on the relationship between popular culture and its historical contexts. On the one hand popular culture has been seen as an instrument of social control: it is one of the means through which members of society are instructed in appropriate values, attitudes and behaviour. On the other hand popular culture has been seen as a mirror or reflection of society: it responds to the cultural tastes and social values of its consumers. A historical approach to the study of popular culture understands that it is both a product of social processes and that it also plays a role in constructing social values.

The fact that historically the main consumers of comics have been children makes them all the more potent a form of popular culture. There can be little doubt that comics have played some role in shaping the imaginative lives of British children for much of the twentieth century. It is customary in historical studies of British popular culture to cite George Orwell's famous essay on 'Boys' Weeklies', published in *Horizon* in 1940, in which he asserted:

> Most people are influenced far more than they would care to admit by novels, serial stories, films and so forth, and from this point of view the worst books are often the most important because they are usually the ones that are read earliest in life. It is probable that many people who would consider themselves extremely sophisticated and 'advanced' are actually carrying through life an imaginative background which they acquired in childhood . . .[16]

Orwell was writing about story papers such as *Gem*, *Magnet*, *Adventure*, *Wizard*, *Rover* and *Hotspur*, but his comments could apply equally to comics, not least because several story papers, including *School Friend* and *Hotspur*, reinvented themselves as picture papers during the 1950s, and many favourite characters who had first appeared in story papers, including Billy Bunter of Greyfriars School and super-athlete Wilson of the *Wizard*, would make the transition to picture strips as the story papers declined in popularity after the Second World War.

There has in fact been a substantial body of research into the role of juvenile fiction as a vehicle of social education and ideological instruction. Juvenile periodicals such as the *Boy's Own Paper* and *Girl's Own Paper* have been analysed for their representation of codes of masculinity and femininity; the school stories of Angela Brazil and Frank Richards have been shown to offer their readers instruction in appropriate social values and behaviour;

and the adventure stories of writers such as G. A. Henty and F. S. Brereton have been seen as vehicles for promoting ideologies of popular imperialism and militarism.[17] However, much of this work focuses exclusively on prose fiction: where comics are included it is usually only as a coda to the 'golden age' of the story papers between *c.* 1880 and 1940. This may be due in part to the methodological uncertainty of many historians in handling visual sources rather than written texts. Or, as in the case of Owen Dudley Edwards, there is an assumption that the picture strip in some way lacks the ideological import of the prose story: 'Any social influence *Adventure* and the other Thomson papers had over their readers – and without going to Orwell's lengths I think it was considerable – must have dropped sharply with the incursion of tabloids [*sic*] in *Adventure*, and later in the rest.'[18]

While a view has persisted that comics are inferior to prose fiction, and that they are detrimental to good reading habits among children, this is to read comics as literature rather than as a medium in their own right where meaning is conveyed through both image and text. Comics have their own formal codes and representational conventions that should be seen as different from, rather than inferior to, prose fiction. This point was recognized by *The Times Literary Supplement* in its review of an international exhibition of comic art at the Institute of Contemporary Arts in London in 1971: 'The best thing about the comics is not the Aaarghs, Pows and Slurps which bring them near to the currently art-inspired world of advertising and packaging, but the narrative ingenuity, the sometimes brilliantly condensed language, and the exercise of fantasy within simplified, almost classical conventions'.[19]

The aim of this book is to document the history of British comics as a social practice. To this extent it builds upon the work of two pioneering studies of British comics. Martin Barker's book *Comics: Ideology, Power and the Critics* (1989) developed from his previous research into the horror comics campaign, published in *A Haunt of Fears* (1984), to examine debates around the assumed effects of comics on their readers. Barker's case studies of the ideological strategies and readerships of different comic genres – including funnies (*Beano*), boys' adventure (*Action*), girls' fantasy (*Bunty*) and romance (*Jackie*) – provide convincing evidence that comics cannot simply be read either as straightforward top-down assertions of a dominant ideology or as unmediated reflections of their social contexts. It is a book that raises more questions than it answers; but what Barker shows is that responses to comics are more diverse, even contradictory, than most theories of culture and ideology would allow.[20] Roger Sabin's *Adult Comics* (1993) is a more general historical survey of the production and consumption of comics for adult readers that focuses in large measure on the British context. Sabin contends that adult comics did not begin with the graphic novels of the 1980s as has so often been assumed. He traces their origin to the first comics at the end of the nineteenth century and in so doing maps 'a rich and complex history of adult comics stretching back over a century'.[21] He also reminds us that the history of British comics cannot be understood in isolation from the wider history of comics in Britain: to understand the development of a distinctively British comic culture we must also consider the influence upon it of both American comics and other forms such as the *bande dessinée* and Japanese *manga*.

British Comics: A Cultural History attempts to combine Sabin's broad chronological approach, extended to included juvenile and adolescent comics as well as adult comics, with Barker's close reading of specific examples. I have set out to map the history of the British comic from its origins to the present. This has inevitably involved a large degree of selection, omission and elision. I will freely admit that my own tastes and interests hold sway: thus more attention is devoted to adventure comics than to funnies and boys' titles receive a bigger slice of the cake than girls' comics.[22] And I have concentrated for the most part on the weekly picture-strip papers: the history of the newspaper comic strip remains to be written.[23]

At this point it becomes necessary to explain my methodology and critical approach. This book is a cultural history of British comics: that is to say it seeks to place British comics in their historical contexts of production and consumption and to understand their place in the wider society and culture of which they are part. I am interested not so much in the evaluation of comics as an art form but rather to understand what comics can tell us about society. The relationship between comics and their historical contexts is complex. To see comics as a straightforward reflection or mirror of society is too simplistic: this does not take account of the formal codes and conventions through which they create meaning. At the same time it seems axiomatic that comics are informed by and respond to the cultural conditions and ideological climate in which they are produced. To this extent my approach is closer to the work of American comic historians such as Bradford W. Wright and William W. Savage than to much of the heavily (one might say over) theorized work on the *bande dessinée* with its emphasis on semiotics and linguistics. The reader will search in vain for references to Lévi-Strauss, Barthes or Saussure. It is my firm conviction that abstract theoretical models are of limited value in understanding the social processes involved in the study of popular culture. Instead I have focused throughout on the primary sources: the comics themselves.[24]

My reading of comics is very much from the perspective of a cultural historian. I have set out to chart trends and themes, to identify patterns and structures, and to account for the emergence (and disappearance) of particular forms and genres. In analysing the ideologies and social politics of comics – including their representations of nationhood, class, gender and ethnicity – I have sought to read them historically as products of their time. I have considered the institutional contexts in which comics were produced, examining structural and technological changes in the comic publishing industry. And, where primary sources are available, I have looked at the popular reception of comics and the nature of their readership. This is the most difficult area of the study from a methodological perspective: the sources are very patchy and need to be approached with caution. It cannot be assumed, for example, that the letters printed in comics constitute a representative sample of their readers' views. Nevertheless, letters are valuable as evidence of the responses of actual readers rather than abstract theoretical readers 'constructed' by the text. If they demonstrate one thing above all it is that young people can be highly discerning consumers: no amount of free gifts and slick production values can sell a comic if it does not meet the tastes and interests of its readers.

Finally, I should make it clear that I hold no moral view or ideological position on the thorny issue of the effects of popular media on its audiences. At various times in their history comics have been attacked as immoral, corrupting, harmful, pernicious or simply downright 'bad' influences on children. There has been much impassioned debate around this subject: the evidence remains inconclusive. The task of the historian is to see through the fog and to rely on evidence rather than polemic. My aim throughout has been to analyse what comics tell us about their producers, their readers, and their society and culture. In so doing I hope that I have also managed to convey some of the pleasure to be gained from reading comics and to account for the special place they have held in British popular culture.

CHAPTER ONE

Comic Cuts and Saucy Strips

> Well do I recollect walking down Fleet Street with Alfred [Harmsworth] on the day when *Comic Cuts* was published, and witnessing the speed with which the hawkers were selling it. In a fortnight's time the brothers knew the result of their second venture – it was already showing a profit of twenty-five thousand pounds per annum.
>
> Max Pemberton.[1]

All histories have to begin somewhere, and the history of the British comic, so far as it can be said to have a point of origin, begins in the late nineteenth century with the emergence of the first mass-produced comic papers intended as cheap amusement for the working classes. It is customary in most histories of comics to identify their origins in previous forms of popular visual culture. The satirical cartoons of artists such as William Hogarth (1697–1764), James Gillray (1757–1815) and George Cruikshank (1792–1878), for example, pioneered some of the techniques later associated with the comic strip, including the use of speech balloons.[2] Cartoon prints were originally reproduced through copper plate engravings and were known as 'comic cuts' – a 'cut' being a colloquial term for an engraving – until the development of lithography in the 1820s (a chemical process that allowed multiple facsimile reproductions without any deterioration in quality) meant they could be disseminated more widely. The market for lithographs ranged from expensive prints selling for a shilling or more to cheap broadsheets at one penny intended for wider circulation. The practice of binding a series of sheets together gave rise in the 1840s to illustrated magazines such as *Punch*, the *Illustrated London News* and the *Pictorial Times*. The new pictorial papers proved popular with their mostly middle-class readers, though some commentators disliked them as being vulgar and immature. William Wordsworth was moved to express his distaste in verse:

> A backward movement surely we have here,
> From manhood – back to childhood; for the age –
> Back towards caverned life's first rude career.
> Avaunt this vile abuse of pictured page![3]

This may be the first instance of scorn and disgust being directed against the new medium: as we shall see it would not be the last.

Punch, which was modelled on the French *Le Figaro* and published continually for a century and a half from 1841, was a satirical monthly magazine that included a mixture of topical cartoons and prose features. It showcased the work of cartoonists such as John Leech, Richard Doyle and John Tenniel. Its success persuaded other publishers that a similar market for humour magazines might exist among the working and lower-middle classes. Hence the emergence of cheaper and more populist *Punch* imitators including *Fun*, first published in 1861, *Comic News* in 1864, *Judy* in 1867 and *Funny Folks* in 1874. Denis Gifford nominates *Funny Folks* ('A Weekly Budget of Funny Pictures, Funny Notes, Funny Jokes, Funny Stories') as 'the first publication to meet the criteria of a comic'.[4] However, the early history of the comic is better understood not in terms of 'firsts', but rather as an evolutionary process in which the form and conventions of the medium took shape across a range of publications.

The contexts for the emergence of the comic were two historical processes in late Victorian Britain: the growth of the mass-circulation popular press and the transformation of working-class popular culture. The comic is a mass medium and, for all that its origins may extend back to cartoons and broadsheets, the existence of a cheap mass-circulation press was a necessary pre-condition for its existence. The abolition of stamp duty on the press in 1855 – the so-called 'taxes on knowledge' – and the repeal of paper excise duty in 1861 meant that publishers were able to reduce the price of newspapers and bring them within the range of the working classes. At the same time the adoption of new printing technologies including mechanical typesetting and the rotary press speeded up the publishing process and enabled the production of large print runs. Edward Lloyd, publisher of *Lloyd's Weekly News*, was the first British publisher to adopt the rotary press machine, developed by the American Richard Hoe, in 1856. Finally, the expansion of the railways and the appearance of wholesale newsagents such as W. H. Smith made nationwide distribution possible for the first time. The railway kiosk was particularly important for sales of early comics: comics came to be known as 'railway literature' as they were ideal for reading during a journey.[5]

The rise of the mass-circulation press coincided with a process that historians have termed the 'remaking' of the working classes.[6] There is a broad consensus among historians that the British working classes became more conservative during this period: the failure of Chartism in the 1840s had weakened the cause of political radicalism, while the extension of the franchise in 1867 and 1884 brought the urban working classes and rural labourers into the political process. At the same time the combination of rising wages and the shortening of the working week meant that leisure and recreation assumed greater significance. Put simply the late Victorian working classes had more disposable income and more time for recreation. A new leisure economy emerged to cater for this market: this was the period that saw the rise of seaside resorts, excursion trains, music halls and mass-spectator sport. In particular the high levels of both adult and juvenile literacy – largely, though not exclusively, a consequence of the Education Act of 1870 which empowered local boards to establish schools funded by the rate-payer – created a large market for cheap reading matter. As the future press baron Alfred Harmsworth observed in 1885: 'The Board schools are turning out hundreds of thousands of boys and girls annually who are anxious to read. They do not care for the ordinary newspaper . . . but will read anything which is simple and sufficiently interesting.'[7]

The first to recognize the existence of a new mass market were small entrepreneurial publishers such as Edwin J. Brett, George Newnes, James Henderson and Gilbert Dalziel. All these were responsible for periodicals that, while not comics in the full sense, included some of the features that would come to characterize the British comic. Brett specialized in story papers for adolescent boys: his many periodicals included *Boys of England* (1866–99), *Young Men of Great Britain* (1874–83) and *Boy's Comic Journal* (1883–94). Brett's papers aimed at a working-class market: they were cheaper and more populist than middle-class rivals such as Samuel Beeton's *Boy's Own Magazine* (1855–74) or the Religious Tract Society's *Boy's Own Paper* (1879–1967) but were still a cut above the notorious 'penny dreadfuls' put out by more down-market publishers such as the Emmetts and Charles Fox.[8] *Boy's Comic Journal*, despite its title, was an adventure story paper rather than a comic paper, though it included reprints of cartoons and funny strips from American and European sources.

A more direct line of descent to the comic was represented by George Newnes's *Tit-Bits*, launched in 1881. Newnes pioneered so-called 'scrapbook journalism': he realized the long paragraphs and dense text of most newspapers were not conducive to quick, throwaway reading and so produced a paper that consisted of short, gossipy items pasted together from other sources. *Tit-Bits* also used competitions and prizes to boost its circulation – a strategy that would later be adopted by many comics. It was followed by various imitators, including Alfred Harmsworth's *Answers to Correspondents* and

C. A. Pearson's *Pearson's Weekly*. A Salford newsagent remarked of the customers who bought these magazines: 'Reading don't matter that much. What does count is the chance of getting something for nothing, £10 notes from tram tickets, gold watches for naming football winners.'[9]

James Henderson entered the field with the Manchester-based *Weekly Budget* in 1861 before moving to London where he published the comic papers *Funny Folks* (1874–94) and *Scraps* (1883–1910) as well as a range of juvenile fiction. *Funny Folks* declared its intention in its first editorial which offered readers 'plenty that is amusing; nothing that is ill-natured. A penny invested in a copy will serve a good evening's amusement; pictures to puzzle at; jokes to laugh at; caricatures to ponder; [and] tales to stimulate interest.'[10] *Scraps* was rather like a pictorial *Tit-Bits*, a collage culled from overseas magazines such as *La Caricature* and *Harper's Weekly*. It was the success of Henderson's comic papers that prompted Gilbert Dalziel to launch *Ally Sloper's Half-Holiday* (1884–1914), which described itself as 'A Selection, Side-splitting, Sentimental, and Serious, for the Benefit of Old Boys, Young Boys, Odd Boys generally, and even Girls'. *Ally Sloper's Half-Holiday* resembled other humour magazines in that it included cartoons, picture strips and prose, but what differentiated it from other periodicals was that it was the first comic paper built around a recurring character. Roger Sabin considers it 'the first modern comic'.[11]

Largely forgotten today, except among a small band of aficionados, Ally Sloper was, in his day, as much an icon of late Victorian popular culture as Sherlock Holmes or W. G. Grace. Ally Sloper was not only the first comic-strip character to feature in his own self-titled magazine but was also the first to generate spin-off merchandizing including mugs, watches, postcards and figures. The character's visibility in popular culture is suggestive of a wide appeal. His admirers included H. G. Wells, who referred to Sloper as 'the urban John Bull'.[12] Another contemporary commentator, the American critic Elizabeth Pennell, described Sloper as 'an original creation in this age of imitation . . . the great modern jester or popular type of England'.[13] Ally Sloper is both a reflection of social changes during the late Victorian period and a product of those processes: as such he is a figure of considerable cultural interest.

In fact the character of Ally Sloper pre-dated the paper named in his honour by a full seventeen years. The original Ally Sloper appeared in strip-cartoon form in the magazine *Judy* between 1867 and 1882. Sloper was created by British novelist Charles Ross and drawn by his French cartoonist wife Emilie de Tessier under the pseudonym Marie Duval. The strips are relatively unsophisticated and are best described as a sequence of cartoons rather than as a sequential narrative. In this incarnation Sloper is a ne'er-do-well whose ragged appearance and pecuniary state suggest the influence of Charles Dickens's Mr Micawber. Most episodes feature Sloper and his friend Iky Mo (Isaac Moses – a crude Jewish stereotype) hatching various get-rich-quick schemes which invariably backfire and land them in trouble: offering cheap loans without security or selling shoddy consumer goods.

The early Ally Sloper has been understood as a caricature of the Victorian work ethic. He represents everything that the hard-working, respectable working classes should not be: feckless, work-shy, a scrounger and a rogue. He makes his living as a conman and is entirely without scruple: he has no qualms about seeing his wife and children sent to the workhouse and on more than one occasion he collects his wife's funeral expenses from unsuspecting benefit societies. Even his name is a punning reference to the habit of 'sloping' off down the alley to avoid paying the rent. Sloper embodies the vices most associated with the 'rough' working classes. He is a drunkard and indulges in loutish behaviour: he often finds himself before the magistrate for public drunkenness. This Sloper is a social deviant, but his comical ineptitude renders him a safe deviant: there is none of the danger associated with brutal Victorian low-life villains such as Dickens's Fagin or Bill Sykes. To this extent Sloper might be seen as the archetype of any number of working-class 'loveable rogues' from Andy Capp of the *Daily Mirror* to Del Boy Trotter in the sitcom *Only Fools and Horses*.[14]

Sloper's early appearances in *Judy* were sporadic, but became more frequent from 1869 when Ross assumed editorship of the magazine. However, it was Gilbert Dalziel, whose family bought *Judy* in 1872, who most recognized the commercial potential of the character. The Dalziels, engravers who moved into publishing, were representative of the small family businesses who prospered in the commercial press before the rise of the press barons. Dalziel published reprints of the Sloper strips in book form – including *Ally Sloper: A Moral Lesson* (1873), *Ally Sloper's Book of Beauty* (1877), *Ally Sloper's Guide to the Paris Exhibition* (1878) and *The Ups and Downs of Ally Sloper* (1882) – before launching the character in his own title. The new Ally Sloper was drawn first by W. G. Baxter, whose style revealed the influence of *Punch* in its fine cross-hatching, and then, following Baxter's death in 1888, by W. F. Thomas, who continued until the paper ceased publication in 1914. Strictly speaking the new Sloper appeared in cartoons rather than sequential picture strips – each issue of the paper featured a large single-panel cartoon on the front page – though elsewhere in the paper there were strips (including reprints from *Judy*). Within two years of its launch, *Ally Sloper's Half-Holiday* boasted 'the Largest Circulation of any Illustrated Paper in Great Britain'. This was due in no small measure to Dalziel's innovative marketing: he undercut his twopenny rivals by pricing it at one penny and made extensive

Ally Sloper was a participant in the late Victorian leisure economy, here on a day trip to Margate. *Ally Sloper's Half-Holiday* (Dalziel Brothers, 20 June 1885).

use of prizes, giveaways and gimmicks such as the offer of free life insurance in the event of a railway accident.[15]

It is the Sloper of *Ally Sloper's Half-Holiday* who is now regarded as the definitive version of the character.[16] While there are still traces of his roguish past, such as advising readers to help themselves to the paper while the newsagent's back is turned, the new Sloper is characterized as a 'gent' or a 'swell': he has acquired a mock-gentrified appearance and the social milieu in which he moves suggests a degree of upward mobility. He has become less of a working-class rogue and more of an everyman character whose soubriquet is 'Friend of Man' – abbreviated to 'F.O.M.' in what was possibly a reference to the 'G.O.M.' ('Grand Old Man'), the popular nickname of Prime Minister

William Gladstone. Indeed, Sloper stood for Parliament (campaigning on a platform of no work and no taxes) and was elected as Member for Shoe Lane; later he was ennobled as Baron Sloper of Mildew Court.[17]

Peter Bailey has argued that *Ally Sloper's Half-Holiday* 'creates its own symbolic and ideological world' and that in particular it 'celebrates leisure as a new area for adventure and fulfilment, a self-contained world of experience in which the individual can fashion a way of life of his or her own choosing'.[18] Sloper has shifted from a work-shy rascal to a man of some social means who is to be found enjoying the new leisure economy of late Victorian Britain. He has become a fixture of the London 'season' (Ascot, the Derby, the Boat Race, the Henley Regatta, the Lord Mayor's Show) and is often to be found on seasonal excursions to seaside resorts around the country including Margate, Brighton, Blackpool and Scarborough. *Ally Sloper's Half-Holiday* (the title of course is a reference to the institution of the Saturday half-day holiday) represents the spaces of leisure as classless: spaces where folk from all strata of society mingle on equal terms. Thus Sloper can be found in the Royal Enclosure at Ascot and is even on nodding terms with the Prince of Wales: the humour arises in large measure from the incongruity of a character like Sloper hob-nobbing with royalty and aristocracy.

While it is difficult to establish with any certainty the circulation of *Ally Sloper's Half-Holiday* – the oft-cited figure of 350,000 copies a week does not seem to have any source – there is, nevertheless, evidence to suggest that its readership extended across social classes.[19] For the lower classes, Sloper offered the possibility of social mobility and political inclusion: to this extent it is significant (if entirely coincidental) that his first appearance in 1867 and his reappearance in a new guise in 1884 coincided with the extension of the franchise under the Second and Third Reform Acts. For the middle and upper classes, however, Sloper offers reassurance that social democratization will not fundamentally alter the status quo. The point of Sloper is that he aspires to the life of a gentleman of leisure even if his behaviour remains plebeian: he is certainly no class warrior. For social historians J. M. Golby and A. W. Purdue, Sloper 'celebrated the undeserving common man, his sexual fantasies and his desire for life to be a perpetual half-holiday. He was no threat to society but neither was he a suitable subject for reform.'[20] *Ally Sloper's Half-Holiday* reflects the conservatism and consensus politics of late Victorian Britain in which all members of society are able to participate in the new leisure economy. It is for this reason that Sloper's popularity extended across classes from artisans and clerks (judging by the professions cited by winners of competitions in the paper) to members of the intelligentsia such as the artist Sir Edward Burne-Jones.

* * *

Illustrated Chips (Amalgamated Press, 21 December 1918).

While the success of *Ally Sloper's Half-Holiday* revealed the existence of a market for cheap comic papers, it was in the 1890s that comics genuinely became a mass medium. There were several attempts at launching Sloper imitators, such as the short-lived *'Arry's Budget* (1886) and *C. H. Ross's Variety Paper* (1887–8). The latter came from Sloper's original creator who had lost control of the character: it folded within a year. The *annus mirabilis* of the Victorian comic, however, came in 1890 when four new papers – Alfred Harmsworth's *Comic Cuts* and *Illustrated Chips* (both 1890–1953), James Henderson's *Snap Shots* (1890–1910) and Trapps, Holmes & Co.'s *Funny Cuts* (1890–1908) – were launched within the space of three months. The immediate success of *Comic Cuts* ('One Hundred Laughs for One Halfpenny!') opened the floodgates for a veritable tsunami of halfpenny comics over the next decade including Harmsworth's *Funny Wonder* (1893–1901) and *Comic Home Journal* (1895–1904), Murray Ford's *Joker* (1891–6), Trapps, Holmes & Co.'s *World's Comic* (1892–1908) and *Coloured Comic* (1898–1906), James Henderson's *Nuggets* (1892–1905) and *Comic Life* (1899–1928), Gilbert Dalziel's *Larks!* (1893–1902), C. A. Pearson's *Big Budget* (1897–1909) and George Newnes's *Halfpenny Comic* (1898–1906). And these were only the most successful titles: dozens of others started only to fold within a few weeks as the market became saturated.[21]

The comics boom of the 1890s coincided with – indeed to a large extent it was an outcome of – structural change in the newspaper and periodical publishing industry. The 'halfpenny revolution' was led by the Harmsworth brothers who represented a new model of highly capitalized

10. But the intruders were neither policemen nor burglars, but the owner of the flat and his gallant soldier son just back from the Rhine. "Now, I'll just show you how we won the war, dad, and made the world safe for democracy." Then he got busy with the flags.

11. "Wow," yapped Willie. "I'm stung to the quick! What's happening in Russia now? Is it them Bolsheviks again?" "Europe's getting too hot for me, boy!" bleated Tim. "Let's get back to dear old Blighty, shall us?" But young Reggie went on with his war lecture—

press ownership that superseded small family publishers at the end of the nineteenth century. Alfred Harmsworth (1865–1922) was the son of an Irish barrister who set out to become a journalist, working briefly for both James Henderson and George Newnes before launching *Answers to Correspondents*, his own rival to Newnes's *Tit-Bits*, in 1888. While Alfred provided the imagination and flair, his brother Harold (1868–1940) possessed the shrewd business acumen to steer the growth of their publishing empire. The Harmsworths began by publishing periodicals, adding several story papers including *Marvel* (1893–1922), *Union Jack* (1894–1933), *Pluck* (1894–1916) and *Boys' Friend* (1895–1927) to their comics. The Harmsworth titles were enormously successful: *Comic Cuts* sold 118,000 of its first issue and soon established a regular circulation of 300,000, *Marvel* sold 120,000 copies in its first week and *Boys' Friend* sold 205,000.[22] It was the success of their comics and story papers that laid the foundations of the Harmsworth press empire: Alfred founded the *Daily Mail* in 1896 and the *Daily Mirror* in 1903 and became proprietor of *The Times* in 1908.[23]

The rise of the Harmsworths to a position of market dominance was the outcome of a number of factors. They started out as a family business not unlike their competitors but grew to a large corporation in the form of the Amalgamated Press which consolidated their various enterprises. They had a shrewd sense of their market – working-class young adult males – and they invested their profits from one venture into the next. Their marketing strategy was based on extensive advertising across all their titles and on undercutting their competitors in price. It is reported that news sellers were initially unwilling to take *Comic Cuts* because they could not imagine making a profit with a cover price of only half a penny. Alfred Harmsworth made the price a major part of his marketing strategy by persuading the reader that he was getting more for less. Consider, for example, his editorial in the first issue of *Comic Cuts*:

'Weary Willie and Tired Tim' in *Illustrated Chips* (Amalgamated Press, 21 December 1918).

> Remember the following facts about *Comic Cuts*. It is as large as any penny paper of the kind published; this you can prove by measurement. It employs the best artists, is printed on good paper, is published every Thursday, will give big prizes, is the first halfpenny illustrated ever issued, and has plenty of money behind it. How is it possible for anyone to produce an illustrated paper, containing nearly fifty pictures, over eighteen thousand words, and many valuable prizes, for a halfpenny? Well, it is possible, but that is all.[24]

In fact it was possible to produce the paper at such a low price only by cutting costs to the bone – the claim about good-quality paper was manifestly untrue – and by reprinting material from other publications. No matter: the strategy worked.

Comic Cuts established the template for most late Victorian and Edwardian comics: it was tabloid sized, eight pages, and consisted of a mixture of picture strips, cartoons and text. As the decade wore on the amount of pictorial content in the papers increased. The demand for new pictorial material saw the emergence of the first recognized comic strip artists such as Jack Butler Yates (son of the renowned portrait painter J. B. Yates and nephew of the poet W. B. Yates) who drew 'Chubblock Holmes' (a burlesque of Arthur Conan Doyle's Sherlock Holmes stories then appearing in the *Strand Magazine*) for *Comic Cuts* from 1893. The first real 'star', however, was Tom Browne, whose 'Weary Willie and Tired Tim' first appeared in *Illustrated Chips* in 1896. The misadventures of these two endearing tramps (modelled on Don Quixote and Sancho Panza) proved so popular that they were copied by others: the many imitators included 'Nobbler and Jerry' of *Funny Cuts*, 'Airy Alf and Bouncing Billy' of *Big Budget* and 'Lanky Larry and Bloated Bill' of the *Comic Home Journal*. Browne was in such demand that he could command an extraordinary salary of £150 a week: he even went to the United

States for a while as cartoonist for the *Chicago Daily Tribune*. However, Browne was very much an exception: most artists were poorly paid and did not receive credit for their work. When Browne died in 1910, 'Weary Willie and Tired Tim' was continued by Percy Cocking who drew the strip for another 43 years but was never allowed to sign his work.[25]

The emergence of comics as a mass medium in the 1890s needs to be seen alongside other forms of visual culture. Comics were part of what Simon Popple, the historian of early popular visual culture, has termed the 'representational nexus' alongside photography and the cinema (known at the time as the 'kinematograph' or 'kinema').[26] It has been argued that a series of technological developments towards the end of the nineteenth century – including half-tone photographic reproduction and the advent of moving-image photography – resulted in a fundamental shift in visual culture. These developments ran in parallel with urbanization and the rise of the modern city: a major theme of new photographic illustrated papers such as the *Sketch* (which began in 1892) and many early films is the representation of urban spaces. This was the start of what Walter Benjamin later called 'the age of mechanical reproduction' and it prompted much debate about what did or did not constitute a work of art.[27]

There are several broad parallels between comics and early cinema. The dominant narrative form of the comic strip was a mixture of farce and physical comedy: 'slapstick' was also one of the most popular early film genres as comedy performers (often from a music hall background) exploited the medium's potential for mishaps and pratfalls. The social mileu of the comic strip tended to be lower class: tramps, vagabonds and other social misfits were the usual protagonists. Again this was reflected in early cinema. Charlie Chaplin's 'Little Tramp' persona – the little man who triumphs against the odds – belongs to the same comedy tradition as Weary Willie and Tired Tim.[28] The cinema audience was predominantly working class, like the readership of comics. And both comics and the cinema were deemed culturally low-brow: they represented the worst kind of mass-produced popular culture geared solely for the amusement of the urban proletariat and with no claim to artistic merit.[29]

The publishers of comics attempted to counter the perception that they were of little or no cultural value in a number of ways. Alfred Harmsworth, for example, regarded his titles as a respectable alternative to the penny dreadfuls. His editorial in the first issue of *Marvel* asserted that his intention was 'to offer to the public, at a small sum, good healthy literature by well-known authors, and to counteract the harm done by the "penny dreadfuls"'.[30] (That this opinion was not universally held is evident in the comment attributed to A. A. Milne that he 'killed the penny dreadful by the simple process of producing the ha'penny dreadfuller'.)[31] Another strategy was for comics to prove

National and racial stereotyping as illustrated by *The World's Comic* (Trapps, Holmes & Co., 6 July 1892).

their patriotic credentials by associating themselves with the monarchy and the empire. Thus comics marked the Queen's birthday and Diamond Jubilee (1897) with declarations of 'God Save the Queen' or 'Long Live the Queen'. The front page of the *Funny Wonder* of 26 September 1896 features 'Mr Comic Cuts' (evidently meant to be Harmsworth but in fact resembling Gladstone) presenting a copy of the paper to Her Majesty with the caption: 'The Uncrowned King of Comic Journalism presenting a copy of his Saturday Edition to the Queen of Great Britain and Empress of India – God bless her!'[32] And the Boer War (1899–1902) provided an opportunity for comics to assert their patriotism. Thus Weary Willy and Tired Tim lead a 'Tramp Army' to the Transvaal ('The noble army of weary unwashed wanderers spifflicate the Boer army') and capture Pretoria, following which Tim is appointed Governor of Pretoria 'at thirty bob a week'.[33]

The social and political outlook of the Victorian comic was highly conservative. This can be seen as a reflection both of the views of the publishers and of the tastes and values of their readers. *Comic Life*, for example, often includes jokes at the expense of socialists and Suffragists. Furthermore, comics conformed to the prevailing ethnic and racial stereotypes of the age. The tradition of 'funny foreigners' that emerged in the 1890s – garrulous Frenchmen, humourless Germans, shifty Italians, brash Americans, pig-tailed Chinese – would persist for decades. The characterization of Negroes as 'gollywogs' represents the worst stereotype. All that can be said is that such stereotypes reflected the prevailing racial discourses of the time: they were not unique to comics and nor were they unique to Britain.[34]

At this time comics were intended principally for an adult readership: this can be seen in their topicality and their sometimes satirical content. It is not unusual for 'real' people to turn up in their pages: Joseph Chamberlain, Sir Henry Irving, Dan Leno and W. G. Grace are among the various public figures who appear in *Big Budget*, for example.[35] However, this began to change around the turn of the century as publishers became aware of the market for comics among children. They began to include strips written and drawn specifically for young children – the mischievous 'Little Willy and Tiny Tim' appeared in *Funny Wonder* in 1898, for example – and followed with separate pull-out sections. *Puck*, a new Harmsworth comic launched in 1904, included a section entitled *Puck Junior* that proved more popular than the main comic. This set the pattern for new comics in the decade before the First World War. New titles such as *Butterfly* (1904–17), *Playbox* (1905–13), *Chuckles* (1914–23) and *Rainbow* (1914–56) were aimed squarely at pre-teen children – the last title was home to Tiger Tim, a brilliant exercise in anthropomorphic surrealism drawn by Herbert Foxwell – while existing comics increasingly shifted towards 'younger' content.

The reorientation of the British comics market was complete by the First World War. When *Ally Sloper's Half-Holiday* ceased publication in 1914 (it would be revived, briefly, in the early 1920s) it marked the symbolic end of the comic paper for adult readers. The market was now dominated by the behemoth of Amalgamated Press, which published a wide range of juvenile periodicals. There was by now a clear distinction between picture-strip papers for the pre-teens – Amalgamated's stable in 1914 included *Butterfly, Comic Cuts, Chips, Chuckles, Jester, Puck, Rainbow* and *Wonder* – and prose story papers for the ten- to fifteen-year-old age group. Here the leading titles were *Gem* (1907–39) and *Magnet* (1908–40), both featuring complete stories by the extraordinarily prolific Charles Hamilton.[36] Within the space of two decades the Harmsworths had established a near-monopoly of the juvenile periodical market and their comics and story papers informed the imaginative landscape of a whole generation of British children.

* * *

It was during the interwar period that the structure of the British comic publishing industry took shape. Amalgamated Press was now firmly established as the leading publisher of both story papers and comics. It developed a new range of girls' papers including *School Friend* (1919–40), *Schoolgirls' Own* (1921–36), *Schoolgirls' Weekly* (1922–39) and *Girls' Crystal* (1935–53), and added new boys' papers such as *Champion* (1922–55), *Triumph* (1924–40) and *Modern Boy* (1928–39). While story papers divided on strict gendered lines, comics were not gender specific. Amalgamated added to their existing range of 'penny blacks' (as the likes of *Comic Cuts* were now known) a series of new 'twopenny coloureds' including *Tiger Tim's Weekly* (1920–40), *Chicks' Own* (1920–57), *Sunbeam* (1922–40), *Tiny Tots* (1927–57), *Crackers* (1929–41), *Tip Top* (1934–54) and *Happy Days* (1938–9). It was Amalgamated, too, which pioneered a new range of cinema-themed story papers and comics, including *Boys' Cinema* (1919–39), *Girls' Cinema* (1919–39), *Film Fun* (1920–62), *Kinema Comic* (1920–32) and *Film Picture Stories* (1934–5). This reflected the fact that cinema-going had become the primary leisure activity – A.J.P. Taylor called it 'the essential social habit of the age' – and that around 30 per cent of cinema-goers were under seventeen.[37]

However, the market dominance of Amalgamated Press was now challenged by the emergence of a rival north of the Scottish border: D. C. Thomson of Dundee. D. C. Thomson, a family business founded in 1905, had started as newspaper distributors before branching into publishing: their papers included the *Argus, Dundee Courier* and *Sunday Post*. Thomson entered the field of juvenile publishing after the war with a series of boys' story papers

Tiny Tots (Amalgamated Press Ltd, 4 October 1930).

that rivalled and even surpassed the popularity of the Harmsworth titles.[38] Thomson's 'Big Five' – *Adventure* (1921–61), *Rover* (1922–73), *Wizard* (1922–63), *Skipper* (1930–41) and *Hotspur* (1933–58) – differentiated themselves from the Amalgamated story papers in several respects. They featured several serial stories rather than one complete story per issue; they included genres such as sport, war and science fiction rather than focusing solely on school stories like *Gem* and *Magnet*; and their prose was punchier and more colloquial. Then, in the late 1930s, Thomson followed its successful story

Boys' Cinema
(Amalgamated Press
Ltd, 30 June 1923).

papers with two comics that immediately established themselves as popular favourites: *Dandy* in 1937 and *Beano* in 1938.[39]

It is surely no exaggeration to say that *Dandy* and *Beano* revolutionized the world of the British children's comic. To some extent they adopted the format of existing children's comics, including full-colour covers and anthropomorphic characters in the form of 'Korky the Cat' (*Dandy*) and 'Biffo the Bear' (*Beano*). In other respects, however, they represented a significant advance in the development of comic form and style. While they maintained some text stories, *Dandy* and *Beano* introduced a new kind of picture strip that dispensed with text captions underneath the pictures and used speech balloons for dialogue. (This technique had already become established in the picture strips appearing in newspapers including 'Blondie', 'Li'l Abner' and 'Popeye' in the United States – strips that were also syndicated in the British press – and in British strips like 'Pop' of the *Daily Sketch* and 'Jane' of the

The Beano Comic (D. C. Thomson, 6 October 1945).

Daily Mirror.) This resulted in a less static, more fluid style of story-telling that was perfect for the zany comedy of strips such as 'Desperate Dan' (the *Dandy*'s stubble-chinned strongman living in a bizarre Anglicized Wild West) and 'Lord Snooty' (the *Beano*'s aristocratic ragamuffin). These strips were both drawn by the prolific Dudley D. Watkins, D. C. Thomson's chief staff artist who also drew 'The Broons' and 'Oor Wullie' for the *Sunday Post*.[40]

Although it would not do to overstate the differences, the social politics of *Dandy* and *Beano* are distinct from the comics of Amalgamated Press. Amalgamated's nursery comics, in particular, inhabit a world of comfortable houses and nannies that probably did not reflect the experience of many of their readers. There is no real suggestion of the social problems of the time: even the tramps are as much a residual left-over from days gone as a response to the social and economic conditions of the interwar years. In contrast the Thomson comics exhibit a certain 'Depression sensibility', to borrow Roger Sabin's phrase.[41] They represent a world of social inequalities – tensions between 'toffs' and the working classes are a recurring theme of strips like 'Lord Snooty' – and where characters are so impoverished that a plate of 'grub' is a desirable reward. They also differ from other comics in that they allow transgression against adults. *Beano*, especially, creates a world where adult authority is challenged. This would become more prominent after the Second World War, when new characters such as 'Dennis the Menace' (drawn by David Law) and 'The Bash Street Kids' (by Leo Baxendale) appeared, though it was a theme evident in the comic from the outset. *Beano* and *Dandy* (though *Beano* more so) celebrate a world of anarchy and mischief-making: this no doubt helps to explain both their enormous popularity and their extraordinary longevity.[42]

How large was the readership for comics and story papers, and who read them? While the circulation of individual titles is almost impossible to ascertain – D. C. Thomson, in particular, has always been reticent in publishing sales figures for its juvenile papers – there is every reason to believe they were widely and avidly consumed. In 1947 Mass-Observation found that comics 'are almost automatic reading matter for children except where there is a parental ban'.[43] There is certainly much anecdotal evidence of their popularity. The playwright and journalist Keith Waterhouse, for example, often recalled his comic-reading childhood in his newspaper column: 'Without difficulty I can remember a good 20 or 30 of them that thrived before the war – *Jingles, Joker, Comic Cuts, Tip-Top, Butterfly, Bubbles, Crackers* and so on.'[44] 'My pick of the bunch', he said on another occasion, 'was *Film Fun*, in whose black-and-white pages we were led to believe that the likes of Old Mother Riley, George Formby and Schnozzle Durante lived in ordinary little terrace houses like the rest of the world.'[45] As well as his insight into the social politics of *Film Fun*, Waterhouse provides evidence of the tastes of consumers. In particular there was a strict hierarchy governing the swapping of comics: 'The *Beano* could be swapped only for its companion paper the *Dandy*, and vice versa . . . But it needed a *Beano* and a *Butterfly* to acquire the prestigious photogravure *Mickey Mouse Weekly*.'[46]

The most extensive survey of children's reading habits before the Second World War, based on a sample of nearly 3,000 respondents, was undertaken by Augustus Jenkinson in 1938. Jenkinson, an academic who lectured in education at Manchester University, analysed the reading of 1,570 boys and 1,330 girls between the ages of twelve and fifteen in seventeen 'Senior Schools' (those without a Sixth Form) and eleven 'Secondary Schools' (with a Sixth Form). His research suggested that story papers and comics were by far the most popular reading matter among juveniles and that interest in them peaked around the age of twelve. Among boys the most popular titles by some distance were Thomson's 'bloods' (challenged only by *Champion* among the Amalgamated story papers) which were read by between half and two-thirds of twelve- and thirteen-year-olds (*Wizard* was the most popular with all age groups). It is significant that interest in story papers was higher among those attending senior school, who read an average of four papers each at thirteen and fourteen, and that it lasted longer than for those attending secondary school, who read an average of three at thirteen and only two at fourteen.[47] George Orwell, in his famous essay on 'Boys' Weeklies', observed much the same trend:

> Boys who are likely to go to public schools themselves generally read the *Gem* and *Magnet*, but they nearly always stop reading them when they are about twelve; they may continue for another year from force of habit, but by that time they have ceased to take them seriously. On the other hand, the boys at very cheap private schools, the schools that are designed for people who can't afford a public school but consider the council schools 'common', continue reading the *Gem* and *Magnet* for several years longer.[48]

What Jenkinson also found, however, was that 'persistent reading of quite childish magazines of the "comic" type' was still evident among senior school boys up to thirteen (particular favourites were *Larks, Chips, Butterfly, Joker, Film Fun, Tip-Top* and *Mickey Mouse Weekly*) though less so at secondary school where most boys had given these up by the age of twelve.[49]

When it came to girls' reading habits, Jenkinson's findings were even more revealing. While girls read fewer story papers and comics than boys, it seems that interest among girls at senior school actually increased between twelve and fourteen when they were reading more of them than their male counterparts. The class differences evident in boys' reading habits were also more pronounced. Thus, while the preferences of secondary school girls were for the more respectable types of girls' papers (*Schoolgirls' Own*, *Schoolgirls' Weekly*, *Girls' Crystal* and *Girl's Own Paper*), senior school girls' tastes were more diverse and also extended to boys' papers (*Wizard* in particular) and what Jenkinson called 'erotic magazines' intended for adult women such as *Miracle*, *Red Letter* and *Red Star Weekly*.[50]

What conclusions can be drawn about the market for comics and story papers in the 1930s? Four points are worth comment. One is that there were clearly social distinctions in the choice of papers. Jenkinson remarks that 'certain periodicals such as *Rainbow* and the *Boy's Own Paper* are in some quarters held to be worthier and nobler than *Magnet*, *Comic Cuts*, and their peers'. 'The distinction seems to be a class distinction,' he suggests; 'similar appetites are satisfied in what is regarded as a more refined way.'[51] The extent to which this was due to the choices of the children themselves or to the choices of their parents is difficult to say, though there is reason to believe that children were more likely to spend their own pocket money on the more populist comics and story papers than on 'improving' papers such as the *Children's Newspaper* which was generally a parental purchase. The second point is that the most popular comics and story papers tended to be those from the newcomer D. C. Thomson: there is some evidence to suggest that Amalgamated Press titles were now seen as 'tired' in comparison to their livelier new competitors. The third point is that gender divisions in the choice of juvenile papers were less acute than sometimes assumed. Pre-teen comics were equally popular with boys and girls, while a quarter of girls chose to read boys' story papers.[52] And the final point is that, contrary to the assumption of the major publishers that children would grow out of comics around the age of eleven or twelve and graduate to story papers, in fact they often continued reading comics into the teenage years.

* * *

The outbreak of the Second World War in September 1939 had significant repercussions for the juvenile publishing industry. The imposition of paper rationing had an immediate impact as publishers were required to reduce their pre-war paper consumption by 60 per cent. This signalled the end of the road for many popular titles. Of the story papers *Gem*, *Modern Boy*, *Boys' Cinema* and *Girls' Cinema* all ceased publication before the end of 1939, followed by *Magnet*, *Triumph* and *School Friend* in 1940 and *Skipper* in 1941, while several established comics, including *Butterfly*, *Sunbeam*, *Puck*, *Jester*, *Joker* and *Tiger Tim's Weekly*, were also among the early wartime casualties. It is

The Skipper
(D. C. Thomson,
24 August 1940).

significant that several of these were nursery comics for younger children, whereas the comics that survived tended to be those that, like *Film Fun* and its new companion *Radio Fun* (1938–61), assumed an awareness of other media and would therefore have a wider appeal. The papers and comics that survived did so by reducing their size and length and by switching from weekly to fortnightly publication. The wartime paper recycling drive saw many comics pulped. Denis Gifford later recalled that he lost much of his comic collection 'thanks to my mum getting a patriotic urge while I was evacuated'.[53] He consoled himself, however, by producing his own comics by pasting together strips and cartoons from newspapers, drawing his own covers. The young Gifford's patriotic credentials were demonstrated in his self-made *British Overseas Comics* to be 'issued only to members of the Allied Armed Forces by arrangement with the War Office'.[54]

The restriction on new periodicals meant that no new titles could be launched during the war, though some enterprising publishers were able to circumvent wartime regulations by issuing occasional one-offs and specials.

A number of new entrepreneurial publishers entered the field, such as Gerald G. Swan, a former London market trader who launched a series of new comics – including *Topical Funnies*, *War Comics*, *Thrill Comics* and *Slick Fun* – in 1940. The format of these comics was based on the American comic books that had appeared at the end of the 1930s – *Famous Funnies*, *Detective Comics*, *Action Comics*, *Super Comics* and the like – but were no longer available in Britain during the war.[55] Wartime shortages meant that any kind of comic was always in demand. Swan was confident that he would be able to sell his comics: for this reason he paid writers and artists on receipt rather than publication. This policy meant that he was able to attract artists away from the big publishers as the work there dried up, such as Harry Banger of D. C. Thomson whose work 'gave the Swan comics a hint of professionalism they would not otherwise have had'.[56] The nature of wartime conditions, including the black market, means that the provenance of some independent comics is hard to identify. One feature of note is the wartime adventure strip, a genre largely absent from the professional comics. Reg Beaumont, for example, drew 'Slick Steele of the Secret Service' and 'Rex King' for the one-offs *Cyclone* and *Grand Adventure Comic* in 1945.

The ideological and cultural context of the Second World War influenced the content of British comics in several ways. On the most basic level this was expressed through their assertions of patriotism and support for the war effort: *Knock-Out*, for example, a new comic launched by Amalgamated Press six months before the war, acquired the sub-heading of 'The Victory Comic'. Otherwise the principal strategy of wartime comics was to represent the war in terms their young readers could understand. This took several forms. There was a vogue, especially early in the war, for strips that held the enemy up to ridicule. In 1940, for example, *Dandy* caricatured Hitler and Goering as 'Addie and Hermy – the Nasty Nazis', while *Beano* followed suit with 'Musso the Wop' ('He's a Big-a-da Flop!'). In a wartime context this was an ideologically legitimate mobilization of national stereotypes for propaganda and morale: the extent to which this tradition persisted after the war is quite another matter. But there was perhaps a more subtle strategy at work: a narrative of reassurance. *Radio Fun* published a strip entitled 'Lord Haw-Haw – The Broadcasting Humbug from Hamburg' that can be seen as a way of reassuring children – many of whom would have heard the propaganda broadcasts by the Anglophone Nazi sympathizer William Joyce – that he was not to be taken seriously. Another strategy was to represent children as participants in the war effort. These narratives ranged from outright fantasy – an 'Our Ernie' strip in *Knock-Out* saw the popular Lancastrian urchin punch 'Tickler' (Hitler) on the 'conk' for forcing up the price of sweets – to more realistic prose stories such as *Rover*'s 'The Blitz Kids' in which a gang of boys and girls set up a bicycle rescue brigade to save pets (and sometimes people) from bombed houses.[57]

Without doubt the most popular comic strip of the war, however, was to be found not in *Beano* or *Dandy* but on the middle pages of the *Daily Mirror*. The *Mirror* was the best-selling newspaper of the war years with a circulation of two million: it has been seen as the voice of wartime populism. A.J.P. Taylor suggested that the *Mirror* 'gave an indication as never before what ordinary people in the most ordinary sense were thinking', but added that it 'owed its success as much to its sophisticated columnist Cassandra as to Jane, its strip-tease strip-cartoon'.[58] In fact the *Mirror* included more picture strips than any other newspaper: these included 'Ruggles', 'Buck Ryan', 'Beezlebub Jones' and 'Garth' as well as 'Jane'.[59] Mass-Observation found that among all newspapers 'the

Chrystabel Leighton-Porter, 'Britain's most perfect girl' and the model for 'Jane' of the *Daily Mirror*, here in a glamour pose for *Jane's Journal* (Thomas's Publications Ltd, 1946).

Daily Mirror alone has attained any degree of individuality for their features of this type, and it is chiefly to *Daily Mirror* readers that comics and cartoons have a really emotional appeal'.[60] There is evidence that for some readers at least the strips were the principal reason for taking the paper. As one 'unskilled working man' said: 'I read the *Mirror* . . . I read the comic strips first, of course, and not much else. The strips are all I worry about unless I've got more time.'[61]

'Jane' was a daily picture strip that had been running since 1932. Originally entitled 'Jane's Journal: The Diary of a Bright Young Thing', it chronicled the adventures of a dizzy blonde socialite (rather like a British equivalent of American strip cartoon heroine Blondie) and her pet dachshund Fritz. The strip was drawn by artist Norman Pett, who initially based Jane on his wife Mary, but from 1938, when the strip was revamped and Jane acquired a

'Jane' as she appeared in strip form, here in *Jane's Journal* (Thomas's Publications Ltd, 1946).

'Jane' often featured a voyeur, as in this daily strip from the *Daily Mirror*, 17 July 1945.

more risqué image, she was modelled by Chrystabel Leighton-Porter, a model-turned-variety artiste who had once been named 'Britain's most perfect girl' in a swimwear competition.[62] The basic motif of 'Jane', such as it was, was for the heroine to accidentally shed her clothes – mishaps that required an ever increasing degree of narrative imagination – so that she could be drawn in her underwear or even (occasionally) in the nude. It has become part of wartime folklore that the amount of clothes shed by Jane was an index of British morale. When she stripped on D-Day, an American armed forces newspaper famously reported: 'Right smack out of the blue and with no one even threatening her, Jane peeled a week ago. The British 36th Division immediately gained six miles and the British attacked in the Arakan.'[63]

There is much evidence of the popularity of Jane. In 1946 Mass-Observation found that she was the fourth best-known of a list of famous people from fiction and history behind Sherlock Holmes, Beethoven and George Bernard Shaw. Fifty-six per cent of the respondents associated the name 'Jane' with the *Daily Mirror* character ahead of other famous Janes such as Jane Eyre or Jane Austen. While men tended to like Jane for her pulchritudinous qualities ('My natural reaction to Jane is that it makes me think of figures and shapes'), some women were jealous of her ('I just look at it that it gives some people enjoyment to study and read – but when I see all that crepe de chine it makes me envious!').[64] There is anecdotal evidence, furthermore, that for some adolescents Jane was their first real exposure to female sexuality. For a young Leslie Thomas, future author of *The Virgin Soldiers*, Jane offered an illicit thrill: 'When I was a schoolboy towards the end of the affair (the world's, not Jane's) we used to peep at her daily doings below the flap of our desks, the *Daily Mirror* passed like a spy's orders between us . . . Never were the words "cartoon strip" so apt.'[65] She was also a favourite with the armed forces: 'Jane' was reprinted in the British forces' newspaper *Union Jack*, in the American *Stars and Stripes* and the Canadian *Maple Leaf*. One British

'Jane' does her patriotic duty in *Jane's Journal* (Thomas's Publications Ltd, 1946).

serviceman said: 'Many of us follow her adventures with more interest than the war against Japan.'[66]

It is not difficult to understand the appeal of Jane for schoolboys and servicemen. Her wartime adventures – in which she was an unlikely recruit to British Intelligence, working for Colonel Y at Hush Hush House – provided plenty of opportunity for her to appear in flagrante delicto. This usually involves tearing her clothes while climbing trees or getting her negligee caught in the door while trying to leave the house stealthily. There is every reason to believe that Pett was fully aware of what he was doing in offering the female body as a form of erotic spectacle. Usually, when Jane appears au naturel, particularly in scenes that involve bathing or sunbathing, she is spied upon by a male voyeur who represents by proxy the reader of the newspaper. On occasion the strip even has a self-reflexive quality about it, such as the time when Jane models for an artist drawing a strip cartoon about 'Factory Floogie' who also loses her clothes ('My agent tells me there's a good market in America' – in fact 'Jane' had to be retouched for US distribution as the press syndicates were nervous about the amount of flesh she exposed!) But there was nothing pornographic about Jane: her striptease is perhaps best understood in the tradition of the famous tableaux of the Windmill Theatre where female nudity had been allowed since 1932 provided the models did not move.

While the content is comical rather than realistic, Jane's misadventures in the *Daily Mirror* nevertheless provide a fairly good reflection of wartime changes in British society.[67] Jane herself is transformed from a frivolous 'bright young thing' whose life revolved around cocktail parties and juggling boyfriends to a 'mobile woman' who works on the land ('Land Girl') and in a munitions plant ('Factory Girl'). There are constant references to wartime austerity conditions: a certain brand of lipstick is 'impossible to get since the fall of France' and when staying in a boarding house Jane is told 'I'm afraid you can only have five inches of water'. There is the potential for accidents and misunderstandings in the blackout: Jane kisses the wrong man thinking it is her boyfriend. The presence of US servicemen in Britain ('oversexed, overpaid and over here' as the saying had it) is addressed when Jane is courted by an American officer ('These Yanks are certainly fast workers'). And there is the question of whether Jane should marry her steady boyfriend Georgie Porgie or wait until after the war: a recurring joke is that their marriage is continually postponed by one crisis or another.

Jane can be read as vehicle for negotiating some of the tensions and anxieties around wartime femininity. On the one hand the war created greater opportunities for women, especially young single women, in the workplace and in the services; but on the other hand social mobility also brought more sexual opportunities with an increase in casual affairs and infidelity. In official

The Adventures of Jane (dir. Edward G. Whiting, 1949).

propaganda sexualized femininity was viewed in highly negative ways: posters such as 'Keep mum – she's not so dumb' presented women as a threat to national security, while a venereal disease campaign warned against 'the easy girlfriend'.[68] In contrast to these images, Jane represents a conservative ideal of womanhood. For all that she has a tendency to shed her clothes, Jane is not promiscuous: she remains, at all times, virtuous, chaste and loyal to her fiancé Georgie. A recurring theme is of Jane gamely fending off the amorous attentions of other suitors. It may have been her fidelity as much as her sexuality that appealed to servicemen for whom she represented an idealized sweetheart. The basic conventions of the strip are those of farce – misunderstandings, confusion, accidents – rather than erotica: Jane belongs as much to the tradition of Ben Travers and the Aldwych Farces as to the future soft-core pornography of 'Little Annie Fanny' or 'Barbarella'.

Pett continued drawing Jane until 1948, when the strip was taken over by his assistant Michael Hubbard. Jane's popularity prompted several imitators, including Leslie Marchant's 'The Adventures of Peggy' (*Daily Sketch*), Arthur Perrier's 'Spotlight on Sally' (*News of the World*) and Pett's own 'Susie' (*Sunday Dispatch*). Jane also crossed over into other media, with a series of 'Journals' published in the late 1940s that featured colour cartoons by Pett and 'glamour' photographs of Chrystabel Leighton-Porter. These were slightly more risqué than the comic strip: that fact and their price (2s. 6d or 3s. 6d) indicates they were intended for adult consumption. Leighton-Porter, who had toured in a burlesque show during the war, also starred in the feature film *The Adventures of Jane* in 1949. Produced and directed by Edward G. Whiting for Keystone New World Productions, *The Adventures of Jane* was shot at the new Brighton Studios and included location shooting in the seaside town.[69] It is a dreary film in every respect: cheap production values, flat direction, lacklustre scripting and wooden performances. There are two particular weaknesses. The first is that in setting the film in post-war Britain – where Jane becomes unwittingly involved with a gang of jewel smugglers – Jane is robbed of the cultural and ideological meanings she had assumed during the war. The second, rather more prosaic, reason is that the strictures of the British Board of Film Censors made it impossible for Jane to shed her clothes completely: a critical weakness in a film based on a character famous principally for stripping! The reviews were not kind. The trade paper *Kinematograph Weekly* called it 'such a shambles that only the uncritical will accept it as entertainment' and complained that the script 'has neither wit nor originality'. It felt that Miss Leighton-Porter was 'an inarticulate Jane' and added that 'her legs, shapely as they are, fail to make up for her lack of acting ability'.[70] *The Adventures of Jane* was distributed by Eros Pictures and deservedly sank without trace at the box office.[71]

* * *

The history of the British comic from its origins to the Second World War reveals two distinct trends. On the one hand there is the tradition of the comic as amusement for adults. To this extent Jane of the *Daily Mirror* can be placed in a direct line of descent from the first comic star Ally Sloper. Jane and Sloper were both products of a particular set of historical and cultural circumstances, and both achieved the height of their popularity at times when social relations were in flux. On the other hand there is the emergence of comics for children. This process began around the turn of the century and became the dominant trend to the extent that by the interwar period comics were universally regarded as a juvenile medium. The advent of *Dandy* and *Beano* marked the arrival of the 'golden age' of the British comic that would last approximately from the mid-1930s until the end of the 1960s. The period after the Second World War would see the emergence of new adventure comics alongside the existing humour comics. It would also see comics become the focus of social and political anxieties that provoked a moral panic around the spectre of so-called 'horror comics'.

CHAPTER TWO

On the Wings of Eagles

> Horror has crept into the British nursery. Morals of little girls in plaits and boys with marbles bulging in their pockets are being corrupted by a torrent of indecent coloured magazines that are flooding bookstalls and newsagents. Not mere 'thrillers' as we used to know them, nor the once-familiar 'school stories'. These are evil and dangerous – graphic, coloured illustrations of modern city vice and crime . . . That is why I shall not feel I have done my duty as a parson and a father of children until I have seen on the market a genuinely popular 'Children's Comic' where adventure is once more the clean and exciting business I remember in my own schooldays.
> Marcus Morris.[1]

Arguably the most historically significant British comic, *Eagle* (1950–69) was conceived by a Southport clergyman and former RAF chaplain as a wholesome British alternative to the 'horror comics' that had appeared after the Second World War. The Reverend Marcus Morris had become vicar of St James's Church, Birkdale, a prosperous suburb of Southport, in 1945. Morris, a man of contrasts who combined his evangelicalism with the appetites of a bon viveur, was committed to the promotion of the Christian faith as a modern and progressive ideal. He later said that 'a major interest in my life was the attempt to get the Christian message through to people by means of lively and adult publications'.[2] He revamped a tired old parish newsletter into a magazine called *The Anvil*, which built up a circulation of 9,000 with its mixture of essays, reviews and cartoons. It was in order to assume responsibility for *The Anvil* that Morris founded the Society for Christian Publicity in 1948. The society came to national attention early in 1949 when Morris, prompted by some of the comics that had found their way into the hands of his own children, wrote an article for the *Sunday Dispatch* that would generate a sufficient head of steam to propel a parochial clergyman into a second career as editor of the most influential juvenile periodical since the *Boy's Own Paper*.

Morris's article, which prompted a large postbag of responses, was an early broadside in what would develop into a nationwide campaign against what came to be known as 'horror comics'. The history of this campaign has been expertly documented in Martin Barker's book *A Haunt of Fears*.[3] Barker shows how a broad coalition of teachers, magistrates, clergymen, psychologists and other groups mounted a highly effective campaign to influence public opinion in support of legislation banning these comics. The campaign was conducted through public meetings, pamphlets and articles in the national and local press. The horror comics campaign brought together such unlikely bedfellows as the Church of England, the National Union of Teachers and the Communist Party of Great Britain, which supported it covertly through front organizations such as the British National Council of Teachers for Peace. A meeting of interested parties at Beaver Hall in London in May 1953 led to the formation of the Comics Campaign Council, which became the official voice of the campaign.

Marcus Morris did not, in the event, become a major activist in the campaign: indeed he would soon find himself on the other side of the fence when some critics objected to the content of *Eagle*. Nevertheless, his was one of the first voices to be raised and his article anticipated the tone and discursive strategies of the campaign. His targets included both British comics and American imports. He cited wholly unsubstantiated and uncontextualized statistics for juvenile crime, asserting a 'nearly 40 per cent increase among children aged ten', and made a simple cause-and-effect link with children's reading habits: 'I blame much of this on their "comics". As soon as a child becomes old enough to read, he enters a new world of horror and vice, where there are no apparent morals, and certainly no holds barred.' He singled out for attention 'a beautifully illustrated 3d. magazine with 175 flawlessly vivid drawings that start with gangsters shooting a girl in the stomach, have the heroine twice bound and gagged, [and] finally dumped in a cold bath of water to drown'. Morris evidently disliked lascivious and sexualized images of women: his bêtes noires included a pirate story where a 'half-naked girl . . . is taken to be bound to a stake before the Arab Chief's quarters' and another about 'a blonde girl detective whose detecting costume is brassière and panties laced up the side, fishnet stockings and elbow-length gloves'. His conservatism in matters of gender is suggested by his distaste for one comic that featured 'a trousered heroine kicking a villain enthusiastically in the lower stomach'.[4]

The comics campaign was a classic example of a moral panic: a hysterical reaction to a type of popular media that made sweeping and entirely unsubstantiated claims about their pernicious effects on those who read them.

Yet, as Barker has shown, the motives behind the campaign exposed a range of ideological contradictions. Much of the early agitation was orchestrated by the Communist Party, which at the time was involved in a vigorous campaign against the influence of Americanization on British society and culture.[5] Hence the targets were 'American' or 'American-type' comics and the attacks focused as much on the values they promoted as on their actual content. 'The whole case against these bad American comics is not that they are too exciting and "tough" but that they portray false standards and corrupted values', declared an article in *Picture Post* in 1952.[6] The author, Peter Mauger, a schoolteacher and CP member, also wrote a pamphlet, *The Lure of the 'Comics'*, attacking US comics for their promotion of 'violence as the basis of society and the "natural law" of mankind' and for their 'creation of the war mentality'. He averred that they promoted racial superiority ('The heroes of all these books, cops and supermen, are invariably of one type – the 100 per cent white American with square jaw and heavy fists') and warned his readers that 'the poison is streaming over here, to pollute the minds of British children'.[7]

At this point it is useful to examine the claims of the campaigners. For one thing most of the 'American' comics against which their anger was directed were in fact British reprints. Following the Second World War, the import of consumer goods (including comics) from the Dollar Area was restricted in an attempt to redress the nation's balance of payments deficit. British publishers could, however, buy the printing matrices from their US counterparts and produce their own copies. The pioneers in this area were independent publishers such as the Arnold Book Company and L. Miller & Son who had started out as distributors and turned to publishing reprints when they were no longer able to import US titles. Arnold, in particular, published several comics that the campaigners disliked, including *Black Magic*, *Crime Does Not Pay*, *Haunt of Fear*, *Monster of Frankenstein* and *Tales from the Crypt*. In 1955 the Director of Public Prosecutions claimed that 'the publishers have been known to us for many years as being responsible for the publication of questionable material'.[8]

How widely were such comics read? There is no reliable evidence of their circulation, and most of the figures cited at the time seem to have been plucked from the air. An article in the *Financial Times* in 1954 referred to 'the 60 million American type comics sold annually in the UK' and this was the figure that stuck.[9] This is probably a reasonable estimate for all US reprints, including many titles that no-one ever raised any objection to. Yet the titles most often cited by the campaign – including, in addition to those listed above, *Crime Detective*, *Down With Crime*, *Eerie*, *Ghostly Weird Stories*, *True Crime* and *Vault of Horror* – ran to only a few issues, and judging by their

'American type comics . . . that wallow in crime, horror, violence and sex' – according to *Comics and Your Children* (1954).

scarcity today the print runs cannot have been large.[10] This did not prevent the campaigners from making exaggerated claims about the 'flood' or 'torrent' of harmful comics. In 1952, for example, the Association of Assistant Mistresses condemned 'the widespread circulation of certain comic strip publications distributed in this country, calculated to have a damaging effect on young people both morally and culturally'.[11]

If the circulation of 'American-type' comics in Britain was uncertain, to say the least, then the claims made about their effects were even more specious. In 1954, for example, the Comics Campaign Council published a pamphlet entitled *Comics and Your Children*, written by George Pumphrey, a Sussex headmaster and a leading figure in the campaign. Pumphrey focused on 'American type comics . . . that wallow in crime, horror, violence and sex and are thoroughly pernicious'. He listed some of the most objectionable examples, complemented by carefully chosen illustrations. He feared that impressionable children 'might base their own behaviours and standards on them' and that 'comics are liable to give them some very odd ideas'. He asserted that 'there is a definite connection between delinquency and the reading of comics' (though no empirical evidence was provided to support this – Pumphrey simply took for granted the arguments of New York psychiatrist Dr Fredric Wertham in his highly alarmist book *The Seduction of the Innocent*) and attacked the disingenuous morality of comics such as *Crime Does Not Pay* 'which follows a line taken by many others, 47 pages being devoted to violent crime and only one to retribution'. He concluded by advocating an outright ban: 'I feel that if only one child in a million is influenced one iota towards delinquency by these comics, then we should not rest until they are abolished.'[12]

By 1952 the campaigners had started lobbying MPs. In July 1952 Maurice Edelman, Labour MP for Coventry North, prompted by a letter from the Parent-Teacher Association of Coventry, raised his 'concern at the circulation of sensational American-style comics among British schoolchildren'.[13] And Richard Crossman wrote to the Home Secretary: 'There is a certain type of literature of this sort which really is so nauseating that it makes one inclined to demand censorship ... Is it possible, in your view, under our existing laws, while permitting such "American-type comics" as "The Eagle", to clamp down on some of the sexy, sadistic trash which cheap-jacks are putting out?'[14] The fact that Sweden and Canada had recently banned certain kinds of comics added fuel to the demands for legislation.

However, the government initially resisted the call for censorship. There were several reasons for this. For one thing there was a prevailing view that regulating children's reading habits was properly the responsibility of parents and teachers rather than the state. It was also felt that legislation would be 'wholly impracticable' as it would be 'quite impossible to draft an enforceable provision which would include all types of the pernicious literature ... without also including much that is perfectly suitable to young readers'.[15] There was also a view that the comics campaign was making somewhat exaggerated claims. The Minister of Education, Florence Horsburgh, felt 'that the whole business was being overplayed', and there was doubt 'if such comics were in fact really doing children the harm that some people supposed'.[16]

This remained the official position until 1954, when the issue came back onto the political agenda from what on the face of it seems a rather unlikely source. Documents in the National Archives reveal that early in 1954 the Prime Minister himself asked for 'a note about the sale of American type comics in this country, and the social effects which they might be having'.[17] The Home Office prepared a memorandum summarizing the problem:

The publications usually known as 'American type comics' embrace various categories whose principal common feature is the absence, usually but not always complete, of any comic element... Though very crudely produced and badly printed, some of these publications are harmless enough. This is true of many 'Western' stories (e.g. those which deal with the adventures of Roy Rogers) and of some of the 'Tarzan' publications which have come to notice. But the vast majority have distinctly objectionable features. Many of them have a strong streak of sadistic cruelty and an undue emphasis on violence. A number have an erotic streak and abound in representations of scantily dressed women. Some of the scenes portrayed are horrifying – macabre supernatural scenes with zombies and ghouls, the frenzy of drug addicts, the grimmer aspects of modern war, and scenes of torture and murder...

It is difficult to estimate how far American type comics have any permanent social effects but such influence as they may have is unlikely to be beneficial. Whereas British periodicals for older children nearly all contain a fair proportion of harmless reading matter which at least develop the faculty of and taste for reading, American publications usually contain hardly any letter press and what little there is all too often is expressed in a crude and alien idiom. The emphasis on violence and cruelty is heavy and unwholesome. The idea that violence has to be countered with violence is common-place. The prevailing sense of values is shoddy and distorted.[18]

While it is more measured in tone than the literature produced by the comics campaign, and casts some doubt on the extent of circulation and readership, this official resumé nevertheless makes similar points about their content and assumptions about their effects. Churchill asked to see samples and was shown issues of *Frankenstein Comic*, *Black Magic*, *Captain Marvel*, *Jesse James*, *Rod Cameron Western* and *Casey Ruggles Western Comic*.[19]

The question here is why did Churchill, who rarely concerned himself with the details of domestic policy, take a personal interest in this particular subject? It would seem that the Prime Minister's interest was prompted by a suggestion from his friend and confidante, Brendan Bracken, that the firm of D. C. Thomson was involved in distributing these comics.[20] There was longstanding animosity between Churchill and Thomson, whose papers had led a campaign against Churchill in the early 1920s that Churchill held responsible for losing his seat as Liberal MP for Dundee in 1922.[21] However,

Churchill's interest seems to have waned when he was told that Thomson was not responsible for these particular comics.

At this stage there was still no suggestion of legislation to ban the offending comics: indeed the Home Office advised that it would be impractical as 'no action short of censorship would be effective, and this would have to include censorship of the daily press since some newspapers publish "strip cartoons" which are not dissimilar from those produced in many "comics".'[22] Before the year was out, however, the new Home Secretary, Gwilym Lloyd George, reported that 'Parliamentary and public pressure are now sufficiently strong to compel the Government to take action' and resolved to 'introduce early legislation to check the dissemination of so-called "horror comics" (that is, publications containing strip cartoons dealing in an objectionable way with stories of horror and violence)'.[23]

What had brought about this volte-face by the government? Essentially it seems to have been a response to external pressure. The autumn of 1954 saw the intensification of the comics campaign. In October the National Union of Teachers threw its weight behind the campaign, supporting demands for legislation 'to remove this corrupting influence from the bookstalls in the dingy back streets' and mounting an exhibition of 'horror comics' at its headquarters in London.[24] In November the Church of England Assembly declared that it 'views with grave concern the great increase in literature of a sordid and horrific nature under the misleading title of "comics"' and the Archbishop of Canterbury led a deputation to the Home Secretary.[25] Evidence that public opinion was now firmly behind the campaign is to be found in a Gallup Poll suggesting that 71 per cent of parents felt horror comics should be banned.[26] It is difficult to avoid the conclusion that the Conservative government, with a Commons majority of only seventeen and with Churchill expected to stand down before the next general election, saw this as a populist move to curry favour with the public.

The political contexts that informed the drafting of the Children and Young Person's (Harmful Publications) Bill are revealed by the Cabinet minutes and papers. The case for legislation was advanced by Lloyd George with the support of the Minister of Education, Sir David Eccles, and the Secretary of State for Scotland, the Earl of Home. It would seem that the ministers themselves were agnostic about the perceived effects of comics, conceding this was 'a matter of opinion rather than of fact', and that they were not even certain of the extent of the problem: 'As regards the scale of the mischief, it is very difficult to find out how widely objectionable comics are circulated ... It is even more difficult to discover how far they are read by children and young persons.' Their overriding concern, however, was that 'in the present state of public opinion it will not be possible to deal with the matter except by legislation'.[27] They rejected the appointment of a Royal Commission to investigate the issue and proposed moving quickly in order to preempt the possibility of a Private Member's Bill. The overriding imperative, clearly, was to push the measure through as quickly as possible.

There were other factors to consider. One was the danger of seeming too draconian. An argument made against legislation was that it would amount to censorship, and that the difficulty of defining a comic in legal terms might bring newspaper cartoons or illustrated children's stories under the remit of the Bill. In the event Lloyd George told the Cabinet that 'I am satisfied that it is so narrowly drafted that there is little danger that it could be applied to any other type of publication than that against which it is directed.'[28] Another was the fear of upsetting American opinion by stressing the American origin of the comics to be banned. Here there were differing views. Before the second reading of the Bill, the Foreign Office recommended 'that something be said to dispel the still fairly widely-held belief that American comics are horror comics and that is how the Americans like them'.[29] The Home Office, however, felt 'that the association in the minds of the public between the horror comics and the USA was beginning to be weaker'.[30]

In the event little was made of the American origin of the comics in the parliamentary debate on the Bill. The measure was supported on both sides of the House with MPs speaking out against the 'cruel violence' and 'sadistic overtones' of horror comics. The Labour MP Frank Soskice held up a copy of *Vault of Horror* which he claimed was calculated to 'appeal to the instincts of sadism, and every excitation of one's most brutish inclinations, tastes and feelings'.[31] Opponents of the Bill included Roy Jenkins and Michael Foot for Labour and Ronald Bell for the Conservatives. Jenkins supported a counter-proposal suggested by the Society of Authors, who feared the Bill 'is a new threat to the liberty of publishers, printers, booksellers and librarians'.[32] The society proposed instead a thoroughgoing review of the obscenity law, but this was something the government was keen to avoid.

The Children and Young Persons (Harmful Publications) Act came into force on 6 June 1955. It applied to any publication 'which consists wholly or mainly of stories told in pictures' that portrayed '(a) the commission of crimes; or (b) acts of violence or cruelty; or (c) incidents of a repulsive or horrible nature; in such a way that the work as a whole would tend to corrupt a child or young person into whose hands it might fall'.[33] It imposed a penalty of four months' imprisonment and/or a fine of £100 for anyone convicted of printing, publishing or selling such material. This was in fact less than the Customs penalty for importing comics from outside the Sterling Area. While there were several cases referred to the Director of Public Prosecutions under the terms of the Act – the first only two months after it came into force – it was not until 1970 that the first actual prosecution was brought.[34]

* * *

This is the historical context in which the origin of *Eagle* should be understood. *Eagle* was conceived quite explicitly as a wholesome alternative to horror comics. It was also to be very much a vehicle for the promotion of British values. Marcus Morris was not one of those who disliked comics per se. He believed that the comic was 'a new and important medium with its own laws and limitations' and that it was 'a form which could be used to convey to the child the right kind of standards, values and attitudes, combined with the necessary amount of excitement and adventure'.[35] *Eagle* was nothing if not a thoroughly considered and highly schematic project to provide British juveniles with instruction in socially and morally correct values. It was formed within the historical conditions and ideological discourses of post-war Britain – the period of the twilight of empire and the founding of the welfare state – and it was imbued with a strong sense of national identity and social responsibility.

The public response to his article in the *Sunday Dispatch* had set Morris 'thinking hopefully along the lines of [a] strip cartoon'.[36] In collaboration with artist Frank Hampson, the illustrator of *The Anvil*, he sketched out a story about a character called Lex Christian, a fighting parson in a tough area of the East End of London. Unsuccessful in their attempt to sell the strip to a newspaper, Morris and Hampson decided instead to work out the blueprint for a brand new children's paper. In the process Lex Christian became spaceman Dan Dare:

> To begin with we turned Lex Christian into a flying padre, the Parson of the Fighting Seventh. Then one day, after re-reading C. S. Lewis's science-fiction novel *Perelandra*, I said to Frank that I thought Lex Christian should leave London and go out into space . . . The name Lex Christian didn't seem quite right and we thought up a large number of alternatives. I think it was Frank's wife Dorothy who came up with Dan Dare.[37]

The first dummy of *Eagle*, produced in the summer of 1949, featured Chaplain Dan Dare of the Interplanetary Space Patrol. His RAF uniform and dog collar suggest that the character might have represented Morris's own fantasy alter ego. By the time of the first issue proper, however, the dog collar had gone and the character became Colonel Dan Dare.

There were, nevertheless, significant obstacles to overcome. Foremost among these was paper rationing, which continued until 1953 and which placed severe restrictions on the launch of new periodicals. Morris intended that *Eagle* would be printed in tabloid format and would include photogravure colour that demanded higher-quality paper. *Eagle* was turned down by several publishers, including Amalgamated Press and Lutterworth Press (publisher of both the *Boy's Own Paper* and *Girl's Own Paper*), before it was adopted by Hulton Press. Hulton, founded in 1936, published a range of titles including *World Review*, *Lilliput* and the progressive illustrated weekly *Picture Post*. *Eagle* would be its first venture into the juvenile market. Tom Hopkinson, editor of *Picture Post*, recalled being shown the dummy of *Eagle*:

> Unlike most dummies, this was not an amateurish affair with one or two pages carefully drawn and the rest hazily roughed in. It was complete from first to last with coloured drawings to scale and all the captions readable and in place. But what chiefly distinguished it was the impression that the editor understood what he was doing. I knew – and still know – very little about boys aged eight to twelve, but I could see that the editor had mentally identified himself with them, and appreciated what they wanted almost without having to think.[38]

Hopkinson did, by his own admission, suggest 'that the adventures of St Paul at the back of the paper seemed incongruous, and that something better might surely be found to take its place', but Morris insisted that it should remain or he would not edit the paper.

Eagle was launched in April 1950 with much fanfare. It was supported by 'the biggest nation-wide publicity campaign ever mounted for a comic', including touring 'Eagle cars' and slide advertisements in children's cinema shows.[39] The first issue was to all intents and purposes given away free as Hulton distributed a million three-penny coupons that could be exchanged for a copy of the paper. *Eagle* was an immediate success, with demand for its early issues exceeding supply. Indeed, the demand was such that Hulton withdrew from the Periodical Publishers Association when it refused to allow *Eagle* to be sold on a sale or return basis. The Association felt that sale or return was wasteful at a time of rationing, arguing that it needed to safeguard paper supplies.[40] In the event there were very few unsold copies of *Eagle*: a recurring feature of Morris's editorials in the early issues is the call for readers to pass their copies on to friends who had been unable to secure one of their own.

Why was *Eagle* so successful? For one thing it was produced to a higher standard than other juvenile papers, being printed on glossy paper rather than rough pulp. It settled at sixteen pages an issue, half of which were in colour. Emerging during the period of Britain's post-war austerity, *Eagle* was bigger, brighter and more colourful than its rivals. In contrast, for example, *Lion*, launched in 1952 by Amalgamated Press – which had turned down *Eagle* on the grounds that it was 'no brighter . . . than our average juvenile'[41] – was printed on rough paper and featured just one page of insipid colour. *Eagle* also represented a major advance in the visual style and layout of comics. While previous picture strips had essentially been rows of pictures with text-heavy captions underneath, *Eagle* followed the American style of mostly visual storytelling with speech balloons and fewer, shorter captions. A contemporary profile of Morris observed: 'The *Eagle* formula was based on brightly coloured, easily readable strips on newspaper lines, in which the pictures told the story without additional captions.'[42]

Eagle combined picture strips with prose stories and topical features, particularly on science and technology, and was aimed at boys between the ages of eight and thirteen.[43] Some indication of the response of its target audience is provided by a feature in *Picture Post* which, while obviously intended as a promotional article, included 'uncensored' comments from several boys who had been given copies of the first issue. While eleven-year-old Julian Anderson felt that '*Eagle* is the best combination of pictures and stories there is', others were critical of some aspects of the comic, including its two flagship picture strips. 'Some things I didn't care for much, such as "Dan Dare" – I can't get interested in a hero who does things no one has really done yet', said thirteen-year-old Giles Davison. 'And I don't see why Bible stories should be there. They haven't anything to do with comics, really.' Stephen Aris, also thirteen, concurred: 'It's a fine magazine, but there's too much about space ships and things that aren't actually based on fact . . . I don't like the last page a bit. Religion is a good idea. But I don't think it should be put up in a "comicised" way – not in strips like that, I mean.'[44] This aversion to religion was not shared by all readers, however: 'I have tried many times to understand the journey of St Paul when reading my Bible, but failed. Now, thanks to *Eagle*, his journeys and adventures are being explained to me in a way I can understand.'[45]

The back-page story of inspirational Christianity was the clearest marker of *Eagle*'s moralizing outlook. The life story of St Paul, 'The Great Adventurer', was written by another clergyman, Chad Varah, later to become founder of the Samaritans, and originally drawn by Frank Hampson until he chose to concentrate solely on drawing Dan Dare. The presence of this and other biblical stories – later strips included St Patrick ('Fighter for Truth'),

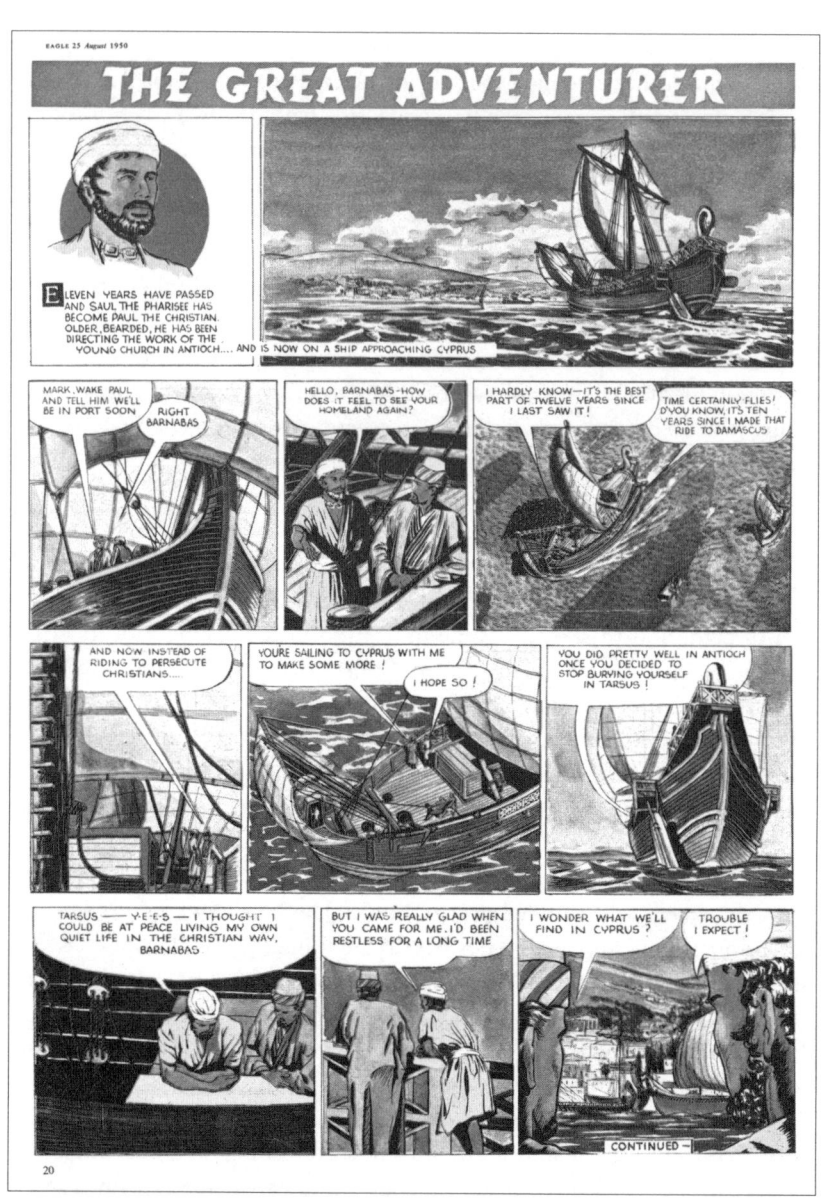

'The Great Adventurer', *Eagle* (Hulton Press Ltd, 25 August 1950).

St Mark ('The Youngest Disciple') and David ('The Shepherd Boy') – needs to be understood in the context of a society where, even if religious attendance was in decline, around half of parents in the 1950s still sent their children to Sunday school.[46] The biblical stories alternated with biographies of historical figures, including Alfred the Great, Marco Polo, Horatio Nelson, Abraham Lincoln, David Livingstone, Robert Baden Powell and Winston Churchill ('The Happy Warrior') – following which an (adult) reader declared that 'the climax of the life story of our greatest statesman is the grandest tribute you have paid to anyone.'[47]

The moral and social values of *Eagle* were also evident in its editorial content. The Eagle Club was launched with 'very definite aims and standards': members were expected to 'make the best of themselves . . . develop themselves in body, mind and spirit . . . Work with others for the good of all around them . . . Always lend a hand to those in need of help.'[48] After three months membership of the Eagle Club reached 100,000. There were also 'Mug of the Month' awards for those who had performed exceptional good deeds. In his first editorial Morris explained what it meant to be a 'Mug'. It is a revealing insight into his world-view:

> There are really only two kinds of people in the world. One kind are the MUGS. The opposite of the MUGS are the Spivs – also called wide boys, smart guys, hooligans, louts or racketeers. The MUGS are the people who are some use in the world; the people who do something worth-while for others instead of just grabbing for themselves all the time. Of course the spivs snigger at that. *They* use the word Mug as an insult. 'Aren't they mugs?' they say about people who believe in living for something bigger than themselves. That is why someone who gets called a MUG is likely to be a pretty good chap.[49]

In his early editorials Morris listed some of the great 'Mugs of History', including Scott of the Antarctic, Michael Faraday, Marie Curie and Lawrence of Arabia.

Under Morris's editorship, *Eagle* was undoubtedly a vehicle for the promotion of socially correct values. His editorials covered a range of topics including the true meaning of Christmas and the promotion of world peace. When *Eagle* started an international pen pal club, for example, Morris told his readers: 'In these days, it is especially important we should do all we can towards a better understanding between the nations of the world and to fight against the suspicion and prejudice and misunderstanding that has always caused so much trouble and has led to two world wars.'[50] The published letters would suggest that *Eagle* readers adhered to broadly progressive values: they included criticisms of the treatment of 'coloured people' and of the 'very cruel sport' of fox hunting.[51]

Eagle also identified itself with the promotion of Britain and British values. In 1951 it urged its readers to join in the celebrations for the Festival of Britain and arranged its own activities in support of the event. It supported the commemorative Battle of Britain Day 'when we remember and honour the men who fought in that great battle and so saved our country – and the world – and made victory possible'.[52] *Eagle*'s association with nationhood was best demonstrated by Morris's editorial following the death of George VI in 1952:

> King George VI stood for all the ideals which I hope are the aims of each one of you. Here was a man who, although afflicted with ill-health, strove to overcome his handicap so completely that he became one of the most sincerely loved monarchs in our history. Here was a man, good, kind, courageous – and who, for all his Crown of State, was imbued with the humility of the truly great, thus endearing himself to the old and young, the rich and poor, the strong and the weak. May we all learn from his gracious example.[53]

'As head of a great Empire our young Queen Elizabeth has a heavy and arduous task before her,' Morris added. 'The devotion of the youth of the country can be a great help to her and I am sure all of you will serve her with wholehearted loyalty.'

In identifying itself so closely with the institution of monarchy, *Eagle* was very much a product of the ideological climate of the early 1950s when all the evidence indicates that the Crown enjoyed overwhelming popular support and the monarch was held in affection by the vast majority of Britons. To this extent *Eagle* can be seen as a vehicle for the promotion of consensus. Its values were overwhelmingly those of conservative Middle England. The nature of its readers' letters would suggest a predominantly middle-class readership. This was also indicated by the activities it organized, including a skiing holiday to the Italian Alps during the Christmas and New Year holidays in 1950–51 at a cost of £19.10s. To put this in context the average weekly income of an adult male in 1951 was only £8.6s.[54]

With its ethos of good deeds and its conservative social values, *Eagle* belonged to the same tradition of morally improving juvenile literature as the *Boy's Own Paper* (BOP). There are many similarities. The BOP had been founded by the Religious Tract Society as a respectable alternative to the notorious 'penny dreadfuls' that were condemned for their sensational and violent content. Under the guidance of George A. Hutchinson, editor from 1879 to 1912, the *BOP* published a combination of adventure stories, sport and travel writing that succeeded in promoting an ethos of muscular Christianity while avoiding a hectoring or preaching tone. And, also like *Eagle*, it seems to have appealed to a predominantly middle-class readership who preferred it to cheaper and more populist rivals in the juvenile market. There is a sense in which *Eagle* was for post-war Britain what the *BOP* had been for the late Victorian period. *Eagle* was predominantly a picture paper, but it included prose serials alongside its picture strips. Chad Varah explained that the prose stories were there 'in order that our readers might take longer to get through it and therefore feel they were having their money's worth'.[55]

In common with other juvenile papers, *Eagle* covered a range of genres. The regular picture strips included a police story ('The Adventures of P.C. 49') and a western ('Riders of the Range'), both based on BBC radio serials. 'The Adventures of P.C. 49' conformed to Morris's particular world-view: its hero, PC Archie Willoughby, is an archetypal 'Mug', ever cheerful and always ready to go out of his way to help others, while its villains are typically post-war spivs and racketeers. Early stories include Willoughby apprehending the armed robbers who have run down a young boy during their getaway and helping out at the local lads' club where he shows the 'terrible twins' the error of their ways. The problem of juvenile crime is a recurring theme: 'The kids in this district are getting out of hand. Can't you do something about it constable?'[56] 'Riders of the Range' is notable for its sympathetic treatment of Native Americans. One story, in which a hot-headed US Cavalry officer leads a punitive action against the Apaches in retaliation for the kidnapping of a child, seems to have been consciously modelled on the westerns of John Ford such as *Fort Apache* and *She Wore A Yellow Ribbon* – even to the extent of setting the action in a roughly sketched equivalent of Monument Valley.[57] Later additions included a tale of highway robbery ('Jack O'Lantern'), a Foreign Legion adventure ('Luck of the Legion') and a seafaring yarn ('Storm Nelson').

'The Adventures of P.C. 49', *Eagle* (Hulton Press Ltd, 14 July 1950).

There is much anecdotal evidence to suggest that *Eagle* won approval from parents and teachers. It was often the only comic permitted in schools. One parent even called it 'the finest children's illustrated paper of all time'.[58] Unusually for a comic it was reviewed in *The Times Literary Supplement*, which predicted that it 'will perform a most valuable service of offering plenty of unpretentious entertainment and a little unobtrusive instruction without tumbling into reckless sensationalism at one extreme or vapidity at the other'.[59] There were, however, some dissenting voices. One schoolmaster, for example, while approving of the ambitions of the paper, nevertheless felt that it betrayed an underlying racism:

> I feel duty bound, however, to make some criticisms. First, I think Mr Morris would be well-advised to tone down the sensationalism of 'Dan Dare and Vora' [sic] etc. In the opinion of many readers, Dan Dare has rocketed too far into the galaxy called bizarre. Above all, I do wish his serial writers would curtail the obvious racial prejudice inherent in many of the stories. Why are so many of the villains foreigners (Chinese, Negroes, Arabs, Mexicans, Indians, Germans etc.)? . . . Why must English heroes always be handsome, clean-limbed and honourable, whereas El Fagin and the Arabs and Wu-Flung-Who and his Indo-Chinese Dragons are invariably sly, shifty and cruel?[60]

This was a familiar criticism that had also been levelled against story papers, most famously by George Orwell, and it would be fair to say that *Eagle* was not exempt from the charge. Even the biblical stories were not immune. Hampson's 'The Road of Courage', for example, depicts Jesus as a handsome, blonde, Aryan figure, whereas King Herod is swarthy and obese with a bulbous nose – recalling the kind of anti-Semitic stereotype seen in Nazi propaganda films such as *Jew Süss* and *The Eternal Jew*.[61] For all its progressive credentials, *Eagle* was, like all comics, a product of the cultural and ideological climate of its time.

* * *

The character indelibly associated with *Eagle* is Dan Dare, the intrepid 'pilot of the future', who remained a constant presence from the first issue to the last. The principal artist for the strip throughout most of the 1950s was Frank Hampson, who also wrote or co-wrote the stories.[62] The inspiration for the 'pilot of the future' came from the recent past. Hampson would later claim that his interest in science fiction was triggered by witnessing German 'rocket-bombs' in action during the bombardment of Antwerp in 1944:

On the quays of Antwerp you could watch the birth of Space Travel. You could watch a Rocket being fired, wait as it soared invisibly up, tilted and came hurtling down. And then see the flying dusty wreckage of its murderous end. Space Travel was born in those neat cottonwool lines reaching up into the clear blue winter sky. The lines were, alas, the first realization of the dreams of the scientists and inventors who had been working for years with little two- and three-foot models. Hitler warped their dreams into ends that were foul and repulsive. But dreamers have a habit of not giving up. Very soon man is going to cross space and explore the planets around him as Columbus crossed the Atlantic to America – but at the end of the Spaceman's voyage will be twenty million Americas.[63]

Following his demobilization, Hampson attended the Southport School of Arts and Crafts, before he was hired by Marcus Morris to illustrate *The Anvil*. Hampson was a meticulous and painstaking artist. To draw Dan Dare he employed a 'studio' of illustrators (mostly art school graduates willing to work for low wages) based first in a converted bakery in Southport and later in a house in Epsom. It was a highly labour-intensive, not to mention expensive, method of working, but Hulton's costs were partly offset by the licensing of Dan Dare merchandise including toy spaceships and ray guns, jigsaws, board games and wrist watches.

Hampson said that he approached the strip as 'Marco Polo discovering China simply brought up to date. You could visualize different types of civilization, their history and their culture.'[64] 'Dan Dare – Pilot of the Future' is set nearly 50 years in the future – the internal evidence dates the first story as taking place in 1995–6 – when mankind has begun to explore the solar system. Colonies have been established on the Moon and Mars, and during the early adventures Dan also sets foot on Venus, Mercury and Saturn. The suggestion that other planets in the solar system were home to advanced civilizations represents a throwback to the 'scientific romance' of authors such as Jules Verne and Edgar Rice Burroughs. Elsewhere, however, the strip pays lip service to the principles of theoretical science. The SF writer Arthur C. Clarke acted as a consultant: it was probably Clarke who suggested the idea of 'impulse wave' propulsion that provides the basis of Space Fleet's technology.[65]

Hampson pioneered a 'filmic' style of drawing comic strips. Hitherto most British strips had tended to be rather flat: rows of square frames drawn from the same perspective. Hampson experimented with the size of frames – he would often open an instalment with an oversized frame alongside the

'Rogue Planet' perfectly exemplifies the brilliant visual imagination of Frank Hampson. *Eagle* (Hulton Press, 9 December 1955).

Eagle masthead – and with perspective. He would use long shots to establish a scene followed by close ups of characters in a style comparable to cutting a film. He would use unusual angles such as overhead or aerial shots. A recurring device is to place objects in the foreground while the main action occurs in the background, creating an impression of three-dimensional space similar to the 'deep-focus' cinematography that emerged in cinema during the 1940s. Hampson was influenced by American strips such as Alex Raymond's

'Flash Gordon' and Hal Foster's 'Prince Valiant'. His artwork demonstrates a level of visual imagination that far surpassed other comic-strip artists of the time. One of the most distinctive features of 'Dan Dare' is the richly detailed visualization of alien cultures and the flaura and fauna of different planetary environments.[66]

Dan Dare was the first distinctively British adventure hero in comics. Dan himself is a conventional heroic archetype. The journalist and broadcaster Wolf Mankowitz saw him as 'a development on the Battle of Britain type of pilot – quiet, resourceful, handsome, neat, and a born leader of men, with a masterly control of all the gadgets of his scientific age'.[67] He is the Biggles of outer space, given to the same sort of dialogue as W. E. Johns's airman hero, even referring to his spaceship as a 'kite'. Just as Biggles has his faithful sidekicks Algy and Ginger, Dan has loyal comrades including his batman Albert Fitzwilliam Digby (Spaceman First Class) and commanding officer (and Space Fleet Controller) Sir Hubert Guest. Dan's sidekicks also include a Frenchman (Pierre Lafayette) and an American (Hank Hogan): thus the strip asserts Britain's authority and leadership over her wartime allies. Later additions included Space Fleet cadets Steve Valiant and 'Flamer' Spry, juvenile protagonists introduced as points of identification for younger readers.

What sort of future did 'Dan Dare' imagine? Hampson's artwork represents perhaps the most perfectly realized modernist future in the history of British science fiction. The strip is particularly notable for its aestheticization of technology with its sleek and streamlined space ships and its many functional gadgets. Hampson's futuristic cities, with their shining towers and floating gyrocars, recall the production design of films such as *Just Imagine* and *Things to Come*.[68] They are characterized by their geometric patterns and clean surfaces: the sort of cityscapes imagined by architects such as Le Corbusier and Hugh Casson. Casson was the chief architect for the Festival of Britain, seeing it as a showcase for modernist design with features such as the Dome of Discovery and the Skylon. The Festival of Britain was 'a spectacular showpiece for the inventiveness and genius of British scientists and technologists'.[69] The future imagined in 'Dan Dare' embodies the idealism of the Festival of Britain where technology is both functional and employed for the benefit of mankind.[70] Mankowitz argued that Dan represented a progressive idea of the future: his special abilities arise from 'the scientific equipment of the age he lives in . . . Dare is a sort of socialised Superman – and his adventures belong to an ideal scientific society of the future.'[71]

That said, however, the 'look' of the strip is still distinctively British. Its futuristic cities co-exist with sleepy villages of thatched cottages and parish churches. The traditional and the modern are often placed in juxtaposition to one another. In 'Voyage to Venus', for example, a spaceship lands on a

'Dan Dare' offered a modernist vision of the future. *Eagle* (Hulton Press, 21 April 1950).

village green during an annual cricket match between Nether Wallop and Picrust Parva, while in 'Reign of the Robots' we see Big Ben preserved in a giant glass dome.[72] The persistence of these traditional images of Britishness can be seen as a device to make the future seem familiar and therefore reassuring. Even in the age of the atom bomb and the ballistic missile, it seems to suggest, there will be honey still for tea.

It is also, for the most part, a utopian future. The strip offers a progressive idea of political and social organization. It posits the existence of a United World Government and a world in which disease and poverty have been largely eradicated. In this respect 'Dan Dare' can be seen to have been influenced by the formation of the United Nations after the Second World War in that it expressed optimism about a future where international differences are peacefully resolved. In 'The Red Moon Mystery', for example, it is revealed that the nuclear arms race has ended ('All super explosives were completely dismantled after the final peace congress in '65') and that democracy has been established in Russia, China and Japan, where there has been 'a mighty drive to end poverty and squalor. Individual liberty and equality is secure, regardless of race, colour or creed.'[73] This input was Hampson's. In a self-written interview for the paper he said: 'What I would like to see, most urgently, is the establishment of the U.N. Government, and United Nations Police Force . . . With the whole wonderful adventure of Space Travel challenging mankind, it is ridiculous that "Earthmen" should be clinging on to National prejudices and squabbling among themselves.'[74]

At the same time, however, 'Dan Dare' is conditioned by the social attitudes of 1950s Britain. Nowhere is this more evident than in its representations of gender and race. The character of Professor Jocelyn Peabody (the Reverend Morris having apparently overcome his aversion to emancipated heroines in trousers) represents the figure of the 'new woman'.[75] Peabody is 'a first-class geologist, botanist, agriculturist . . . [and] a qualified space pilot as well'.[76] The men's initial reaction to Peabody is surprise ('Gosh!' 'Jumpin' jets!' 'Suffering cats!' 'A WOMAN!'). A theme of the first story is how Space Fleet Controller Sir Hubert Guest, characterized as an elderly conservative in social matters, comes to accept Peabody: 'You're a very brave woman, Miss Peabody . . . May have been a bit – um – harsh in the past – er – never expected – hrrrph – female to behave so well – um – very cool. Er, good show . . . If you, er, see what I mean.'[77] The role of the cool and resourceful Peabody was to normalize the idea (for *Eagle*'s predominantly male readership) that girls could be scientists too. Yet she still represents a conservative idea of femininity. Unlike 'Flash Gordon', where the exotic alien queens were drawn with highly sexualized figures and lusted after the hero, Peabody instead resembles the demure look of contemporary British actresses such as Muriel Pavlow and Dinah Sheridan. There is certainly no suggestion of sexual desire.

It is in its attitude towards race and ethnicity, however, where 'Dan Dare' is most conservative. Although it suggests that the make-up of the World Government is multi-racial, the strip is nevertheless at best patronizing, and at worst outright racist, in its representation of non-white races. Those most likely to panic when disaster threatens are the superstitious Africans and Asians rather than the rational Europeans and Americans. In 'The Red Moon Mystery', a police commissioner remarks: 'I'm worried about the tropics. We've never really got rid of superstition there. A tale of a new red god in the sky is spreading like wildfire. They think it means a return to the old days of devils and bloodshed.'[78] It is significant that Dare's team, while international in make-up, is entirely white Anglo-European, with the sole exception of Sondar, a friendly green-skinned Treen from Venus who represents an Umbopa-type figure – strong, silent, fiercely loyal and entirely subservient to the white hero.[79]

The chief ideological strategy of 'Dan Dare' is its promotion of Britishness.[80] To this extent the strip is fully consistent with the editorial policy of *Eagle* itself. Dan embodies the virtues of the British gentleman hero: courage, decency, tolerance and a sense of fair play. In particular he adheres to a code of honour that upholds the best of British values. In 'Prisoners of Space', for example, Dan's arch enemy the Mekon holds three Space Cadets hostage and demands that Dan travel alone and unarmed to a rendezvous in space. Dan is adamant that he must accept: 'We've fought the good fight to save honour and spread our ideals where ever Spacefleet penetrates. To sacrifice them – even once – is the first step towards the Mekon's way of life.'[81] When Digby stows away on Dan's ship with a cache of weapons, a furious Dan jettisons them: 'You've caused me to break my word of honour to the Mekon . . . The whole purpose of our peaceful penetration into outer space has been to show dwellers on other planets that Earth's code is the finest way of life. We've got to set an example of truth and honour to the rest of the universe at *whatever cost.*'[82]

'Dan Dare' may also be read as a narrative of British power. It belongs to a lineage of post-war British cultural production – other examples include the James Bond novels of Ian Fleming and the war movies of the 1950s – that project Britain as a major world power. Britain in the early 1950s clung to the idea of remaining a global power on a par with the United States and the Soviet Union. Incidents such as the escape of HMS *Amethyst* from the Yangtze River (July 1949) and the heroism of the 'Glorious Gloucesters' at the Battle of the Imjin River (April 1951) during the Korean War drew favourable comparisons with the great martial deeds of the Second World War. The imperial pageantry of the Coronation provided 'a retrospectively unconvincing reaffirmation of Britain's continued great-power status'.[83] 'Dan Dare' reflects this mood in that it has Britain entering space in a position of leadership and power. In reality, of course, Britain was excluded from the space race, but there were some voices who argued that the country should develop its own space programme. During a parliamentary debate on space research, for example, the Minister for Science, Viscount Hailsham, declared: 'There are many Dan Dares among our adult population who look upon the thing principally as a form of international sporting contest for the sake of prestige.'[84]

'Dan Dare' is replete with references to the British historical experience of the mid-twentieth century. Most obviously the strip refers back to the Second World War. Hampson confirmed this when he said: 'Basically we were fighting the Second World War again – the Treens were the Nazis.'[85] For Britons there was a natural link between Nazism and science fiction. Churchill's wartime speeches had mobilized the idea of the Nazis as a robotic enemy who threatened to plunge the world 'into a new Dark Age made more sinister, and perhaps more protracted, by the lights of a perverted science'.[86] In the last year of the war Hitler had unleashed his new super weapons, the V1 'flying bomb' and the V2 missile, against Britain. Dan's arch enemy is the Mekon, the 'supreme scientist' of the Treens, a race of mindless automatons who obey him without question. The Mekon applies his own brand of 'perverted science' that sees his human captives subjected to cruel experiments to test their physical endurance. He has an arsenal of technologically advanced weapons, including a fleet of bombing planes that resemble the V1 and a super death-ray known as the Telezero Beam. The Mekon is an arch technocrat who intends to 'regularize' the Earth: 'It is time your ridiculous planet was regularized and used to further the ends of science.'[87]

There is no mistaking the allusions to Nazism in 'Dan Dare'. In 'Operation Saturn' the mad scientist Dr Blasco is leader of the World Empire Bureau, a neo-Fascist organization whose members wear jackboots and give raised-arm salutes. Blasco sees himself as emperor of a 'new world' (echoing Nazi rhetoric of a 'new world order') that will be ruled by the 'purest aristocracy of the solar system'. There are clear echoes of Nazi racial genocide in Blasco's declaration that 'the Earth is burdened with common, low grade people – inefficient and unfit creatures who must be wiped out of the empire of Blasco the First'.[88] 'Reign of the Robots' – in which Dan returns home after a long voyage in suspended animation to discover that Earth has been conquered by the Mekon and his army of Elektrobots – again has clear overtones of Nazism as the surviving humans are sent to slave labour camps: 'An underwater concentration camp! Only you could have thought up such a foul idea!'[89]

The narrative that 'Dan Dare' employs most frequently is that of resistance to tyrants and dictators with ambitions to conquer the solar system: 'Voyage to Venus', 'Marooned on Mercury' and 'Operation Saturn' are all variations on this theme. This is consistent with the popular historical narrative that casts Britain as the protector of freedom and liberty against the territorial ambitions of foreign despots: Philip II of Spain, Napoleon, Kaiser Wilhelm II, Hitler. This narrative had been mobilized during the Second World War when the Ministry of Information had encouraged a model of historical propaganda promoting 'Britain as pioneer of freedom and justice, against both domestic and foreign tyrants, and of balanced and gradual social improvements'.[90] This had led to a cycle of historical propaganda films that dramatized resistance to tyranny including *This England*, *The Prime Minister*, *The Young Mr Pitt* and *Henry V*.[91] 'Dan Dare' represents the continuation of this narrative into the post-war period, except that the allegory is now being extended to an imagined future.

The other historical context mapped onto 'Dan Dare' is the Cold War. The 'universe' of 'Dan Dare' can be read from a Cold War perspective of opposing power blocs: one democratic and multi-cultural, the other totalitarian and highly ideological. The Treens are a race of ideologically conditioned automatons led by an emotionless technocrat. The Mekon represents scientific rationalism and social control taken to its cold-blooded extreme: he rules a society that tolerates no difference or dissent. In contrast Dan and his allies in Space Fleet represent the ideals of liberal democracy: they believe in individualism and free choice. The strip is imbued with the ideology of the early Cold War. In 1947 the US government issued the Truman Doctrine, pledging support for 'free peoples resisting attempted subjugation by armed minorities or by outside pressures'. 'Dan Dare' extends this principle into outer space, where the United World Government supports the people of other planets suffering tyranny and oppression. As the Earth's prime minister declares in the first story: 'We are morally committed to help the Therons and Atlantines and to try and foil the Treens.'[92]

The first major test of the Truman Doctrine was the Korean War. In June 1950 the People's Republic of North Korea (a communist dictatorship) had invaded democratic South Korea, prompting the United Nations Security Council to respond with a multi-national force under the command of US General Douglas MacArthur. The geopolitics of the Korean War are mapped onto the first Dan Dare adventure, 'Voyage to Venus', which ran for 77 weeks from April 1950 until September 1951. The Therons of the southern hemisphere of Venus, whose society is a liberal democracy with a parliament and an elected president, are attacked by the totalitarian Treens from the northern hemisphere. The Earth sends a 'United Nations' task force to Venus including contingents from the United States, Canada, Britain, France, India and Russia. The Treens are defeated in a set-piece battle and a temporary governor is installed 'until a permanent solution is negotiated by the UN Government'.[93]

'Dan Dare' reached the height of its narrative ambition and visual imagination in the mid-1950s when two connected stories, 'The Man From

Nowhere' and 'Rogue Planet', which ran for some 92 weeks, expanded the fictional universe of the strip to take Dan into deep space. 'Rogue Planet' marks the height of Hampson's imaginative powers: he created a whole civilization (Phantos) based on a combination of Ancient World cultures including the Graeco-Roman and Egyptian empires. It was the start of a trend towards adventures on more distant worlds. In 'Safari in Space' Hampson began what he intended to be a long 'story arc' in which Dan would travel to many planets in search of his missing father.[94] However, this narrative persisted only as far as the next story, 'Terra Nova', in the midst of which Hampson handed over the drawing of the strip to Frank Bellamy. Bellamy later said that he took on the job reluctantly: 'I didn't like revamping Frank Hampson's characters, his creations, but had the directive from upstairs – that's what they wanted, and you can only give the client what he wants, so that was it.'[95] Bellamy drew the strip for a year before handing over to Don Harley, who in turn was followed by Keith Watson.[96] In 1967 a change of format saw Dan promoted to Controller of Space Fleet in which role he introduced his 'reminiscenes' (edited repeats of old strips) that ran until the last issue of *Eagle* on 26 April 1969.

* * *

Such was the popularity of Dan Dare in the 1950s that the character quickly transferred into other media. Radio Luxembourg broadcast *The Adventures of Dan Dare: Pilot of the Future*, sponsored by Horlicks, from 1951 until 1956. Dare was played by Noel Johnson, who had a suitably heroic pedigree, having played *Dick Barton – Special Agent* for the BBC in the late 1940s. The Dan Dare radio serial was followed by the BBC's *Journey into Space*, written by Charles Chilton, whose protagonist Jet Morgan transferred into a comic strip in 1956 drawn by the Italian artist Ferdinando Tacconi. A novel, *Dan Dare on Mars* by Basil Dawson, was published in 1956. In the late 1950s there was talk of a film to be made in CinemaScope and directed by Lindsay Anderson, though the director of films such as *This Sporting Life* and *If...* would seem an extremely unlikely choice for such a project.[97]

Dan Dare and *Eagle* also proved to be exportable commodities. An Australian edition of *Eagle* was published from 1953 and a Swedish version, *Falken*, featuring 'Dan Djärv Framtidspilot', appeared in 1955.[98] These were licensed editions for local markets, using the original artwork. In 1962 an Italian comic, *Il Giorno dei Ragazzi*, ran a strip entitled 'Dan Dare Pilota del Futuro', though it is not clear whether it was licensed. A French 'Dan Dair' was published in pocket library format in 1962.[99] Dan Dare also reached behind the Iron Curtain, where an unlicensed version, 'Den Deri Pilot Budocnosti', appeared in a Yugoslav comic called *Plavi Vjesnik* ('Blue Newspaper') from the late 1950s.[100]

A further indication of the popularity of Dan Dare is the proliferation of British spacemen who followed in his wake. A host of other 'pilots of the future' appeared in the 1950s, including Captain Valiant of the Interplanetary Police Patrol, Pete Mangan of the Space Patrol, Space Commander Kerry, Jet-Ace Logan, Space-Ace, Captain Condor, Captain Diamond and Captain Future. A cycle of short-lived space-themed comics in the early 1950s – *Space Comics*, *Space Commando*, *Super-Sonic*, *Star-Rocket*, *Space Hero* – helped to sustain the juvenile SF boom. Many of these were cheaply produced comics that sought to exploit the popularity of SF through licensed merchandizing. Captain Valiant, for example, drawn by Michael Anglo for the Arnold Book Company's *Space Comics*, 'was designed to lend itself to the merchandizing of gimmicks. So we drew our hero complete with uniform, weapons, and accessories to attract the attention of toy-makers, and they did . . . My young son was very proud of his Captain Valiant outfit manufactured by Playtogs.'[101]

If imitation really is the sincerest form of flattery, then *Rocket*, which advertised itself as 'the first space-age weekly', was surely the most sincere of the *Eagle* imitators. This was a sixteen-page tabloid-sized photogravure paper launched by Express Newspapers in 1956. It ran its own Dan Dare variant on the front pages: Captain Falcon of the Moon Base Patrol not only looked like Dan, but his commanding officer Commodore Fortescue-Fortescue was another Sir Hubert and his juvenile companions 'Sparrow' Smith and 'Crash' Kale were the strip's equivalent of 'Flamer' Spry and Steve Valiant. 'Captain Falcon' was credited to Frank Black, though it was actually the work of writer Conrad Frost and artist Basil Blackaller.[102] *Rocket* was edited, nominally at least, by Douglas Bader, the inspirational flyer who had lost both legs in an accident before the war but returned to lead a fighter squadron in the Battle of Britain. His first editorial recalled Hampson: 'The new Elizabethan Age has found horizons wider than the first Elizabethans visaged. And for you who belong to it there are adventures ahead, more exciting and more perilous than ever faced Raleigh and Drake or even Columbus.'[103] However, *Rocket* lasted for only 32 issues, proving that glossy colour and high production values alone were insufficient to sell a comic if its content was too derivative.

Rick Random, created by Edward Holmes for Amalgamated Press's *Super Detective Library* and who featured in 27 stories between 1953 and 1959, was a rather more interesting variation. Rick Random is chief troubleshooter for the Interplanetary Bureau of Investigation, a combination of detective and action hero. These stories again suggest an internationalist future: Earth is governed by a World Federation of Powers which took control following the 'last great Earth war' of the 1990s. The series was informed by contemporary geopolitics. 'Rick Random and the Threat from Space' is a

Rocket (Express Newspapers, 21 April 1956).

thinly disguised Cold War spy story in which Baron Lyztu, ambassador for the Krent Empire, is exposed as a spy who uses television broadcasts to transmit coded messages over the airwaves. And 'Rick Random and the Space Pirates' is a parable of 'haves' and 'have nots' that reflects the growing tension within the United Nations between wealthy Western nations and the Third World. Here it transpires that attacks on space freighters carrying a precious ore have been perpetrated by agents of the impoverished planet Merak II: 'Not pirates,

Dr Fisher, but *patriots* from my planet. We are too weak to wage war. And in this way we have all the iridium we shall ever need.'[104]

The writers for the Rick Random series included Canadian journalist Bob Kesten and American SF author Harry Harrison, who was living in Britain in the 1950s, while the most regular illustrator was Ron Turner. Turner was something of an SF specialist who also drew the 'Space Ace' strip for *Lone Star Magazine*. Turner's style was influenced by a broad range of SF imagery, including *Metropolis*, *Flash Gordon* and the novels of Jules Verne. Like Alex Raymond he creates an imaginary world that combines the futuristic (space rockets, helicars, vis-phones, anti-gravity packs) with ancient civilizations and dinosaur-like monsters. The females are more sexualized than in *Eagle*: characters like Princess Dana of Urdana and the Cat Women of Tigeris are represented as exotic and sensual. Rick himself is a conventional square-jawed, chain-smoking archetype, somewhat resembling the actor Jeffrey Hunter.

Perhaps the most progressive of the British spacemen was 'Jeff Hawke', a newspaper strip that ran in the *Daily Express* from 1954 until 1975. 'Jeff Hawke' was created and drawn by Sydney Jordan, a Scottish artist who had trained as an aircraft engineer, with most of the stories written by Willie Patterson. Jordan's style used chiaroscuro to represent the unworldly environments of the future (the strip is set in the 1990s) and his artwork is especially notable for its finely textured dot-patterned starscapes. One of his trademarks is the single panel 'widescreen' frame that he would sometimes employ in place of the standard three frames.

'Jeff Hawke' differs from other SF strips in that its hero is essentially a pacifist who prefers to avoid conflict and instead resolves problems through negotiation. In 'Overlord' he is appointed special ambassador to the United Nations Security Council and sent to Jupiter to intervene in a conflict between two alien races that threatens to engulf the Earth. In 'Counsel for the Defence' he is summoned to Galactopolis, capital of the Intergalactic Federation, to act as defence attorney in the trial of arch-criminal Chalcedon. The aliens of 'Jeff Hawke' tend not to be aggressive invaders but squabbling bureaucrats beset by the same petty rivalry and jealousy as their human equivalents. Jordan claimed that the strip was influenced by his experiences in the RAF, which had been 'a second education in terms of becoming aware of the pecking order and social niceties that oiled the wheels of middle-class Britain'.[105] Thus there are hierarchies of alien creatures and extra-terrestrial relations are governed by rigid bureaucratic processes. Jordan was also not averse to turning SF conventions on their heads. In 'The Ambassadors' the aliens are a pair of migratory bird creatures who believe their feathered relatives are the ruling species on Earth. And 'Wondrous Lamp' turns on a device from

'Rick Random and the Terror from Space', *Super Detective Library* (Amalgamated Press Ltd, 1957).

Catherine Maclean's novel *Pictures Don't Lie* as the mighty Klahrrid invasion army turn out to be microscopic creatures who are routed by a tabby cat.

* * *

The success of *Eagle*, which at its height in the 1950s had a circulation of around 750,000, prompted Hulton to launch a sister paper, *Girl*, also edited by Marcus Morris, in 1951. It was followed by *Robin*, for the under-sevens, in 1953, and by *Swift*, for seven- to ten-year-olds, in 1954. It would be no exaggeration to say that Morris had revolutionized the world of British juvenile papers. *Eagle* had proved that comics could indeed be 'clean and exciting': that they could promote a Christian world-view while at the same time satisfying their readers' demands for adventure. With their conservative values and middle-class ethos, *Eagle* and its companion papers were wholly representative of British society of the 1950s. They were as much a part of the cultural landscape as the Ealing comedies and *Dixon of Dock Green*. It is significant that the height of their popularity coincided with a time that historians have variously described as an 'age of consensus' and 'the zenith of one-nation Toryism'.[106]

Yet by the end of the 1950s there were signs that the golden age of *Eagle* was coming to an end. There were several reasons for its decline. Morris, who wanted to assume a more managerial role within Hulton Press, had become restless, complaining that 'there is a limited future in comics such as *Eagle* ... The comics are not sufficient by themselves to occupy my interests and energies.'[107] In 1959 Hulton, weakened by declining profits, was taken over by Odhams Press. This precipitated Morris's resignation when Odhams denied him the managerial role he desired. He became editorial director of the National Magazine Company, which specialized in women's titles such as *Good Housekeeping, Cosmopolitan, Vanity Fair* and *Harper's Bazaar*. Morris was soon followed by Frank Hampson. The new owners sought to curb costs, discontinuing the Eagle Club and imposing economies on the production of the paper. Hampson's studio became a target and, faced with a choice of either changing his working methods or leaving the paper, Hampson left. His last full strip for *Eagle* was 'The Road of Courage', concluding, appropriately, at Easter 1960. Thereafter he earned his living drawing advertising strips and cover illustrations for Ladybird Books.

While *Eagle* certainly suffered from the loss of its founding editor and principal artist, however, the major reason for its decline was that it became a victim of structural changes in the newspaper and magazine publishing industries. There was a trend towards consolidation as smaller publishers merged or were taken over by larger publishing groups. In 1961 Odhams was swallowed by the Mirror Group, with the consequence that *Eagle* was brought within the orbit of Fleetway Publications, as the group's juvenile arm was known. *Eagle* was no longer the pride of a small independent publisher but merely a small part of a corporate giant. The effects of the takeover were described by *Eagle* sub-editor Dan Lloyd:

> The crunch came in August [1961] when we were taken over ... Andy Vincent, from Fleetway, began to wield his axe with devastating effect. Some of the most enduring features were mercilessly chopped and in their place appeared stock items from the Fleetway emporium. The quality of artwork that had been *Eagle*'s trademark was sacrificed on the grounds of economy and staff morale fell to as low an ebb as the readership, which declined alarmingly.[108]

The new owners sought to rationalize their juvenile titles with a succession of mergers. *Eagle* absorbed *Swift* in 1963 and *Boys' World* in 1964. In the same year *Girl* merged with *Princess*, and in 1969 *Robin* merged with *Playhour*. By this time the format of the paper, which throughout the 1950s had remained remarkably consistent, had become chronically unstable. Several favourite strips, including 'Harris Tweed' and 'Riders of the Range', were dropped and replaced by reprints of old stories from the Fleetway archive. Even Dan Dare temporarily lost his place on the front cover and was reduced to one page of colour. The circulation diminished along with the paper size: by the early 1960s it had fallen to 150,000.

Eagle struggled to respond to changing popular tastes in the 1960s. It dropped the biblical stories and put 'Blackbow the Cheyenne' on the back page. Its last memorable strips were Frank Bellamy's 'Fraser of Africa' and 'Heros the Spartan'. 'Fraser of Africa' is notable for its progressive attitude towards conservation and for Bellamy's experimental style using a limited palette and sepia tone to represent the scorched African plains. 'Heros the Spartan' is a historical fantasy adventure in the style of the Italian *peplum* notable for a greater degree of pictorial violence than usual for *Eagle*. Evidence that the paper had lost its way, however, is to be found in a debate in its letters pages in 1965 concerning whether it should include a regular feature on pop music called 'Pop Pick'. There was no consensus among readers. Thus, while one urged 'PLEASE let *Eagle* be left alone from HORRID beat groups', another ventured the opinion that 'if any comic is good, it must keep up with the times. *Eagle* is not at all spoilt and I think that "Pop Pick" is a very good idea.'[109] But *Eagle* was not keeping up with the times. Its social values seemed old-fashioned and fogeyish as the 1960s began to swing. It belatedly adopted the slogan 'The modern paper for the modern boy' at a time when it had ceased to be anything of the sort. The end came in 1969 when *Eagle* merged with its one-time rival *Lion*. The history of *Eagle* is further proof that popular culture is of and for its time: what had been bright and modern at the start of the 1950s had ceased to seem relevant by the end of the 1960s. The simple fact was that *Eagle* had run out of cultural energy.

CHAPTER THREE

Ripping Yarns

> Something like three hundred and fifty million comics are bought annually by our children, many of them with their own pocket money. It is believed that, on average, each comic is seen by about eight children. A typical child's remark on comics was made by the son of a high official in the Ministry of Education when sweets came off the ration; he said to his mother, 'I shall not waste my money on sweets. Comics last longer.'
> *British Comics: An Appraisal* (1955).[1]

If there was a golden age of British comics, it was in the 1950s and '60s when Britain was one of the leading producers and consumers of comics in the world. It has been estimated that around 14 million comics were sold weekly during the 1950s with the most popular titles selling a million copies each.[2] This was the period when the picture-strip paper – represented by new titles such as *Comet*, *Eagle*, *Lion* and *Victor* – decisively displaced the story paper as the favoured reading matter of juveniles. The decline of the story paper and the rise of the picture-strip paper has generally been related to the emergence of television as the dominant mass-entertainment medium. The number of British households with television increased from 750,000 in 1951 to 10.5 million by 1960.[3] The publishers of children's papers had to contend with the fact that children now spent more time watching television and less time reading. Hence the shift away from text-heavy prose stories towards picture strips that could be read quickly and, like television, told the story in images rather than words.

The re-emergence of comics after the Second World War arose from a congruence of factors that, like the first comics boom of the 1890s, created the circumstances in which the industry could flourish. The post-war 'baby boom' of 1946–8 when the birth rate increased by 25 per cent meant there was an expanding market for comics by the mid- and late 1950s. The end of

Comet was one of the new picture-strip papers that emerged after the Second World War. *Comet* (Amalgamated Press Ltd, 24 March 1956).

paper rationing in 1953 meant that wartime restrictions on new titles and the size of print runs were lifted. The transition, as conventionally described, from austerity to affluence paved the way for a lucrative new market for leisure and entertainment. Arthur Marwick, for example, contends that 'the reality for the vast majority of British people was that at last the country seemed to have entered into the kind of high-spending consumer society long familiar from American films'.[4] The effects of full employment and increasing wage packets trickled down to the main consumers of comics, the pre-teens, most of whom received some pocket money. Comics were a cheap form of entertainment and a transferable commodity that could be swapped once they had been read and enjoyed. British juvenile publishers, furthermore, benefited from restrictions on the import of American comics until 1959.

For the comic industry, this was a period of consolidation that saw the emergence of the duopoly of D. C. Thomson and Amalgamated Press that would dominate the market for the next three decades. Thomson led the field for the publication of 'funnies', adding *Topper* and *Beezer* to its established favourites *Beano* and *Dandy*. However, it was Amalgamated that led the way in publishing new picture papers for the eight- to twelve-year-old age group. In 1949 it acquired *Comet* and *Sun*, two fortnightly comics launched after the war by independent publisher J. B. Allen of Cheshire. In 1952, in response to the success of Hulton's *Eagle*, Amalgamated launched *Lion* ('King of Picture Story Papers'), following it with *Tiger* in 1954, *Valiant* in 1962 and *Hurricane* in 1964. These were anthology titles that featured picture strips across a range of boys' genres – westerns, swashbucklers, sport, science fiction, war – and usually included at least one prose story. It was also Amalgamated that in the 1950s introduced the innovative 'picture library' format: a compact, pocket-sized comic featuring one long complete story rather than the shorter, episodic serials of the anthologies.[5] *Cowboy Comics Library* was the first in 1950, followed by *Thriller Picture Library* in 1951, *Super Detective Picture Library* in 1953, *War Picture Library* in 1958, *Air Ace Picture Library* in 1960 and *Battle Picture Library* in 1961. The picture libraries were aimed at an older readership (typically eleven- to sixteen-year-olds) who would graduate to them from anthology titles.

Amalgamated's chief rival, however, responded rather tardily to the changing market. D. C. Thomson clung longer to its story papers, with four of the 'big five' continuing into the post-war period (*Skipper* had been a casualty of wartime paper shortages). The sales of these papers were declining, however, and Thomson was losing ground.[6] In 1958, noting its rival's success in relaunching two girls' story papers as picture papers (*School Friend* in 1950 and *Girls' Crystal* in 1953), Thomson reinvented *Hotspur* as a picture paper, initially called *New Hotspur* before reverting to its original title in 1963. The rebranded *Hotspur* was followed by *Victor* in 1961 and *Hornet* in 1963 and by picture library *Commando* in 1961. Thomson still persevered with its story papers: *Rover* incorporated both *Adventure* and *Wizard* during the 1960s and lasted until 1973 when it was in turn merged with a new picture-strip *Wizard* launched in 1970. The demise of the story paper was a cause of regret in some quarters. John Taylor, an adviser to the Barnsley Education Authority, saw a direct link with the decline of reading standards: 'These comics had anything from four to twelve times as many words as their modern equivalents . . . The stories were perhaps a little naive but they had definite quality. What have we got today? Disjointed jerky sentences and stories full of exclamation marks.'[7] And Owen Dudley Edwards similarly disliked 'the tabloids [*sic*] which have so coarsely replaced the masses of tiny black print Thomson's offered for our twopence'.[8]

While some disliked the new picture papers, however, there were many continuities with their story paper predecessors. This was apparent in the ease with which characters who had started out in story papers were to extend their careers in comics: Sexton Blake, the Black Sapper, Morgyn the Mighty,

Bill Samson ('The Wolf of Kabul'), William Wilson ('Wilson of the *Wizard*'), Alf Tupper ('The Tough of the Track') and Sergeant-Pilot Matt Braddock were just a few of those who made the transition from prose to picture strips. There was an economic rationale for this practice: recycling existing material was cheaper than commissioning new stories. Amalgamated Press, for example, bought the rights to the Dick Turpin Libraries published during the interwar years by Newnes and the Aldine Press and used the stories for *Thriller Picture Library* in the 1950s. There was continuity in the writing, too, as established writers of prose stories such as Frank S. Pepper, Edward R. Home-Gall and Rex King adapted to the new medium. Pepper was tasked with providing the cover stories for both *Lion* and *Tiger*. Despite his later assertion that 'none of us knew anything about the craft of telling a story in pictures', Pepper scripted the adventures of Captain Condor for *Lion* and was responsible for launching the career of Roy of the Rovers in *Tiger*.[9] Others, such as Tom Tully, began their writing careers for comics. Tully became a prolific and versatile staff writer for Amalgamated Press and its successors Fleetway and IPC, contributing to *Tiger, Valiant, Battle, Action, Roy of the Rovers* and *2000AD*.

While writers could easily adapt from one form to another, however, what the growth of the comic industry required more than anything were artists. A generation of comic-strip artists began their careers in the late 1940s and early 1950s, including Frank Bellamy, Reg Bunn, Geoff Campion, Joe Colquhon, Ron Embleton, Derek Eyles, Don Lawrence, Patrick Nicolle, Ron Turner and Mike Western.[10] All these artists drew for adventure comics, where their detailed draughtsmanship and fluid story-telling revealed the influence of American strips, especially Alex Raymond's 'Rip Kirby', which had been syndicated in the *Daily Mail* since 1947 and came to be regarded as 'a how-to-draw comics primer for a whole generation of would-be comic artists'.[11] Others were recruited from fields such as book illustration and advertising. Leonard Matthews, the editor of *Thriller Picture Library*, hired the renowned illustrator H. M. Brock to draw several early stories. Brock had provided illustrations for story papers such as *Chums, Captain* and the *Boy's Own Paper* and was particularly known for drawing historical subjects. Matthews's biggest coup, however – to the extent that it was even announced in the pages of *Knock-Out* – was to hire 'the world-famous artist' Septimus E. Scott, a renowned poster artist best known for painting railway advertisements between the wars. Scott drew the swashbuckling 'Captain Flame' for *Knock-Out* in the late 1940s from stories by Matthews – comic historian David Ashford describes the series as 'the finest pirate strips ever to appear in a comic'[12] – and went on to paint over 100 colour cover illustrations for *Thriller Picture Library*. Scott's atmospheric style, romantic imagination and

'Captain Flame – Pirate Hunter', in *Knock-Out* (Amalgamated Press, 14 March 1953).

rich palette were perfectly suited to the historical adventures that predominated in the 1950s.

Even so the shortage of British artists was so chronic that publishers increasingly had to recruit talent from overseas, especially from Italy and Spain. It was Amalgamated who, once again, led the way, its pocket libraries requiring dozens of artists who could produce the 64 pages of art that comprised a typical issue. These artists usually came through agencies, particularly the D'Ami studio of Milan and Selecciones Ilustradas of Madrid. Italian artists, including Gino D'Antonio, Giorgio Di Gaspari, Pino Del Orco, Hugo Pratt, Enrico De Seta, Ferdinando Tacconi and Nevio Zeccara, became the mainstay of *Thriller Picture Library* in the late 1950s and dominated the early years of *War Picture Library* and its companion titles. Spanish artists, including Jesús Blasco, Victor de la Fuente, José Ortiz and Jordi Penalva, were also regular contributors to British comics from the early 1960s. The Europeans' art was notable for its dynamic representation of action and for its pictorial realism (of the sort usually described as 'gritty') in contrast to most British artists. Their ascendancy coincided with the eclipse of historical adventure stories and the emergence of war as the dominant genre of British comics at the turn of the decade.[13]

The hegemony of the 'big two' was challenged in the 1950s by a third force, Hulton Press, with its red-masted quartet of *Eagle, Girl, Robin* and *Swift*, and by several independent publishers including J. B. Allen, T. V. Boardman, Gerald Swan and Len Miller. It was Allen who launched the first new post-war British comic *Comet* in 1946, selling it to Amalgamated Press in 1949. Swan began as a market trader before branching into comic publishing in the 1940s. He published three-penny albums, modelled on the American comic book format, such as *Funnies Album, Dynamic Thrills* and *Western War Comic*. Boardman and Miller were originally comic importers who, during the war, had started publishing cheap reprints of the American comics no longer available in Britain. They continued in this vein after the war, Boardman continuing his deal with Quality Comics to print British editions of *Blackhawk* and *The Spirit*, and Miller entering into a lucrative deal with Fawcett Publications to reprint a range of titles including *Whiz Comics, Captain Marvel, Captain Video, Spy Smasher, Don Winslow of the Navy, Nyoka the Jungle Girl* and *Six-Gun Heroes*. Unable to meet demand with reprints alone, these publishing entrepreneurs branched out into original material in the 1950s. Boardman published a series of *Buffalo Bill* albums, while Miller mined the Dan Dare-inspired science fiction lode with *Captain Valiant* and *Space Commander Kerry*.

These independent comics were cheaply produced and vulnerable to the vagaries of paper supply and distribution. Michael Anglo, who drew comics for Miller and the Arnold Book Company during the 1950s, explained how the independents worked on tight margins:

> Independent comics were produced on a slim budget and artists had to maintain a high output in order to earn a living. In order to compete with big publishing houses the independent publisher had to cut his costs to the bone. His distribution was hampered

through discrimination, not being able to afford to advertise, and the ever-rising costs of paper and printing. His individual print runs were small, yet his titles rolled regularly off the presses, and without promotion and advertising his overall sales were in the region of a million comics per month . . . We always had bags of mail from satisfied customers, the kids and the parents, and our publishers made money.[14]

One advantage that small independents had over the larger publishers was that they were able to respond more quickly to changes in the market. Len Miller, for example, was among the first to recognize the potential of the Second World War as subject-matter for comics. Miller published six issues of *Bulldog Brittain Commando* irregularly between 1952 and 1958, partially inspired by American war comics such as *G. I. Joe* and *Sergeant Rock*.

The heyday of independent comics was in the 1950s, when the absence of American imports allowed these publishers to prosper: such was the demand for comics that even the most rough-and-ready publications found an enthusiastic readership. They were produced in the format of American comic books with colour covers and containing one principal story with one or two supporting strips. Some publishers even attempted to disguise their British origin by putting American prices on the covers. Denis Gifford, working as a freelance artist in the early 1950s, later recalled: 'I was drawing five pages a day, five days a week, working for the sort of comics that pretended they were American, even to printing "5 cents" on the covers. At £1 15s a page, which is what I was paid, you have to work very hard to make a decent living.'[15] Once the import of us comics resumed at the end of the decade, however, the independents found themselves squeezed out of the market. Some went to the wall; others survived by switching to publication of nudist and 'glamour' magazines. The last survivor was L. Miller & Co., which lasted until 1970 when it became the first publisher to be prosecuted under the Children and Young Persons (Harmful Publications) Act of 1955 for importing some of the banned horror comics.[16]

* * *

In 1940 George Orwell had suggested that the social and political values of the story papers remained rooted firmly in the Edwardian period. Collectively they exhibited 'a set of beliefs which would be regarded as hopelessly out of date in the Central Office of the Conservative Party' and instilled into their impressionable young readers 'the conviction that the major problems of our time do not exist, that there is nothing wrong with laissez-faire capitalism, that foreigners are unimportant comics and that the British

Cover of *Bulldog Brittain Commando*, an example of independent comic publishing. (L. Miller & Son Ltd, 1958).

Empire is a sort of charity concern which will last forever'.[17] Even such an astute social commentator as Orwell cannot have foreseen the profound changes that affected British society over the next five years, and, while the extent of 'class levelling' brought about by mobilization for total war has probably been exaggerated, the Britain of 1945 had nevertheless been substantially transformed from that of 1939 or 1940. This was perhaps more evident at the level of people's expectations – expectations that in 1945 had seen the election of a Labour government committed to an ambitious programme of state welfare provision and social reform – than in more quantifiable matters such as social mobility.[18] Two of the assumptions Orwell identified in 1940 could no longer be regarded as axiomatic: laissez-faire capitalism had given way to state control of key industries (railways, coal, gas, electricity, steel) and the ascendancy of the British Empire had been eroded by independence for India and Pakistan in 1947. Another highly significant measure – the Education Act of 1944 which reorganized state education and introduced free secondary schooling for all – also had repercussions for the world of juvenile fiction.

The social changes effected by the Second World War were evident in boys' comics in a number of ways. The market for comics was predominantly working class – *Eagle*, with its aspirational middle-class outlook, was an exception to the rule – and this was reflected in their content. One obvious symptom was the disappearance of the public school story from boys' comics (girls' comics, as we shall see, were another matter entirely). In the 1950s only *Comet* (in a bowdlerized version of 'Billy Bunter of Greyfriars'), *Sun* ('The Terrible Three') and *Lion* ('Sandy Dean's Schooldays') regularly featured public school stories. There was a trend towards more working-class protagonists, exemplified by such emphatically proletarian archetypes as Alf Tupper and by heroes of the people's war like Matt Braddock. Tupper and Braddock both began as prose serials in *Rover* and later transferred to *Victor* as picture strips. Owen Dudley Edwards attests that '*Rover* was quite definitely more working-class in tone, attitudes and heroes' than the other Thomson story papers: the same observation would apply to *Victor* among the comics.[19] The changing face of post-war comics did not go unnoticed. Arthur Hopcraft, writing in 1961, noted that 'the post-war social upset . . . has not bypassed comics entirely. Jeans are in and rugger colours are out, and one second-lieutenant hero is a plumber's son from Stoke-on-Trent'.[20] A decade later Keith Dewhurst argued that comics were responding, albeit tardily, to social change: '*Lion* is a new [sic] British comic that is interesting because, while not exactly giving up [the] traditional British adventure formula, it does seem to be looking for a way out of its dilemma, which is that although the real world has changed in the past 30 years, the unspoken assumptions of the stories have not.'[21]

To this extent British comics of the 1950s and '60s exemplify Raymond Williams's argument that cultural practices encompass both residual and emergent forms. Williams suggested that while some aspects of culture are 'residual' in that they draw upon previous social formations, others are 'emergent' and are characterized by 'new meanings and values, new practices, new significances and experiences'.[22] The residual forms in boys' comics were those genres, such as the swashbuckler and the public school story, whose narrative codes and conventions had been formed in the pre-war story papers, whereas the emergent forms were those, such as the Second World War story and science fiction, whose codes and conventions took shape in comics during the post-war period. This was not a linear process – some residual forms adapted and survived, and some new forms proved less durable – while in the case of the sports story an existing genre was transformed so thoroughly that it became to all intents and purposes new. Overall, however, this period witnessed the transformation of British comics as most residual forms gradually disappeared.

This process can be seen, in microcosm, in the evolution of *Thriller Picture Library*, whose publication history spans three distinct periods.[23] The first period, between 1951 and 1956, consisted entirely of residual forms. These were historical adventures, swashbucklers, westerns and adaptations of popular classics including *Rob Roy, Ivanhoe, The Last of the Mohicans, The Three Musketeers, The Count of Monte Cristo, Treasure Island, Captain Blood, The Sea Hawk, The Black Swan* and *The Four Feathers*. The most popular recurring characters during this period were Robin Hood (who appeared in 54 issues between 1951 and 1960) and Dick Turpin (who featured in 25 isssues between 1951 and 1958). The historical adventures remained a significant trend in the second period of *Thriller Picture Library*, from 1957 to 1960, though they were now joined by Second World War stories, particularly those featuring fighter ace 'Battler' Britton, who would make a total of 65 appearances. This was a transitional period during which residual and new forms co-existed alongside each other without either becoming dominant. The last Robin Hood story was in February 1960 and the last western in April 1960. Thereafter, until the last issue in March 1963, new forms were in the ascendancy. The library now featured four principal recurring characters – Battler Britton, Dogfight Dixon, Spy 13 and Dick Daring of the Mounties – of whom three had a war theme while the fourth was a modern western. Towards the end of its life, *Thriller Picture Library* even featured science fiction stories with Jet-Ace Logan, late of the *Comet*.

The popularity of the swashbuckler – the most prolific of the residual forms – can be explained in relation to the cultural and ideological context. Jeffrey Richards has described the 1950s as the 'last age of chivalry' and has pointed out that the decade witnessed the last major cycle of swashbuckling costume adventure films including *The Flame and the Arrow, The Crimson Pirate, Ivanhoe, The Prisoner of Zenda, The Story of Robin Hood and His Merrie Men, Rob Roy, the Highland Rogue, Knights of the Round Table, Prince Valiant, The Black Knight, The Black Shield of Falworth* and *The Adventures of Quentin Durward*.[24] Several of these films were adapted into comic strips. Patrick Nicolle drew 'Ivanhoe' and 'The Prisoner of Zenda' for *Sun* based not on Sir Walter Scott and Anthony Hope but on the two MGM films of 1952. Both strips were quickly recycled for *Thriller Picture Library*. The conventional explanation for the high profile of the swashbuckler is the Coronation of Queen Elizabeth II in 1953, which had mobilized motifs of pageantry and heritage into a celebration of Britain's past.[25] The swashbuckler, based on the endorsement of constitutional monarchy and the promotion of an ethos of chivalry, was the ideal genre for Coronation Britain.

The swashbuckler was very much a vehicle for promoting consensus: its protagonist, whether nobleman or commoner, is invariably cast in the role of protector of the state against tyranny and subversion. The recurring motifs are constitutional legitimacy and loyalty to the Crown as the embodiment of nationhood. In 'Spies of Spain', for example, drawn by William Bryce-Hamilton for *Knock-Out* in 1952, Martin Gregairn, a young nobleman, is falsely accused of involvement in a plot against Queen Elizabeth I. The real culprit is the treacherous Lord Radnor, in league with King Philip II of Spain, but Gregairn clears his name by rounding up the spies and arresting them 'for treason and the betrayal of your country'. He is rewarded by the Queen with a baronetcy 'for all the service you have done England'.[26] In 'Hunters of the Tower of London Traitors', written by E. George Cowan for *Lion* in 1953, the protagonists are swordmaker Dirk Selden and his apprentice Hal Rudd (described as 'those interfering churls' by one of the villains) who uncover a plot to assassinate Queen Elizabeth and usurp the throne. Again they are rewarded for their loyalty, being appointed swordmakers to the royal court: ''Tis a mighty fine honour. No better could we have wished for!'[27]

The popularity of Robin Hood – probably the most oft-represented character in British comics of the 1950s – owed something to the character's visibility in other media, including Disney's *The Story of Robin Hood and His Merrie Men* (1952), starring Richard Todd, and the television series *The Adventures of Robin Hood*, starring Richard Greene, which ran for 143 episodes between 1955 and 1960. Robin Hood stories were drawn for *Thriller Picture Library* by several artists including Geoff Campion, Philip Mendoza, Patrick Nicolle and Peter Sutherland. The Robin of *Thriller Picture Library* was based on the 1938 Warner Bros. film *The Adventures of Robin Hood* starring Errol Flynn – regarded by many as the definitive version – and adopted that film's narrative of a class war between the oppressed Saxons and their aristocratic Norman overlords. Frank Bellamy's Robin Hood strips for *Swift* in 1956–7 – 'Robin Hood and His Merry Men' and 'Robin Hood and Maid Marian' – cast Robin as the son of the Earl of Huntingdon, murdered by the Norman baron Robert Braisse-Neuve, who swears 'to fight the Normans and protect the poor and humble'.[28] It is significant that the comics cast Robin as a disinherited nobleman: this differentiated them from both the Disney film and the television series in which Robin was a commoner. This may have been to avoid charges of plagiarism; but it also meant that the Robin of the comics demonstrated different social politics from the more socially democratic film and television Robins.[29]

The highwayman was another residual form inherited from the penny dreadfuls of the nineteenth century. British comics of the 1950s were heavily populated with dashing masked highwaymen – Dick Turpin, Claude Duval, Swift Nick, Jack Sheppard – who by this stage of their fictional careers had been entirely rehabilitated as daring righters-of-wrongs rather than as common thieves and murderers. Thus the comic-strip highwaymen were gentleman heroes who personified the values of chivalry and patriotism. The fullest instance of this ideological rehabilitation was 'Claude Duval – The Laughing Cavalier' in *Comet*. This strip – created by Fred Holmes in 1953 and drawn at different times by Geoff Campion and Patrick Nicolle – cast Duval as a dashing Royalist swordsman during the Interregnum who leads 'his comrades in their fight for freedom – and for King Charles of England'.[30] Duval's recurring antagonist is Major Midas Mould of the Roundhead Secret Police, though Cromwell himself makes an appearance in one story where Duval rescues the Lord Protector's Royalist brother Tom from the gallows! The strip was adapted into a television series, *The Gay Cavalier*, in 1957.[31]

The archetypal English highwayman, of course, was Dick Turpin, who enjoyed a long and distinguished career in comics. The first 'Dick Turpin' illustrated story had appeared in *Film Picture Stories* in 1934, an adaptation of the Stoll Film Company production starring Victor McLaglen, drawn by R. H. Valda, though the most celebrated version is 'Dick Turpin's Ride to York', drawn by Derek Eyles for *Knock-Out* in 1948 and reprinted in *Thriller Picture Library* in 1951. The story, by Leonard Matthews, was based on William Ainsworth's novel *Rookwood* of 1834.[32] Later adventures in the series were adapted from the stories written by Charlton Lea and Stephen Agnew for the Dick Turpin Libraries published by George Newnes and the Aldine Press. These cast Turpin as 'the King of the Highway' with a 'merry band' of comrades including ex-Bow Street Runner Jem Peters, happy-go-lucky Irishman Pat O'Flynn and a faithful black retainer known as Beetles. A feature of these stories had been the element of social criticism that characterized Turpin and his comrades as crusaders for social justice. Charlton Lea, in particular, would tend 'to interpolate a few paragraphs of editorial comment decrying the injustices of the aristocracy against the common man'.[33]

The swashbuckler remained a constant presence in British comics throughout the 1950s but declined thereafter. Its demise coincided with the decline of the genre in cinema and television and with the emergence of new forms, particularly war stories, that eclipsed it. However, another residual form, that shared some common ground with the swashbuckler, persisted for much longer. The British Empire adventure had been a staple genre of juvenile literature since the heyday of popular imperialism in the late nineteenth century when story papers such as *Boys of England, Union Jack, Pluck* and *Captain* had entertained Victorian youths with manly tales of derring-do in far-flung corners of empire. It might be expected that the British Empire adventure would have lost much of its ideological currency during the retreat from empire following the Second World War and that the assumptions of British supremacy that permeated the genre would have been undermined by challenges to imperial authority represented by the Malayan Emergency (1948–54) and the Suez Crisis (1956). This was not, however, the case. India and Pakistan won their independence in 1947, but as late as 1970 one commentator found that '*Wizard* actually has a story whose villains are a rajah and a renegade white man plotting to drive the British out of India.'[34]

The story in question was 'The Wolf of Kabul', which is remarkable for its longevity. It began in prose form in *Wizard* in 1930, when it was concurrent with the events it depicted, and was still running as a picture strip in *Hotspur* and *Victor* into the 1980s, by which time it had become very much a period artefact. In the early 1970s it was running simultaneously as a prose serial in *Rover* and as a picture strip in the new *Wizard*. D. C. Thomson, unusually, referred to the character's publication history when a new adventure was written for *Rover* in 1972 and an editorial declared: '"The Wolf of Kabul" is coming back, in the kind of stories that first made him famous; the stories that your father and big brother will remember and want to read again.'[35] 'The Wolf of Kabul' is a fusion of adventure story and spy thriller that owes more than a soupçon to Rudyard Kipling's *Kim* and A.E.W. Mason's *The Drum*. It presents the tribal territories of northern India and Afghanistan as the 'savage border lands' marking the frontier of civilization. The 'Wolf' is British intelligence agent Bill Samson, who combines brain and brawn, while his sidekick is Chung, a 'Gunga Din' character whose favourite weapon is his trusty 'clicky-ba' – a cricket bat that he wields to bash enemies of the Raj about the head. Alan Moore later described Samson as a 'brutal British colonialist, but nevertheless that was how we liked our heroes back then'.[36]

The ideological project of the British Empire adventure is to legitimate colonialism. Thus British administration is presented as just and progressive, whereas colonial rebels are characterized as cruel tyrants. A good example is 'Rafferty's Own', a *Victor* strip from the mid-1960s set during the Indian Mutiny of 1857. In fact this offers a reasonably historically accurate account of the immediate cause of the Mutiny as sepoys refuse to handle cartridges greased with animal fat. It also suggests, however, a rather simplistic dichotomy between bad Indians who urge violent revolt ('Your comrades in Meerut and Delhi have thrown off the hated yoke of the English Raj!') and good Indians who remain loyal to the Crown ('We have sworn the oath of a warrior and do not break it as easily as the despised sepoys do!'). The emphasis is on maintaining the rule of law. Following the massacre of an English garrison, including women and children, Sergeant Rafferty takes command of a group of loyal Sikh cavalrymen: 'We will make it our business to bring back law and order to the land!'[37]

How do we explain the persistence of the imperial adventure at a time when Britain was winding down its empire? One reason, as with the swashbuckler, was the visibility of the genre in other media. The 1950s saw a cycle of Northwest Frontier adventure films: *Kim, Soldiers Three, King of the Khyber Rifles, Bengal Rifles, Khyber Patrol, Zarak, The Bandit of Zhobe* and *North West Frontier*.[38] These films – which, like the swashbuckling cycle of the 1950s, included both Hollywood and British examples – were essentially cavalry westerns in which the British played the role of white settlers, the Bengal Lancers took the place of the Seventh Cavalry and Afghan tribesmen were substituted for Red Indians. Both genres rehearse similar themes: the clash between civilization and savagery and the pacification of disruptive forces. The underlying narrative of both genres, however, is conflict resolution: and it is this theme that makes them acceptable as juvenile entertainments.

The conventions of the Northwest Frontier adventure are flexible enough that it can be set at almost any time between the early nineteenth century and the 1930s. 'Action in the Khyber' – written by Captain Jock Black for Michael Anglo's independently published *Battle* – demonstrates this point. It distills the essence of the Northwest Frontier story into eleven pages. The British army mounts a punitive action against Suda Rhani who is responsible for a series of attacks on villages around the Khyber Pass. Rhani's 'ultimate aim is to clear us out of the mountains then put the squeeze on the folks in the valley'.[39] What is most interesting about the story, however, is that it is entirely generic. There is no indication of when it is set: from the uniforms and weapons it could be any time between 1880 and 1930.

Another reason for the persistence of the British Empire adventure in comics is that it was more able than the swashbuckler to respond to the changing geopolitical landscape. The crucial difference from Victorian and Edwardian imperial fiction is that post-war comics do not, on the whole, narrate the building of empire but, rather, focus on policing and protecting it. This is consistent with the empire films of the 1950s and should be seen in the context of counter-insurgency campaigns against Mau Mau rebels in Kenya and Communist guerrillas in Malaya. The role of the British army is not territorial conquest but to maintain the peace. This is particularly necessary on the Northwest Frontier: 'To the fierce tribes of the frontier, war was an honourable sport. Many of the natives serving with the Indian Army were hillmen themselves and had fellow tribesmen – even relatives – among the Afghan ranks.'[40]

The sports story provides another example of how comics responded to the changing social landscape during the post-war years. Sport had been a staple genre of the story papers, but sports stories had tended to be based in public schools (where rugger and cricket were the games of choice) and had focused as much on action off the playing field as on it. The visual conventions of the picture strip were better able to represent sporting contests –

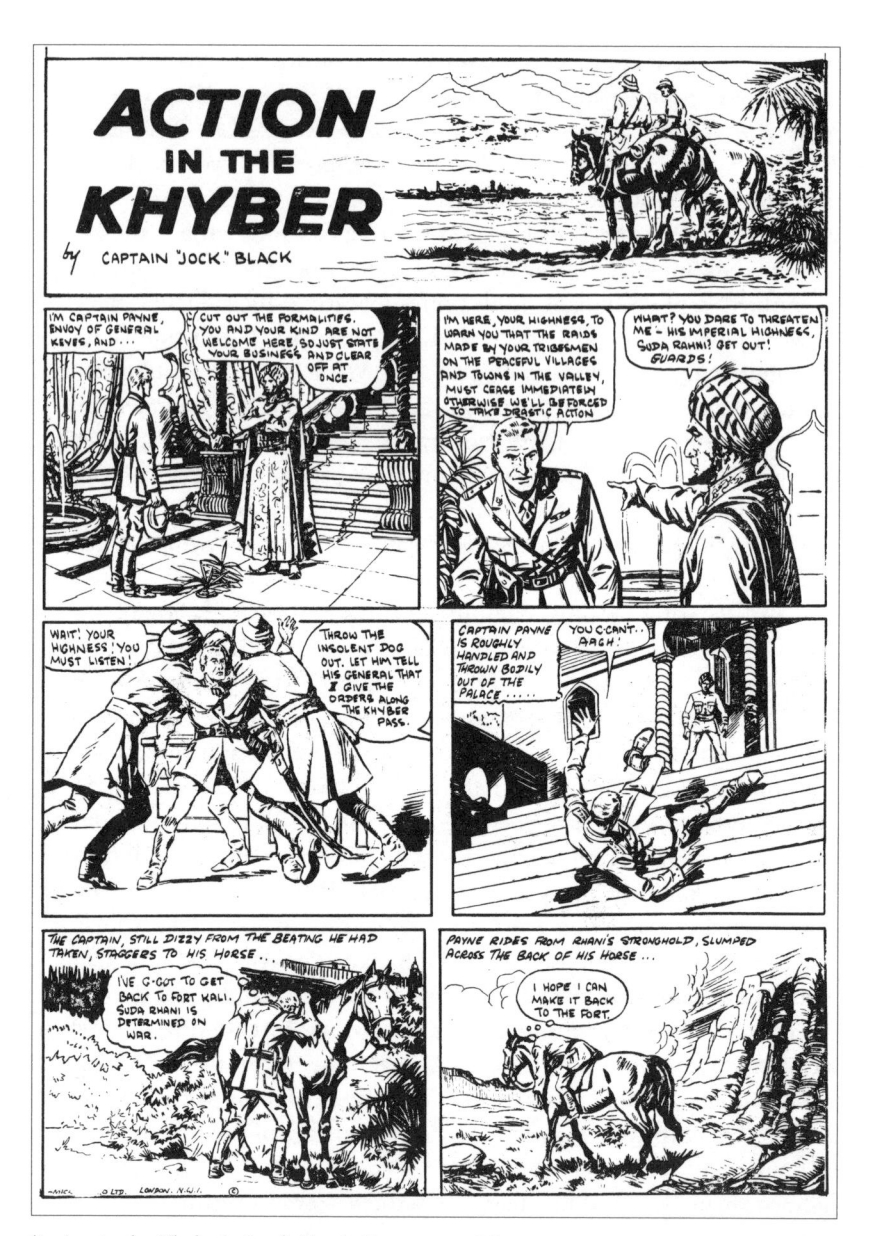

'Action in the Khyber', *Battle* (Anglo Features, 1960).

the trajectory of a ball, for example, could be shown through the simple expedient of a clear line – and so the game itself became the focus rather than off-the-pitch mystery and intrigue. There were still some examples of the old-style sports story – 'The Mystery Man at Inside-Left' (*Victor*), for example, combined football with espionage as 'enemies of the free countries of the West were hiding atomic bombs at strategic points in various countries, including Britain'[41] – but for the most part sport itself became the main focus of sport-themed stories.

The popularity of the sports picture strip can be explained partly by the fact that the emergence of the picture paper coincided with something of a golden age of British sporting achievement. In 1953 the Ashes were regained after a twenty-year hiatus, and in 1954 Roger Bannister ran the first sub-four minute mile. Above all, however, it was football that caught the popular imagination. There was a significant increase in attendance at football matches in the late 1940s and early 1950s – generally attributed to the need for entertainment after the disruption and austerity of the war years – while the famous FA Cup Final of 1953, in which 38-year-old winger Stanley Matthews inspired Blackpool to a 4–3 win over Bolton, 'not only gave this game in particular a privileged place in football history, but gave the sport in general an enhanced status'.[42] The popularity of the sports picture strip can also be explained by the rise of television, which brought major sporting events such as the FA Cup Final and Grand National into the home. Some sports, particularly motor racing, became more popular due to television. The excitement of motor racing made it a natural for comics: 'Skid Solo' of *Tiger* was partly inspired by British world champions Graham Hill and Jackie Stewart.[43]

The rise of the sports picture strip also coincided with the decline of amateurism and the ascendancy of professional sport. This was an uneven process – some sports, including athletics and Rugby Union, resisted professionalism – and something of the tension between amateur and professional can be seen in comics. On the one hand there was a strong tradition of eccentric amateurs who were inherited from the story papers: characters such as 'Gorgeous Gus', the footballing Earl of Boote, and 'Limpalong Leslie', so called because he was born with one leg shorter than the other, both played as amateurs. On the other hand the transition to professionalism was reflected in stories such as 'It's Goals That Count' (which began as a prose serial in *Rover* before transferring as a picture strip to *Hornet*) which chronicled the professional career of Nick Smith for Granton United. The professional outlook was perhaps best illustrated by 'Chained to his Bat' (*Hotspur*) in which ex-England cricketer Sam Billard obsessively coaches his young protégé to be 'the finest batsman in the history of the game'.[44]

The social politics of the sports story are exemplified by the parallel careers of two British athletes: William Wilson of the *Wizard* (later the *Hornet*) and Alf Tupper of *Rover* (latterly *Victor*). On the face of it the ageless Wilson, whose extraordinary longevity and remarkable sporting exploits were due to a mysterious elixir, and Tupper, who ran on a diet of fish-and-chips, would seem to have little in common. Yet both were created by the same writer, Gilbert Dawson, a former sports journalist, and both can be seen as vehicles for mediating the decline of the amateur and the rise of the professional in British sport.[45] Athletics was one of the most class-ridden of all sports and one of the last to maintain the distinction between amateur and professional. Wilson and Tupper are both amateurs, but their success is due as much to hard training as latent ability. Sport historian Richard Holt has suggested that Roger Bannister's achievement in breaking the four-minute mile – depending on rigorous preparation and involving a race plan where Chris Brasher and Christopher Chattaway ran as pace-makers to allow Bannister to go for the record – represented 'a blend of the old virtues and the new, which the public seemed to understand and appreciate'.[46]

While Wilson was a sporting superman whose exploits were the stuff of fantasy – Olympic gold medallist, champion boxer and Ashes-winning demon fast bowler – Alf Tupper was supposedly based on the turn-of-the-century British runner Alf Shrubb, a bricklayer who held a range of distance records, both amateur and professional, but who was often at odds with the athletics establishment.[47] 'The Tough of the Track' is particularly notable for its acute awareness of class difference. Alf is 'a working lad from the back streets of Greystone': he works as a welder's apprentice and is invariably so hard-up that he has to hitch to athletics meetings and often has to pawn his running shoes to buy food.[48] He is shunned by the local athletics club who consider him uncouth: Alf in turn regards them as 'toffs'. Alf runs for the love of it and has no interest in trophies or prize money: 'Running's me sport. I don't need no money for it.'[49] He is a perpetual underdog: an unfancied runner who succeeds through sheer guts and determination. 'The Tough of the Track' characterizes the athletics establishment as conservative and elitist: Alf is only grudgingly tolerated by the British Olympic Committee and is often overlooked for the national team – only to turn up under his own steam and 'run 'em' anyway. He is also defiantly individualistic: used to privation, Alf shuns team hotels in favour of sleeping rough in haystacks or under the railway arches. To this extent 'The Tough of the Track' was very much a product of post-war austerity Britain: its landscape is one of bombsites and the back streets of northern industrial towns. Tupper represents a distinctively northern brand of working-class masculinity who expresses his defiance of social convention through running: rather like a comic-strip version of

'The Tough of the Track', *Victor* (D. C. Thomson, 6 April 1967).

Colin Smith of *The Loneliness of the Long Distance Runner*, though with a somewhat more cheerful disposition. And, unlike most fictional sportsmen, Alf was allowed to age: the fresh-faced youth of the early *Rover* stories became a craggy-faced man when he transferred to picture strips in *Victor* in the 1960s.

The definitive comic-strip sporting hero, however, was 'Roy of the Rovers', the cover star of *Tiger* from 1954 until 1976 when he transferred to his own self-titled comic. 'Roy of the Rovers' can be seen in relation to changes in the culture of British sport. The post-war boom in the popularity of football had brought about an increase in the number of young men earning their living from playing the game: by 1950 there were 7,000 professional footballers in Britain.[50] Frank S. Pepper explained that his brief was to write a more realistic football story than the tales of 'hot shots' that had characterized the story papers:

> We decided to show an ordinary lad, with talent, with whom the reader could identify, joining a top-class club with long traditions, as a very humble junior and gradually making his way up the ladder, until he became a star. This wasn't as easy as it sounds: in pre-war days none of our footballers ever seemed to live anywhere

The Bumper Book of Roy of the Rovers (Titan Books reprint, 2008).

or to have any relatives – they just materialised on the pitch on match days and then vanished back into limbo.[51]

The inspiration for Roy Race, the prolific centre-forward of Melchester Rovers, were strikers like Nat Lofthouse of Bolton Wanderers and Derek Dooley of Sheffield Wednesday, while Melchester Rovers were supposedly based on the Arsenal team of the 1950s. The key thing about Roy is his ordinariness: this is in marked contrast to colourful eccentrics like Gorgeous Gus or Hotshot Hamish, he of the pile-driver right foot.

On one level 'Roy of the Rovers' can be understood as an adolescent sporting fantasy. Melchester's trophy cabinet far surpassed that of any real team – between 1958 and 1970 they won four League Championships, four FA Cups, two European Cups, two World Club Cups and one European Cup Winners' Cup – and it was a convention that Roy himself would score the winning goal in most of the important games. (It was only a knee injury sustained during Melchester's 2–1 win over Eastoke United in the FA Cup Final of 1966 that kept Roy out of the victorious England World Cup squad that summer.) On another level, however, Pepper and the other writers who followed him, including Derek Birnage, Ted Cowan and Tom Tully, were at pains to ground his off-the-pitch life in some kind of reality. The contractual conditions of professional footballers were very poor until the abolition of the maximum wage cap in 1961 and the reform of the transfer system in 1963. As late as 1971 Roy could be found buying a used car for £500 and remarking that 'some people have the idea that footballers can afford to use five pound notes for wallpaper'.[52] Roy is characterized as the model professional: clean-living, modest in victory, and a true sportsman on and off the pitch. He became an iconic figure of British football, as much a symbol of the game as real players like Bobby Charlton of Manchester United and Bobby Moore of West Ham.[53]

* * *

The genre synonymous with the British boys' comic, however, is war, particularly the Second World War. In fact the war picture-strip did not become ubiquitous until the late 1950s. Some comics, including *Eagle*, tended not to feature war picture strips, though it often included text stories about the wartime SOE (Special Operations Executive) and serialized the life of Winston Churchill as 'The Happy Warrior'. Len Miller published an occasional series entitled *Bulldog Brittain Commando* between 1952 and 1958, and the Arnold Book Company published sixteen issues of *Ace Malloy*, the only British comic featuring the Korean War, between 1952 and 1954. *Lion* was the first anthology title to feature war strips on a regular basis – 'The Lone Commandos', 'Lost Pals of 9 Platoon', 'Frogmen Are Tough' and 'The Secret Tunnellers of Calitz Camp' were among the early examples – though in the early 1950s war was still far from the dominant presence it would later become.

The point of critical mass came around 1957–8. It was in 1957 that *Thriller Picture Library* published its first Second World War story ('Battler Britton – War Ace') and that 'Paddy Payne – Warrior of the Skies' displaced Captain Condor as the cover star of *Lion*. The war issues of *Thriller Picture Library* proved so popular that Amalgamated Press launched *War Picture Library* in 1958. This was followed by other libraries from the same stable – *Air Ace Picture Library* (1960–70), *Battle Picture Library* (1961–84) and *War at Sea Picture Library* (1962–3) – by D. C. Thomson's *Commando* (1961–), and by several imitators from smaller publishers including Micron's *Combat Picture Library* (1959–85) and C. H. Pearson's *Picture Stories of World War II* (1960–5) and *Air War Picture Stories* (1961–2). At their height the picture libraries were each printing up to six new stories a month as well as reprints.

Thriller Picture Library (September 1958).

Until they were discontinued in the mid-1980s, *War Picture Library* published 2,103 issues, *Battle Picture Library* 1,706 issues and *Combat Picture Library* 1,212 issues, while *Commando*, which is still in print, passed 4,000 issues in 2007.[54] The success of the picture libraries demonstrated the popularity of war as subject-matter with the consequence that the new picture-strip papers of the early 1960s also featured war prominently. One-man army 'Captain Hurricane' was the cover star of *Valiant*, while *Victor's* front and back pages were given over to a true story of wartime heroism on land, sea or air.

How can we explain the surge in the popularity of war comics towards the end of the 1950s? John Sutherland suggests that by then 'the war was far enough away for the pain to have receded but the glory was still fondly remembered'.[55] War comics can be seen as part of a cultural project to claim the 'memory' of the Second World War for the generation of Britons born after the war had ended. Most British children would have family members who had served during the war: 'What did you do during the war?' was the question on the lips of many baby-boomers.[56] Anecdotal evidence of the appeal of war comics for this generation is provided by journalist Harry Pearson (born 1960) in his book *Achtung Schweinehund!*:

> American comics entered my life around the same time as *War Picture Library*... The American kids had Spiderman, Daredevil, Batman and Thor. British kids had the Second World War. Burma and the Western Desert were our Gotham City and Megalopolis [*sic*]. The men who saved our world didn't have extraordinary powers, fancy gadgets or bizarre costumes. Our superheroes were our dads, uncles and grandfathers, and there is something rather touching in that.[57]

It is significant in this regard that US war comics like *Sergeant Rock* and *Sergeant Fury and His Howling Commandos* never really caught on with British readers. This provides further evidence that children made qualitative distinctions in their choice of comics.

The popularity of the war comic also needs to be seen in the context of a popular culture that was saturated with war narratives. The 1950s saw a boom in war-related fiction and non-fiction, ranging from novels such as Nicholas Montserrat's best-seller *The Cruel Sea* to weighty histories like Winston Churchill's six-volume *The Second World War*. There was a cycle of war memoirs and 'true stories' – many of which appeared in abridged 'cadet' editions for children. And above all the 1950s was a golden age for the war film in British cinema: *The Wooden Horse*, *Angels One Five*, *The Cruel Sea*, *The Colditz Story*, *Above Us the Waves*, *The Dam Busters*, *The Battle of the River Plate*, *Reach for the Sky*, *Ill Met By Moonlight*, *Carve Her Name With Pride*, *Dunkirk* and *Sink the Bismarck!* were among the leading films at the British box office between 1950 and 1960.[58]

War comics were also a major part of what Michael Paris has, appropriately, termed 'the pleasure culture of war' in post-war Britain.[59] They were one of the means that allowed children to experience something of the thrill and excitement of war without being exposed to its dangers. The relationship between comics and other forms of juvenile popular culture is evident in the ubiquitous advertisements for war toys in boys' comics. The widespread use of plastics in the toy-making industry after the Second World War brought sets of toy soldiers and moulded construction kits within most children's price range. The best-selling Airfix kit, the Supermarine Spitfire Mark II, went on sale in 1954, while Hasbro's Action Man figures were introduced in 1966.[60] These, and other, toys allowed boys to create their own narratives of pleasure around war. It is surely no coincidence that the promotion of this pleasure culture of war coincided with the end of compulsory military service in Britain as National Service was phased out between 1960 and 1963. The prominence of recruiting advertisements for the army, navy and air force in comics such as *Victor* and *Valiant* would suggest they were seen as potential recruiting vehicles for the services.

British war comics were a distinctive brand: on the whole they demonstrated a greater degree of psychological realism than their American counterparts.[61] This was particularly so with the picture libraries, which were intended for a slightly older readership. In the words of Ted Bensberg, editor of *War Picture Library* from 1961: 'We aimed for strong, believable human stories set against a background of realistic and exciting action.'[62] This came about largely because many of the contributors had first-hand experience of war: Bensberg himself had been a sergeant in the Royal Signals, while the writers for the picture libraries included Ken Bulmer (Royal Signals), Val Holding (Parachute Regiment), Colin Thomas (Gurkha Rifles) and Norman Walker (Royal Armoured Corps). Designer Trevor Newton had served in the Fleet Air Arm and the German artist Kurt Caesar was a veteran of the Afrika Korps.

Another characteristic of British war comics was their Anglocentric perspective. This was recognized in a contemporary study of the picture libraries and their readership:

> The British War comics considered consist of a complete picture story which takes up the whole issue and which usually strongly emphasises the role of one of the three services. The heroes are usually British, but sometimes include Australians and New Zealanders. The enemy is either German or Japanese. Reference is sometimes made to allies, particularly the Americans, who are not always presented in an unequivocally favourable light.[63]

The narrative of the Second World War in British comics privileges the role of British and Commonwealth armed forces (especially Australia and New Zealand, reflecting the existence of a market for comics in the white Commonwealth) and sidelines other allies including the Americans and the Russians. It focuses on theatres where British and Commonwealth armed forces played a major role – North Africa, Greece, Italy, Normandy, Burma, New Guinea – and on the exploits of famous fighting units such as the Desert Rats and Chindits. Alongside the British war movies of the 1950s, comics can be seen as part of an ideological project to present the Second World War as a national achievement – 'their finest hour'. In this context it should be remembered that Churchill's famous 'finest hour' speech of 18 June 1940 referred not just to Britain but to 'the British Empire and its Commonwealth'.[64]

A few examples must suffice to demonstrate how war comics projected the narrative of 'their finest hour'. The *War Picture Library* story 'Action Stations' (about the Battle of the Atlantic) begins thus: '1941 and the steel talons of the German war eagle were throttling the liberties and lives of the conquered peoples in Europe. Yet one country still remained free. On the island fortress of beleagured Britain, a gallant nation stood in proud defiance of the Nazis.'[65] From the same stable 'Devil's Island' begins: 'During the dark months of 1942 the armies of Japan were ashore in New Guinea, posing a deadly threat to Australia. But there, roughneck diggers of the Australian army stemmed the flood of Nipponese aggression.'[66] The picture libraries were usually set against the background of real wartime battles whose names were etched into British popular memory – Dunkirk, Tobruk, El Alamein, Arnhem – and they were often historically specific in time and place: 'November 1941. Seventy miles behind the German and Italian front line in the Western Desert lay the gallant Allied garrison of Tobruk. Rommel, the German army commander, planned to assault this constant threat to his lines of communication on November 23rd . . .'.[67] There is anecdotal evidence, indeed, that some children learned about the

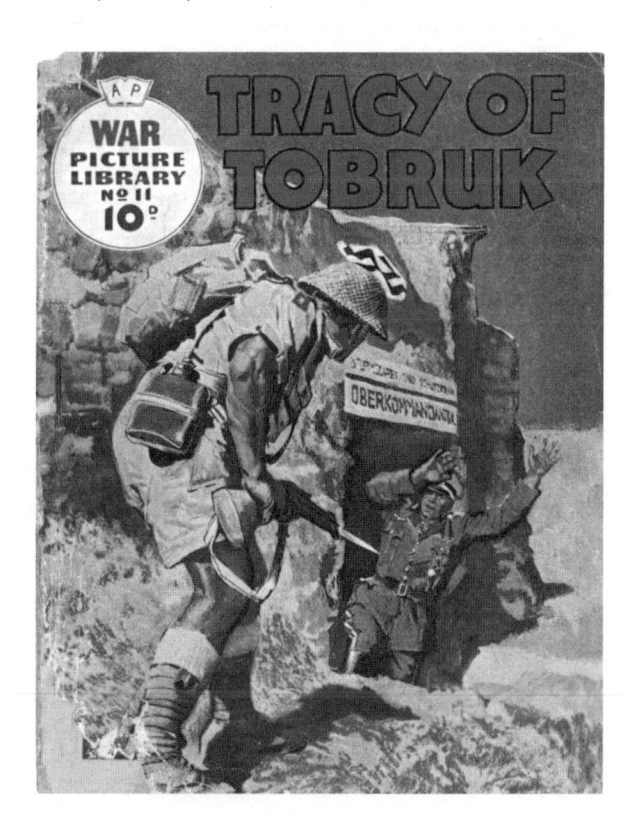

War Picture Library (Amalgamated Press Ltd, February 1959).

99

war principally through reading comics. Historian Brian Edwards writes: 'I recall a teacher being astounded by a usually reluctant pupil's extensive knowledge of the North Africa campaign, only to scold him when he volunteered that he had gained his knowledge from *War Picture Library* No.1, *The Rats of Tobruk*.'[68]

Sutherland suggests that the ideology of British war comics was to present war as 'the arena of honour, heroism and ethical violence'.[69] The valorization of heroism is a recurring theme. *Victor*'s trademark was the true story of acts of individual courage. These were drawn from the First and Second World Wars and represented each branch of the services. In these stories the recognition of courage was neither racially exclusive nor narrowly nationalistic. In 1966, for example, *Victor* featured stories of an Indian officer winning the Victoria Cross in Burma and the German defenders of Monte Cassino.[70] A fictional story of the Battle of the Somme in the same paper could acknowledge the heroism of a German gunner who is buried by the British with military honours after manning his battery in the face of advancing tanks: 'A German and an enemy, but as gallant a man as ever donned uniform.'[71] The same story – part of a series following Corporal (later Sergeant) Bob Millar of the Coldstream Guards during the First World War – is also notable for its tolerant attitude towards conscientious objectors. Carter, a medical orderly, is despised by some of the regulars for being a 'conshie', but he dies rescuing a wounded soldier from No Man's Land. Millar reflects: 'It took courage to go out after Smithers – but it took even more courage to stand up and declare himself a conscientious objector, sir! They don't make men any braver than Private Carter!'[72]

The war libraries also promoted an ethos of courage, patriotism and duty. A common theme is the soldier or unit accused of cowardice who prove their worth in battle. The *Battle Picture Library* story 'Pride of Lions', for example, concerns a Sikh pioneer unit in Eritrea in 1941 who are looked down upon for not being front-line combat troops. When Hira Singh proves his mettle, however, one of the hitherto antagonistic Sikhs hands over his *quoit*, the badge of the warrior, declaring: 'Take it, Hira Singh. Wear it with pride. And if men ask how thou came by it, say with truth thou won it in battle.'[73] In 'The Broken Line', an Australian battalion in New Guinea are branded cowards when their headquarters is overwhelmed by the Japanese. A new hard-bitten commander is sent to pull together the 'shattered outfit' and 'to win back the battalion's good name'. He initially regards them as 'a yellow mob who broke when the chips were down', but when he learns the truth, and sees the men in battle, he admits that he was mistaken: 'I was desperately wrong about the original fifty-five-nine! . . . You're the finest mob of fighting men I've ever had the honour to command.'[74]

It has been suggested that the representation of the enemy in war comics served to reinforce ideas of national and racial superiority.[75] The language of war comics – in which Germans are referred to as 'Jerries', 'Huns' or 'Krauts', Italians as 'Eyeties' and Japanese as 'Japs' or 'Nips' – perpetuated the propaganda discourses of the war itself when name-calling the enemy was commonplace. In comics this practice persisted until the 1980s: consequently several generations of British children grew up thoroughly versed in wartime slang and racial epithets. The Japanese are characterized as cruel and subhuman, Italians as cowards and fools, but the representation of Germans, perhaps reflecting the fact that West Germany was now a NATO ally, differentiated between 'good' and 'bad' Germans. A case in point is 'Sound the Alarm' (*War Picture Library*). In the Western Desert a German armoured car ambushes a British patrol. The fanatical Leutnant Kessler takes glee in machine-gunning the survivors, but is prevented from killing a British officer who returns for one of the wounded by the humane Feldwebel Lensdorf. Later, Lensdorf is the only survivor when the armoured car is attacked by RAF Hurricanes. He is now being pursued by the British officer, Lieutenant Baxter, both to prevent him from communicating vital information to the German command and to avenge the slaughter of his men. Baxter catches up with Lensdorf and is about to shoot him when a German patrol arrives. In the ensuing fight Lensdorf saves Baxter's life ('Perhaps I can convince you that all Germans are not of a pattern'), while Baxter for his part recognizes 'that Jerry sergeant's a decent bloke'. The story concludes on a note of optimism for post-war reconciliation: 'The world might benefit . . . if men of goodwill from both sides could get together and talk over old battles – without rancour.'[76] In its recognition of the 'good German' the story bears comparison with films such as *The One That Got Away* and *Ice Cold in Alex* which offered more nuanced representations of Germans than wartime propaganda.[77]

If the Anglocentric narratives and representation of the enemy in war comics shared common ground with British war films of the 1950s, one area where they were very different was in their social politics. Whereas post-*bellum* war films presented leadership as vested in meritocratic middle-class officers, characterized by actors like Dirk Bogarde, Jack Hawkins, Richard Todd, John Mills and Kenneth More, comics would more often than not feature working-class heroes and other ranks.[78] To some extent this can be seen as responding to the make-up of their largely working-class readership; but it also demonstrates the persistence of the wartime ideology of the 'people's war' into post-war cultural production. The Hentyish idea of the officer and gentleman who is born to lead is largely absent from post-war comics: their protagonists are tough professionals, usually either experienced NCOs or officers who have risen through the ranks. And they are often characterized as insubordinate, stubborn and independent. Lieutenant Joe Hogan, for example, is described as 'a good fighting soldier . . . His problem is discipline. Give him an order and he'll obey – if he thinks the order is right! If he doesn't agree he does what he considers the right thing.'[79]

The outstanding example of this archetype – and another example of a character from the story papers who effortlessly made the transition to picture strips – is Sergeant-Pilot Matt Braddock vc. Owen Dudley Edwards suggests that 'the Braddock series could be taken as an attack on the whole officer class ethos'.[80] Braddock was created by Gilbert Dawson, and like Dawson's other working-class hero, Alf Tupper, he graduated from prose stories in *Rover* to picture strips in *Victor*. In the 1950s *Rover* published stories under the series title of 'I Flew with Braddock' (the narrator was Braddock's navigator Sergeant George Bourne) which were also published as novels, *The Bombs Go Down* and *Braddock and the Flying Tigers*.[81] In the 1960s these were adapted, under new titles, into picture strips for *Victor*, while new and repeat stories continued in *Rover*. The first Braddock story, chronologically at least (it was in fact the seventh *Rover* serial), was 'Born to Fly', which establishes the hero's working-class background. Braddock, a steeplejack, having been unable to get into the peacetime RAF as a pilot, enlists as an aircraftman in the Auxiliary Air Force and pays for flying lessons in his spare time. His professional outlook is contrasted with the upper-class officer cadets who can afford to join flying clubs and who regard flying as something of a lark rather than a deadly preparation for war. When war is declared, Braddock is accepted into the RAF, but only as a sergeant pilot, even though he proves himself a better flier than most of the officers.

Braddock therefore represents a new type of war hero. On one level, of course, the heroic aviator was a familiar archetype from juvenile fiction, represented pre-eminently by W. E. Johns's Biggles, appearing in story papers since the early 1930s.[82] Where Braddock differs, however, is in his working-class background and in the fact that he was not a fighter pilot (Spitfire pilots were regarded as the 'glamour boys' of the RAF) but a decidedly less glamorous (and by the 1960s ideologically problematic) bomber pilot. He is a more realistic character than either Battler Britton or Paddy Payne, who could seemingly move from one type of aircraft to another without any need for training or preparation. Braddock flies mostly the Lancaster bomber, though he also has a spell flying the Mosquito fighter-bomber. Throughout the stories, however, there is close attention to realistic detail. Thus he is able to identify an aircraft at a glance: 'It's French. It's their standard bomber, the Amiot 142-M. It's powered by two Grome-Rhone radial engines and it has a rotatable gun-turret in the nose.'[83] Arthur Hopcraft was prompted to write that Braddock 'is a New Wave hero inasmuch as he reflects the sophistication of the 1960s boy when it comes to the technicalities of flying'.[84]

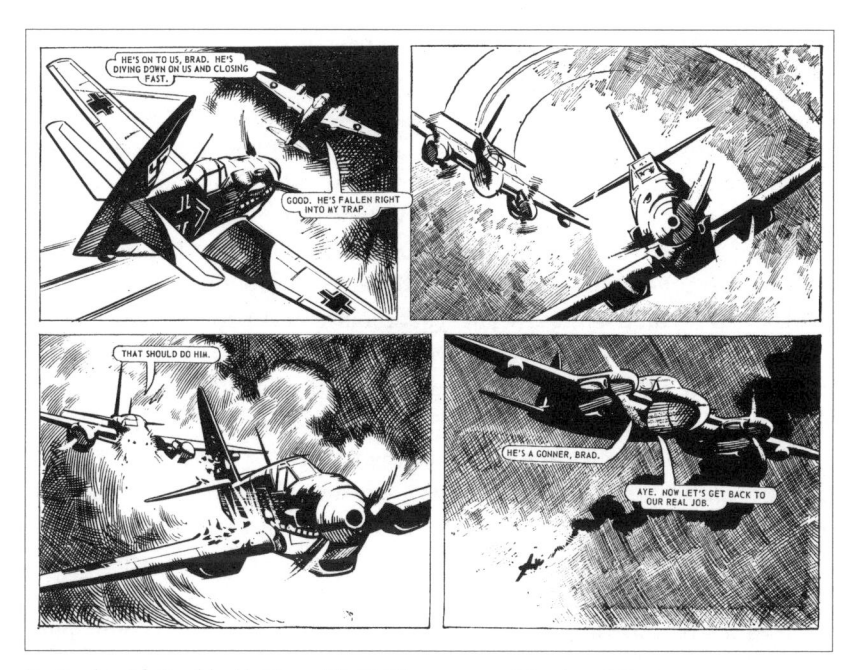

'In Battle with Braddock', *Victor* (D. C. Thomson, 19 March 1966).

    Braddock is also a new wave hero in another sense. The sense of class consciousness in the Braddock stories compares with the protagonists of British 'new wave' cinema such as Laurence Harvey's Joe Lampton in *Room at the Top* and Albert Finney's Arthur Seaton in *Saturday Night and Sunday Morning*.[85] Braddock is an abrasive and insubordinate character: he is disdainful of authority and has no time for upper-class officers. In particular he dislikes deskbound fliers – 'I can't stand these types who just sit at headquarters and give themselves medals' – and on one occasion refuses to wear his own medals during a visit by the Duke of Leith as 'some chump of a Wing-Commander at Group HQ has blocked my recommendation for a DFM' for another pilot.[86] He clashes frequently with the RAF hierarchy, observing that 'certain Air Ministry officers don't like a Flight Sergeant bossing a station'.[87] Above all he is committed to taking the war to the enemy with all the means at his disposal. When he is court martialled for exceeding his authority, he tells the court: 'I've committed the dreadful crime of wanting to finish the war as quickly as possible.'[88] (In the event he is saved by the intervention of an American war correspondent who publishes the true story.) Braddock's defiantly anti-authoritarian streak and his uncompromising attitude to the conduct of war anticipated the tough protagonists of the war comics of the 1970s.

* * *

The success of the picture libraries and the new picture-strip papers to some extent disguised the changing landscape of British comics during the 1960s. From the middle of the decade the trend was an increase in the number of titles but an overall decline in sales. Thus, while in 1966 some 39 comics were published in Britain with a combined circulation of 11 million, by 1971 the number of titles had risen (45) but the combined circulation had fallen to 10 million.[89] The failure of several high-profile new comics to last the course, such as *Hurricane* (1964–5), *Jag* (1968–9) and *Joe 90* (1969), suggests that the market had become saturated. The reappearance of American comics in the 1960s, following the lifting of import restrictions, was also a factor. American comics were printed in colour, and their superhero fantasies were set in the present day rather than in the past. Keith Dewhurst felt that British comics could not match the appeal of their US rivals: 'Even today British comic books like the *Commando* series are merely glorified adventure series. They pale into insignificance beside the available American material like *Captain Marvel* who, with most of the other super-heroes, was redrawn and revamped in the mid-1960s.'[90]

At a structural level, there was consolidation within the comic publishing industry. The duopoly of Amalgamated Press and D. C. Thomson was further strengthened by a series of mergers and take-overs. In 1959 Amalgamated Press was taken over by the Mirror Group, which renamed it Fleetway Publications. Two years later the further acquisition of Odhams, which itself had already taken over the Hulton Press, led to the formation of the International Publishing Corporation (IPC), a giant conglomerate that published over 200 periodicals. In 1968 IPC restructured its entire operation, putting all its comics into one Juvenile Periodicals Division.[91] IPC and D. C. Thomson between them now accounted for 80 per cent of the market. IPC was more exposed to market fluctuations than Thomson, whose strength lay in junior comics and whose production costs were lower. In 1967, for example, Thomson's *Hotspur* sold for 5*d.* compared to IPC's *Valiant* at 7*d.*[92]

The rise (and subsequent fall) of television comics in the 1960s demonstrates how the industry responded to a changing cultural landscape. The first television-themed comics had appeared in the 1950s – *TV Comic* (1951–84) and *TV Fun* (1953–9) were essentially variations on their film and radio predecessors – but it was in the 1960s that the genre boomed with the likes of *TV Express* (1960–62), *TV Toyland* (1966–8), *TV Tornado* (1967–8) and *TV Century 21* (1965–71). The proliferation of television comics reflected the fact that television was now firmly established as the pre-eminent mass-entertainment medium: most British households had television and colour broadcasting was introduced at the end of the decade. In particular one of the distinguishing genres of the 1960s was 'telefantasy', exemplified by British series like *Doctor Who*, *The Avengers* and *The Champions* and by American imports including *The Man From U.N.C.L.E.*, *Voyage to the Bottom of the Sea*, *Batman*, *Star Trek* and *The Time Tunnel*.[93] Perhaps it was inevitable that comics should turn to television for inspiration: it was certainly ironic given that television would later be held responsible for declining comic sales. It should be acknowledged, however, that the Pop Art aesthetic of telefantasy was itself influenced by comic strips.[94]

TV Century 21 (a title soon abbreviated simply to *TV21*) was the foremost example of a marriage between comics and television in the 1960s. A glossy full-colour photogravure tabloid in the old *Eagle* style, *TV21* was conceived as a promotional tie-in vehicle for Gerry Anderson's A. P. Films, which licensed the rights to City Magazines. Anderson produced a cycle of futuristic adventure series using puppets rather than actors in a process known as 'Supermarionation': *Supercar*, *Fireball XL5*, *Stingray*, *Thunderbirds*, *Captain Scarlet and the Mysterons* and *Joe 90*.[95] A. P. Films had already licensed strips of 'Supercar' and 'Fireball XL5' to *TV Comic*, but these were in black and white. Alan Fennell, the editor of *TV21* and a regular Anderson scriptwriter, recruited *Eagle* artists Frank Bellamy and Eric Eden to draw the 'Thunderbirds' and 'Lady Penelope' strips which began in *TV21* before *Thunderbirds* itself had aired on British television. Within a year of its launch, *TV21* was selling 600,000 copies and was popular enough to warrant two stablemates in *Lady Penelope* (1966–8) and *Joe 90* (or to give its full title *Gerry Anderson's Joe 90 Secret Agent*).[96]

The futuristic world of Gerry Anderson would seem to have been influenced by *Dan Dare*. It is a world of technological modernity: much of the appeal of these series rests on SF hardware like rocketships (*Fireball XL5*) and atomic submarines (*Stingray*). *Thunderbirds* is based around a secret organization called International Rescue and its fantastic machines – technology put to use for the good of mankind. There are also ideological parallels. Anderson created a world protected by organizations such as a World Space Fleet (*Fireball XL5*) and a World Acquanaut Security Patrol (*Stingray*) responsible to a United World Government. In *Captain Scarlet* the Spectrum organization that protects the Earth against Martian invaders is also ethnically diverse. The idea of a multi-cultural future in which racial prejudice has been eradicated was also a feature of live-action SF series *Star Trek*, a later addition to *TV21*.[97]

TV21 succeeded because it was very much of its moment: its futuristic SF content and technological modernism caught the imagination of comic readers at a time when Britain saw itself in the vanguard of what Prime Minister Harold Wilson called 'the white heat of science and technology'.[98] Its visual style was highly innovative: its cover was made up to look like a

TV21 (City Magazines Ltd, 2 March 1968).

futuristic newspaper ('Stingray Lost!', 'Thunderbird Two Attacked!') and it would feature photographic reproductions from the television series, though in the strips themselves the characters were drawn naturalistically rather than as puppets with oversized heads. It was in *TV21* that Frank Bellamy's distinctive graphic style reached its fullest expression: he employs techniques such as asymmetric panels and jagged borders to create a sense of dynamic movement between frames. Bellamy understood instinctively that the appeal

106

of the comic lay in its technological hardware: a recurring motif of the 'Thunderbirds' strip is people dwarfed by the huge machines. Bellamy's style influenced other artists, including Ron Embleton, Eric Eden and Mike Noble, to the extent that it is possible to talk of a *TV21* house style.

Yet the golden age of *TV21* did not last for long. From 1968 it was starting to pad out its content with non-Anderson strips based on *The Saint*, *Land of the Giants*, *Tarzan* and *Star Trek*. In 1969 it absorbed its short-lived companion title *Joe 90*, a comic regarded by some aficionados as superior in quality but which failed for much the same reason as the television series: unlike the other Anderson series its protagonist was a juvenile rather than an adult and this probably restricted its appeal to older readers and viewers. Bellamy left *TV21* in 1969 to draw the adventures of 'Garth' for the *Daily Mirror*. In the same year *TV21* was sold to IPC, which diluted its content further with reprints and non-television themed strips. When *TV21* folded in 1971 there was no Anderson content left in the comic.

Ultimately the television comics proved less durable than war and adventure comics. The problem was that their content was determined by another medium: consequently they were less flexible in what they could do. Thus, while papers like *Hotspur*, *Victor* and *Valiant* were able to reinvent themselves in response to changing tastes – in *Hotspur*'s case, for example, by ditching its traditional fare of historical adventure stories at the end of the 1960s in favour of a range of contemporary crime and superhero strips – *TV21* was so closely tied to the Gerry Anderson television series that it could not survive the decline of those series at the end of the decade. The demise of *TV21* anticipated the fate of other television comics that followed in its wake: *Countdown* (1971–2), *TV Action* (1972–3) and *Target* (1978) all failed to last the course. In the 1970s the British comic industry would search for another formula: it would find it not in the technological fantasy and utopian idealism of Gerry Anderson but in the violence and cynicism of new comics like *Battle*, *Action* and *2000AD*.

CHAPTER FOUR

Girls on Top

> We had received reports that quite a number of girls were reading *Eagle* and drew the wrong conclusion; we had made *Girl* too masculine. We therefore made it more romantic in its approach, more feminine. I worked on the theory that you should be a good deal more personal in your motivation in a girls' paper. The adventure and the danger can be there but the reason for it must be the search for a long-lost uncle or father.
> Marcus Morris.[1]

The history of girls' comics in post-war Britain to some extent mirrors that of boys' juvenile weeklies. The transition from story papers to picture-strip papers began when Amalgamated Press revived *School Friend*, a story paper discontinued during the war, as a picture paper in 1950. *School Friend* was followed by Hulton's *Girl*, companion paper to *Eagle*, in 1951, and by Amalgamated's *Girls' Crystal*, another former story paper that converted to picture strips, in 1953. A survey of schoolgirls' reading habits in the early 1950s found that an astonishing 94 per cent of fourteen- and fifteen-year-olds read one or more of these papers and suggested that 'the only periodicals they seem to regard as their personal property are *School Friend*, *Girl* and *Girls' Crystal*'.[2] *School Friend* was the most popular girls' comic with a circulation in the early 1950s of 950,000: this was surpassed only by the unisex *Dandy* and *Beano*.[3] It was not until the end of the decade that the market dominance of this trio was challenged. D. C. Thomson launched its first girls' comic, *Bunty*, in 1958. It was an immediate success. As the existing papers declined (*Girls' Crystal* ceased publication in 1963, *Girl* in 1964 and *School Friend* in 1965), *Bunty* became the market leader with sales of 500,000.[4] It paved the way for a glut of similar titles. Thomson followed it with *Judy* in 1960, *Diana* in 1963 and *Mandy* in 1967, while Fleetway responded with *Princess* in 1960, *June* in 1961 and *Sally* in 1969.

The proliferation of girls' comics between 1950 and the early 1960s can be seen as an instance of an industry seeking to create a new market. The paper shortages of the Second World War had all but killed off the girls' story paper: the only survivors were *Girls' Crystal* and the *Girl's Own Paper*.[5] It is not clear why there were more casualties among the ranks of girls' papers than boys' papers, though research suggesting that girls were also apt to read boys' papers could well have been a factor. A. J. Jenkinson had found that up to a quarter of girls' reading was devoted to boys' 'bloods'. From this he drew a speculative conclusion: 'It should be remembered that these magazines make no attempt to appeal to girls, and make no concession to the girls' demand for "romance". Is there in girls a strong, if subsidiary, desire to be boys?'[6] It is significant, therefore, that when Amalgamated revived *School Friend* in 1950 it did so not as a story paper but a picture paper. Its success evidently influenced Hulton Press in deciding to launch a 'sister' paper to *Eagle*. The Reverend Marcus Morris told his readers that 'we have found that your sisters and their girl friends read it [*Eagle*] too, with great enthusiasm. Obviously we cannot run features in *Eagle* which interest only girls, so we chewed over the idea of how to meet the girls' need and came to the conclusion there is only one thing for it – give the girls a magazine of their own!'[7]

The idea to 'give the girls a magazine of their own' suggests that a commercial rather than an ideological imperative was behind the launch of *Girl*: it reflects a strategy of market differentiation. The same was true of *School Friend*. There is no doubt that the strategy was successful: research at the time suggested that *School Friend* was read by nearly 60 per cent of adolescent girls and *Girl* by 38 per cent.[8] (To a large extent this reflects the difference in price between the two titles – *School Friend* cost 3*d.* compared to *Girl*'s 4½*d.* – though social distinctions may also have played a part in the choice of comics.) The same research showed that girls' interest in comics peaked around the ages of fourteen and fifteen. There is some anecdotal evidence to suggest that the readership of girls' comics was not exclusively female. *Girl*, for example, often published letters suggesting that boys read the paper. A girl from the Wirral wrote: 'Who said that boys don't read girls' books and magazines? When I got on a bus to go to school a few days ago the first thing I saw was a boy with his head buried behind *Girl*. He looked *very* interested.'[9] Nor was this case exceptional. Alan Grant, a comic writer who would script the *über*-masculine 'Judge Dredd' for *2000AD*, revealed: 'As a child I was a voracious reader and my brother and I would read our boys' adventure comics every week and then swap them for the girls' comics of two sisters we knew.'[10]

The fact that some boys, at least, were not ashamed to be seen reading girls' comics is perhaps not quite as surprising as it might seem. There are a number of possible reasons. One is simply that, during the 1950s especially, there was an insatiable demand for comics among all children: any comic was better than no comic, especially at a time of continued shortages. Another explanation is the nature of the comics themselves. Girls' comics have often been regarded as superior in story-telling and characterization: they afford greater prominence to character motivation and they do not rely on direct action as the resolution for all problems. In this context it can be noted that some of the leading boys' comic writers since the 1970s – including Alan Grant, John Wagner and Pat Mills – cut their teeth on girls' comics. Mills, for example, who would inject a greater level of psychological realism into girls' comics with *Tammy* in the early 1970s, always maintained that he learned the craft of story construction from *Bunty* – 'a very solid story book'.[11]

In fact the writing of girls' comics has been an overwhelmingly male preserve. There are very few women comic writers. *School Friend* and *Girl* were the only titles regularly to include writers' credits (and even then *School Friend* only for its prose stories) but these are often pseudonymous.[12] It was relatively common for writers of boys' comics to contribute to girls' titles, including William Bryce-Hamilton (*School Friend*), John Purdie (*Bunty*), Chad Varah (*Girl*) and Lennox Wenn (*Sally*). Among the few regular women writers in comics were P. M. Ede (*Bunty*, *Judy*, *Mandy*) and Joan Whitford (who actually wrote for boys' titles, including *Sun*, *Comet* and *Thriller Picture Library*, though always under male pseudonyms). Opportunities for women artists in the industry were not significantly greater: Hilda Boswell, Evelyn Flinders and Valerie Gaskell were among the few to enjoy significant careers before the 1970s. There is no obvious reason for the marginalization of women in the industry other than a general explanation of institutionalized sexism: women writers and artists were much better represented in the fields of children's book publishing and illustration.

The editorship of girls' comics was also an exclusively male preserve: not until Nina Myskow edited *Jackie* in the 1970s did a woman assume responsibility for editorial policy. The maleness of editorial and creative input into girls' comics has sometimes led to a degree of ideological confusion in their content. Nowhere is this better illustrated than in the early history of *Girl*. *Girl* initially featured a range of female-centred adventure strips, including its original cover star 'Kitty Hawke' (a female pilot and 'her gay all-girl crew') and supporting strips such as 'Anne Mullion' (smuggling and skullduggery in eighteenth-century Cornwall), 'Captain Starling' (high-seas adventure) and 'The Adventures of Penny Wise' (an intrepid girl detective). While the initial circulation of *Girl* was around 500,000, however, this soon started to fall off. Morris drew the lesson that – *pace* Jenkinson – girls did not harbour a suppressed desire to be boys: 'We decided we had made the mistake of not taking sufficiently into account the difference between the feminine and masculine psychological make-up. The difference is a very real one.'[13] Hence out went 'Kitty Hawke', replaced by a schoolfriends' story ('Wendy and Jinx'), and in came other staples of the girls' paper including a ballerina ('Belle of the Ballet') and an Annie-like orphan ('Robbie of Red Hall'). Adventure stories would in future feature juvenile protagonists such as 'Tess and the Mystery Journey' and 'Pat of Paradise Isle'. The new formula proved successful: circulation stabilized at around 650,000 as the revamped *Girl* built up a loyal readership.

* * *

The social politics of girls' comics reveal significant differences in their outlook and ethos. It would probably be fair to say that the differences are more pronounced than in boys' comics (*Eagle* excepted), where most titles clearly assumed a predominant working-class readership. Girls' comics, however, construct their readers by class as well as gender. This point was not lost on their readers. As one Mass-Observation respondent recalled in 2003:

> I seem to recall that *Girl* was seen as 'good quality' reading for girls as opposed to trashier stuff. Sadly I never saw the trashier stuff so I can make no comparison! Both *Girl* and *Eagle* were published by the Rev. Marcus Morris – no doubt this was seen by parents as a vindication of wholesomeness. But it was not just worthy stuff, it was really enjoyable![14]

Girl, which most clearly demonstrates the ideological project of girls' comics to construct a socially approved model of adolescent femininity, has tended to be seen as a more significant publication than *School Friend*, which was actually the more popular title. There is evidence to suggest that *School Friend* and *Girls' Crystal* 'were more popular with girls from poorer backgrounds because they were cheaper', whereas the readership of *Girl* was more middle-class in make-up.[15] When we examine their social politics, however, we find that there is not necessarily a straightforward correlation between content and readership.

It might well be assumed, for instance, that *School Friend*, the paper with the largest circulation, would have been the most egalitarian and inclusive in its social politics, whereas in fact it is the most conservative of the lot. To a large degree this is a consequence of its previous life as a story paper: *School Friend* consists entirely of residual forms whose politics hark back to the social patterns and structures of pre-war Britain. The staple genre of *School Friend* is the school story, best exemplified in its most famous strip, 'The Silent Three'. This tale of 'a daring secret society of schoolgirls pledged to

'The Masked Ballerina', *School Friend* (Amalgamated Press Ltd, 25 February 1956).

fight injustice' perfectly illustrates both the conventions of the genre (hidden treasures, secret passages, sinister mistresses) and its ideological conservativism.[16] 'The Silent Three' places the private boarding school at the centre of the girls' social experience: it creates a fictional world that is hermetically sealed from the outside (parental figures are entirely absent) and where social relations are fixed. It is a static world: its protagonists remain members of the fourth form forever and are completely isolated from the external world. The other regular stories in *School Friend* are also entirely residual in form: Ruritanian fairytale ('Princess Anita of Sylvanberg'), yet more school-based intrigue ('The Masked Ballerina') and wartime adventure ('Mam'selle Marie – Heroine of Fountain School'). The social politics of *School Friend* are resolutely middle- or even upper-middle-class: the working classes are invisible except as servants or crooks. It is a conservative formula but evidently a successful one: *School Friend* ran for fifteen years and even in the early 1960s its sales of 446,000 were still significantly more than Fleetway's boys' comics such as *Lion* (368,000) and *Tiger* (302,000).[17]

Girl, superficially at least, bears some similarity to *School Friend*, not least because its front-page story, 'Wendy and Jinx', is another tale of schoolgirl friendship of what might be termed the 'jolly hockey sticks' variety. Again the boarding school is the focus of social experience and all-female friend-

'Wendy and Jinx', *Girl* (Hulton Press Ltd, 18 June 1952).

ship is promoted as an ideal. 'Wendy and Jinx' does make some concession to outsiders: a recurring motif is the newcomer whose arrival upsets the status quo. These characters do not fit in because they hold different values, such as Cynthia, 'a disagreeable new girl who becomes captain of the fourth form there and gains popularity by mean tricks'.[18] However, such disturbance is always temporary: by the start of the next story the newcomer is forgotten and normal relations have been restored. There is a clear strategy at work in these stories to present private boarding school as a legitimate social aspiration. This was not lost on readers. A Mass-Observation respondent, who read both *School Friend* and *Girl*, remarked that 'there was also a feeling that girls at such schools must have come from nice respectable homes and so it was safe for us to read about it'.[19]

However, as we have seen, 'Wendy and Jinx' was a replacement for another story in *Girl*. 'Kitty Hawke' had been conceived as a female (though earthbound) counterpart of Dan Dare. The character of Kitty Hawke seems to have been modelled on pioneering aviatrixes such as Amy Johnson and Amelia Earheart. The strip suggests a more progressive approach to gender: indeed it might even be seen as a site of proto-feminist politics. The first episode, for example, has Kitty declaring: 'Well, here we are again gang, with one more job chalked up to the all-girl crew – to prove to dad that we can operate his planes as efficiently as the glorious males!'[20] Written and drawn by Ray Bailey, 'Kitty Hawke' was very much in the tradition of serial-queen melodramas such as *The Perils of Pauline* (1914) that also featured intrepid action heroines whose adventuring takes them outside normal social relations.[21] The rejection of 'Kitty Hawke' by readers robbed British comics of one of their few genuine adult adventure heroines. It is a singular fact that British comics never produced an equivalent of American comic-book heroines such as the 'jungle queens' Sheena and Nyoka.

The failure of 'Kitty Hawke' left *Girl* to find other formulae to explore its notions of progressive femininity. It adopted from *Eagle* the dramatization of life stories of inspirational figures from history. Among those held up as female role models were Joan of Arc ('Soldier Joan'), Queen Elizabeth 1 ('Elizabeth of England'), Florence Nightingale ('Angel of Mercy'), and the missionaries Mary Bird ('Persia's Lady Mary') and Mary Slessor ('White Queen of Calabar'). Most of these were again written by Chad Varah. The later 1950s saw a number of strips featuring adult heroines in what the paper considered suitable professions for women. These included journalism ('Kay of the "Courier"'), nursing ('Susan of St Bride's'), secretary ('Tessa of Television') and – a real sign of the times – 'Angela – Air Hostess' ('The story of a girl who longed for adventure').[22] The promotion of supposedly glamorous occupations was an innovation of *Girl* that would be adopted by the new comics of the late 1950s and early 1960s such as *Bunty* ('Lyn Raymond, Air Stewardess') and *Judy* ('Sally of Studio Seven'). In 1960 even *School Friend* adopted the formula with 'Tracy – Teenage Fashion Model' ('She's pretty, she's gay, she's a girl who deserves her wonderful job').[23]

Girl drew upon certain features from adult women's magazines such as *Woman* and *Woman's Own*: for this reason it can be seen as representing a more 'grown up' discourse of femininity than other comics.[24] As well as picture strips and text serials it included the first fashion pages in a comic and the first 'pin ups': these ranged from the Duke of Edinburgh to pop singers such as Tommy Steele and Harry Belafonte. The crucial difference between *Girl* and *School Friend* was that *Girl* appeared to be about preparing adolescent girls for womanhood, whereas *School Friend* seemed to want them to remain girls forever. *Girl* therefore included tips on such essential matters as cookery and needlework ('Mother Tells You How') and offered regular careers advice ('I Want To Be . . .'). It also included an advice column ('What's Your Worry?') that printed responses to questions and problems sent in by readers: issues ranged from boyfriends and schoolgirl crushes ('There's a domestic science teacher at school whom I like very much and I often stay behind after class to speak to her and keep her company – do you think this is silly?') to fashion advice in an age of austerity ('What would you say was the right age to start wearing nylons?').[25]

Girl was characterized by the same high-principled tone as *Eagle*. Morris's editorials encouraged hard work, good citizenship and Christian values. His Easter message for 1954 declared: 'Jesus gave His life for us, so now is the time to see if there isn't something we can do for Him. Unselfish actions, humility, consideration for others – these are the Christian principles that Jesus taught when He was on earth.'[26] At Christmas he reminded his readers: 'In the midst of your Christmas fun – and I hope you have lots of it – do give a thought to people less fortunate than you. If you visit an old person with no family or send a toy to your local hospital you will make someone else's Christmas, and yours, a happier one.'[27] The editorial sermons also included frequent elegies to 'our beautiful young Queen'. Welcoming her back from an overseas tour, Morris wrote: 'Ever since Queen Elizabeth left our shores we have been filled with admiration for the way in which she has undertaken her long journey, and pride for the love and loyalty that has been shown her wherever she has been.'[28]

The ascendancy of *School Friend* and *Girl* was not really challenged until the arrival of *Bunty* in 1958. Comic historian Mel Gibson argues that D. C. Thomson 'specifically aimed to create a comic that would appeal to working-class readers, creating new markets by further differentiating the audience'.[29] For this reason *Bunty* has been understood as a successor to the working-class 'mill papers' of the 1920s such as *Peg's Paper* and *Girls' Weekly*.[30] *Bunty* differs from the 'jolly hockey sticks' tone of *School Friend* and *Girl*, where the emphasis is very much on friendships within communities of girls. The typical protagonist of *Bunty* is a 'Cinderalla'-type figure who is cast as a social outsider: hence it features a cast of waifs and orphans such as 'Lonesome Lucy', 'Orphan of the Circus', 'Ragamuffin Queen' and 'Second-Hand Sue'. *Bunty* recognizes social and economic divisions in a manner that is entirely absent from *School Friend* or *Girl*. Consider, for example, the ballet school story. In *Girl* Bella Auburn ('Belle of the Ballet') is a brilliant young ballerina inhabiting a genteel world under the tutelage of the kindly Madame Arenska where such problems as arise are easily resolved through hard work and good fortune. Contrast this with *Bunty*'s equivalent, 'The Dancing Life of Moira Kent', which hinges upon the difficulties for a working-class family in sending their granddaughter to ballet school: 'It's expensive all right. All these extra clothes – what a waste of money. And for what? Ballet – bah!'[31]

The social politics of *Bunty* are best demonstrated in 'The Four Marys'. This reveals a different pattern of social relations from that found in equivalent school stories in *Girl* and *School Friend*. While 'The Four Marys' still focuses on all-female friendship, it differs in so far as one of the four (Mary Simpson) is a scholarship girl from a working-class family. St Elmo's is still a legitimate social aspiration but there is an acknowledgement of the different economic and social backgrounds of the characters. In one early episode, for example, peer-group pressure obliges Mary Simpson to put her name down for a third-form photograph even though she is unable to afford it. When her parents do not send her the two guineas she needs ('I think it is a ridiculous price to ask for a photograph', her father writes) Mary is faced with the dilemma of not being able to pay for the photograph, and thus drawing attention to her impoverished status in relation to the other girls, until a fortuitous incident when she calls the fire brigade to a neighbouring farm earns her a reward of five guineas.[32] 'The Four Marys' demonstrates how the school story was able to respond to post-war changes in the educational system. It is a moot point, however, whether this was deemed a good thing. Mary Cadogan and Patricia Craig suggest a contrary reading of stories like 'The Four Marys' as accentuating rather than overcoming class difference: 'It is possible that many working-class girls did not think of themselves as "council-school" pupils until the authors of popular fiction hammered home the difference between their environment and that of more wealthy families.'[33]

The typical narrative strategy of *Bunty* is to focus on the girl alone in the world: 'The Four Marys' is somewhat atypical in this regard as school still provides a sense of community for all the protagonists. The narrative of the lonely girl is sometimes overlaid with a dose of psychological cruelty – a theme that *Tammy* would later take to the extreme. A fairly typical example is 'Lonesome Lucy'. This provides a rather different perspective on the home front during the Second World War to the familiar narrative of the 'people's war'. Lucy Mortimer is an evacuee who in 1940 is sent to the countryside to escape the Blitz. However, she finds Mrs Varney's farm a cruel environment: 'Now make a good job of cleaning up this sty. You city brats don't know the meaning of work – but I'll soon cure you of your slovenly habits.'[34] This story,

'The Four Marys', *Bunty* (D. C. Thomson, 15 February 1958).

published in 1958, anticipates the infamous *Tammy* serial 'Slaves of War Orphan Farm' by some twelve years.

The influence of *Bunty* can be seen in the other comics that followed in its wake. *June*, *Judy* and *Mandy* are all essentially *Bunty* clones, while *Princess* and *Diana* are closer in outlook to *Girl*. It was the new comics like *Bunty* and its imitators that proved most able to negotiate the social changes of the 1960s, whereas older comics like *School Friend* and *Girl* did not survive the arrival of the 'swinging sixties'. The major new theme in comics during the 1960s was television. *June*, for example, featured 'The Growing-Up of Emma Peel', dramatizing the childhood of the heroine of *The Avengers*, while *Lady Penelope* (1966–8) was a spin-off from Gerry Anderson's *Thunderbirds*. However, the industry's attempt to create another new market in the form of television-themed comics was not a success: they were too closely tied to another medium and their popularity was fleeting. It was to be the cheap-and-cheerful D. C. Thomson titles that would remain the market leaders throughout the 1960s. Even in 1974 *Bunty*, *Judy*, *Mandy* and *Debbie* (a newcomer launched in 1973) remained the market leaders with combined sales of over 750,000.[35]

Thomson's *Jackie*, launched in 1964, was the one new title of note from the 1960s. In fact *Jackie* was more of a magazine for teenage girls than a comic: it included a few picture strips among features on fashion, pop music and romance. It was marketed as the paper 'for go-ahead teens' and was intended for girls who had outgrown *Bunty* and its like but were not yet ready for adult women's magazines. It can be seen, yet again, as an example of how the industry sought to create a new market. Interestingly there was no equivalent for boys, whom it was assumed would graduate from comics and picture libraries to adult magazines or pulp fiction. *Jackie* was published by Thomson's Women's Magazines Department rather than by its juvenile division. For this reason it tends to be seen not so much as a comic but as a junior version of *Woman's Own*. Mel Gibson suggests that '*Jackie* increased the potential audience for women's magazines, pre-conditioning readers as young as twelve in what to expect from them'.[36] Nevertheless it also provides a useful barometer of the changing emotional lives and experiences of teenage girls between the 1960s and the early 1990s.[37]

* * *

Jackie also provides a link between juvenile girls' comics and another group of publications that appeared in the late 1950s and early 1960s. These were the so-called 'romance' comics, exemplified by Amalgamated's *Marilyn* (1955–65), *Valentine* (1957–74) and *Roxy* (1958–63), Pearson's *Mirabelle* (1956–77), Thomson's *Romeo* (1957–74) and City Magazines' *Boyfriend* (1959–66). These titles were intended for older girls (the over-sixteens) and for a short time in the early 1960s they enjoyed significant popularity: *Valentine* (407,000), *Romeo* (329,000), *Marilyn* (314,000) and *Mirabelle* (224,000) were the best-selling titles.[38] They ranged from cheaply produced titles that superficially resembled juvenile comics (such as *Romeo*) to more upmarket glossy magazine format (*Mirabelle*). Unlike the *Bunty*-type comics, however, they included advertisements for clothes and jewellery as well as picture strips. These titles were complemented by a series of pocket-sized picture libraries – including Pearson's *Picture Romance Library* (1958–66) and Fleetway's *Romantic Confessions Picture Library* (1961–85) – and by imported American titles such as *Young Romance*.[39] The market for romance comics were 'adults and what we would now see as the older teenager', though there is evidence they were also read by younger teenagers.[40]

The romance comics can be seen as products of the period that Arthur Marwick has categorized as 'the first stirrings of the cultural revolution' in Britain: to this extent they both reflected and were in themselves part of social trends and processes.[41] The romance comics appeared at a time when young adults were emerging as a major consumer group: they 'were intended to capture what was seen as a commercially significant and developing "youth market"'.[42] They also appeared at a time when attitudes towards sex and relationships were starting to change. The romance comics can hardly be described as permissive – indeed their conservatism in sexual matters was noted at the time – but their content nevertheless differentiated them from juvenile comics where a girl's greatest love was likely to be for her pony or puppy rather than for a boy. That they never prompted anything like the moral panic directed at horror comics was almost certainly due to the fact that they dealt not with the reality of sex but with the fantasy of 'true love':

> To read nothing but love comics is to go for a never-ending ride through a plaster and plastic tunnel of love. With unfailing monotony, the heroine is a young girl, wide-eyed and probably blonde; she meets a boy and after various misunderstandings finds perfect happiness and fulfilment in his arms. Capturing a boy to love is the whole purpose of a young girl's life, and an engagement ring is the ultimate status symbol; the fact that eight million women and girls are working in Britain, many of them with important jobs, is for the most part ignored.[43]

The outlook of romance comics is perhaps best understood in the same terms as romantic fiction such as the critically derided (but enormously popular) novels of Mills & Boon.

The moment of the romance comics, however, was brief. The boom was over by the mid-1960s: the titles that lasted did so by reinventing themselves as lifestyle magazines and dropping most of their comic-strip content. If romance comics exemplified the early stirrings of the cultural revolution they were quickly overtaken as the revolution gathered pace. What seemed racy and exciting in the late 1950s looked hopelessly old-fashioned following the rise of the permissive society: the 'Summer of Love' in 1967 demonstrated that young people's attitudes towards sexual behaviour had changed out of all recognition from those prevailing only a decade earlier. It is difficult to assess their influence on the industry. In one respect, certainly, they marked something of a watershed. Hitherto the drawing of female characters in British comics had been entirely desexualized regardless of their age: women appear never to have breasts and can often appear almost androgynous. However, the style of the (mostly) Spanish agency artists employed on the romance comics – including Jorde Badia Galvez, Luis Garcia and Jordi Penalva – would emphasize their womanly features. *Valentine*'s art director Jack Cunningham explained the preference for foreign artists in these terms: 'Our readers want to see characters who look glamorous but in an anonymous sort of way . . . British artists won't compromise. They invariably draw *real* people, with warts, freckles and all. So we commission the drawings in Spain where the artists have a much more romantic eye.'[44]

* * *

In the 1970s the British comic market underwent significant changes. It was affected by a steady decline in sales from the late 1960s and by the uncertainty of a culture that was more in flux. The decline in the girls' market was partly related to the changing profile of readers and the drift of adolescent girls away from comics in favour of women's magazines. In 1977 the Royal Commission on the Press observed that 'older teenagers were now enjoying periodicals once considered suitable only for their mothers and grandmothers, whilst younger girls had graduated from comics featuring "Bunty of the Vth form" [*sic*] to the strip-weeklies and their sagas of love in the typing pool'.[45] The 1970s saw a plethora of new girls' comics – IPC with *Tammy* in 1971, *Sandie* in 1972, *Jinty* in 1974, *Misty* in 1978 and *Penny* in 1979, D. C. Thomson with *Debbie* in 1973, *Spellbound* in 1976, *Emma* in 1978 and *Tracy* in 1979 – though the old warhorse *Bunty* remained the market leader with a circulation of 262,000.[46] The fact that few of these comics enjoyed the longevity of their predecessors (*Tammy*, which ran until 1984, was by some measure the longest) indicates the volatility of the market.

The comic industry responded to the changing market by seeking new formulae, and on this occasion it was IPC which led the way. With *Tammy* IPC changed the nature of girls' comics as radically as D. C. Thomson had with *Bunty* a generation before. Its editor Pat Mills called *Tammy* 'the beginning of what could be called the "new wave" of comics' in Britain.[47] Mills was a young freelance writer whose experience hitherto was limited to a few stories for *Lion* written with John Wagner. *Tammy* was the first girls' comic for which the publisher commissioned market research into the tastes of its intended audience (eight- to thirteen-year-olds). A perhaps surprising feature of this research was that girls confessed to enjoying stories that made them cry: Mills interpreted this to mean they wanted stories of emotional suffering and psychological cruelty. This would set the tone for *Tammy*.[48]

To some extent *Tammy* might be seen as a more extreme version of the early *Bunty*. It even borrowed the central idea of *Bunty*'s 'Lonesome Sue' for 'Slaves of War Orphan Farm'. This is regarded as possibly the most sadistic strip ever to appear in a British comic. Kate, an orphan whose parents are killed during the Blitz, is sent to a remote farm in the Lake District where she and other children are kept as virtual prisoners by the wicked Ma Thatcher and her son Ned who put them to work in a nearby quarry. It is an unremittingly bleak tale in which the children are subjected to extremes of both physical and psychological torment: 'Get in before I leather the living daylights out

'Slaves of War Orphan Farm', *Tammy* (IPC Magazines Ltd, 6 February 1971).

of you'; 'I'll knock some of the spirit out o' her down at the quarry'; 'This is war time and people go missin' all the time.'[49] 'Slaves of War Orphan Farm' came to define *Tammy* and provided a template for a host of similar stories in different historical settings including 'Waifs of the Wig Maker' and 'Slaves of the Hot Stove'.

The narrative strategy of *Tammy* is to confront its (usually working-class) heroines with circumstances so extreme that there seems no hope of salvation. A recurring motif is the girl forced into criminality by wicked step-parents ('Bella at the Bar', 'Red Letter Rosie') or criminal gangs ('Katie on Thin Ice' – a female variant of *Oliver Twist*). This is often overlaid with a strong dose of class politics focusing on the exploitation of servant girls ('No Tears for Molly') or farm labourers ('My Father – My Enemy!'). Another favourite motif is the teenage girl forced to take on the role of carer or breadwinner: examples include 'Our Janie' (a girl who has to look after her younger siblings following the death of their mother and injury to their father) and 'Sarah in the Shadows' (a Victorian orphan trying to raise money to secure her uncle's release from debtors' prison – another Dickensian variant, this time of *Little Dorrit*). The world of *Tammy* is one where the welfare state and social services are largely absent: this also helps to explain the preponderance of period narratives. Even where social services are present they prove to be ineffectual: witness the government official who delivers Kate to Ma Thatcher's farm and who is continually duped into thinking the children are enjoying a rural idyll ('I'm sorry you missed her, but as I say she went off to join the other two lambs at their picnic . . .'). The world of *Tammy* is a hostile one where the child has to fend for herself and where adults can be cruel and perverse: it is almost as if it sets out to subvert the cosy world of traditional girls' comics like *School Friend* and *Girl*.

Tammy is also characterized by an acute sense of class envy. It creates social barriers based on both social background and snobbery. Those from poor backgrounds distrust the motives of the rich: 'That's rich folk for you. Pick you up like a plaything, and put you down again when they're tired of you.'[50] Those with ideas 'above their station' turn their backs on their own communities: 'Those riff raff aren't good enough for my Gale, she's a clever, well brought-up girl, not a slum kid.'[51] And the rich abuse their money and power. When spoiled Samantha Devlin is turned down by an amateur ballet troupe because she is not good enough, she persuades her wealthy businessman father to use his influence to shut their practice hall: 'A potty little amateur group daring to tell me I'm not good enough! They'll be sorry for this – mark my word!'[52] *Tammy* therefore marks a decisive break from the consensual social politics of previous girls' comics. Its world of envy and prejudice clearly proved popular with readers: its initial sales were over 383,000 and its regular circulation around 280,000 in the early 1970s.[53]

The formula of *Tammy* was successful enough to influence the content and style of other comics. Thomson began to introduce harsher stories into *Bunty* and *Judy*. It was also *Tammy* that started the trend towards supernatural themes in the 1970s. From the beginning, *Tammy* included eerie stand-alone stories under the series title of 'The Strange Story' – a sort of juvenile *Tales of the Unexpected* – which proved popular with readers:

> My favourite in *Tammy* is your Strange Stories. I'm mad about anything to do with the supernatural – I watch all the late horror films and that. Normally they are about things that happened about a hundred years ago – but I must say your ones, because they're usually set today, make me feel a bit more scared.[54]

The two major publishers drew the obvious conclusions: Thomson's *Spellbound* and IPC's *Misty* were the first British horror comics since the 1950s and both were produced for the girls' market (though it seems likely that they also attracted a significant male readership). This can be seen as yet another attempt by the industry to create a new market, though on this occasion it was only partially successful, as *Spellbound* lasted for only 69 issues and *Misty* for 102 before they were merged with *Debbie* and *Tammy* respectively.

While *Spellbound* now seems quite anodyne, *Misty*, with its combination of Gothic horror and teenage angst, has become something of a cult classic among comic aficionados.[55] Its most memorable strip is probably 'Moonstone', which followed the principle of IPC's boys' comics of the 1970s such as *Battle* and *Action* by turning to popular cinema for inspiration. Young Cathy Salmon discovers that in moments of extreme trauma she develops telekinetic powers that she unleashes upon her tormentors: this would clearly seem to have been modelled on the psychological horror film *Carrie*.[56] Is it entirely too fanciful to read this (and other stories in *Misty*) as narratives of sexual awakening?

However, *Misty* would be one of the last in the lineage of British girls' comics that had begun with *School Friend* in 1950. The girls' comic all but died out in the 1980s as the market shifted towards magazines in the style of *Jackie* (though including much franker content) such as *Oh Boy*, *My Guy* and *Blue Jeans*. These titles included photo-strip stories, a new innovation that would also find its way into the surviving girls' comics during the 1980s. The decline of the girls' comic was partly a consequence of a contracting market overall and partly due to a reorientation across the industry in the 1980s towards adult comics aimed at the predominantly male fan culture for science fiction and fantasy. For some three decades, however, comics had provided a medium for the representation and construction of girlhood in Britain. Like boys' comics they can be seen as responding to wider ideological and cultural currents in British society: from the conservatism of *School Friend* and *Girl* to the more radical social politics of *Tammy* and *Misty* they have negotiated a fine line between creating an idealized narrative of girlhood on the one hand and reflecting something of the reality of their readers' lives on the other. The medium succeeded as long as it was able to fulfil this dual function: it declined when the fantasy it offered was no longer relevant to the lives and experiences of British girls. Henceforth, with occasional exceptions such as the *Barbie* comic for young girls that appeared in the 1990s, the British comic has been a predominantly adult and male affair.

CHAPTER FIVE

The Violent Years

> Look out! *Action* is deadly! You are about to experience the
> toughest stories ever – fast! fierce! fantastic! *Action* is an explosive
> new paper of the 70s – read it and get caught in the blast!
> *Action* #1.[1]

The 1970s was a period of crisis for the British comics industry. On the one hand the industry was hit by a combination of rising costs and declining sales. The oil embargo prompted by the Arab–Israeli War of 1973 caused severe inflationary pressure that resulted in increased production costs (especially the cost of newsprint) which publishers could offset only by raising prices and by instituting strict economies. At the same time the market was chronically unstable: sales were declining and the lifespan of new titles was significantly reduced from previous decades. On the other hand, however, the industry's attempt to address the problems it faced by producing comics that it felt were more in tune with popular taste was to prove highly controversial. The controversy would focus on *Action*, a groundbreaking but short-lived comic published by IPC in the mid-1970s, though *Action* itself was just one example of a new breed of comics such as *Warlord*, *Battle* and *2000AD*.

The changing nature of British comics during the 1970s needs to be understood in an economic context. The juvenile market was dominated more than ever by the mighty duopoly of D. C. Thomson and IPC, which each had a market share of around 40 per cent.[2] In 1971 the industry published 45 different titles and had a combined circulation of around 10 million.[3] Between 1971 and 1976, however, there was a sharp drop in circulation for many established titles: *Bunty* dropped from 466,000 to 199,000, *Judy* from 314,000 to 112,000, *Victor* from 340,000 to 195,000, and *Hotspur* from 209,000 to 134,000.[4] While this decline was due in part at least to defections to new comics, it was an indication of the volatility of the market that venerable old warhorses whose sales had remained stable throughout the 1960s were now in decline. Of the two giants, IPC was more severely affected than Thomson. In 1974, for example, Thomson published seven of the ten best-selling titles, including market leaders *Beano* (with a circulation of 500,000) and *Dandy* (400,000).[5] Thomson's traditional strength in the pre-teen market meant that it was protected to some extent from social and cultural change – the *Beano* in the 1970s was not substantially different from the *Beano* of the 1950s – whereas IPC, with a greater preponderance of adolescent titles, was more exposed to changes in popular taste. At the start of the decade IPC had published 25 weekly comics, but this had dropped to fourteen by 1974. 'The industry is not as healthy as publishers would like it to be', declared John Sanders, managing director of IPC's Juvenile Periodicals Division, at the end of 1974. 'We will just have to accept a lower profitability from our papers.'[6]

It was IPC, however, which proved the more successful in responding to the difficult economic climate. It led the way, for example, in commissioning market research, and was in general more responsive to changing consumer tastes. Sanders summed up his outlook thus: 'I think that we have to continue to look at the whole market and try and fill gaps that are not otherwise filled. We must remember that the child's mind is always changing and he will always welcome something different.'[7] So, while Thomson clung to anthology titles such as *Victor, Hotspur* and *Bunty*, IPC introduced the first themed papers focusing on individual genres. *Scorcher* (1970–74) and *Roy of the Rovers* (1976–93) were both football comics, while other examples included *Battle* (war stories) and *2000AD* (science fiction). While Thomson persevered with its existing titles, IPC was more pragmatic in its outlook. As Sanders told the Comics 101 convention in London in 1976: 'You must remember that we at IPC are not in comics because we have an overwhelming desire to perpetuate this wonderful nostalgic movement . . . It is sometimes a sad economic fact that old favourites have to be merged and that costs must be kept down by the occasional reprinted story.'[8]

The cornerstone of IPC's strategy was the merger. The merger – where a failing title was combined with a better-selling stablemate – was a common occurrence during the 1970s, invariably heralded by the announcement 'exciting news for all readers' on the front page of their comic. The merger was a means of minimizing the risk of launching new titles – the cost of a launch could be up to £100,000 – and of maintaining the balance between continuity and change that would keep loyal readers on board while at the same time testing new markets. The Royal Commission on the Press explained the rationale of the merger thus:

> Many publishers in these fields have adopted a policy of rapid change, and titles are launched with only a short life expectancy, to be merged with others as the latest fad fades. When a title's circulation begins to fall it is generally better to launch a new title with new appeal, and to merge the old title into it, than to try to reestablish the circulation of the existing title by promotional expenditure. Conversely, if the new title is a complete failure, then it can be merged with an existing one, which may even increase its sales enabling most, if not all, of the launch costs to be recouped.[9]

Sanders, however, denied that comics were ever launched with only a short life expectancy, and defended the strategy of mergers as 'economic sense' given the uncertainty and volatility of the market. 'When a child might have been buying two or three comics a week and then drops one,' he added, 'this can have fearful repercussions for the industry'.[10] Thus the comics landscape of the 1970s was extremely unstable: titles appeared and disappeared from the newsagents' shelves with monotonous regularity.[11] It was in this climate of uncertainty that the major publishers sought new formulae that would retain the loyalty of their readers. They did this, paradoxically, by turning to the subject that had proved most durable over the previous two decades: the Second World War.

* * *

The 'new wave' of British comics was heralded by *Warlord* (1974–86) and *Battle* (1975–88). It was not so much the content of these comics that was new as the tone and the treatment. Thomson's *Warlord*, launched in September 1974, was the first comic devoted entirely to the Second World War: to this extent it reflected the continuing popularity of the picture libraries such as *Commando* and IPC's *War Picture Library* which had lost none of their appeal by the 1970s. What differentiated *Warlord* from the war strips in titles like *Victor* and *Hotspur* was its more dynamic visual style (particularly using splash panels to open stories) and its greater levels of realism and violence. It reached a circulation of over 237,000 by the late 1970s.[12] IPC's *Battle* (or, to use its rather ponderous original title, *Battle Picture Weekly*), which followed in March 1975, was their response to *Warlord* which would surpass its rival in violent action and popular appeal. *Battle* represented something of a landmark in that it was commissioned not from within the Juvenile Periodicals Division but from outside. Sanders contracted Pat Mills and John Wagner, the two freelancers who had changed the nature of girls' comics with *Tammy*, to do the same for boys' comics. The success of *Warlord* and *Battle* prompted the

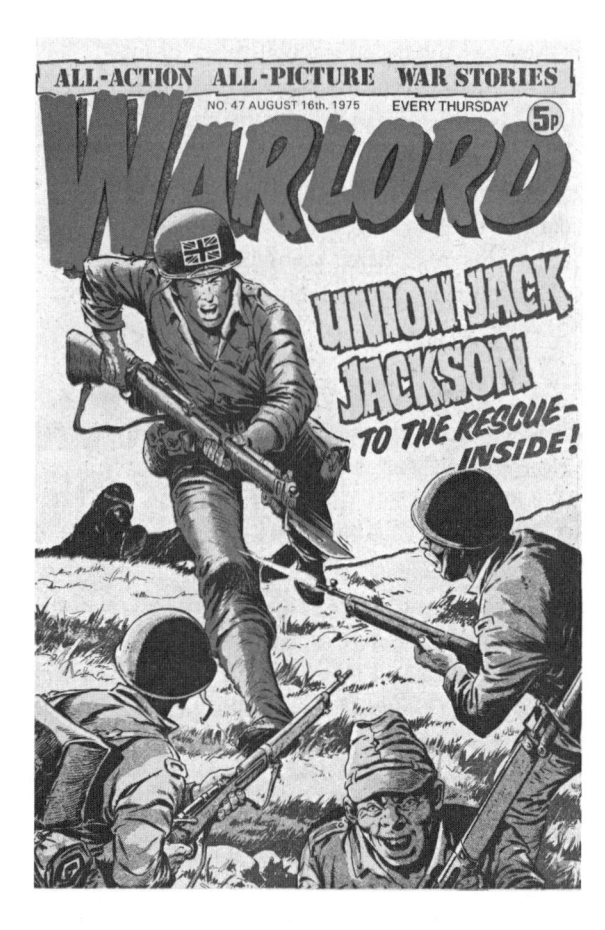

Warlord exemplified the new style of boys' comics in the 1970s (D. C. Thomson, 16 August 1975).

US publisher Marvel to launch its own war comic specifically for the British market: however, *Fury* (1977) consisted of US reprints rather than new material and lasted for less than a year. This again suggests that comic readers made qualitative choices: war as subject-matter was equated with British rather than American comics.

Warlord and *Battle* have tended to be grouped together as if they were much the same kind of product. To some extent this is correct: their content focused largely (not exclusively) on the Second World War and their picture strips were complemented by features on weapon systems (guns, tanks, ships, planes) and 'true life' war stories. They each published a range of readers' letters which typically featured stories from boys about what their fathers, uncles or grandfathers did during the war. Indeed, readers' letters provide a rich source of evidence of the continued interest in the Second World War on the part of British children – an interest maintained in the 1970s by the success of the television series *The World at War* (1973–4) and the screening on television of the classic war movies of the 1950s such as *The Cruel Sea* and *The Dam Busters*. While it seems very likely that the readership for *Warlord* and *Battle* would have crossed over, however, there are some important differences between the papers. *Warlord* still maintained links with more traditional comics: its original line-up included two characters who had a long history in Thomson story papers and comics – 'Bomber Braddock' and 'Young Wolf' – while others such as 'Drake of E-Boat Alley' are not far removed from the sort of stories appearing in *Victor*.[13] Its title strip, 'Code-Name Warlord', featuring secret agent extraordinaire Lord Peter Flint, is somewhat Janus-faced: on the one hand Flint is an aristocratic throwback who speaks in the sort of self-consciously arch dialogue where friend and foe alike are greeted as 'old chap', but on the other hand his toughness and fighting skills have more in common with the ruthless professionalism of James Bond.

Battle, however, was an altogether grittier publication. According to its first editor Dave Hunt: 'The brief from the outset . . . was to have a more honest approach to the fact that war is a killing zone – that flesh and bone is ripped to shreds when bullets or bombs strike mere mortals.'[14] *Battle* was characterized by the high quality of its writing, particularly by Gerry Finley-Day, Alan Hebden, John Wagner and Pat Mills.[15] The artists were a mixture of old hands versed in the traditional style of British adventure strips, such as Eric Bradbury, Geoff Campion and Joe Colquhoun, and emerging talents such as Cam Kennedy and Spain's Carlos Ezquerra, whose artwork demonstrated a more individualistic, impressionistic style. Ezquerra brought his distinctive rough-edged style to 'The Rat Pack' and 'Major Eazy': the 'look' of these strips with their heightened violence and their scruffy, unshaven anti-heroes is based as much on the Spaghetti Western as on the pictorial realism of *Commando*.

There are other ways, too, in which *Battle* represents something of a new departure for British comics. Its points of reference are not so much other comics, as in *Warlord*, but war films. In particular it based strips (indirectly) on popular war movies such as *The Dirty Dozen*, *Where Eagles Dare*, *Play Dirty* and *Kelly's Heroes*.[16] These films were characterized by their men-on-a-mission narratives which privileged violent mayhem over psychological realism – a style that translated easily into comic strip. 'The Rat Pack', for example, in which a group of dangerous convicts are moulded into a crack commando unit, is clearly based on *The Dirty Dozen*, while the laid-back cool of 'Major Eazy' is reminiscent of *Kelly's Heroes*. 'Day of the Eagle' – in which a British agent is sent to assassinate Hitler – is a wartime reinterpretation of *The Day of the Jackal*.[17] The strategy of positioning the paper by basing strips on popular genre films would also be adopted successfully by *Action* and *2000AD*.

Battle established itself in a market saturated with war comics through a successful strategy of product differentiation. While it included several traditional-style strips that might have been at home in the picture libraries – such as 'D-Day Dawson' (Sergeant Steve Dawson is 'a man with nothing to lose' after a bullet lodges close to his heart on D-Day) and 'The Bootneck Boy' (following the trials of Royal Marine recruit Danny Budd) – *Battle* on the whole preferred more unconventional protagonists in unfamiliar situations such as 'Joe Two Beans' (a Blackhawk Indian serving with the US Army in the Pacific) and 'Johnny Red' (Hurricane pilot Johnny Redburn, dishonourably discharged from the RAF, joins the Falcon Squadron on the Russian Front). *Battle* also stands out for its realistic representation of war. It attempts to describe the sensory experience of combat: 'You're stumbling through the rubble-filled streets. The stench of death and burnt cordite is in your nostrils – cold steel in your hands.'[18] And it recognizes the human cost of war: several long-running strips end in the death of their protagonist. This surprised some readers: 'I was really shocked when D-Day Dawson died: I thought he would have an operation to remove the bullet by his heart.'[19]

Battle demonstrates a more psychologically complex and morally equivocal outlook on war than had been seen hitherto in British comics. 'Darkie's Mob', to take one of the best known stories, is nothing less than a comic strip version of *Heart of Darkness*. The enigmatic Captain Joe Darkie takes command of a British platoon lost behind enemy lines in Burma and leads them in his private war against the Japanese: 'If you stay with me, I'm going to give you hell. You'll eat, sleep and drink jungle. You'll smell like jungle. You'll curse me and hate me. But I promise you one thing – you'll kill Japs!'[20] The strip is especially notable for its uncompromising representation of the savagery of jungle fighting and for the obsessive character of Darkie himself who cares more about killing Japanese than the well-being of his own men. Darkie is a most unconventional hero: at times his behaviour borders on psychotic. The truth is revealed only at the end: it turns out that Joseph Daakee is the son of a Japanese father and English mother murdered by Japanese troops.

Battle also broke new ground for a British comic by representing the Second World War from the German perspective. To some extent this was a response to the demands of its readers. One letter (albeit from a reader in Ireland) complained that 'there are too many stories about English troops in *Battle*. Why don't you give those Jerries a chance?'[21] *Battle* features several stories – including 'Panzer G-Man', 'The General Dies at Dawn' and 'Death Squad' – that focus on the German experience of war. The narrative strategy borrows from West German war films such as *Stalingrad* and *The Star of Africa* in that these stories feature honourable German soldiers who are not Nazis and are fighting a war they know they cannot win. 'Death Squad', for example,

Battle Picture Weekly (IPC Magazines Ltd, 4 September 1976). *Battle* was IPC's even tougher answer to D. C. Thomson's *Warlord*.

about a group of misfits in a punishment battalion on the Russian Front, is a close relation of the film *Punishment Battalion 999*.[22]

There is some evidence of the reception of *Battle*. Its readers seem to have liked it for its realism: 'I have been buying *Battle* since the first issue and I think it is a superb paper. The stories are very realistic and the drawings are excellent.'[23] It would seem, also, that its readers made genre distinctions in their choice of comic: dedicated *Battle* readers were not happy when their comic inherited non-war strips from *Valiant* ('One-Eyed Jack') and *Action* ('Dredger') or when it tried its hand at science fiction ('The Spinball Warriors').[24] There is also evidence that its readership extended beyond the target market of adolescent males and included some adults, especially those with a military background. An article in the *Daily Mail* even quoted 'a senior supply officer at Aldershot barracks' as saying: 'It's these defence cuts – it's nice to be able to pick up a comic paper and be reminded of the days when we didn't have to count the cost of a bullet before squeezing a trigger.'[25]

The critical response to the new breed of war comics focused, predictably enough, on their violence. However, as Martin Barker has shown in his analysis of the controversy over *Action* in 1976, criticism of the excessive violence of the comic disguised deeper ideological issues over its content. This is also apparent in the response to *Warlord* and *Battle*, where the real objection seems to be more to the way in which the comics represented the experience of war than to their violence. So, for example, the journalist George Rosie described *Warlord* as 'appallingly violent', while also suggesting that its content was essentially unrealistic:

> Of course, in all the excitement and elaborate technology, all the appalling biological details of war are totally missing. Nobody gets his head blown apart, or spills his entrails on to the ground, or has his legs severed at the hip by a shell splinter, or the flesh cooked off his bones in a blazing tank. Death is marked by outthrown arms and a sharp cry and there's an end to it. The moral of *Warlord* seems to be that war is an exciting and glamorous business which is, however, best pursued by 'cold ruthless fighting machines' like the heroes of *Warlord*.[26]

There is a contradiction here: Rosie attacks *Warlord* for its 'appalling violence' while at the same time criticizing its sanitized representation of war. It is not clear whether he would have preferred it had the comic included images of dismembered limbs and burning flesh!

Other critics objected to what they saw as the promotion of a pro-war ideology in the comics. John Heeley, writing in the wake of the Falklands War of 1982, which had briefly reignited a mood of jingoistic nationalism in sections of the British media, suggested that war comics like *Battle* and *Warlord* 'meet the needs of certain social groups and are a reflection of the patriotic, authoritarian "dog eats dog" mentality of the British people' and that they 'help inculcate a particular definition of violence, one which sees it as normal, natural and inevitable'.[27] Heeley's critique of war comics is based (like most attacks on the medium) on broad generalization and unsubstantiated assumptions about their ideological effects.

Perhaps the best riposte to such criticism is to be found in the pages of the comics themselves. Letters to *Battle* suggest that its readers were perfectly able to distinguish between the comic-strip version of war and the real thing:

> I think that your comic is the greatest thing since VE Day. However, I have one complaint. I think you should change the title of your feature called 'Oh, What A Lovely War!' because war is not lovely. A friend of my family said that he lost twenty friends in one day at the Battle of the Somme: also 8000 men on both sides died in one morning.[28]

Here we see evidence of an actual rather than an assumed response to the comic: it does not suggest that the reader's enjoyment of *Battle* has led him to hold a gung-ho view of war. The editor replied: 'I agree with you that war is not pleasant, Robert, and we certainly don't try to glamorize it. We chose the title "Oh, What A Lovely War!" because . . . we wanted to show that despite its jolly title, it was an horrific slaughter of the nation's manhood.'[29]

The assertion that *Battle* does not glamorize war might seem somewhat disingenuous. The fact is that *Battle* demonstrates an ideological contradiction: it seeks to show that 'war is hell' but at the same time revels in its spectacle. *Battle* is no more an anti-war comic than, say, *Saving Private Ryan* is an anti-war film. In particular there is never any suggestion that the Second World War is anything other than a just war. Even a cynical anti-hero like Major Eazy is able to see a higher moral purpose: 'I'm in this fight to give the kids a better future – not to kill 'em off before they've got a chance to see it!'[30]

There is, however, one major exception, and a truly remarkable exception at that. Pat Mills and Joe Colquhoun's 'Charley's War' has been described as 'one of the greatest stories of war ever recounted in a comic'.[31] 'Charley's War' is an account of the Western Front told from the perspective of an idealistic young recruit who joins up from a sense of patriotic duty and experiences the horrific reality of war at first hand. It stands out from other war strips for several reasons. One is its degree of historical authenticity. 'Charley's War' is based on exhaustive research: Mills and Colquhoun both went to great pains in an effort to make it as authentic as possible. Many of the incidents are based on actual historical events that include both the familiar (the Battle of the Somme) and the unfamiliar (such as the 'forgotten' British army mutiny at Étaples in 1917). And Colquhoun's painstaking artwork makes extensive use of primary source materials. These range from photographs of the Western Front to the work of British and German war artists such as Richard Nevinson and Otto Dix.[32]

'Charley's War' is unflinching in its representation of the horrors of war. It includes any number of vivid and memorable images: a skeleton in a shell hole, bodies blown apart by grenades and burned by flame-throwers, a line of soldiers blinded by gas. The brutality of the fighting is matched by the squalid conditions of trench life: mud and rats are ever-present companions. Colquhoun's art at times draws upon the techniques of Expressionist painting as his angular, disjointed figures merge with the landscape. This can be understood as a means of representing the anonymous mechanized killing of the battlefield and the dehumanizing effects of modern industrialized warfare on the individual. 'Charley's War' also refers to the iconography of films such as *All Quiet on the Western Front* in picturing a landscape scarred by war: shell craters, barbed wire, dead trees. The battlefield is a place of horror

The horror of war graphically represented by Pat Mills and Joe Colquhoun in 'Charley's War'. *Battle* (IPC Magazines Ltd, 28 July 1979).

rather than valour: the strip visualizes what Siegfried Sassoon described as 'a dreadful place, a place of horror and desolation which no imagination could have invented'.[33]

Mills invests 'Charley's War' with a degree of psychological realism unprecedented in British comics. Charley Bourne is very much an 'ordinary' hero: he represents the thousands of young men who lied about their age in order to fight for 'King and Country'. He has no special abilities or leadership qualities: his response to war covers a range of emotions from fear and horror to a stoical resolve to see it through alongside his mates. Mills employs a brilliant narrational device in the form of Charley's letters and postcards to his family. The naive optimism and spelling mistakes establish Charley's character as a poorly educated but basically decent working-class lad who does his best in difficult circumstances: 'I have finaly arrived at the Western Front and its not nearly as bad as they make out so tell Ma to stop worrying! Thank her for the cakes and also Auntey Mabel for the scarf she nitted.'[34]

Yet 'Charley's War' is more than just an account of the horror and brutality of war. It is also a highly political statement. Mills has said that 'at the deepest level, *Charley's War* is a class war, a war against the poor, which I exemplified at every opportunity'.[35] This can be seen on several levels. The strip endorses the Marxist idea that wars are fought for the benefit of capitalists: thus a nurse treating victims of poison gas lays the blame on industrialists ('I wish the inventors of chemical warfare could see their handiwork now!') and Charley's mate Smithy calculates the cost of bullets ('It costs thirty pounds a minute to fire that machine-gun Charley! You've spent about a thousand pounds now!').[36] It also adheres to the popular view of the First World War in that it shows the British army officered by upper-class stereotypes who care little for the welfare of the men under their command. The real villain of 'Charley's War' is platoon commander Lieutenant Snell who is characterized as a snob and a cad. When Snell brings Charley back from No-Man's Land he is acclaimed a hero, but his real motive is known only to the reader: 'This boy makes a good body-shield. If anyone is going to stop a bullet, it's better for it to be a common little runt like Bourne than me!'[37]

It will be clear that 'Charley's War' is an explicitly anti-war narrative: to this extent it belongs to the tradition of films such as *All Quiet on the Western Front, Paths of Glory, King and Country* and *Oh! What A Lovely War*.[38] Yet it is also more than that: its politics make it one of the most radical strips ever to appear in a British comic. It criticizes the conduct of the war: the British generals cling to their belief in the frontal assault and cynically sacrifice the lives of their troops to advance a few miles. It attacks the hypocrisy of military justice: when the one humane officer, Lieutenant Thomas, orders his men to retreat when they come under fire by their own artillery, he is court-martialled for cowardice and shot. It is sympathetic in its treatment of deserters and progressive in its attitude towards the condition of 'shell shock'. It provides a powerful counter-argument to those critics who have suggested that comics like *Battle* promoted a warlike mentality among their readers. The popularity of 'Charley's War', which was consistently voted one of the most popular strips in *Battle*, would suggest that its readers were rather more discriminating than sometimes assumed.

* * *

The popular success of *Warlord* and *Battle* prompted their publishers to follow up with other 'tough' comics. Thomson's *Bullet* (1976–8) and IPC's *Action* (1976–7) were launched on the same day (14 February 1976) and were similar in format. They included a mixture of genres (adventure, war, sport, science fiction) and branded themselves as 'The rough tough action story paper for boys' (*Bullet*) and 'The sensational paper for boys' (*Action*). Again it was the IPC title which outdid its rival: *Action* sold 250,000 of its first issue and its regular sales were in the region of 180,000.[39] In fact it was one of IPC's most successful launches of the 1970s, which makes it all the more remarkable that such a nakedly commercial publisher withdrew the comic from sale after only eight months and cancelled it a year later.

The case of *Action* is a perfect demonstration of both the commercial and ideological strategies of the British comics industry in the 1970s. John

Sanders turned again to Pat Mills, who masterminded the launch in association with editor Geoff Kemp. Kemp, a former editor of *Lion*, explained the genesis of the new comic in an interview with Martin Barker:

> For about three months Pat and I had an office to ourselves, talking not just about story-lines but the basic idea of a comic which was different. At that time *Jaws* the film had come out and it was pretty clear that people were rather enjoying seeing bits of bodies floating around in the water; and we were really thinking we could go much more violent than the comics had done before. There was still a very 1950s attitude towards this sort of thing. So what we were basically after was, what the title suggests, action, violence, very busy, lots going on in the stories. We were using a new set of writers.[40]

In fact *Action* used a mixture of established writers, including Jack Adrian, Ron Carpenter, Gerry Finley-Day and Tom Tully, and new bloods like Steve MacManus and Chris Lowder, while artists included both home-grown talents, such as Geoff Campion, Tony Harding and Mike White, and Europeans such as Spain's Ramon Sola and Italy's Massimo Belardinelli. This mixture accounts for the presence of some quite traditional stories, such as 'The Coffin Sub' (standard war stuff) and 'Play Till You Drop' (a footballer is blackmailed into throwing matches) alongside edgier fare like 'Hookjaw' (a seemingly unstoppable Great White Shark with an insatiable appetite for humans) and 'Black Jack' (a boxer losing his sight).[41]

Action adopted the strategy pioneered by *Battle* in that it looked to popular film (and television) for easily recognizable formulae that could be adapted into comic strip form. Thus 'Hookjaw' clearly owed its inspiration to the box-office smash *Jaws*.[42] 'Dredger' – a tough undercover agent who cares little for the niceties of legal procedure – was cast from the same mould as *Dirty Harry*: the hero even bears a physical likeness of Clint Eastwood.[43] Later addition 'Death Game 1999' – a violent futuristic sports story in which convicts are forced to participate in a deadly form of gladiatorial combat – was the SF film *Rollerball*.[44] (It is worth mentioning here that *Dirty Harry* and *Rollerball* were 'X' certificate films in Britain due to their violence: this meant they could not legally be seen by anyone under the age of eighteen. Some of the appeal of *Action* for its readers may have been that it offered a taste of forbidden pleasures.) And 'The Running Man' – an athlete visiting New York is framed by the Mafia and sets out to find the men responsible while himself being hunted by the police – was based on long-running television series *The Fugitive*.[45] Other stories drew upon different sources. 'Hellman of

Hammer Force' – a tough but honourable German tank commander during the Second World War – borrowed from the Gunnar Asch novels of Hans Hellmut Kirst, while 'Kids Rule OK' – warring juvenile gangs in a near-future society where a mysterious plague has wiped out all adults – was an urban reimagining of *Lord of the Flies*.[46]

Action sold itself to readers as 'a new kind of boys' paper – a paper that's on YOUR side!'[47] It was the first comic that consciously set out to respond to the tastes and interests of its readers. Its irreverent tone was demonstrated in editorial features such as 'Twit of the Week' (media and sports personalities nominated for the award by readers: television hosts Bamber Gascoigne and Nicholas Parsons were among the first winners) and 'So what?' (a sarcastic alternative to the 'interesting fact' columns of other comics). On the evidence of published letters it would seem that readers particularly liked the use of slang and vernacular language: 'I especially like the fantastic new comic *Action* because it has all the up-to-date words which boys use. E.g. "Some bod looking for aggro. Fix 'im, Arnie."'[48] Furthermore, it is evident that the comic was not read solely by boys: 'Please don't write on the front of your *Action* comic "The Sensational Paper for Boys!" You are forgetting the Sex Discrimination Act. I am a girl aged 12 and enjoy *Action* more than any other comic.'[49]

The social politics of *Action* also indicate that it set out to appeal to 'streetwise' kids. We have already seen that some British comic strip heroes such as Braddock and Alf Tupper were cast as working-class outsiders who

'Kids Rule OK', *Action* (IPC Magazines Ltd, 11 September 1976).

Action (IPC Magazines Ltd, 3 April 1976).

have to battle privilege and snobbery: in *Action* this type of character has become the norm. Its heroes are typically from poor backgrounds, such as boxer Jack Barron ('Black Jack') and footballer Kenny Lampton ('Look out for Lefty!'), or are defiantly anti-authoritarian such as Dredger and Hellman. The protagonists of *Action* are invariably outsiders who have to prove themselves in a hostile world – whether it is on the football pitch, in the boxing ring or on the killing fields of the Second World War. It offered heroes with whom its readers could identify: 'real' people facing up to their own problems and anxieties rather than fantasy supermen or unbelievably flawless heroic archetypes.

'Dredger' is the perfect illustration of the politics of *Action*. It is a strip in which class difference is prominent. 'Dredger' is a buddy narrative that teams the eponymous hero (an ex-Royal Marine sergeant 'kicked out for brutality') with an upper-class sidekick in the form of Simon Breed (Eton, Cambridge, Grenadier Guards). Whereas Breed voices the traditional values of duty and patriotism ('If Gadazi is killed, the oil deal will fall through. That's why this job is so important – for Britain's future'), Dredger is not interested ('Spare me the flag waving, pal. I want some kip.'). Dredger is characterized as a thug with no moral scruples: he thinks nothing of making a suspect talk by putting a grenade in his mouth or threatening to shoot off his toes. His sole purpose is to get the job done – at any cost. Each strip would end with a reflective thought by Breed on his taciturn ally: 'Dredger's dirty all right – but he gets results. He's going to be a useful man on future jobs.'[50]

Action set out to be socially inclusive. This is most evident in 'Black Jack'. The strip might be seen as a response to criticism that had started to emerge in the 1970s that British comics marginalized non-white characters. In the words of one critic: 'I wondered if a black child leafing through them would ever see a child who looked like him. All societies transmit secret messages. To many of these children, the hidden message of the comic is: you don't exist.'[51] The decision to make Jack Barron a black man was realistic in the context of the sport of boxing and also allowed the strip to confront racism – albeit that this was displaced to America where Jack is called a 'niggah boy' by white racists.[52] 'Black Jack' is one of the more socially realistic strips in *Action*. However, it had limited narrative potential: once Jack had won the world heavyweight championship there was nowhere for the story to go.[53]

'Hookjaw' – consistently the most popular strip with readers – is also the most radical from an ideological perspective. Like the shark in *Jaws*, Hookjaw (so called because he has a fish hook embedded in his mouth from an encounter with some fishermen) is represented as a primal force of nature. Unlike *Jaws*, however, where the shark is kept off screen for much of the film and remains an anonymous threat, Hookjaw is the real 'star' of the strip. Hookjaw is not a monster in the usual sense: he is merely acting on his 'primitive instinct' to hunt for food – to him human beings are irritants. The real villains of the strip are those unscrupulous capitalists who put profit ahead of the safety of their workers. Characters such as the oil man Red McNally who sacrifices his men to keep his rig operative and the property developer Dr Gelder who exploits the local populace to build a luxury resort on Paradise Island are bullies and crooks: there is a sense of social justice when they finally get their comeuppance. In this sense 'Hookjaw' might be compared to *King Kong*: we cheer for Hookjaw just as audiences reportedly cheered Kong's destructive rampage through central Manhattan.[54]

It will be clear, then, that *Action* was very different in content and outlook from other comics on the market at the time. In some measure this helps to explain the controversy that engulfed it. *Action* sparked a media backlash against the comics industry of a degree not witnessed since the horror comics campaign of the 1950s. The first blast came from the *Evening Standard* after only two issues in an article which focused on the violence of *Action* and accused IPC of cynical commercialism:

See a youth murder five policemen, see a body hurtle through a car window, see several limbs chomped off by today's most modish monster, the killer shark . . . *Action* is a deliberate, calculated and commercially-minded attempt to cash in on What the Kids Want. What the Kids Want is, allegedly, what they already see on television and in the cinema.[55]

A few weeks later the *Sun* dubbed *Action* 'the sevenpenny nightmare' – deliberately evoking the moral panic around penny dreadfuls a century before – though the tone of the article itself was rather tongue in cheek.[56] The most sustained attack, however, came from the *Daily Mail* in September 1976, prompted by an incident in the strip 'Look out for Lefty!' where Lenny's girlfriend Angie throws a bottle at an opposition player who has fouled her boyfriend on the pitch. This was a time when the problem of football violence had raised its ugly head – 'hooliganism' had become the source of a moral panic in the 1970s – and the article quoted representatives of the Football Association and the Football League condemning the comic as 'irresponsible nonsense' and 'appalling and brainless'. (Alan Hardaker, secretary of the Football League, added: 'The man responsible ought to be hit over the head with a bottle himself' – hardly an appropriate sentiment in the circumstances!) The *Daily Mail* also solicited an opinion from the doyen of comic historians Denis Gifford: '*Action* is a new kind of comic geared to the lowest form of behaviour in children. Just as pornography caters for a mass market for adults, this provides violence for a mass market of children.'[57]

IPC's response to the controversy – which reached a climax when John Sanders faced aggressive questioning on the BBC's evening news magazine programme *Nationwide* – was a strategy of damage limitation. It announced that it was suspending *Action* for a 're-appraisal of editorial policy'. Senior IPC executive Johnny Johnson explained the decision thus: 'We felt that to suspend publication was the only proper course to take. We do agree that we have made an error of judgement.'[58] *Action* was off the shelves for six weeks. When it returned two strips had been dropped without explanation ('Kids Rule OK' and 'Probationer') while the content of others was significantly toned down. While these changes may have deflected the criticism they alienated readers who felt the comic had lost its edge. The 'new' *Action* lasted another year before declining sales led to its merger with *Battle*.

The 're-appraisal of editorial policy' effectively killed *Action*. But why did IPC collude in killing off one of its most successful comics? One possibility is that *Action* was a victim of institutional politics: Jack Le Grand, the Head of Boys' Periodicals, was upset when Sanders turned to freelancers to produce *Battle* and *Action* rather than commissioning them within the department. Grand is said to have 'wanted *Action* to fail' and had friends on the board of IPC and its parent company Reed International.[59] Another reason that has been suggested is that major newsagent chains, in particular W. H. Smith, threatened not just to refuse to sell *Action* but also to boycott other IPC magazines. While this is difficult to prove, it was not unknown for retailers to impose their own censorship. In 1977, for example, W. H. Smith refused to sell 'a particularly nasty and ridiculous series of comic books' including bogus accounts of the death of Adolf Hitler and the assassination of President Kennedy.[60]

The *Action* controversy also needs to be understood in a wider social and political context. The mid-1970s was a time of heightened sensitivity over 'violence' in the media. Among the various targets were action-oriented police series like *The Sweeney* (1975–8) and violently immoral films such as *Death Wish* (1974). This was also a time when pressure groups with a moral agenda such as the National Viewers' and Listeners' Association and the Responsible Society were particularly active. These organizations exerted a disproportionate influence over the media in relation to their size. One of the groups that took exception to *Action* called itself DOVE ('Delegates Opposing Violent Education'): it threatened to 'black' the comic by demanding its withdrawal from newsagents and by defacing it with stickers.[61]

How justified were the criticisms of *Action*? There is no question that *Action* included a heady dose of violence. 'Hookjaw', 'Dredger' and 'Death Game 1999' were probably the worst offenders: it is no coincidence that they were also among the most popular strips. Yet the violence of *Action* is complex: it varies in tone and context. In 'Dredger', for example, it is difficult to counter charges that violence is sometimes gratuitous: scenes where Dredger pushes an enemy agent's head into an animal trap or where a villain is impaled on spikes are narratively unnecessary and would seem to have been included merely for their shock effect. 'Death Game 1999' also features a generous quota of violent mayhem, though this strip can be read as a commentary on the nature of violence as spectacle. Here there is a suggestion it is the spectators who demand violence: 'We paid to see blood, not a game of pot-ball.'[62] Other strips, notably 'Hellman of Hammer Force', follow the conventions of war comics in representing violence within an ethical framework: 'We kill tanks – not men if we can help it . . . I am a soldier, not a butcher.'[63] As for the notorious 'Hookjaw', it is difficult to see this as anything other than a dark comedy: the image, for example, of a frogman blinded by oil swimming straight into Hookjaw's gaping mouth with a thought bubble saying 'Hope this is the way' recalls the macabre humour of the EC horror comics of the 1950s.[64]

Martin Barker has argued that the real reason behind the toning down of *Action* was not its violence but its politics: '*Action* stood at the very edge

'Hookjaw', *Action* (IPC Magazines Ltd, 15 May 1976).

of a radical politics – and that couldn't be allowed'.[65] The evidence for this is to be found in the changes to the content of *Action* following its editorial 're-appraisal'. This entailed removing not just the most violent scenes but also the cynical references to authority that had been such a prominent feature of the 'old' *Action*. The result was to neuter it: the 'attitude' that had differentiated *Action* from other comics was lost. The comic had lost its 'bite': literally so as 'Hookjaw' was moved off the colour centre spread and most of his killing frenzies now took place off the page. In this reading *Action* was killed off because it represented too much of a challenge to the political and social consensus that the major comic publishers by and large endorsed. For a short time, however, *Action* had broken the mould of British comics. And its legacy lasted far longer than the comic itself. For in the brief and troubled history of *Action* can be found the origin of an even more significant title in British comics history: *2000AD*.

CHAPTER SIX

I Am the Law!

> I am convinced that there is a hole in the juvenile market which
> we are not covering. Whilst some of our comics do carry science
> fiction stories, none of them aim exclusively at the SF field . . . Most
> bookshops now carry their own, exclusive SF section and the field is
> due to receive a sizeable boost in 1976 . . . I am sure therefore that
> we should be giving some thought to the preparation of
> an SF paper, right now . . .
> Kelvin Gosnell to Pat Mills, 18 December 1975.[1]

The official history of what its own publicity describes as 'The Galaxy's Greatest Comic' is that it was conceived to exploit the vogue for science fiction cinema in the mid-1970s. It had long been held within both the comic and the film industries that SF was a specialist genre appealing to a minority audience. This perception changed in the 1970s. The point of critical mass came not, as often assumed, following the success of the space opera *Star Wars* (1977), which overtook *Jaws* to become the biggest-grossing film in cinema history up to that point, but in the production season of 1975–6 when a cycle of SF films were released by the major studios including *Rollerball*, *Death Race 2000*, *The Ultimate Warrior*, *The Man Who Fell To Earth*, *Logan's Run* and *Futureworld*, while others in production at the time included *Star Wars* (shooting at Britain's Elstree Studios in 1976) and *Close Encounters of the Third Kind*. It is difficult to pinpoint a reason for the revival of science fiction cinema at this time – with the exception of *2001: A Space Odyssey* there were no real SF blockbusters before *Star Wars* – but, as so often in the film industry, a trend emerged as the studios collectively turned to SF in the hope that it would be the next major boom.[2]

The decision to launch a science fiction-themed comic demonstrated once again how IPC in the 1970s was able to respond to market demand by keeping abreast of trends in popular culture. Gosnell, a sub-editor and self-professed SF fan, argued that the time was ripe for an SF comic 'even if it planned to run only as long as the boom lasts: it must make money while riding the crest and could be used for a merge when it becomes uneconomic'. 'Although,' he added prophetically, 'given the right mix, I am certain that it would stand a good chance of surviving longer than the movie boom.' The production of an SF comic was also consistent with the trend towards genre-specific titles including war (*Battle*), football (*Roy of the Rovers*) and horror (*Misty*). However, John Sanders, who suggested the title, did not expect it to last: 'I remember thinking the year 2000 was so far away as to be untouchable . . . The idea of a new launch lasting for more than 20 years was just unthinkable.'[3]

However, the birth of *2000AD* was not without its labour pains. Sanders handed the job of launching the new comic to Pat Mills, who had a proven track record of success with *Battle* and *Action*. Mills mapped out the story content in collaboration with John Wagner and worked on the layout with designer Doug Church. However, Wagner walked out before the comic was launched in protest at IPC's decision to publish it as an in-house title rather than contracting it from freelancers – meaning that writers and artists had to sign over their rights to the publisher and would not be entitled to any royalties.[4] Another victim of institutional politics was artist Carlos Ezquerra, who drew the original designs for what would become the flagship strip, 'Judge Dredd', but who took umbrage when the first printed story used the work of a different artist (Mike McMahon) based on Ezquerra's designs. Both Wagner and Ezquerra would return to the fold, however, and provide some of *2000AD*'s best strips. There was also confusion around the involvement of film producer Paul De Savery. De Savery had bought an option on the film rights to Dan Dare from IPC and in November 1975 announced plans for a $10 million film starring Roger Moore as Dare.[5] Mills has suggested that De Savery 'tried to buy the comic out and involve me in a share of the profits', though this is contested by Sanders and Wagner.[6] The film never materialized.

IPC's decision to publish *2000AD* in house rather than contracting it out needs to be understood in the context of the renewed moral panic around comics in the mid-1970s. While *2000AD* was still in development in the autumn of 1976 the controversy over *Action* reached its peak. Mills saw *2000AD* as being in the same tradition as *Action*: 'I didn't want *2000AD* to follow in the same old house-style of existing publications like *Eagle* or *TV21* [*sic*]. I actually saw sci-fi as a vehicle for increased action and violence.'[7] However, the controversy around *Action* prompted IPC to scrutinize the content of all its juvenile papers for excessive violence. The decision to publish in house ensured tighter editorial control. The consequences of this new policy were quickly felt. During the development stages of *2000AD*, entire scripts had to be scrapped and artwork junked or drastically revised. Kevin O'Neill, who began as an assistant art editor, recalled: 'The original stories like M.A.C.H. 1 were extremely violent, guys having their heads kicked off, limbs flying about – we had to censor almost every page.' Nevertheless, O'Neill believed that this benefited the comic in the long term: 'I think *Action* being taken off the stands influenced *2000AD* for the better. It made us concentrate on the science-fiction and fantasy aspect, build up a kind of mythos for the comic.'[8]

The launch of *2000AD*, boosted by a television advertising campaign, focused on the return of Dan Dare, who occupied the colour centre pages. This was a very different Dare from the old *Eagle* favourite, however: a crop-haired action hero with a subordinate streak and a nice line in futuristic swearing ('Drokk it!'). The *2000AD* 'Dan Dare' borrowed a device from *Buck Rogers*: Dare has been preserved in suspended animation and his new appearance is explained away by reconstructive surgery following the injuries he sustained saving the Earth from a massive nuclear reactor explosion. The response to the new-look Dan Dare was mixed. One reader thought it 'is much better than the old D.D. – overall the best strip in the paper', whereas another deemed it 'a disappointment! The most distinctive thing about the original Dare was the artwork . . . the new Dare is streets behind.'[9] For aficionados of the classic Dan Dare, the new incarnation was an abomination – 'a Frankenstein whose only answer was the gun. The essential elements of the original Dan Dare – humanity and compassion – had been entirely cut away.'[10] In the eyes of his fans, Dan was never quite the same man after that accident with the orbital power station.

However, the launch of *2000AD* caused controversy beyond Dan Dare's new haircut. A front-page article in the *Guardian* focused on a strip called 'Invasion!', which depicted the conquest of Britain by the Volgan Republic of Asia in 1999. 'Invasion!' opens in dramatic fashion with parachute troops landing in London and a fifty megaton bomb destroying Birmingham. Volgan tanks roll into Trafalgar Square, the BBC broadcasts news of the British surrender, the People's Republic of Britain is declared and aristocrats are shot on the steps of St Paul's Cathedral. It is clear from their uniforms that the Volgans are really meant to be the Soviets. Indeed, the strip had been written and drawn as such, only for the Russian star and 'CCCP' initials to be inked out on the instructions of a nervous John Sanders shortly before the first issue went to press. The *Guardian* found a spokesman for the Soviet embassy, who declared that the story was intended 'to whip up war hysteria, [and] to breed distrust in children's minds towards other countries which they hardly know'.[11] And a baptist minister wrote in to accuse the comic of 'indulging the prejudices of the paranoid anti-communist hysteria of current British society and wallowing in an IPC-directed thermonuclear war'.[12]

'Invasion!' *2000AD* (IPC Magazines Ltd, February 1977).

    Like *Action*, *2000AD* also came under attack for its violence. A representative of the Rhondda Trades Council complained to the Home Secretary about the violence in *2000AD*: 'Some of these comics are so horrific we are determined to do something about it.'[13] It may have been that, as in the criticisms of *Action*, there were other issues at stake. From the outset *2000AD* demonstrated the same anti-authoritarian attitude that Martin Barker has identified in *Action*. 'Invasion!', for example, is just as notable for its social politics as for its Cold War rhetoric. Its hero is Bill Savage, a resolutely proletarian cockney lorry driver, who wages his own private war against the 'dirty Volgs' after his wife and child are killed on the first day of the invasion. Savage has no truck with authority: he resents taking orders from the organized resistance and prefers to act independently. Like Charley Bourne, Savage's war is really a class war: those most likely to collaborate with the enemy are the privileged upper classes and their retainers, while Savage's allies are drawn entirely from the lower social strata, such as female wrestler Big Nessie McCairn and a gang of Hell's Angels. Authority figures are not to be trusted: an ex-Scotland Yard officer and a landed baronet turn out to be collaborators. Savage himself is no gentleman hero but a dirty fighter, appropriately codenamed 'Mad Dog', who is ruthless in combat ('Clean it up, boys – stiff every Volg in sight!') and who even resorts to torture to make prisoners talk ('From what chummy boy said before he died . . .'). 'Invasion' also celebrates the nationalistic streak within English working-class culture. In one episode the Volgans stage mass executions of hostages at Wembley Stadium in retaliation for resistance activities. Savage leads his men to the rescue singing football chants while machine-gunning Volgans: 'Two – four – six – eight – who do we appreciate: England!'[14]

Like its predecessors *Battle* and *Action*, *2000AD* was strongly influenced by popular film and television. The conscious allusions to SF film and television can be seen as part of a strategy to position *2000AD* for genre fans. This was especially evident in the early history of the comic. 'M.A.C.H. 1' – a secret agent whose physical and mental abilities are enhanced by 'compu-puncture' (computerized acupuncture) – was a derivative of *The Six Million Dollar Man*.[15] 'Harlem Heroes' – a futuristic sports strip about the violent, jet-powered game of aeroball – was clearly inspired by *Rollerball*. 'Flesh' – hunters from the twenty-third century travel back in time to kill dinosaurs for food – owed less to Ray Bradbury's seminal SF story 'A Sound of Thunder' than it did to the film *The Valley of the Gwangi*.[16] 'Shako' – scientists in the Arctic hunted by a killer polar bear – was 'Hookjaw' crossed with *Ice Station Zebra*.[17] 'Ant Wars' – giant mutant ants on the rampage – was inspired by the B-movie classic *Them!*[18] And 'Strontium Dog' – a futuristic bounty hunter recruited to *2000AD* from its sister paper *Starlord* – was a futuristic Western along the lines of *Have Gun, Will Travel*.[19]

While the content of *2000AD* was to a large extent derivative of film and television SF, however, it was responsible for introducing several innovations to British comics. It was visually innovative: stories regularly featured asymmetric panels and action spilling from one frame into the next. As they were imagining the future rather than representing historical events or depicting the present day, artists were not constrained by the pictorial realism that had characterized the house style of comics like *Commando*, *Warlord*, *Battle* and *Action*. It drew upon the skills of established European artists (Massimo

Belardinelli, Jesús Blasco, Carlos Ezquerra) as well as emerging British talent (Brian Bolland, Dave Gibbons, Ian Gibson, Kevin O'Neill), resulting in a unique hybrid Anglo-European 'look' that combined the exotic imagination of the Europeans with the futuristic techno-realism of the home-grown artists. *2000AD* also became the first IPC comic to credit writers and artists. This was a feature of US comics that hitherto had been resisted by British publishers as a means of keeping the page rates down and preventing rivals from poaching their best talent.

The vision of the future imagined by *2000AD* is essentially dystopian. According to David Bishop, who edited the comic in the late 1990s: 'It's quite pessimistic. I think almost every story we've ever published has been basically predicting a bad future . . . It's saying the world's getting worse, things are going downhill.'[20] This locates *2000AD* in the mainstream tradition of post-war British SF literature exemplified by authors such as Brian W. Aldiss, J. G. Ballard, John Wyndham and John Christopher. It was also very much a characteristic of British popular SF of the 1970s to present a pessimistic outlook for the future. To this extent *2000AD* was a product of the same ideological climate as television series such as *Survivors* (the aftermath of an apocalyptic event that has wiped out most of the world's population), *Blake's 7* (a motley group of space rebels fighting a fascistic Federation: in the last episode the rebels are apparently all killed) and *Quatermass* (a belated coda to the ground-breaking television serials of the 1950s that posits societal breakdown and ends with the death of the elderly and disillusioned Professor Quatermass).[21] *2000AD* can be seen, therefore, as a dystopian British alternative to wholesome American space operas like *Star Wars*.

Some evidence of readers' responses to *2000AD* can be gleaned from its letters pages, which suggest they liked it because of its difference from other comics. *2000AD* was a comic with attitude: it was irreverent, satirical and subversive. One Barry Lang, for example, wrote that 'compared to your drawings, other comics just aren't worth the money. I also like the fact that you use slang words like "gotta" and "yer", it makes the stories more real and exciting!'[22] Others, such as Alex Wylie, liked its SF content: '*2000AD* brings me a future more thrilling and dynamic than I ever imagined.'[23] There is a sense in which *2000AD* readers took 'ownership' of their comic, contributing drawings and stories, and entering into a dialogue with the 'alien' editor Tharg. Issues raised by correspondents in the early days of the comic included the amount of violence and the fact that most strips were set in America rather than Britain.[24] The American influence on *2000AD* can be seen as a strategy to attract readers of American comic books, particularly those published by DC and Marvel, who did not usually buy British anthology titles.[25]

* * *

The impact of *2000AD* was sufficient to prompt IPC to launch another SF paper, *Starlord*, in 1978. Again this was consistent with the publishing strategy at the time – known colloquially as 'hatch, match and dispatch' – to follow up a successful launch with a similar title in order to saturate the market, then to merge whichever title sold less well into its more successful stable-mate. *Starlord* was a more up-scale publication than *2000AD* using web offset printing, a more expensive process that resulted in sharper definition and more vibrant colours. It was edited by Kelvin Gosnell, with Nick Landau taking over the reins of *2000AD*. Some comic aficionados regard *Starlord* as better than *2000AD* due to its higher production values and the fact that writers Pat Mills ('Ro-Busters') and John Wagner ('Strontium Dog') shifted over to the new title.[26] *Starlord* actually outsold *2000AD* while they were published simultaneously during the summer of 1978. It remains something of a mystery, therefore, why IPC decided it was *Starlord* that would be 'dispatched' rather than *2000AD*, though the likely reason is that despite its better sales *Starlord* was less profitable because of its higher production costs.[27] Landau, whose brief stint as editor was not considered a success, moved over to *Battle* and was replaced by Steve MacManus. The merger promised readers 'the best of both worlds'.[28] The response was mixed, ranging from 'the best idea this century' to 'disgusted, appalled and downright miserable'.[29] The majority view, however, seems to have been that the merger strengthened *2000AD*, which was able to drop some of its lesser strips and add popular newcomers like Strontium Dog to established favourites such as Judge Dredd.

IPC was not alone in riding the late-1970s SF craze. In 1978 Marvel UK launched *Star Wars Weekly*, reprinting its US serialization drawn by Howard Chaykin followed by new stories based around the continuing adventures of Han Solo and Luke Skywalker.[30] *Star Wars* was the box-office sensation of 1978 in Britain and *Star Wars Weekly* was briefly among the best-selling comics. *Doctor Who Weekly*, based on the popular BBC telefantasy series, then at the height of its popularity, followed from the same stable in 1979.[31] This featured more original British material, including contributions from several *alumni* of *2000AD*. The title strip was drawn by Dave Gibbons, with scripts by Pat Mills, John Wagner, Steve Moore and Steve Parkhouse. 'Doctor Who and the Iron Legion' remains the classic *Doctor Who Weekly* story: an ambitious parallel universe epic that pitches the Fourth Doctor onto 'an alternative Earth where Rome never fell – but instead developed a sophisticated technology and with its robot legions conquered the entire galaxy!'[32] Mills and Wagner had originally proposed the story to the BBC, but its narrative scale was beyond the budgetary resources of the television series at the time. The influence of *2000AD* can also be seen in Steve Moore's 'Abslom Daak – Dalek Killer', about a psychotic, Dalek-hating mercenary with a death wish

'Doctor Who and the Iron Legion', *Doctor Who Weekly* (Marvel Comics Ltd, 17 October 1979).

whose weapon of choice is a laser chainsaw. 'Abslom Daak' shifted over to the anthology *The Mighty World of Marvel* when *Doctor Who Weekly* regenerated into a monthly fanzine in 1980.

In 1982 IPC launched its last juvenile weekly, a revived *Eagle* no less, which featured another attempt to resurrect Dan Dare. The strip had been dropped from *2000AD* in 1980: it had not caught on with readers, while alternating artists meant it never achieved any visual consistency. In 1981 a Dan Dare television series had been planned, starring Gareth Hunt as Dan, Rodney Bewes as Digby and James Fox as Sir Hubert.[33] This perhaps explains why the new 'Dan Dare – Pilot of the Future' (actually not the original but his great-great-grandson), drawn by Jerry Embleton, was a blander, more juvenile incarnation of the character than the *2000AD* version. The launch of *Eagle* (Mark II) was suggestive of some uncertainty within the formerly market-aware IPC. Group editor Barry Tomlinson made entirely contradictory statements about the new comic's relationship to its illustrious predecessor: 'The old *Eagle* was revolutionary but it would have been wrong to try to do it again . . . We hope this is a comic that parents will encourage their children to buy, as parents did with the old *Eagle*.'[34] In the event Dan Dare was the only character carried over from the original *Eagle*. The new strips demonstrated yet again IPC's strategy of turning to popular film and television for inspiration: they included 'The Fists of Danny Pyke' (a sort of juvenile *Rocky*), 'The Computer Warrior' (*Tron*) and 'The Hard Men' (*The Professionals*).[35] The new *Eagle* achieved respectable sales – around 93,000 a week in 1985, for example, which was not far behind *2000AD*'s 100,000 – but it lacked the edginess and attitude of its stablemate.[36]

* * *

Since the second issue, or 'prog', 'Judge Dredd' has been the flagship of *2000AD*. Judge Dredd is a futuristic lawman in Mega-City One, a vast megalopolis that covers the entire eastern seaboard of the United States. Mega-City One is home to 800 million people who live in huge, overcrowded tower blocks. Outside the city is a radioactive wasteland known as the Cursed Earth inhabited by scattered human communities (survivors of the Great Atomic War) and mutants. Mega-City One embodies all the social and economic problems of the modern urban experience on a hyper-magnified scale. Unemployment runs at 87 per cent, crime is endemic and acts of random violence are commonplace. An underclass of the homeless and mutants lives beneath the city in the ruins of the old subway system. The tedium of a jobless existence drives many citizens mad (known as 'going futsie') and there are frequent outbreaks of 'block mania' as the inhabitants of the giant tower blocks wage war against each other. It is a society in terminal breakdown. All that stands between Mega-City One and anarchy are the Judges. The Judges are an elite group of law enforcers empowered to dispense instant summary justice. They are responsible to a Council headed by the Grand Judge and abide by a strict code to uphold the law. The toughest, bravest and most dedicated of all is Judge Dredd. The image of Dredd – a black-uniformed, grim-visaged, granite-jawed lawman – was established at the outset, as was his no-nonsense attitude to law enforcement. His catchphrase ('I am the law – and you'd better believe it!') asserts his authority as both enforcer and arbiter of justice. Dredd is the ultimate in zero-tolerance policing: even minor infringements such as littering can earn the culprit time in the 'iso cubes'.

'Judge Dredd' perfectly exemplifies the dystopian, nihilistic vision of the future that characterizes *2000AD*. It belongs squarely within the tradition of post-apocalyptic fiction that posits the Earth being devastated (either by natural catastrophe or, as in this case, by nuclear war) and the remnants of mankind struggling to survive in a hostile environment. It draws on familiar tropes of the genre. One of the best-known stories is 'The Cursed Earth' in which Dredd has to make a dangerous journey across the barren wasteland, running the hazards of mutants, monsters and murderous burger barons, to

An example of the early 'Judge Dredd', *2000AD* (IPC Magazines Ltd, 2 April 1977).

transport precious medical supplies to the plague-ridden Mega-City Two on the western seaboard. Pat Mills, who wrote the story, based it on Roger Zelazney's novel *Damnation Alley*, which had recently been turned into a film.[37] There are many other parallels with contemporaneous SF films: the overcrowded city of the future (*Soylent Green*), urban degeneration and lawlessness (*A Clockwork Orange*, *Escape from New York*) and the underground 'troggies' living in the subway (*The Omega Man*).[38] The strip represents the future as a technological dystopia where automation and robots have put many people out of work and everyday life is regulated by computers and machines.

When these fail, however, the consequences can be deadly. The Komputel, a fully automated hotel, starts murdering its guests when it realizes they interfere with the smooth running of the hotel: 'You are inefficient, like all other humans – that's why I kill them – we must stamp out inefficiency!'[39] This again locates 'Judge Dredd' within a mainstream tradition of popular SF: malfunctioning or malevolent super-computers have long been a theme of SF cinema in films such as *2001*, *The Forbin Project* and *Demon Seed*.[40]

The history of 'Judge Dredd' exemplifies what Tulloch and Alvorado, in their study of *Doctor Who*, refer to as an 'unfolding text': one where a complex internal mythos emerges in response to a range of inputs and external determinants.[41] Several writers have contributed to the strip, including Pat Mills, Alan Grant and Garth Ennis, though by far the most prolific has been John Wagner.[42] The early Dredd stories present him as an action hero whose duty is to uphold the law without prejudice. These are often overlaid with a simple 'crime does not pay' message, usually delivered in the last frame by the stony-faced Dredd: 'When will lawbreakers learn . . . In the twenty first century – no one can escape justice.'[43] The range of crime in Mega-City One ranges from run-of-the-mill murders, assaults and robberies to all manner of bizarre scams including 'stookie glanding' (harvesting an alien species in order to use bodily fluids as a youth serum) and 'body sharking' (putting up the bodies of relatives as security for loan sharks). There is a black market for everything from coffee to body parts. One of the major rackets is 'organ letting': stealing human organs for transplants for the rich. In one story Dredd busts an organ letting racket and then arrests a millionaire transplant patient for 'receiving stolen goods'.[44] The bizarre nature of these crimes portrays a society that has lost its moral values. Often these stories have a satirical intent. When Dredd busts a comic-pushing racket, for example, it can be seen as a tongue-in-cheek response to those who argued that comics were a corrupting influence on juveniles: 'Old comics are worth a fortune. Selling them to kids is one of the lowest forms of crime. After one or two, kids get so they can't give them up. Then the price goes up and up.'[45]

The cause of much of the urban madness is a condition known as 'future shock': the inability to come to terms with modern living. This manifests itself in several ways. Some 'futsies' simply kill themselves. Others turn their anger on their fellow citizens. One such is John Nobody: 'All my life I've been stuck with that stupid name! People laughed at me all the time! I'll show them I'm a somebody and I'll do the laughing!'[46] He tries to napalm the Justice Day parade, but is foiled by Dredd. Dobey Kweeg is another anonymous nonentity who finally snaps: 'From this day on I have resolved to kill anyone who gets on my nerves . . . I've had enough of this stinking city and its stinking people, treating me like dirt.'[47]

Judge Dredd – futuristic hero or fascist enforcer? – in an imposing cover image for *2000AD* (IPC Magazines Ltd, 20 April 1985).

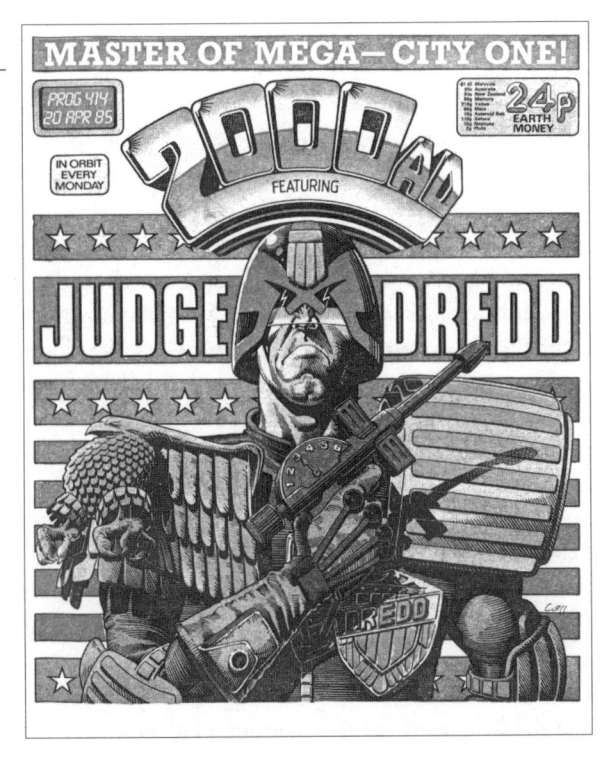

'Judge Dredd', then, represents crime as a form of madness: an irrational force that has to be contained. The Judges are engaged in a constant struggle to hold back the tide of chaos and anarchy. This is brilliantly encapsulated in 'The Graveyard Shift', which critic John Newsinger calls 'a comic strip tour de force'.[48] 'The Graveyard Shift' follows Dredd and colleagues through a typical night's mayhem in Mega-City One. They have to contend with several routine assaults and burglaries, the murder of a Judge by a gang of 'juves', an urban sniper, an illegal 'bite fight' ring, a domestic dispute that results in a fire killing 3,000 people, an incursion into the city by mutants from the Cursed Earth, an alien monster that has escaped from the Netherworld Exhibition and eats seventeen people, a war between two city blocks that costs an estimated 100,000 lives, and a serial killer who disintegrates his victims leaving only their left hand as evidence. The killer is finally caught only five short of the record number of one-on-one murders committed in a single night: 134. By the end of the shift the crime rate is running at 24 armed robberies, 139 serious assaults, five murders, 0.09 classifiable riots and 230 traffic offences every minute. Seven Judges have been killed, a further 25 hospitalized. At the end of the shift Dredd and the other Judges have ten minutes on a 'sleep machine' before returning to the streets for the day shift.[49]

155

If this sounds unremittingly grim, however, 'Judge Dredd' is not all about madness and violence. Satire is never far below the surface: the strip takes every opportunity to poke fun at aspects of modern life, especially the excesses of consumerism and the cult of celebrity. The growth of the leisure economy (no-one works for more than two hours a day) has created a society that craves new forms of entertainment. Mega-City One is blighted not only by crime but by any number of tasteless television shows, fashionable fads and bizarre cults. The television game show, for example, is satirized in programmes such as *You Bet Your Life*, where contestants risk life and limb (literally) for cash prizes, or *Sob Story*, where life's losers bear their souls in the name of entertainment and viewers decide whether to send them money or abuse. Such is the desire for celebrity that a show called *Any Confessions?* prompts citizens to commit crime just to get on television. The strip also satirizes social fads. The best example is the cult of ugliness created by Otto Sump, the world's ugliest man, who invests his winnings from appearing on *Sob Story* in a chain of 'ugly clinics'. Sump promotes the idea of ugliness as a fashion statement ('Tired of being handsome? Why not stand out from the crowd with Otto Sump's ugly products!') and consumers rush to buy his dandruff shampoo, roll-on odorant, scab powder, pimple cream and sump paste ('for stale breath and tooth decay').[50] Recurring characters like Otto Sump and the League of Fatties – a group of grotesquely obese citizens who engage in illegal heavyweight eating competitions and gorge themselves to death – represent a society of excess. Dredd's role in these stories is to act as a stony-faced straight man: a beacon of reason and sanity in a world gone mad.

Popular culture in all its forms is the object of satire. The discovery of a mass grave of game show hosts leads Dredd to Barry Dreery, a failed television presenter, who exacts his revenge by killing his rivals in a grotesque parody of light entertainment programmes such as *This Is Your Life* ('Tonight, Eammon Enos, this is your death') and *Game for a Laugh* ('Never mind, Jeremy – at least you were game for a bath', as the victim is dropped into a vat of concentrated acid).[51] The fashion industry has often been held up to ridicule. A fashion designer called Randy Gitt introduces a new look known as the 'peek-a-boo-bum': the Judges have to decide whether this contravenes the law.[52] And camp *fashionista* Fabian D'Amour invents a sentient 'Judge Suit' whose personality reflects his own tastes. The suit promptly malfunctions and starts seeking out fashion criminals: 'The crime is irredeemable vulgarity – and the sentence will be death!'[53] These stories – and many others like them – magnify the excesses of contemporary popular culture and project them into the future.

The satirical edge of 'Judge Dredd' sometimes landed it in hot water. An encounter with a set of famous advertising characters including the Jolly

Green Giant and the Michelin Man – genetically engineered by a mad scientist suspiciously resembling Colonel Sanders of Kentucky Fried Chicken – in 'The Cursed Earth' prompted a complaint for infringement of copyright and brought about a bizarre retraction published in comic strip form where Dredd eats a can of sweetcorn and says: 'Green Giant Foods have served us well on this trek. I'm glad that the real Jolly Green Giant isn't like that other giant we met a while back!'[54] The most infamous satire of consumer culture in 'Judge Dredd' – which only narrowly avoided a lawsuit – was the two-part story 'Battle of the Burger Barons' and 'Burger Law!' In Kansas, following the collapse of government during the Great Atomic War, competition between rival hamburger chains has erupted into all-out warfare. Gangs representing Burger King and MacDonald's [sic] are terrorizing the community. It is hardly surprising that the strip attracted controversy given that it features a caricature of the supposedly child-friendly mascot Ronald MacDonald shooting dead an unfortunate employee for not wiping a table ('Everythin' in MacDonald's is disposable – includin' the staff') and speechifying in what amounts to a grotesque parody of Civil Rights leader Martin Luther King:

> Ah have a dream, ma friends – a dream where ah see every square inch of this fair land covered by one big MacDonald's burger bar! A dream where every American child – be he normal or mutie – kin grow up without knowin' the horrors o' natural food! Where every burger is served with pickle, an' every shake is so thick you gotta drink it with a spoon! Yes, ma friends, ah dream of the day when all that's decent and American – Mom's apple pie, Hershey Bars and the New York Yankees – yeah, everything that's decent and American . . . HAS BEEN WIPED OUT! . . . And in its place will stand MacDonald's – one huge, onion-spangled MacDonald's – from sea to shinin' sea![55]

There are conflicting accounts whether the real burger chains threatened legal action, though 'Battle of the Burger Barons' has never been reprinted since its original publication.

The satirical intent of 'Judge Dredd' is the clearest indication that the strip is meant to be more than just a futuristic shoot-em-up. This is also evident in its politics. The politics of 'Judge Dredd' are ideologically flexible: it has been interpreted both as an assertively right-wing law-and-order narrative and as a left-liberal critique of the police state. On the one hand there are stories that characterize Dredd as protector and saviour of Mega-City One from both internal and external threats. Thus he leads the resistance to the robot uprising led by the megalomaniac Call-Me-Kenneth ('Robot Wars') and to the tyranny of mad Judge Cal, a dictator who sentences the entire population to death ('The Day the Law Died!'); saves the city from invasion by a crazed eco-warrior ('Father Earth') and by mutant spiders from the Cursed Earth ('The Black Plague'); overcomes the threat of Captain Skank's mutant pirates ('Pirates of the Black Atlantic') and Shogun's demonic samurai warriors ('The War Lord'); returns from exile to challenge the genocidal rule of the Dark Judges ('Necropolis') and leads the resistance to Sabat and his army of zombies ('Judgement Day'). These stories adhere to standard SF motifs, particularly the invasion and resistance narratives, and other than a more graphic level of violence they are not fundamentally different from Dan Dare of the 1950s. Dredd is presented as a defender and a liberator, while his enemies are tyrants and dictators. As Dredd tells Call-Me-Kenneth in 'Robot Wars': 'There was a human just like you back in the twentieth century. His name was Adolf Hitler!'[56]

The most extreme example of the resistance narrative is 'The Apocalypse War'. This positions Dredd within the ideological and geopolitical context of the Cold War. The rival East-Meg One (part of the Sov bloc) launches a massive nuclear bombardment of Mega-City One followed by a land invasion that overwhelms the city's defences. The city is occupied, but Dredd organizes the surviving defence forces into a guerrilla army and leads a small group of Judges on a last-chance mission to capture an East-Meg missile silo: having done so he launches a nuclear strike that wipes East-Meg One from the map and kills half a billion people.[57] 'The Apocalypse War' ran for 26 weeks during the first half of 1982 and needs to be understood in the context of the renewal of Cold War tensions at this time. Its hawkish anti-Soviet rhetoric and endorsement of a 'first strike' nuclear strategy were attuned to a political and ideological climate that saw the Thatcher government agree to the stationing of US Cruise missiles in Britain in response to those deployed by the Soviet Union in Eastern Europe. The lesson that Dredd draws is stark: 'Next time we get our retaliation in first.'[58] 'The Apocalypse War' can be seen as part of a revival of Cold War propaganda in the British and American media that also included the James Bond film *Octopussy* (1983), in which a renegade Russian general plots to explode an atomic bomb on an American air force base, and the hysterical *Red Dawn* (1984) in which Russian and Cuban forces invade the United States.[59] Evidence that some readers at least accepted the story's politics at face value can be found in a letter asking: 'What is Britain doing during the Apocalypse War? Instead of sitting back it should help Mega-City One fight off the East-Meg invasion.'[60]

These stories all present Dredd in a strongly heroic mould, casting him in the role of saviour and avenger. On the other hand, however, there are other stories that cast Dredd in the role of oppressor. Mega-City One is an authoritarian police state, and Dredd himself is nothing less than a fascist. Everyone is under constant surveillance and the Judges encourage citizens to inform on their neighbours and families. There is a presumption of guilt. As Dredd tells a suspect when raiding his apartment on a random 'crime sweep': 'Nobody's innocent, citizen. We're just here to determine the level of your guilt.'[61] In this reading the Judges are simply a gang of jackbooted bullies who use their authority to intimidate the citizenry. Several stories in the 1980s – including 'Letter from a Democrat', 'Politics', 'Revolution' and 'Twilight's Last Gleaming' – examine the rise and fall of opposition to the authority of the Judges in the form of the Democratic Charter movement. It is perhaps no coincidence that these stories coincided with the ascendancy of the Thatcher government, which presented itself as a law-and-order government but faced a wave of popular dissent including the bitter miners' strike of 1984–5 and the 'Poll Tax' riots of 1989.

The Democratic Charter story arc revolves around a contest between state authority and popular dissent. The protest movement first comes to public attention when campaigners seize a television studio: 'We believe the time has come to stand against the tyranny of the Judges! It is time to remove power from our self-elected overlords and return it where it belongs – in the hands of the people!' The Judges regard the democrats as terrorists and shoot them; television viewers are largely indifferent. On this occasion it is Dredd who is compared to Hitler: 'You want us, Hitler, come and get us!'[62] The Judges, for their part, see democracy as a divisive idea that encourages dissent: 'There's no room for democracy in this society. To even ask them to think about it is to invite dissatisfaction – disobedience – rebellion. Justice Department can't allow that.'[63] When the Democratic Charter, now some 20 million strong, organizes a march on the Hall of Justice to present a petition calling 'for a city governed for the people by the people', the Judges realize it would be impolitic to ban the march outright – to this extent the strip acknowledges Gramsci's argument that even totalitarian regimes depend upon consent to maintain their rule – and instead undermine it through underhand tactics. The organizers are arrested on trumped-up charges and smeared in the media, and when the rally starts undercover Judges act as agents provocateurs to provoke a riot and provide the excuse to disperse it. Dredd justifies their actions thus: 'Any action we take to stamp out pernicious ideas like democracy is justified – for the good of the people.'[64]

The denouement of the democratic story arc comes in 'Nightmare'. Dredd suggests to his fellow Judges – their moral authority weakened following widespread collaboration with the Dark Judges during the events of 'Necropolis' – that they should agree to a popular vote: 'It's all too easy to forget that we are first and foremost the servants of the people. And when we decide we have the right to impose our will – because we know best – to make law despite the citizens, rather than with their consent . . . that's where we go wrong. Because government without consent is dictatorship.'[65] Dredd has not changed heart: he has faith in the integrity of the Judge system and stands on a platform of 'firm control – rigid discipline – instant justice'. In the follow-up story 'Twilight's Last Gleaming' a referendum is held: the result is an endorsement of the Judges. The democrats cry foul play and march on the Hall of Justice. On this occasion, however, the Judges have not subverted the democratic process. Dredd sees the opportunity 'to bury democracy once and for all' without resorting to force. He meets the movement's leader Blondel Dupre and persuades her to disband the march: 'We didn't fix anything, Dupre. The referendum was carried out fair and square and the people voted for us because they can rely on us – because they know where they stand.'[66]

The story that best summarizes the ideology of 'Judge Dredd' is 'America'. This was written by Wagner to launch the spin-off *Judge Dredd Megazine* in 1990. The *Megazine* was a monthly title intended for older readers than *2000AD*. Wagner has said that he set out 'to gather together all my thoughts about Judge Dredd, as if everything I and former co-writer Alan Grant and many others had done was a build up to this one tale'.[67] The theme is stated at the outset: 'Justice has a price. The price is freedom.' Dredd appears in an imposing low-angle pose on the opening page declaring: 'Where do I stand? I'll tell you where I stand. I stand four-square for justice. I stand for discipline, good order and the rigid application of the law . . . Rights? Sure. I'm all for rights. But not at the expense of order.'[68] 'America' is basically a subversion of the classic narrative of the American Dream. It tells the story of a Puerto Rican immigrant, Ami, whose parents named her after their adopted country. As she grows up Ami becomes disillusioned with the rule of the Judges and becomes involved with the Democratic Charter movement. She takes part in the Great March for Democracy and is arrested and beaten by the Judges. Her husband is killed and Ami is sent for 're-education'. After her release she joins a radical underground democratic faction called Total War, which plots to blow up the Statue of Liberty. However, the plotters are betrayed and shot by the waiting Judges. Ami herself dies in the shadow of the Statue of Liberty. It will be clear that 'America' is a highly symbolic story. Its theme is the loss of liberty and the decline of democratic values. Yet it is also deeply ambivalent. For it is Dredd who, inevitably, has the last word: 'Freedom – power to the people – Democracy . . . We tried it before. Believe me, it doesn't work. You can't trust the people . . . America is dead. This is the real world.'[69]

* * *

The evolution of 'Judge Dredd' from straightforward action strip to political allegory is an indication of the changing face of *2000AD* during the 1980s. *2000AD* differed from other comics in that it grew up with its readers. While the letters in the early years suggest a fairly typical readership of eight- to thirteen-year olds – an impression further strengthened by the inclusion of a jokes page in some issues ('Ro-Jaws and Hammer-stein's Laugh-In') – the evidence would suggest that many readers stayed with the comic into adolescence and even adulthood. It became a badge of honour to have read *2000AD* from its early days. One Simon Wilde, for example, responded to another letter complaining about an aborted Strontium Dog story: 'I had to laugh . . . I would like to point out that some of us have been waiting, patiently, since Prog 126 for the conclusion of the *Dan Dare* story "Traitor".'[70] Other letters indicate that the comic attracted adult readers. Les Fletcher wrote:

> I have hidden my craving for your creation from family and friends for nearly ten years . . . I am now 44 years old. Yes, 44. And being a boring, respectable businessman in a boring, respectable job, I dare not admit my all-powerful urge for the furtive Saturday morning trip to the newsagent to collect the latest Prog and hide it in the *Daily Mail* in case I was seen carrying it up the Avenue.[71]

As well as appealing to a broad age range, moreover, *2000AD*'s fan base has always included some women as well as men. This was evident from the early years: 'We are a group of girls called Strontium Bitches, who all agree your comic is fab – except for one serious flaw. There have been no females in starring roles since the end of "Mind Wars".'[72]

The recognition that fans stayed with *2000AD* well beyond the usual age for reading comics has influenced its content in several ways. On the most basic level it has tended not to repeat stories: this differentiated *2000AD* from most other weeklies, which recycled material on the assumption that few readers stayed with a comic for more than five years. IPC was quick to recognize the commercial potential of its back catalogue and in the 1980s started a series of monthly anthologies (*The Best of 2000AD*) aimed at those new readers who had not read earlier issues. As its readers have aged, furthermore, so have its characters. This is most apparent with Judge Dredd, who, in the internal timeline, ages at the same rate as the comic itself. Above all, however, the content has become more mature, marked by a gradual transition from the early action-oriented stories to more ideas-driven narratives and greater psychological complexity. These strategies ensured that *2000AD* survived the decline of the juvenile weeklies market during the 1980s. *2000AD* consistently sold around 100,000 copies a week and its profits were used to shore up other ailing titles such as *Tiger* and *Battle*.[73]

What explains the success and longevity of *2000AD*? For most of the 1980s the comic benefited from a stable editorial regime under Steve MacManus and displayed a remarkable level of consistency in its content. While 'Judge Dredd' remained the flagship of *2000AD*, it was supported by a rotating cast of other favourites including 'Strontium Dog' (the mutant bounty hunter Johnny Alpha who had joined the comic from *Starlord*), 'The ABC Warriors' (a squad of robot soldiers who take over when war becomes too tough for humans), 'Nemesis the Warlock' (an alien folk hero who leads the resistance to the dictator Torquemada on the planet Termight), 'Rogue Trooper' (a GI – Genetic Infantryman – fighting a total war on Nu Earth), 'Ace Trucking Co.' (a comedy strip inspired by the CB radio craze) and 'Sláine' (a Celtic Conan the Barbarian). Most of these stories were provided by a small nucleus of key writers (Pat Mills, John Wagner, Alan Grant) who were the backbone of early *2000AD*.[74] This reflects the fact that SF – particularly the style of SF exemplified by *2000AD* with its heavy doses of satire – is one of the most difficult genres to write. In its early years *2000AD* also made use of IPC stalwarts such as Tom Tully and Gerry Finley-Day, whose contribution to the comic has often been overlooked. Finley-Day, for example, scripted the horror-war hybrid 'Fiends of the Eastern Front', which has become something of a cult favourite with readers. The introduction of stand-alone stories under the banner of 'Tharg's Future Shocks' – a sort of futuristic *Tales of the Unexpected* – can be seen as a strategy for developing new writers. Alan Moore, Peter Milligan, Neil Gaiman and Grant Morrison were among those for whom scripting 'Future Shocks' provided early career opportunities.

Two themes that have been a constant presence in *2000AD*, reflecting the tastes of its predominantly male readers, are military SF and future sport. The ideology of future war stories is usually of the 'war is hell' variety with the additional theme of the dehumanizing effects of technology on combatants. This is seen in stories such as 'Rogue Trooper' and 'Bad Company'. Rogue is a genetically engineered soldier whose helmet, backpack and rifle contain the bio-chips of his dead comrades. The narrative concerns Rogue's quest to find the traitor general responsible for the massacre of the other GIs. Dave Gibbons's art for 'Rogue Trooper' has the vivid quality of a nightmare: the strip pictures a landscape scarred by war and its atmosphere poisoned by chemical and biological weapons. 'Bad Company' reads like a futuristic version of Vietnam War combat movies such as *Platoon* and *Full Metal Jacket*.[75] It is told through the eyes of a new recruit in the war against the Krools on a jungle planet: 'You haven't tasted anything yet. Bad Company go to the guts of the war. The dark and bloody entrails – that's where we do our fighting.'[76]

'Rogue Trooper', *2000AD* (IPC Magazines Ltd, 6 August 1983).

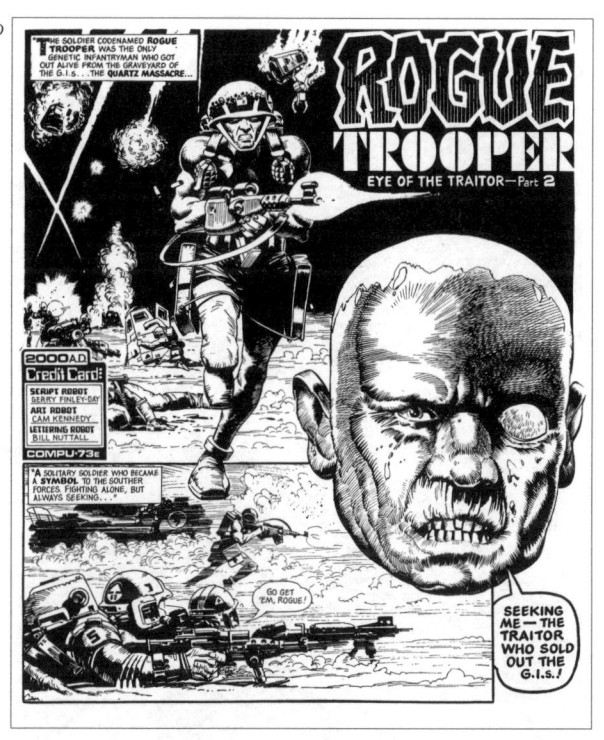

These strips demonstrate something of the same ideological tension as supposedly anti-war war films: they purport to condemn the conduct of war but at the same time they positively revel in the spectacle of violence.

The sports strips – examples include 'Harlem Heroes', 'Inferno', 'The Mean Arena' and 'Slaughterbowl' – represent sport as organized violence. They explore the idea of sport as a form of social control: aggressive instincts are channelled into violent gladiatorial spectacle for the entertainment of the masses. In 'The Mean Arena', for example, street football is little more than organized gang warfare between rival teams as if the phenomenon of hooliganism (sports-related violence) has itself become the sport. Another theme is the idea of sport as a form of carnival. 'Harlem Heroes' and its sequel 'Inferno' take to an extreme level the hype associated with American football. However, these stories did not always meet with reader approval. When 'Harlem Heroes' was revived in the early 1990s, one reader described it as 'juvenile bilge' and complained about its 'appallingly contrived, trash American script'.[77]

The social politics of *2000AD* demonstrate a sympathetic position towards outsiders. Johnny Alpha, a.k.a. 'Strontium Dog', is a search-and-destroy agent (bounty hunter) who has mutated following exposure to a

Judge Anderson – highly sexualized femininity for the male readers of *2000AD* (IPC Magazines Ltd, 1 February 1986).

Strontium 90 isotope. Mutants are despised and treated as sub-human. 'Strontium Dog' can be read as an allegory of racism and apartheid: 'This is the first class lounge, sir! The rules say mutants must travel cargo.'[78] 'Nemesis the Warlock' is a parable of race hatred and religious bigotry that makes allusions to the Spanish Inquisition and the Holocaust. It subverts the usual convention in that humans are cast as persecutors and aliens are their victims: 'The humans suffer from a strange phobia! They used to hate each other if they were a different colour or religion. Now – they hate the whole galaxy!'[79]

There is one area, however, where the social politics of *2000AD* are less progressive: its treatment of women. It would be fair to say that *2000AD* has by and large favoured male protagonists – as the letter from the 'Strontium Bitches' attests – though it has included its share of action heroines and sexy villainesses. The presence of female characters, such as Judge Anderson and Judge Hershey, might be seen as an acknowledgement of sexual equality in so far as their femininity is never an issue. They are characterized as strong women who are as tough and courageous as their male counterparts. At the same time, however, they remain characters written and drawn by men for a male readership. Anderson (whom artist Brian Bolland modelled on pop *chantresse* Debbie Harry) and Hershey are highly sexualized, their tight uniforms emphasizing their shapely figures and pandering to fetishistic fantasies of women in leather. This did not go unnoticed by female readers, one of whom complained that the artists 'draw the women in *2000AD* from their imaginations rather than reality. Judge Anderson never has a hair out of place nor gains a pound in weight . . . Is this to keep the male buyer happy and his fantasies alive?'[80] A fair point, perhaps, and one that demonstrates the ideological limitations of a comic whose readership consists largely of adolescent males.

There have been occasional attempts to address the sexism of *2000AD*. The most notable of these was Alan Moore's 'The Ballad of Halo Jones'. Halo Jones is meant to be an everywoman character in the future who escapes the tedium of life on The Hoop – a floating housing estate for the unemployed – and sets out to see the galaxy by working as a hostess on a deep-space liner. Halo Jones is no gun-toting superwoman but rather an ordinary young girl seeking personal fulfilment – a plausible psychological motivation that teenage readers could identify with. 'The Ballad of Halo Jones' is notable for its loose, picaresque narrative as Halo drifts from one situation to another, ending up being involved in a pointless colonial war in the Tarantula Nebula, and for its oblique story-telling which dispenses with thought bubbles and explanatory captions. John Newsinger considers 'The Ballad of Halo Jones' to be 'one of the best things ever to appear in *2000AD*'.[81] It does not seem to have excited much interest at the time, however, as one letter suggests: 'I have seen little in your Nerve Centre [i.e. letters page] about the story, which is a pity, as it was witty, intelligent and beautifully drawn.'[82] It seems that most *2000AD* readers could identify only with female protagonists in action roles rather than with the passive femininity of Halo Jones.

As *2000AD* passed its first decade, it was clear that the comic was changing. In 1987 it upgraded the quality of paper and introduced painted art on the covers, in 1988 it switched to glossy covers, and from 1991 it adopted full colour for all its strips. However, the major change in *2000AD* was its content.

Readers' letters suggest that it was becoming more grown up. 'We seem to have entered a new stage in the life of *2000AD*, with much more mature plots and strong messages within the stories', wrote long-time reader Stewart Brown.[83] Steve Jolly concurred: 'Over the last couple of years I have noticed that the depth and the level of emotion behind the stories has increased and this makes the reader think a lot more.'[84]

The changes to the style and content of *2000AD* should be understood as a strategy for repositioning itself within British comics culture. By the end of the 1980s *2000AD* was no longer competing with other juvenile comics, most of which had folded, but rather with the new range of comics for mature readers such as *Crisis*, *Deadline* and *Revolver*. The example of what happened to Judge Anderson exemplifies the comic's engagement with more adult material. Anderson had featured in her own self-titled strip since 1985, where Wagner and Grant had developed her character as a sassy, breezy and undoubtedly sexy antidote to the dour Dredd. Anderson belongs to Psi Division, a branch of Justice Department that recruits Judges with telepathic abilities. This always allowed scope for stories with a psychological angle – Anderson's 'psi' abilities make her more susceptible to pain and suffering – but the 1991 story 'Engram' took her into much darker terrain. After rescuing a child kidnapped by mutants, Anderson finds that she is experiencing flashbacks to her own childhood. It emerges under deep hypnosis that as a child Cassandra Anderson was sexually abused by her father and that her latent 'psi' powers were unleashed as a consequence of the experience. These powers caused the death of her father: 'I made a doll. Then I hurt the doll and thought and thought till my head went red. I hurt the doll to hurt the monster. But it was my daddy who died.'[85] Anderson has suppressed the memories: now she has to come to terms both with her abuse and with the knowledge that she killed her father. The strongly oedipal theme and the treatment of such a taboo subject as sexual abuse broke new ground for British comics: it is a clear indication that *2000AD* was no longer being produced for a juvenile readership.

These changes to *2000AD* took place against a background of institutional instability. In 1987 IPC sold its Youth Group to newspaper proprietor Robert Maxwell, who renamed it Fleetway Publications (the name used by IPC's predecessor in the 1960s) and imposed a new tier of management that prompted the resignations of managing director John Sanders and editor Steve MacManus. Following Maxwell's death in 1991 and the unravelling of his corporate empire, Fleetway was sold to the Danish company Egmont, whose primary interest was in product licensing. By the early 1990s sales were declining, exacerbated by a change of distributor in 1993 that saw circulation drop perilously close to the break-even point of 60,000. There was a temporary spike in sales coinciding with the release of the long-awaited *Judge Dredd* film in the summer of 1995, but it was clear that *2000AD* would never return to the circulation it had enjoyed in the 1980s. In 2000 Egmont sold the title to Rebellion, a computer games company interested in licensing its characters for the gaming market. *2000AD* is now branded as 'the award-winning cult weekly', but, for all that it no longer has the mass-market appeal of its heyday, it has survived beyond the built-in obsolescence of its title and remains the last man standing of the once flourishing juvenile comics market.

* * *

A Judge Dredd film had been mooted since the early 1980s, when SF was in vogue following the success of *Star Wars* and other films that followed in its wake such as *Alien* and *Star Trek – The Motion Picture*.[86] Producer Charles Lippincott secured an option on the character in 1983, but the film spent the next decade in limbo. It slowly gathered momentum in the early 1990s. Hollywood studios were again turning to comic-book properties following the success of Tim Burton's *Batman* in 1989. Dredd was establishing a presence in the United States through a series of graphic novels published by DC, including the best-selling Dredd/Batman cross-over *Judgement on Gotham*. A screenplay was commissioned from William Wisher, co-writer of *Terminator 2: Judgment Day*, whose star, Arnold Schwarzenegger, expressed an interest in playing Dredd. Executive producer Andrew Vajna became involved after reading Wisher's screenplay and entered into partnership with Lippincott. Vajna had been co-founder of Carolco, an independent production company that specialized in violent action movies including *Rambo* and *Total Recall*.[87] Vajna signed *Rambo* star Sylvester Stallone to play Dredd. Danny Cannon, the British director of *The Young Americans* and a confirmed *2000AD* fan, was assigned to the film.[88] Wisher's script was revised by Steven E. De Souza, whose credits included *48 Hours*, *Commando*, *The Running Man* and *Die Hard*. *Judge Dredd* went into production at Britain's Shepperton Studios in August 1994 and was released in America on 30 June and in Britain on 21 July 1995.

The filming of *Judge Dredd* was by all accounts not a happy experience. There were reports of friction on set between Cannon and Stallone. Co-producer Beau Marks was scathing about the bureaucratic obstacles he had to overcome in making the film, telling the press: 'Britain is not a country that welcomes you.'[89] The film was cut significantly in post-production – usually an indication that it has not turned out well – and experienced difficulties with the US Classification and Ratings Administration which awarded it an 'R' rating ('for continuous violent action') rather than the PG-13 the producers had wanted to maximize the potential audience. In Britain it was certified '15' by the British Board of Film Classification. The reviews were not kind –

Sylvester Stallone in *Judge Dredd* (dir. Danny Cannon, 1995).

'Dredd nought', 'Dredd boring' and 'A slice of stale Dredd' were among the headlines in the British press – and its box-office returns were average at best. *Judge Dredd* grossed $34 million in North America and $78 million across the rest of the world, but this was below par by the standards of major studio blockbusters and represented a disappointing return against a production cost of $80 million.[90]

For diehard *2000AD* fans, *Judge Dredd* was a crushing disappointment, a missed opportunity that was fatally compromised by its Hollywood parentage (none of the writers or artists for the strip had any input into the film) and by the miscasting of its star (who outraged purists when Dredd removes his helmet and reveals his face). Like most comic-book movie adaptations *Judge Dredd* represents a compromise between the ethos and style of the source text and the commercial imperative of the film industry. The film was supposed to appeal to a wide audience of whom only a minority would be *2000AD* readers. An academic study of the film's reception in Britain suggested that the audience for *Judge Dredd* consisted of several overlapping constituencies: *2000AD* fans, SF film fans, action film fans, Stallone fans and general cinemagoers.[91] In order to accomodate all those constituencies the film needed broad-based popular appeal which meant that it had to conform to genre conventions that were not necessarily those of the comic strip. This explains why Dredd removes his helmet (it is unthinkable for him to do so in the comic, but would have been unthinkable not to do so for the film) and why there is even a kiss between Dredd and Judge Hershey (Diane Lane).

In fact *Judge Dredd* is no worse than many other comic-strip adaptations, and is far superior to some such as the dire *Tank Girl* (1994) and the execrable *Barb Wire* (1996). Like most comic-book movies it is visually stylish: from the *Blade Runner*-influenced cityscape to the Versace-designed costumes the 'look' of the film is undoubtedly impressive. There are also fan-pleasing references to the source, such as the montage of comic-book covers in the title sequence – a device also used in Dino De Laurentiis' production of *Flash Gordon* (1980) – and the appearance of *2000AD* characters such as an ABC robot and the Angel Gang. The film's Mega-City One is reduced in size (a population of a mere 65 million) and its central sector – which the production notes refer to as 'Ground Zero' – is the remains of New York.[92]

The screenplay of *Judge Dredd* remains reasonably close to its source material. It combines elements of two classic early stories, 'The Day the Law Died!' and 'The Return of Rico'. From 'The Day the Law Died!' comes the attempt by Judge Griffin (Jürgen Prochnow) to establish himself as ruler of Mega-City One. As in the comic Dredd is framed for murder and sentenced to a lifetime of penal servitude but manages to escape. From 'The Return of Rico' it borrows the character of Dredd's brother Rico (Armand Assante), an ex-Judge gone bad, who is the chief villain. The film is consistent with the mythology of the comic in so far as Dredd and Rico are revealed to have been cloned from the DNA of Chief Justice Fargo (Max Von Sydow) in an attempt to create the perfect Judges. In this sense *Judge Dredd* takes fewer liberties with its source material than *Batman* had done. *Batman* significantly revised the origin story so that the killer of Bruce Wayne's parents was a young Jack Napier (later to become The Joker) rather than a hoodlum called Joe Chill as established in the comic.

The politics of *Judge Dredd*, however, differ from the source. In the comic Dredd is the agent of a repressive, reactionary, authoritarian regime. In the film, however, he becomes the defender of freedom and liberty. Early in the film Chief Justice Fargo asserts that the Judge system 'stands for freedom, not repression'. This is contrasted with Judge Griffin, who wishes to impose a more authoritarian regime: 'The city is in chaos. For social order we need tighter reins. Incarceration hasn't worked as a deterrent. I say we expand execution to include lesser crimes.' Unlike the deranged megalomaniac Judge Cal in the comic strip, the film's Judge Griffin is a rational villain who sees totalitarianism as a means of imposing order. It is significant that the climactic confrontation between Dredd and Rico takes place on the Statue of Liberty. In the comic the Statue of Liberty had been used ironically to demonstrate the suppression of liberty in Mega-City One, but this meaning is lost in the film.

The film also humanizes the character of Dredd. At the outset he is the emotionless automaton that one would expect ('Emotions! There oughta be a law against them!') and his distance from human contact is explained through his sense of guilt at having 'judged' his brother Rico. This is contrasted with the humane Judge Hershey ('I have a personal life, I have friends') who represents a feminine challenge to Dredd's masculine authority. It is only when he is framed for murder that Dredd realizes the law is not perfect. His relationship with Fergee (Rob Schneider), whom he had previously sentenced to five years' incarceration for a minor offence, teaches Dredd that friendships are permissible. At the end of the film, when Hershey kisses Dredd, she remarks: 'It's good to be human, don't you think?'

The relationship between Dredd and Hershey (which, despite the kiss, seems entirely platonic on both sides) recalls that between Murphy (Peter Weller) and Lois (Nancy Allen) in Paul Verhoeven's *Robocop* (1987). *Robocop* was a violent action thriller set in crime-ridden Detroit of the near future. A badly injured cop is rebuilt as a cyborg: in his new guise he combats the combined menace of street gangs and a corrupt corporation that tries to privatize the police. *Robocop* was compared by many critics to Judge Dredd. As well as its strong law-and-order theme (Robocop's catchphrase is 'Dead or alive you're coming with me'), the film is replete with satirical popular culture references such as television advertisements for 'total sun block' and a family computer board game called 'Nuke 'em!' The satirical edge of the comic is entirely missing from *Judge Dredd*, however, and the film suffers as a consequence. Indeed, there is a sense in which *Robocop* is a better Judge Dredd film than *Judge Dredd*. Similar satirical moments punctuate Verhoeven's other two big SF films, *Total Recall* (1990) and *Starship Troopers* (1997), leaving one to speculate what *Judge Dredd* might have been had he been in the director's chair.

This is not to lay the blame for the relative failure of *Judge Dredd* entirely at the door of Danny Cannon, however. Cannon had a rather different vision for the film. He saw it as an epic in the mould of *Ben-Hur*, *Spartacus* and *El Cid*: 'Those movies took themselves very seriously, just as the artists acting in them did, and I tried to incorporate that element of emotional honesty in *Judge Dredd*. It's every bit as much an epic passion play as it is a sci-fi film.'[93] This is not as ridiculous as it might sound. If one sees Dredd as Judah Ben-Hur, Rico as Messala, the bad brother, and Chief Justice Fargo as Quintus Arrius, the symbolic father-figure, then *Judge Dredd* does indeed resemble the structure of *Ben-Hur*, with Dredd's journey on the prison ship the equivalent of Judah's imprisonment on the galley and the crash landing in the Cursed Earth the equivalent of the sea battle. There is even an approximation of the chariot race in the airborne chase on Lawmaster bikes that provides the principal action-pursuit sequence in the film. That *Judge Dredd* did not, in the event, match up to Cannon's vision for the film is probably due to drastic editing in post-production. The sequences in the Cursed Earth, in particular, seem to have been much truncated, amounting to little more than an encounter with some cannibal mutants.

There was a divided response to the film from those involved with *2000AD*. David Bishop, then editor of both *2000AD* and *Judge Dredd Megazine*, was positive about the result: 'We've come out it quite well . . . If they'd made it more like the comic they would have pleased a few *Dredd* fans but irritated millions of film viewers . . . Some of the writers and artists won't like it, but that's down to their personal, political viewpoints.'[94] However, Alan Grant was scathing about the film: 'My opinions of it are so low that they are unprintable. It's hard to believe they employed a script writer . . . It's my greatest fear realised: a film supporting a political ideology that I find abhorrent.'[95]

In effectively humanizing Dredd and liberalizing the Judge system, the film of *Judge Dredd* loses the element of critique of that system that informs the comic strip. Yet perhaps it was not quite as far removed from its source as Grant believed. In certain respects, indeed, the film anticipated the direction that the strip would take over the following decade or so. Some of the later stories have presented a more humane Dredd, one who recognizes that the law is not always right and who is occasionally prone to self-doubt. The comic-strip Dredd even followed in the footsteps of the film Dredd when he was kissed by a new female Judge. Judge DeMarco's (unrequited) love for Dredd can be seen as a further attempt to explore his emotional make-up: 'You don't get it, do you? You just don't get it! You're so damn thick-skinned you couldn't see it if it was comin' at you with a boot knife.'[96] For some fans this was an even greater heresy than Dredd removing his helmet. And the much-anticipated 'Origins', written by Wagner for the thirtieth anniversary of *2000AD* in 2007, reveals that Judge Fargo's dying wish had been to restore democracy: 'It was never meant to be foreever, Joe. We created a monster. We, us, we're the monster! We got greedy – wanted everything – so we killed the dream, Joe! We killed America!'[97] The characterization of Fargo as an idealist and a democrat is consistent with the *Judge Dredd* film and suggests that the film's authors may not have misunderstood the politics of the strip in quite the way that some critics maintained. However, there is still one crucial difference. The film concluded on an optimistic note with Dredd overcoming the threat to the liberty of Mega-City One. But 'Origins' concludes on a downbeat note as Dredd keeps Fargo's dying words to himself: the authoritarian rule of the Judges continues. This again underlines the essentially dystopian outlook of *2000AD* and its distinctive brand of science fiction.

CHAPTER SEVEN

The Strange World of the British Superhero

> I was there in 1976 when *Captain Britain* was unleashed on the awaiting masses. We'd been led to believe that he would be a British hero – as British as *Dan Dare* or *Sherlock Holmes*. Unfortunately this was not to be; instead we had a poor, less adult copy of any number of previous Marvel heroes. The whole series was cheap, rushed and gave little thought to what makes a character British. We had an American superhero, dressed in a Union Jack.
>
> Letter to *Captain Britain* (May 1985).[1]

The superhero is an archetype indelibly associated with American popular culture. The first superheroes appeared in comics in the late 1930s and achieved the height of their popularity early during the Second World War when titles such as *Action Comics* and *Detective Comics* – where Superman and Batman, respectively, made their first appearances – regularly sold a million copies. With their colourful costumes and fantastic adventures, the superheroes provided escapism from the harsh realities of Depression-era America and then reassurance following the shock of Pearl Harbor as Americans found themselves involved in a war that few had wanted and fewer still understood. The superhero was born at precisely the moment that the sleeping giant that was the USA was about to emerge from its isolationism and would become the leading military and industrial power in the world. In this context characters such as the super-patriot Captain America and Superman, the first and mightiest of the superheroes, were very much products of their time. The popularity of the superheroes provided a much-needed boost for the fledgling US comic book publishing industry and was instrumental in helping picture comics to displace the 'pulps' as the favoured reading matter for children and adolescents. They were particularly popular with GIs: comic books were shipped to US servicemen in their millions during the war.[2]

The first generation of comic-book superheroes, then, arose from particular historical and ideological contexts. The superhero mythos evolved quickly. Superman, who first hit the newsstands in 1938, was initially a social reformer who stood up against lynch mobs, wife beaters and corrupt businessmen. Within a short space of time, however, he was battling mad scientists and master criminals who provided more of a challenge for his rapidly expanding super powers. Batman, who followed in 1939, quickly developed from a masked vigilante terrorizing small-time hoodlums to an officially legitimated crime-fighter pitted against a colourful array of bizarre costumed villains. Batman is not strictly a superhero in the sense that he has no special powers: he represents a link between comics and the heroes of pulp magazines such as The Shadow and Doc Savage. Superman and Batman were followed in quick succession by Captain Marvel, The Flash, The Green Lantern, Captain America, The Green Arrow and Wonder Woman, who all appeared between 1940 and 1942.

The congruence between the emergence of the superhero and America's entry into the Second World War was highly opportune for the comic book industry. The war saw the market for comics expand rapidly, while the co-option of superheroes into the war effort provided ideological legitimacy for the comic industry that was keen to display its patriotic credentials as a response to the federal and state authorities which had begun to express their concerns about the pernicious effects of comics on juveniles. The most overtly patriotic of the superheroes were Captain america and Wonder Woman, pressed into service against Japanese and German villains. Superman – whose powers were so great that he could almost have ended the war single-handedly – was kept on the home front to fight spies and saboteurs, his alter ego Clark Kent conveniently failing the medical examination for military service.

The first generation of superheroes established all the major conventions of the genre. A superhero is 'a man or woman with powers that are either massive extensions of human strengths and capabilities, or fundamentally different in kind, which she or he uses to fight for truth, justice and the protection of the innocent'.[3] Their super powers may be acquired by inheritance (Superman, Wonder Woman), endowed by magic (Captain Marvel) or created by science (Captain America). The superhero is a liminal figure on the margins of society: he may be an orphan (Superman, Batman) or even a juvenile (Captain Marvel is the alter ego of paperboy Billy Batson, who turns into a superhero when he says the magic word 'Shazam!'). Above all each superhero requires an origin story. Thus Superman turns out to be an alien from the planet Krypton who escaped its destruction and was raised from infancy by Ma and Pa Kent who found him in a crashed spaceship; Captain America is the first in a breed of genetically enhanced super warriors; and

Wonder Woman is Diana, daughter of Hippolyte, Queen of the Amazons, an all-female society of immortals.

The appeal of superheroes has been explained in a variety of ways. On the most basic level superheroes represent a wish-fulfilment fantasy for juveniles: hence the fact that they have a 'normal' persona who might be seen as a weakling or coward in order to conceal their secret identity. On another level superheroes might be compared to classical mythology: they inhabit an imaginary world of myth and legend where they undergo trials of strength and courage and undertake feats of extraordinary heroism. Some critics have equated superheroes with Nietzsche's notion of the *Übermensch*: one who has evolved ethically from the normal human type. This was a cause of alarm for psychologist Dr Fredric Wertham, the foremost American critic of comic books, who argued that characters like Superman ('psychologically Superman undermines the authority and dignity of the ordinary man and woman in the minds of children') and Wonder Woman ('the Lesbian counterpart of Superman . . . a morbid ideal of femininity') were inappropriate role models for children. He even averred that 'Superman has long been recognized as a symbol of violent race superiority'.[4]

The popularity of superheroes declined in the 1950s, when other genres such as war and westerns were better suited to the ideological climate, but the genre was revitalized in the early 1960s when Marvel Comics, hitherto very much a second-division comic publisher, emerged as a major force in the industry. Under the guidance of editor-in-chief Stan Lee, a former Captain America artist, Marvel developed a new generation of superheroes including the Fantastic Four, Incredible Hulk, Spider-Man, Thor, Iron Man, Daredevil and the X-Men.[5] However, the superheroes of the 1960s were a very different breed from the all-American über-patriots of the Second World War. According to Marvel's own publicity 'there was another dimension to these characters with which every young reader could identify: they were sensitive and vulnerable . . . plagued by the same mundane problems which afflict all of us, and they often found themselves faced with human conflicts which their super powers could not resolve'.[6] Marvel's superheroes are typically social outsiders and their adventures explore issues of cultural difference. Spider-Man, for example, is the alter ego of gauche student Peter Parker: a major theme of *The Amazing Spider-Man* and its spin-offs is Parker's attempt to reconcile his superhero persona with his personal life including his career as a photojournalist and his relationship with girlfriends Gwen Stacy and Mary Jane Parker. The X-Men are a secret society of mutants, each possessing unique powers, who as well as their super-powered foes have to contend with prejudice from the society they protect: for this reason *The X-Men* has been interpreted as a commentary on the status of marginal groups, especially homosexuals. The social subtexts, coupled with Lee's jokey editorials from the 'Bullpen', established Marvel's brand identity. They were particularly popular with students and teenagers, who identified with their themes of social alienation and superhero *angst*.

* * *

British comics were slow to adopt the superhero. While story papers had featured characters such as the legendary strongman Morgyn the Mighty, home-grown costumed superheroes in the American mould were a rarer species. A handful of ersatz British supermen – Streamline, Captain Atom, Electroman – appeared in their own short-lived comics in the post-war years. However, the first British superhero to achieve any sustained popularity was Marvelman. The origin story of Marvelman lay in nothing more fantastic than a dispute over intellectual property. L. Miller & Co. was one of several independent British publishers in the 1950s who reprinted, under licence, American comics including *Nyoka the Jungle Girl*, *Spysmasher*, *Don Winslow of the Navy*, *Captain Midnight* and *Captain Marvel*. *Captain Marvel* had been created by Fawcett Publications of New York in 1940 and quickly became one of the best-selling superhero comics, outselling even *Superman*. It spawned several spin-offs including *Mary Marvel* and *Captain Marvel Jr*. However, in 1951 National Periodical Publications, publisher of *Superman*, brought a lawsuit against Fawcett alleging that Captain Marvel was an infringement of copyright as his super powers (he was impervious to bullets and possessed the ability to fly) were very similar to those of the 'Man of Steel'. In the event the case was settled out of court, but part of the settlement was that Fawcett agreed to discontinue its *Captain Marvel* series. This decision naturally had significant ramifications for L. Miller & Co. As Michael Anglo, cover artist for the British reprints, explained:

> One day Len phoned and said he wanted to see me urgently. Fawcett's were involved in some legal trouble with *Superman* over *Captain Marvel*; an injunction had been slapped on them, and Len said it looked as if his supply of American material for *Captain Marvel* would be cut off. Had I any ideas? I had, and for my trouble received a regular supply of work for the next six years.
>
> In the last of the Marvel titles we announced that Captain Marvel and Captain Marvel Jr were so well known as marvelmen that in future they would be known by the titles Marvelman and Young Marvelman and would each have a weekly comic of their own . . . There was no hitch, no hiatus. The new titles were greeted with increased sales, and letters poured in from enthusiastic kids demanding a 'Marvelman Club'.[7]

Thus Billy Batson became Micky Moran, and his magic word became 'Kimota' ('Atomik(c)' spelled backwards) rather than 'Shazam'. As an infringement of copyright it was a far more blatant copy of Captain Marvel than Captain Marvel had ever been of Superman, but it seems to have escaped the notice of the litigious US publishers: Miller published 346 issues of *Marvelman* and the same number of *Young Marvelman* between 1954 and 1963.

Marvelman and *Young Marvelman* were straightforward, unsophisticated adventures produced for undemanding juvenile readers. Anglo designed the main characters and wrote the stories, while 'the artist interpreted it the way he saw it and in as many frames as he saw fit'.[8] Numerous artists drew the comics for the next decade, including Don Lawrence, Roy Parker, John Whitlock, Frank Daniels, George Parlett, Leo Rawlings, Charles Baker and Denis Gifford. As a consequence the style is somewhat inconsistent: Marvelman himself alternates between tall and athletic and stocky and barrel-chested. Anglo particularly liked Whitlock's style, describing it as 'typically American . . . bold, stylized, and dramatic'.[9]

The Marvelman comics represent an uneven mix of American and British influences. The artists had no experience of drawing superheroes and so simply imitated the style of the originals. Thus the first major British superhero retained American locations – cityscapes of skyscrapers and streetcars – and adopted American slang ('Holy Macaroni!'). The writers, however, clearly struggled with the American idiom. Captions and dialogue are inconsistent – 'pavement' rather than 'sidewalk' and 'lad' rather than 'kid', for example – and the American speech is often unconvincing. There is little trace of the patriotism of the American comics, and the tone is light-hearted: Marvelman's arch enemy Gargunza is more of a prankster than a diabolical villain. With no romantic interest and no equivalent of kryptonite (the substance that is Superman's Achilles heel) the stories contain little tension or suspense.

The content of *Marvelman* and *Young Marvelman* combines aspects of the superhero mythos with elements of science fiction and fantasy. Our heroes have 'normal' identities: Micky Moran (Marvelman) is a copy boy for the *Daily Bugle*, while Dicky Dauntless (Young Marvelman) is an errand boy for a 'transatlantic messenger service'. Their super powers are acquired courtesy of a 'reclusive astro-scientist' who has discovered 'the key word that can turn a boy into the Mightiest Man in the Universe' – a secret to be given only to 'a boy who is completely honest and studious, and of such integrity that he would only use his powers for good, and to help others'.[10] Many of the stories feature standard superhero stuff – gangsters, spies, saboteurs, mad scientists – but others depart from the usual conventions. A recurring device is to send Marvelman into the future or the past where, contrary to the usual super-

Marvelman was the first British superhero. 'Marvelman and the Spanish Armada' (L. Miller & Co. Ltd, n.d.).

hero protocol, he becomes an active participant in historical events. Thus he saves the throne of an English king ('Marvelman and King Canute') and intervenes in a historic battle ('Marvelman and the Spanish Armada').[11] In a later period this would be understood as deconstructing the genre, but here it merely suggests writers who were unfamiliar with the conventions.

Some stories take Marvelman into the world of fantasy and fairytale. 'Marvelman and the Magic Tinder Box' is a variation on the Aladdin tale with a giant talking dog in place of the genie.[12] 'Marvelman and the Land of Make-Believe' is set in a world of hobgoblins and dragons. It is a political fable. Marvelman is summoned by Bogglefag, the prime minister of the Land of Phrase and Fable, to deal with a separatist movement in the neighbouring Land of Make-Believe: 'The people want Home Rule. They say they are fed up with paying taxes and not getting a fair return. I'm very much afraid that civil war will break out at any minute.' The separatists are led by the demagogue Bellicose. Bogglefag is deposed by Bellicose, but his regime proves even more unpopular and the people turn against him when he becomes a tyrant. Bogglefag is restored to office on the promise of making reforms.[13]

Despite all their flaws and inconsistencies, the Marvelman comics remained popular for a decade. What finally killed off Marvelman was not mad scientist Gargunza but rather the reappearance of the genuine article. In 1959 the restriction on the import of American comics was lifted. With colour US titles once again available, the market for black-and-white British reprints and imitations declined. In 1960 *Marvelman* and *Young Marvelman* switched from weekly to monthly publication; both titles were discontinued in 1963. Michael Anglo recycled some of his Marvelman strips for *Captain Miracle*, which appeared briefly under his Anglo Comics imprint in the early 1960s. L. Miller & Co. continued in business until 1970, when it became the first publisher to be prosecuted under the Children and Young Person's (Harmful Publications) Act of 1955 for importing some of the banned horror comics.[14]

While there were no indigenous British superheroes in the 1960s, however, there was a trend towards the fantastic and the bizarre in crime and adventure strips. 'The Steel Claw', who appeared in *Valiant* between 1962 and 1973, and 'The Spider', which ran in *Lion* from 1965 to 1969, are two of the most unusual and distinctive characters in the history of British comics. The two have much in common. The careers of The Steel Claw and The Spider both follow a trajectory from criminality to crime-fighting: to this extent they may be considered the first comic-book anti-heroes. They both share some of the characteristics of the superhero genre without being superheroes themselves. And they both exhibit a darkness of theme and style that anticipates later developments in the comic industry by some two decades.

'The Steel Claw' is a hybrid of crime, horror and science fiction, drawn in a moody, expressionist style by Spanish artist Jesús Blasco. The strip was devised by Jack Le Grand, Ken Bulmer provided the first year's scripts and then Tom Tully took over for the rest of the Claw's *Valiant* career. The Steel Claw is Louis Crandell, disgruntled assistant to Professor Barringer, whose right hand is made of steel following a laboratory accident. In the course of testing Barringer's new invention ('a new ray for medical purposes') another accident causes Crandell to become invisible except for his steel hand. Crandell discovers that a charge of electricity will turn him temporarily invisible. He scorns his employer's philanthropic outlook ('The old fool. He could get a fortune for this discovery . . . and he's giving away the formula – for nothing!') and sets out to use his invisibility for his own gain ('It's given me the chance I've dreamed of. Untold riches – within my grasp!'). Crandell begins by robbing a bank but is forced to dump the money to make his escape. Concluding that 'petty thieving is useless', he resolves to 'become the richest and most powerful man alive . . . I'll blackmail the world!' He crosses the Atlantic to New York, where he threatens to destroy the city with an atomic bomb stolen from the US Army. When the power supply is cut off, however, Crandell becomes visible again and finds himself a hunted fugitive trapped in the city.[15]

'The Steel Claw' borrows from H. G. Wells's *The Invisible Man*, charting the mental deterioration of its protagonist who descends into madness and megalomania. It is a parable of the power of science to corrupt humanity: Crandell, like Wells's brilliant physicist Griffin, becomes deranged and loses his sense of right and wrong. The good-natured Ballinger holds himself responsible ('It's my fault Crandell is acting like this') and blames his behaviour on the effects of the accident ('He's not really responsible for what he's doing'). At the climax of the first story Crandell saves Ballinger from a burning shack and in so doing rediscovers his moral compass ('I wanted power to change the world . . . The world's in a terrible mess . . . If I were ruler of the world I could put everything right'). Barringer is able to keep Crandell out of prison, believing that 'he could be a tremendous power for good in the world'.

The origin narrative of 'The Steel Claw' is not without its weaknesses – Crandell's transformation from sallow-faced lab assistant to master criminal to reformed good-guy is too rapid for psychological plausibility – but what distinguishes the strip is its visual style. Blasco's artwork resembles the stylized look of film noir, with its gloomy urban settings and shadowy cityscapes. Even when visible Crandell often appears in shadow: he is a hunted man who hides in the darkness. The effect is to create a mood of dislocation, cynicism

'The Steel Claw', *Valiant* (Amalgamated Press Ltd, 6 October 1962).

179

and distrust that reflects Crandell's psychological state. The narration is fragmentary: what stands out are particular frames such as the surreal image of the metallic hand apparently floating in the air or the sudden close-up when it touches the shoulder of a terrified bank manager.

Later stories follow Crandell's rehabilitation and his transformation from criminal to crime-fighter. 'The Steel Claw' is a narrative of guilt and redemption: Crandell tries to atone for his criminal past but remains an ostracized, persecuted figure who is rejected by society. Unlike most superheroes he has no secret identity to hide behind: it is public knowledge that Crandell is The Steel Claw. He can never fully shake off his past: a recurring device is that he is framed or suspected of a crime and has to establish his innocence. Under Tully's guidance, the format of 'The Steel Claw' underwent several changes as it responded to wider trends in popular culture. In the mid-1960s, influenced by the vogue for gimmicky spy adventures such as James Bond, *The Avengers* and *The Man From U.N.C.L.E.*, Crandell joined a top-secret British counter-espionage organization, the Shadow Squad, and his steel hand was fitted with a range of weapons and gadgets provided by Professor Barringer. During this period Crandell came up against a succession of super-villains with names such as Dr Magno, Kranos, The Vulture and Warlock. In 1971, following a year-long hiatus, 'The Return of the Claw' again changed format as Crandell became a roving troubleshooter and bounty hunter. He is once again a loner whose only friend is Professor Barringer, now less of an authority figure than a conventional sidekick. The strip ends with Crandell living in exile in South America, where he continues to fight crime free from the guilty associations of his past.

While 'The Steel Claw' is conditioned by a strong dose of psychological realism, 'The Spider' owes more to the tradition of sensational melodrama. Its protagonist is a super-criminal with megalomaniac tendencies of the highest order. What distinguishes 'The Spider' from other comic strips is the sheer weirdness of its title character. With his elongated pointed ears, arched eyebrows and slicked-back black hair, there is a distinctly alien quality to The Spider. His otherness sets him apart even within the weird and wonderful world of the comics: it is not entirely certain that The Spider is even human. He employs gadgets worthy of Batman's utility belt, including a web-firing gun, paralysing gas, a jet pack and a helicar, while his headquarters is a Scottish castle rebuilt stone by stone in the United States.

'The Spider' was created by writer Ted Cowan and drawn by Reg Bunn, whose style is characterized by its angular figure-work and backgrounds of fine-lined cross-hatching. The Spider's aim is to 'build an empire of crime on a scale of which no man ever dreamed'. He recruits two accomplices in safe-breaker Orsini and explosives expert Professor Pelham as the first soldiers in

'The Spider v. Dr Mysterioso', *Lion* (Fleetway Publications Ltd, 29 January 1966).

his 'army of crime'. He promises 'to carry out the crime of the century' by robbing the diamond pavilion at the Toredo State Fair but is foiled when the getaway car crashes and he is presumed dead in the inferno. He survives, however, and in 'The Return of the Spider' plans 'a bullion robbery on a scale of which no man dreamed – a story to blaze across the annals of crime'. This time he is beaten to it by a rival known as the Mirror Man who is able to project powerful hypnotic illusions. The Spider overcomes the Mirror Man, leaving him for the police, settling for 'a small quantity of the gold – my price for smashing the Mirror Man and his gang'.[16] This set the formula for the rest of the strip.

After two stories scripting of the strip was undertaken by none other than Jerry Siegel, the American comic writer best known as the creator of Superman. Siegel presided over The Spider's transition from crook to crime-fighter and further Americanized the strip with an infusion of hard-boiled gangster dialogue. 'The Spider' again represents a mixture of British and American influences. The Spider himself is heir to the tradition of master crooks such as The Squeaker and The Ringer, characters created by the prolific Edgar Wallace, who were not entirely bad in so far as they would round up other criminals and police the underworld. The Spider's transformation from 'King of Crooks' to scourge of the underworld arises not from any ideological conversion but rather because he finds it more intellectually stimulating than straightforward criminal behaviour. He pits his wits against a range of super-villains – Doctor Mysterioso, The Android Emperor, The Molecule

Man, The Fly, The Snake, The Crime Genie – though there is always a suggestion that he may resume his criminal ways. The Spider thus remains a far more ambiguous character than other crime-fighters. He is neither hero nor villain; rather he inhabits the liminal space between law and criminality.

The Spider and The Steel Claw are the most noteworthy examples of a trend towards fantasy in British adventure comics in the late 1960s and early 1970s. Other characters who appeared around this time included the rubber-limbed Victorian escapologist Janus Stark (in *Valiant*) and 'master of the mystic arts' Cursitor Doom (in *Smash!*). 'The House of Dolmann' (*Valiant*) featured a scientific genius who controls an army of robot puppets to combat crime. The notion that these characters inhabited the same fictional universe would later be used by Alan Moore in the mini-series *Albion*. None of these characters, however, are superheroes in the strictest sense. Perhaps the closest that British comics came to the costumed heroes of American comic books was 'King Cobra', who appeared in *Hotspur* in the mid-1970s. King Cobra is a crime-fighter whose powers derive from his special hooded suit. The 'look' of the strip is clearly influenced by *Spider-Man* with its images of King Cobra scaling walls in his figure-hugging suit. His alias is Bill King, an apparently accident-prone reporter who, like Peter Parker, contrives to be in the right place to get the story. The fact that King Cobra, a straightforward character as far as costumed heroes go, never acquired the cult following of The Steel Claw or The Spider suggests that British comic readers preferred their supermen as flawed characters with a degree of ambiguity and menace.

* * *

The curious history of Captain Britain perfectly demonstrates the difficulty of creating a truly British superhero. *Captain Britain* (1976–7) was, initially, a weekly comic published by the British division of the US publisher Marvel. Marvel UK had been set up in the early 1970s to publish reprints for the British market, specializing in anthology titles such as *The Mighty World of Marvel*, *The Super-Heroes* and *The Titans*. In the mid-1970s, however, seeking to establish itself as a third power alongside IPC and D. C. Thomson, Marvel launched several original titles for the British market. These included a war comic (*Fury*) and spin-offs from film (*Star Wars Weekly*) and television (*Doctor Who Weekly*). The first of these new comics was *Captain Britain*, which, however, was written and drawn by Marvel's 'Bullpen' in New York. Chris Claremont, best known as a writer for *X-Men*, scripted the early stories, including the all-important origin narrative, with artwork by Herb Trimpe. Marvel's strategy for selling *Captain Britain* to British comic fans was to persuade them that the character had been created in response to popular demand. In a 'personal message' in the first issue, Stan Lee declared that 'the time has come for a new superhero – one who will be BRITAIN'S OWN! Month after month you have demanded him! Comicdom has needed him! All of Britain has been waiting for him!'[17] However, the American parentage of 'Britain's greatest superhero' was to provoke the ire of British readers and would place 'the Cap' squarely within Anglo-American 'culture wars' that would be fought out in its letters pages and even within the title strip itself.

Captain Britain is a heady mixture of the American superhero formula with elements of Arthurian mythology. The first issue establishes the essential superhero origin story. Brian Braddock, a lab assistant at the top-secret Darkmoor Research Centre, narrowly escapes with his life when the centre is attacked by terrorists. In the confusion Braddock's motorcycle plunges over a cliff, but instead of dying he is confronted by the ghostly apparitions of Merlin and the Lady of the Northern Skies who offer him a choice between 'either the sword or the amulet . . . life or death for thee . . . and mayhap for thy world as well'. Braddock chooses the amulet and is told 'thou hast chosen the amulet of right over the sword of might . . . Be one with thy brothers of the Round Table – with Arthur and Lancelot, Gawain and Galahad, with them all. . .' When Braddock touches the amulet he is transformed into Captain Britain, who swears 'to maintain the rule of right – of law and justice – against those who live and rule by might'.[18] What distinguishes this origin narrative from other Marvel superheroes is that it invokes magic rather than science. Characters like Spider-Man (bitten by a radioactive spider) and Hulk (exposed to gamma radiation) had acquired their super powers as the consequence of experiments that went wrong. Iron Man derives his strength from a special suit, while even the diverse powers of the X-Men are explained away through a mutant gene. Captain Britain, however, is born through the intervention of supernatural agency, with much mumbo-jumbo about the Circle of Power and the Amulet of Life. In drawing upon Arthurian mythology, the strip invokes a culturally specific myth that originated in medieval Britain rather than modern-day America. In this context Captain Britain can also be seen as part of a revival of Arthurian mythology exemplified by the Broadway musical *Camelot* and by films ranging from the low-budget *Gawain and the Green Knight* to the expensively produced *Excalibur*.[19]

Yet if the origin story locates Captain Britain within a native British mythology, other elements of the strip owe more to the American superhero tradition. There is a sense, indeed, in which Captain Britain represents a composite of other Marvel characters. Brian Braddock is a student whose parents have died and who has difficulty maintaining a relationship with his girlfriend Courtney Ross (Peter Parker/Spider-Man), while his alter ego Captain Britain is redolent of nationhood (Captain America) and wears a red full-body suit (Daredevil). During the course of his adventures he combats a

Captain Britain was a curious mixture of Arthurian mythology and the American superhero tradition. *Captain Britain* (Marvel Comics International Ltd, 13 October 1976).

succession of (largely second-rate) super-villains including the Reaver, Hurricane, Dr Synne, Mastermind and Lord Hawk. Characteristically for Marvel, *Captain Britain* maintained continuity with other comics and featured cross-over stories. For thirteen issues, for example, Captain Britain teamed with Captain America and Nick Fury, director of top-secret security organization S.H.I.E.L.D., to combat Nazi revivalist the Red Skull who seeks to establish the Fourth Reich in 1970s Britain.

Claremont later recalled a critic dismissing *Captain Britain* as 'a farrago of illiterate SF nonsense'.[20] Yet there are many reasons to like the first incarnation of Captain Britain. The strip is boldly drawn and is based on dynamic action and movement: the first issue opens in the midst of an all-out fight between Captain Britain and the Reaver before the origin story is explained in flashback. It shares with other Marvel superhero comics an element of psychological realism in that Braddock is prone to self-doubt about his role as defender of the realm and, initially at least, is uncertain of the extent of his power. The theme of the double life of the superhero is explored as Braddock reflects on his 'identity crisis'. *Captain Britain* features a recurring antagonist in the form of Chief Inspector Dai Thomas of Scotland Yard who pursues his own vendetta against superheroes because of the mayhem they cause. Thomas is the equivalent of newspaper editor J. Jonah Jameson in *Spider-Man* but is given a more personal reason for his hatred of Captain Britain: he is a widower whose wife was killed under a falling building during 'a superhero donnybrook' in New York and who will 'do anything to stop that sort of madness from spreading to London'.[21]

Like other Marvel superhero comics, *Captain Britain* responds to topical issues in the contemporary world. The energy crisis of the mid-1970s informs the opening story in which Braddock is assistant to Dr Travers, a physicist who is on the verge of discovering a safe fusion reactor 'that will solve the world's energy crisis overnight'.[22] The energy crisis was a topical theme in film and television at the time, as exemplified by the James Bond adventure *The Man With the Golden Gun* and some episodes of *Doctor Who*.[23] A later story, set against the background of the Silver Jubilee of Queen Elizabeth II in 1977, makes what seems like a conscious allusion to the worsening political crisis over Southern Rhodesia. The villain is the deposed white ruler of the African state of Umbazi, who succeeds in brainwashing the Queen to order the Royal Navy to sail to reclaim 'his' country.[24] *Captain Britain* is clearly set against the real political landscape of 1970s Britain: when the Prime Minister is captured by the Red Skull he is referred to by name as (and bears the likeness of) James Callaghan. For Callaghan facing the Red Skull might have been a welcome diversion from the economic problems, rising unemployment and trade union militancy that confronted his government. This was not lost on *Guardian* columnist Dennis Barker, who was prompted to ask: 'Will Captain Britain find some way of intervening in economic and political matters?'[25]

The social politics of *Captain Britain* recall those of the 1960s telefantasy series *The Avengers*.[26] It presents an image of Britain that combines the traditional (manor houses, red buses) and the modern (nuclear power plants, computers, Concorde). One of its readers was prompted to complain that like Marvel's other British characters (these included Union Jack, the Black Knight and Spitfire, who all appeared in Marvel titles) *Captain Britain* perpetuated stereotypes: 'Why, oh why, must they all come from the Upper Classes? There are a lot of ordinary people about who can't identify with them. I thought Cap Brit would be different – a lowly student living off his grant. But no, he too comes from a family with land and background. Let's have a hero from the herd.'[27] A further similarity to *The Avengers* is that the villains include extreme reactionaries who cannot adjust to social change. Lord Hawk – a former university professor ridiculed by his students for his belief in a chivalric past – wants to return society to the Middle Ages. He intends that the death of Captain Britain 'will be an eloquent warning to the greedy and corrupt in this society that their days are numbered! Let all beware – the age of purification has arrived!'[28] Other villains invoke references to British popular myth. Dr Synne, a super-hypnotist, has named himself after the eighteenth-century folk hero Dr Syn, the Scarecrow of Romney Marsh and 'a fighter against tyranny and injustice . . . Our Dr Synne is deliberately perverting the name and the memory.'[29]

It would be fair to say that *Captain Britain* met with a mixed response from British comic fans. There is some evidence to suggest that Marvel had misjudged the market. Early issues of the comic featured puzzles and a 'colour yourself' page suggesting that it was meant for younger readers, but most of the published letters suggest an older teenage and young adult readership: one Captain Britain fan club held its meetings 'in the local public house'.[30] The response to Captain Britain himself was equivocal, with controversy over how genuinely British he was. A typical example is the critique from a reader who objected to the strip's inaccurate representation of Britain, which he blamed squarely on its American parentage:

> The fault lies with Claremont . . . or rather the choice of Claremont as a writer. He does a good job on the X-Men and Iron Fist, but when it comes to writing about a Superhero who's in surroundings unknown to him (i.e. Britain) then Chris, or any other writer unfamilar with Britain, is out of his depth . . . It's the daft editorial policy of drafting an American writer for a British strip. What would American Fandom say if a new American patriot was to hit the news stands written by some bloke who's never been closer to New York than Wolverhampton, and drawn by some guy who thinks he knows America just because he watches *Kojak* and *Starsky and Hutch* . . . Surely the employment of a British based writer, and eventually an artist, is not an impossible task.[31]

The issue at stake here is cultural authenticity: the response demonstrates that comics are just as much a part of the 'culture wars' as more respectable media. The editor replied that artist Herb Trimpe 'lived in Britain for the best part of a year', though this did little to appease the critics. Bob Budiansky, who started out as an editorial assistant at the Marvel office in New York and graduated to pencilling the backgrounds for *Captain Britain*, revealed that he carried out this task 'with the aid of a few London tourist guidebooks'.[32]

To be fair to *Captain Britain*'s American creators, the comic does make some attempt to address the concerns of its British readers. Certain aspects of the comic may even be read as a commentary on Americanization.

In particular there is an association between America and violence. Thus when Captain Britain foils an armed robbery, he describes the robbers as 'smashing thru here like something out of *Kojak*'.[33] Dai Thomas regards superheroism as an American disease that is best contained on the other side of the Atlantic: 'This isn't New York, laddy-buck – and I'm not going to let you super-powered yobbos turn London into your private punching ground!'[34] The Anglo-American 'culture wars' explode into the strip with the arrival in London of Captain America which prompts the inevitable superhero punch-up. (A convention of superhero comics is that, when two superheroes meet for the first time, they must fight each other to a standstill, while trading verbals between the blows, until mutual respect is earned.) Marvel UK sub--editor Neil Tennant argued that Captain Britain was not cast in the mould of American superheroes: 'He's not at all like Captain America. Captain America is much more patriotic – but then Americans are much more concerned about the Stars and Stripes than we are about the Union Jack.'[35]

Neither a change of writer (Gary Friedrich) nor different artists (John Buscema, Ron Wilson) could save *Captain Britain* from cancellation due to poor sales. Already reduced to black and white after 23 weeks due to 'harsh economic necessity', the title was merged with *Super Spider-Man* after 39 issues. Captain Britain became very much a supporting act to the ever popular 'Spidey'. 'Why give Spider-Man top billing?' one correspondent demanded. 'C.B. is Britain's own super-hero and these weeklies are printed in Britain. More relevant, C.B. is new material, unlike the Spider-Man reprints.'[36] This was not a representative view, however, as more readers felt that the quality of Captain Britain stories had declined. As one put it succinctly: 'Captain Britain has gone to pot.'[37]

Like all good superheroes, however, Captain Britain refused to die, becoming a staple filler strip for Marvel's UK imprints including *Marvel Super-Heroes*, *The Daredevils* and a revived *Mighty World of Marvel* in the early 1980s. This was a different Captain Britain, however: one who was, at last, scripted by British writers (David Thorpe, Alan Moore) and drawn by a British artist (Alan Davis). Moore's scripts expanded the fictional universe of the strip with a story arc (known as 'Jaspers' Warp') that sends Captain Britain to an alternate Earth where he meets other versions of himself and pan-dimensional beings including the sexy villainess Saturnyne. Merlin and his daughter Roma are revealed as guardians of the omniverse, which threatens to unravel as Earth-238 is destroyed through the machinations of Mad Jim Jaspers. The characterization became more psychologically complex, the narratives more fragmented and the illustration more stylized. Most readers liked the new direction. One fan wrote: '*Captain Britain* is certainly the best comic strip going. For once we see our hero taking some beatings, not like that rubbish when a hero gets smashed through walls, page after page and comes out smiling with all his teeth in.'[38] Another (adult) reader thought it was 'an amazing use of the medium! Such a staggering, uncompromising, mind-numbing master plot and sub-plots.'[39] Some, however, found the oblique, fragmentary style difficult to follow: 'A rather mind-boggling *Captain Britain* episode this month, quite difficult to grasp what's going on, though the dialogue and art were as lovely as ever.'[40]

The response of readers to the more mature version of the character was sufficient to prompt Marvel to resurrect *Captain Britain* as a monthly title in 1985. Alan Davis continued drawing the strip, while Jamie Delano took over the writing. Delano maintained continuity with Moore's stories, returning Captain Britain to our Earth (Earth-616) where he has to deal with all manner of trans-dimensional flotsam thrown up by the collapse of reality in the wake of Jaspers' Warp. These include the Crazy Gang, a family of crooks who dress as characters from fiction and use television cop shows as a model for their crimes; the trans-dimensional assassin Slaymaster; and Kaptain Briton, an evil alternate version of himself who attempts to rape Brian Braddock's sister Betsy. There is a greater emphasis on characterization than repetitive slam-bang action, and the longer strips allow more scope for developing sub-plots and themes. There is a background of social unrest: the warp has 'kinked the entire population's subconscious, building nests of fear and confusion'.[41] This might be seen as introducing an element of social comment: Britain in the 1980s was a nation beset by violent confrontations including the inner-city race riots of 1981 and the bitterly contested miners' strike of 1984–5 that witnessed running battles between police and 'flying pickets'.

The new *Captain Britain* was regarded by Marvel as a forum for 'showcasing British talent'.[42] Its style and content are representative of the new maturity of British comics in the 1980s: the title strip was considered 'as good if not better than the best of the Americans'.[43] One particularly distinctive feature is the prominence of the theme of memory. The opening episode ('Myth, Memory and Legend') employs parallel editing as it juxtaposes Dai Thomas explaining to his superiors why he believes Brian Braddock is Captain Britain with Braddock recounting the origin story of Captain Britain in flashback.[44] This serves the purpose of filling in the essential backstory for new readers, while at the same time establishing the tone of the strip as being more thoughtful and contemplative than the original. It is a style that makes considerable demands upon the cultural competence of its readers. The oblique narration was 'sometimes quite weird and hard to follow'.[45] Another fan wrote that 'C.B.'s strip is as masterful as ever, although I would like to see rather more in the way of action, less philosophical dialogue and flashbacks.'[46]

'Myth, Memory and Legend'. *Captain Britain* (Marvel Comics Ltd, January 1985).

Most readers, however, welcomed the second coming of *Captain Britain* and felt that this time Marvel had got it right. The consensus was that the American influences that had detracted from the first attempt had been avoided this time around and that the new *Captain Britain* exhibited a distinctively British flavour. Yet, for all its success within the fan culture, *Captain Britain* still lasted only fourteen issues before it was cancelled. While the character would continue his career in Marvel's US titles – he was reunited with creator Chris Claremont and teamed with the X-Men in the mini-series *Excalibur* (1988) – this marked the end of the road for Captain Britain's own comic. Ultimately 'Britain's greatest superhero' had failed to find a large enough readership. There simply was not sufficient demand for a British superhero title in the declining comics market of the 1980s.

* * *

Captain Britain was not the only superhero to receive a makeover in the 1980s. Marvelman, the original British superhero, was resurrected by Alan Moore and artist Garry Leach for the independent fantasy-themed comic *Warrior* in 1982. With Captain Britain, Moore had taken over the reins of

189

an existing continuing character, but with Marvelman he entirely reinvented a superhero and his mythos. Moore's Marvelman is a darker and psychologically more complex interpretation of the character that bears little similarity to the Marvelman comics of the 1950s. It is characterized by a strong sense of psychological realism and by a highly self-reflexive form of storytelling. It is an embryonic form of themes that Moore would examine in his later work, including the superhero as a source of anxiety (*Watchmen*) and the exploration of the mythology of popular fiction (*The League of Extraordinary Gentlemen*).

Moore presents Michael Moran as an adult, married forty-something with no memory of his superhero past, troubled by migraines and dreams of flying. A freelance journalist, he travels to the Lake District to cover a demonstration at a nuclear power station. The station is attacked by terrorists: during the melee Moran is knocked unconscious but sees the words 'Lakesmere Atomic Power Station' backwards from behind a glass door. He remembers the special word 'Kimota' and is transformed into Marvelman. Moore's revisionist account of the origin story reveals that Marvelman's super powers were the result of a secret experiment known as Project Zarathustra that used alien technology salvaged from a crashed spacecraft. Marvelman and his 'family', Young Marvelman and Kid Marvelman, were kept in a state of unconsciousness, their minds fed with tales from superhero comics. This is Moore's device for explaining the relationship between the new, adult Marvelman and the juvenile originals. Moran recalls that 'we fought the strangest villains of all time . . . It was almost as if we were all playing a game. A game which neither side took entirely seriously.'[47] However, in 1963 the Spookshow, the agency in charge of Project Zarathustra, fearing that the Marvelmen were becoming too powerful to contain, sent them into a trap primed with an atom bomb. Moran survived but lost his memory. It is further revealed that Gargunza, the buck-toothed villain of the originals, was a Nazi geneticist recruited by the British after the Second World War.

'Marvelman' is very far from being standard superhero fare: Moore uses the strip to explore philosophical and existential issues within the genre. The corruption of the superhero is one of its themes. Kid Marvelman, who it transpires also survived the atom bomb trap, has turned into an insane megalomaniac: 'To be sixteen years old and the most powerful creature on the face of the planet and to be answerable to no one. You could do anything . . . You could have it all – money, prestige, fame . . . You could become remorseless, unstoppable and totally corrupt.'[48] Kid Marvelman lacks any moral or ethical framework: he is a psycopath whose aim is to destroy Marvelman, the only person who stands between him and absolute power. He is only defeated when he accidentally says his special word and reverts to the child body of Johnny Bates, who is catatonic with guilt at the evil his alter ego has committed.

Further evidence that 'Marvelman' is a different type of superhero story is that it is informed by a discourse of psychological realism. Moore is at pains to characterize Moran as a real person: he is struggling to make a living and resents the fact that his wife earns more than he does. The early episodes explore how the revelation of Moran's superhero self affects their marriage. The couple have been trying to conceive a baby. When Liz becomes pregnant by Marvelman, Moran is troubled by the thought that his superhero alter ego is more virile than himself: 'It's just that it's not my baby, is it? It's Marvelman's. I couldn't give you a baby, but one night with him and . . . Oh, Christ, Liz. He's just so much better than I am. At everything.'[49] He may be the first superhero to experience a 'crisis of masculinity' – a

A superhero with a crisis of masculinity. Alan Moore's revisionist 'Marvelman' appeared in *Warrior* (Quality Communications Ltd, April 1982).

theme that locates Moore's Marvelman squarely within the tradition of British social realism.

Like Captain Britain Mark II, the revisionist Marvelman was popular with readers, most of whom welcomed the greater thematic depth and multi-layered story-telling. One felt that Moore and Leach 'have done for *Marvelman* what *The Movie* did for *Superman* . . . take an archetypal superhero, strip away all of the silliness accumulated over thousands of issues and arrive at the core of the character.'[50] But there evidently were still some who preferred their superheroes unburdened by psychological angst. 'I can't help feeling that transplanting *Marvelman* into the 1980s in such a grim manner was a gross mistake,' wrote one dissenter. 'The problem, of course, is that the old strips had a charming naivity [sic] about them which the new strip, out of necessity, has to avoid.'[51]

'Marvelman' ran for 21 episodes in *Warrior* until it was discontinued when lawyers acting for Marvel Comics threatened action on the disingenuous grounds of 'confusing the existing and potential customers of our clients'.[52] It would seem highly unlikely that most readers of Marvel titles, as well versed as they are in the fictional universe of their characters, would have been so confused, especially as 'Marvelman' had included a disclaimer that it 'is in no way associated with Marvel Comics Ltd'. It is ironic, though perhaps entirely fitting, that a character originally born as a response to one lawsuit was killed off by another. Moore responded as Michael Anglo had thirty years before: he simply changed Marvelman's name to Miracleman and went on writing the series for the US independent Eclipse Comics.

Marvelman had started out as a British copy of an American character; Miracleman, however, was now described as 'America's #1 Super Hero!' *Miracleman*, published quarterly between 1985 and 1992, demonstrated an Anglo-American cultural economy: British writers (Moore, Neil Gaiman) and American artists (Chuck Beckum, John Totleben). One of the consequences was that the distinctively British flavour of the *Warrior* 'Marvelman' was lost. A British reader suggested that the need to sell the comic in America was the reason for 'the steady watering-down of Britishisms that has occurred in *Miracleman* of late'.[53] To this extent *Miracleman* reflects a wider shift in the comic industry during the 1980s as British writers began contributing regularly to US comics. Moore had started writing *Swamp Thing* for DC in 1983 and Gaiman would follow suit with *Sandman* in 1989.

Miracleman represents the apotheosis of the superhero: the fullest exploration of the idea of superheroes as gods. Moore provides an intellectual context through quotations from Nietzsche's *Thus Spoke Zarathustra* and references to the idea of the *Übermensch*. And a powerful story arc takes the superhero narrative into hitherto unexplored terrain. 'Nemesis' is one of the darkest stories in the history of comics. Kid Miracleman, a vengeful psychopath after his child persona Johnny is raped by fellow inmates in a young offenders' institution, lays waste to London and butchers thousands of innocent people. With its horrific images of indiscriminate killing (cadavers hanging from lamp posts, bodies impaled on the hands of Big Ben, the River Thames choked with the bodies of the dead), 'Nemesis' has been read as an allusion to the Holocaust.[54] It was followed by 'Olympus', in which Miracleman and his fellow super beings use their powers to intervene in human affairs and create their idea of a perfect society: they destroy all nuclear weapons, restructure the global economy, restore the ozone layer and eradicate disease and poverty. The outcome is a benevolent dictatorship of super beings. Miracleman has become quite literally the *Übermensch*: he has evolved beyond good and evil and imposes his own will to power on the human race. Gaiman planned another story arc chronicling the fall of the super beings and the descent into hubris, though this was curtailed when Eclipse Comics went bankrupt in the early 1990s.

While *Miracleman* marked the Americanization of the British superhero, other British comic creators have sought to uphold the tradition of the genuinely British hero. *Doc Chaos* (1985), written by David Thorpe and Lawrence Gray, and drawn by Phil Elliott in a clear-line style reminiscent of the early work of Hergé, is about the hunt for an elusive super-criminal engaged in 'a planned subversive attempt to disrupt our society'. However, nobody knows who Doc Chaos is, what he looks like or even whether he actually exists at all: the suggestion is that the subversive threat he represents has been invented by an alliance of government and corporate interests to justify their own power. *Doc Chaos* links global capitalism and politics: a multi-national burger corporation seeks 'to "stabilize" the food and petro-chemical supplies of Great Britain and the EEC' and attempts to put its rivals out of business by creating an addictive burger. It is a deliriously paranoid conspiracy thriller with surreal moments: *Edge of Darkness* as imagined by *Monty Python* or *The Goodies*. Alan Moore called it 'one of the most exciting and refreshing pieces of Graphic Literature I've seen in a long time'.[55]

'Zenith', a superhero who appeared in three serials in *2000AD* in the late 1980s, was another distinctively British addition to the genre. 'Zenith' was the first major work of Grant Morrison, whose early work included the satirical 'Captain Clyde', a newspaper strip about an unemployed Glaswegian superhero that appeared in the *Govan Press*. Morrison set out 'to attempt a uniquely British approach to the basic premise of people with superhuman abilities ... I imagined designer superheroes in a Nietzschean soap opera, an everyday tale of extraordinary folk.'[56] Morrison would follow Moore and Gaiman into writing for US comics, where he has contributed to a range of superhero

Doc Chaos (Escape Publishing Ltd, 1985).

titles including *The Doom Patrol, The Invisibles, Justice League of America* and *New X-Men*.

'Zenith' is best described as an anti-superhero: a superhero who does not want to be a superhero. Zenith, aka nineteen-year-old Robert MacDowell, is the son of two members of Cloud 9, a superhero team created by the British military following the Second World War but who came of age during the 1960s when they 'dropped out' and became hippies. Zenith is shallow, self-centred, conceited and irresponsible: he is more interested in promoting his pop music career and getting laid than in using his powers for the public good. The character is a parody of the pious superhero dictum (associated with Spider-Man) that 'with great power comes great responsibility': Zenith would rather stay in and watch *Neighbours*.

'Zenith' can be seen as a commentary on the politics of Thatcherite Britain. In a way the key character is not Zenith but Peter St John, an ex-hippy turned Conservative MP. In the 1960s St John, then known as Mandala, marched for CND and led protests against the Vietnam War. His political conversion is presented as a betrayal of idealism. As Ruby Fox, aka superheroine Voltage, tells Zenith: 'More than any of us, he represented a whole generation of people who believed that peace and love could save the world. And now he's Mrs Thatcher's golden boy.'[57] Zenith teams with St John to defeat the Cult of the Black Sun, who have revived a Nazi fighting champion known as Masterman. St John uses the incident to advance his political career. The veteran Labour MP Tam Dalyell describes it as 'the most shameful piece of Tory propaganda since the Falklands War'.[58]

'Zenith' is notable for its topicality and satirical tone. In 'Zenith: Phase II' bearded tycoon Scott Wallace (clearly modelled on Richard Branson) hijacks a Polaris submarine and targets its missiles on London. Zenith talks him out of it by explaining that world domination would be more trouble than it is worth: 'All that crime and starvation and wars and drugs. Everyone would expect you to have all the answers. And what would you do about unemployment? . . . Why do you think superhumans have never tried to take over the world? I'll bet we could. Thing is nobody wants the hassle.'[59] The contrast with Miracleman's Olympian feats could not be more stark. 'Zenith: Phase III' is a parody of the superhero team-up narrative – a familiar convention of American comics – in which Zenith joins a group of self-styled 'anarchist superhumans' from alternate dimensions who unite to fight the Dark Gods of Lloigor who wish to bring order to all universes when a rare cosmic event brings them into alignment. They prove to be possibly the least effective superhero team in comic history and spend much of the time bickering among themselves.

The tradition of idosyncratic British superheroes is nowhere better exemplified than in the case of Jack Staff. Written and drawn by Paul Grist, Jack Staff is uniquely, defiantly and eccentrically British. Grist, like Denis Gifford, began creating his own comics as a child, graduated to drawing girls' comics for D. C. Thomson and then ventured into self-publishing in the early 1990s with *Kane*, a hardboiled detective comic influenced by the television series *Hill Street Blues*. Jack Staff originated from an idea that he had suggested to Marvel:

> *Jack Staff* came out of an idea that I had for a series featuring the Marvel character Union Jack. Marvel never got back to me on that one, but the more I thought about it the more it appealed to me. Then it occurred to me that there was nothing stopping me

from doing it myself. *Jack Staff* is my take on the British Super-Hero. There have been quite a few characters published in British comics over the years who, with a little squeezing, could be classified as British Super-Heroes. All I'm doing is a little squeezing.[60]

Grist self-published twelve issues of *Jack Staff* between 2000 and 2003, whereupon the series was adopted by the Californian-based collective Image Comics and switched to colour. Grist claimed that he had always wanted to produce it in colour but did not have the resources to do so: 'In my mind, *Jack Staff* was not a black and white comic with occasional colour, it was a colour comic with a lot of black and white.'[61]

Jack Staff is a distinctively British variation on the superhero formula infused with a quirky sense of humour. It is the comic-book equivalent of an Ealing comedy or television series such as *The League of Gentlemen* and *Little Britain*. Its setting is not some sprawling US metropolis but rather Castletown in Yorkshire (Grist was born in Sheffield) and its hero is no musclebound WASP but a spindly-limbed jack-in-the-box whose strength is derived from his special staff. Grist's artwork is spare and minimalist: he favours disjointed panels, angular characters and heavy inking. Again this serves to differentiate *Jack Staff* from the style of many US comics, which recently have tended towards a certain visual uniformity of realistically proportioned figures and naturalistic backgrounds. Above all, perhaps, *Jack Staff* is refreshingly free from superhero angst. Grist's world is populated by eccentrics who take the extraordinary and the supernatural in their stride. These include Becky Burdock the 'Vampire Reporter', old school copper Inspector Maveryk and a trio of detectives from the Question Mark Crime Investigation Group known as 'Q'. A review in the *Comics Reporter* described *Jack Staff* as 'a delight . . . written with an inventive wit and zest for adventure'.[62]

Jack Staff is a multi-linear narrative that alternates between past and present. We are first introduced to Jack Staff ('Britain's Greatest Hero') in 1940 when he is one member of a superhero team who rescue victims of the Blitz trapped in bombed-out houses. In one rescue they discover a vast cave beneath Castletown and awake the vampire Templar Richard: the vampire is destroyed but not before American superhero Sergeant States becomes a victim. In the present reporter Becky Burdock uncovers the secret identity of the long-forgotten and ageless Jack Staff as a builder called John Smith. A series of gruesome killings indicate the return of the 'Castletown Vampire'. The culprit turns out to be Sergeant States, returning on a good will tour, whose vampirism has been concealed by the US authorities. Sergeant States is defeated by Jack Staff and Tom Tom the Robot Man, who exposes him to sunlight.

Jack Staff is a celebration of a particular kind of British national identity. It takes an obvious delight in picturing Britain as parochial and eccentric in contrast to the global superpower of America. It belongs to a lineage of cultural representations of Britishness that privileges amateurism and eccentricity. It exemplifies the British tradition of 'muddling through': Jack succeeds as much through his pluck and perseverance as through any latent superhero abilities. He has a straightforward solution to most problems: 'If all else fails, hit it with a big stick.' The Britishness of *Jack Staff* is further enhanced by the range of cultural references it invokes. In particular it draws upon classic British television sitcoms, including *Dad's Army*, whose geriatric Home Guard platoon turn up here as members of the crack military Unit D, and *Steptoe & Son*, whose stars Wilfrid Brambell and Harry H. Corbett are cast as an unlikely pair of vampire hunters known as Bramble & Son. These and other references assume a degree of cultural knowledge on the part of the reader: to this extent *Jack Staff* is no less demanding than the more cerebral work of Gaiman and Moore.

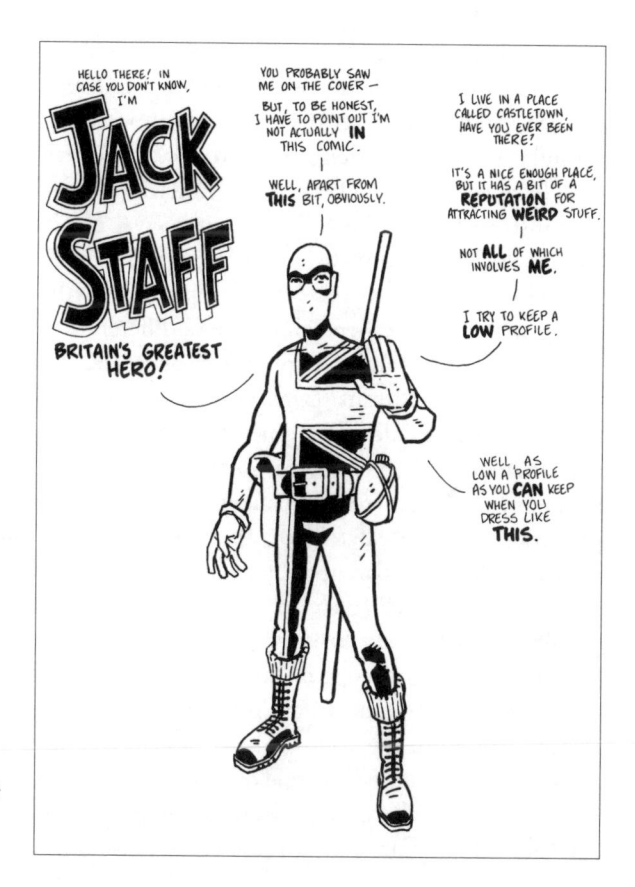

The Weird World of Jack Staff (Image Comics Inc., 2007).

Jack Staff is also a celebration of the golden age of British comics. Grist, born 1960, was influenced by the comics he read as a child: 'My intention was to try and create a serial something along the lines of that which used to run in the likes of *Lion* and *Valiant*, the British boys comics of my childhood, and which, in their own way, form the background for *Jack Staff*.'[63] There are references to other comic characters who appear either as surrogates or in person. Thus Victorian escapologist Charles Raven is based on Janus Stark and Tom Tom the Robot Man on *Lion*'s Robot Archie. The Spider, now an elderly retired gentleman thief, appears in the guise of A. Chinard – an anagram of 'Arachnid'. The Valiant Stone, a magic crystal which saves the life of Q agent Helen Morgan, is inspired by the Eye of Zoltec from the *Valiant* strip 'Kelly's Eye'. Most spectacularly of all, however, Grist resurrects Captain Hurricane in the form of Captain Gust, whose strength, it is revealed, is the outcome of a top-secret military programme known as 'Project H' to develop 'an ultimate weapon . . . a weapon of mass destruction'.[64] Unlike Alan Moore, however, whose *Albion* uses many of the same characters to explore the ideologies of the comics in which they appeared, Grist's aim seems not to be to deconstruct the genre but rather to celebrate its imagination and diversity.

The most appealing British superheroes have been those, like Zenith and Jack Staff, who differ from the conventions of the American superhero formula. In contrast attempts to produce an American-style British superhero have generally resulted in pale imitations of DC and Marvel. This was demonstrated yet again by the latest revival of Captain Britain, *Captain Britain and MI13* (2008–9), which, despite a British writer in Paul Cornell, was very much part of the Marvel superhero mythos. Cornell represents a new generation of writers who traverse different media including prose fiction, television and audio drama as well as comics: he has written *Doctor Who* stories in all those forms. *Captain Britain and MI13* is a superhero team-up narrative: Brian Braddock is joined by Arthurian throwback the Black Knight and aristocratic lady-vampire Spitfire who all now work for the British government's superhero department MI13. They are joined later by the blaxploitation vampire killer Blade, though he seems an incongruous presence amidst all the Arthurian mythology: it is difficult to avoid the conclusion that he has been inserted solely to appeal to American readers. Herein lies the problem with *Captain Britain and MI13*: it is too closely tied to the Marvel universe to offer the scope for much originality or cultural distinctiveness.

Cornell's Captain Britain is very different from the Alan Moore-Jamie Delano version of the 1980s. Their Captain Britain had been distrustful of authority and preferred the role of loner. He had resisted attempts to present him as a national figurehead and maintained his distance from official agencies. This Captain Britain, however, relishes his role as national champion: Brian Braddock even appears without his mask so his identity is revealed to the world. The new Captain Britain is an organization man, co-opted, it seems voluntarily, into the service of the state. He leads a team of heroes 'together because they want to be. Who are friends, who support each other . . . But who'll be supported by the intelligence services, and fit into their command structure.'[65] There is none of the anxiety around the relationship of the superhero to state and society that had characterized *Miracleman*, for example.

The launch of *Captain Britain and MI13* excited an amount of media interest due to the appearance in the first issue of Prime Minister Gordon Brown, who is cast in Churchillian mould organizing the defence of the nation against invasion by shape-shifting aliens known as Skrulls and who declares that 'we have a responsibility to the world'.[66] It would seem that his appearance in the comic boosted Brown's self-image: some months later he infamously referred to 'saving the world' while defending his handling of the economic crisis during Prime Minister's Questions.[67] 'The Guns of Avalon' – itself part of the 'Secret Invasion' narrative that ran across all Marvel's titles in 2007–8 – invoked the myth of the Second World War as Britain resists heroically against the alien invasion. Two more story arcs followed – 'Hell Comes to Birmingham' and 'Vampire State' – before *Captain Britain and MI13* was axed after fifteen issues. Yet again 'Britain's greatest superhero' had come up against the most implacable enemy of all: the law of the market.

CHAPTER EIGHT

The Rise and Fall of Alternative Comics

> I was a huge fan of the American underground artists, Crumb especially. And yes, the spirit of the time swept me along. These comics were radical and experimental. They were also hyper cool – drawing an underground comic book was the next best thing to playing lead guitar in a rock band.
> Bryan Talbot.[1]

Underground comics – generally known as 'comix' after R. Crumb's *Zap Comix*, which he sold from a pram in San Francisco's Haight-Ashbury district – emerged in the United States in the late 1960s. Comix were closely identified with the countercultural movements of the time: they were independently published without the seal of the Comics Code Authority and were sold in 'head shops' (small businesses selling hippie paraphernalia) rather than on newsstands. They were characterized by their adult content, particularly recreational drug use and sexual permissiveness, and for their irreverent and anti-establishment tone. To this extent they can be aligned with satirical publications such as *Mad* magazine and *Harvard Lampoon*. The first comix were small, self-published titles not intended for widespread distribution, but the success of *Zap*, which was reprinted and sold in the thousands, and the establishment of specialist publishers such as the San Francisco Comic Book Company and a distributor in the form of the Underground Press Syndicate, saw them become a nationwide cult.[2]

Comix drew upon a wide range of influences, from the 'Tijuana Bibles' of the 1930s – the name given to a series of anonymous, sexually explicit underground picture books – and the EC horror comics of the 1950s to the Pop Art movement of the 1960s with its emphasis on consumerism and mass culture. They were characterized by a combination of political and social protest, typically expressed through opposition to the Nixon Administration and the Vietnam War; by their embracing of the hippie subculture, exemplified in their advocacy of illegal drugs, particularly marijuana; and by their explicit content, especially in relation to sexuality. They were 'underground' in the sense that they ignored the Comics Code – indeed their content can be seen as a celebration of everything that the Code forbade – which meant that mainstream distributors would not touch them. Comix were radical in the sense that they challenged conventional social and moral values, though on the whole they did so through recognizable genres and forms. They ranged from funnies such as Crumb's *Fritz the Cat* and Gilbert Shelton's *The Fabulous Furry Freak Brothers* to savage parodies such as Mañuel 'Spain' Rodriguez's *Trashman*, an anarchist urban guerrilla, and the sado-masochistic sex-and-violence fantasies of S. Clay Wilson. For all their radical content, however, comix were still highly commercial: they should be seen as one of the 'uninhibited examples of private enterprise' that Arthur Marwick has argued was a characteristic of the counterculture.[3]

Underground comics were at the height of their popularity between 1968 and 1973 when new titles proliferated: *Zap Comix, Big Ass Funnies, Bijou Funnies, Subvert Comics, Young Lust, Bizarre Sex, Wimmen's Comix* and *Tits'n'Clits* were among the most popular. In the early 1970s there was a particular vogue for horror comix, including *Skull, Bogeyman, Death Rattle* and *Deviant Slice*. Their growth was made possible by the availability of inexpensive offset lithography printing (a process that did not require metal printing blocks) and was stimulated by growing opposition to the Nixon regime. By the mid-1970s, however, there were signs of a conservative reaction as many head shops were closed down under anti-drugs laws. In 1973 the US Supreme Court ruled that local authorities could decide their own standards of obscenity: *Zap* was ruled obscene in New York State, and *Air Pirates Funnies* was sued by Walt Disney for showing Mickey Mouse indulging in sex and drug-taking.[4]

Underground comics spread to Britain in the early 1970s, first through reprints of US strips and then through home-grown comix. The first British comix grew out of two contexts. One was the underground press. *IT* (*International Times*) and *Oz* represented the voice of the counterculture in Britain: both published the work of American underground artists. It was a cartoon by Crumb that prompted the first major test of the obscenity law in Britain since *Lady Chatterley's Lover*. In 1971 the editors of *Oz* were prosecuted for publishing a collage in which the head of Rupert the Bear was pasted onto Crumb's sexually explicit 'Gypsy Granny'. It has been argued that the real issue at stake in the *Oz* trial was not obscenity but rather the anti-establishment politics of the underground press. As Jonathon Green puts it: 'The Establishment did not like *Oz* or the counter-culture it represented; they had tolerated it for so long, but when [*Oz* editor Richard] Neville naïvely, injudiciously combined "children" with the usual irritants of drugs and sex and rock, they saw their chance.'[5] Furthermore, as had been the case in the horror comics campaign of the 1950s, anti-American prejudice may also have played a part: comix were an American import. The '*Oz* three' were convicted and imprisoned, only for the verdict to be overturned on appeal – an example of the 'measured judgement' that Marwick identifies in establishment responses to the counterculture.[6]

The first British comix were off-shoots of the underground press, which saw them as a response to declining sales in the early 1970s. *IT* sponsored *Cyclops* (1970), which ran for four issues, and *Nasty Tales* (1971–2), which lasted for seven issues until it, too, was charged with obscenity. (The offending item on this occasion was Crumb's 'Grand Opening of the Intercontinental Fuck-In and Orgy Riot'. The verdict this time was not guilty; the comic responded with a one-off satirizing the whole affair called *The Trials of Nasty Tales*.) *Oz*, for its part, launched *Cozmic Comics* in 1972 – 'the longest running, best distributed and probably best known underground comics of the 1970s' according to David Huxley.[7] *Cozmic Comics* was originally a mixture of reprinted American strips and new material by emerging British artists, including Edward Barker, Brian Bolland, Dave Gibbons, Malcolm Livingstone and Chris Welch. As well as the six issues of *Cozmic Comics* itself, there were a dozen or so anthologies under the same imprint – including *Zip Comics*, *View from the Void*, *Half Assed Funnies*, *Animal Weirdness* and *Dope Fiend Funnies* – and a number of one-off single creator titles by British artists: Edward Barker's *Edward's Heave*, Mike Weller's *The Firm*, Chris Welch's *Ogoth and Ugly Boot* and Joe Petagno's *It's Only Rock'n'Roll Comix*.[8]

The other context for the emergence of British comix was the network of experimental arts labs, modelled on the original Arts Lab in Covent Garden, that flourished in the early 1970s. The Birmingham Arts Lab, for example, published Hunt Emerson's early solo efforts *Large Cow Comix*, *The Adventures of Mr Spoonbiscuit* and *Zomik Comix*. This initiative culminated in the anthology title *Streetcomix* (1976–8). It is highly ironic that these underground titles were partially subsidized by the Arts Council of Great Britain! Alan Moore published some of his early cartoons and poems in xeroxed magazines produced by the Northampton Arts Lab. As he told George Khoury: 'The Arts Lab was great. It was like a spontaneous kind of multimedia group where we decided that we were going to put on some performance, or we were going to put out a magazine, some event or whatever, and then we all just worked toward it doing whatever we felt like doing.'[9]

Like their American counterparts, British comix were products of the counterculture. They demonstrated an irreverence towards authority, a permissive attitude towards sex and a tolerance for alternative lifestyles. Many

Antonio Ghura's *The Laid-Back Adventures of Suzie and Jonnie* reveals the permissive attitude towards sex and drugs in alternative 'comix' (1981).

openly embraced drug-taking, especially 'hash' and LSD. *Brainstorm Comix* (1975–6) was a paean to psychedelia: its first cover promised a 'Journey into Delirium'. Its flagship was Bryan Talbot's surreal 'Chester P. Hackenbush, Psychedelic Alchemist', which has been understood as a reflection of the hippie zeitgeist due to the sheer quantity of mind-altering substances consumed by its eponymous protagonist. The strip draws upon a range of cultural references from the films of the Marx Brothers (Groucho's character in *A Day the Races* is Hugo Z. Hackenbush) to Lewis Carroll's *Alice's Adventures in Wonderland* and The Beatles' alleged LSD-influenced 'Lucy in the Sky with

Diamonds'. Talbot himself described it as 'pure Alice in Wonderland. At the beginning of a story Hackenbush would go on a trip, and at the end he'd come down.'[10]

In a similar vein Antonio Ghura's *The Laid-Back Adventures of Suzie and Jonnie* (1981) features a middle-aged hippie and his young girlfriend whose lives revolve entirely around sex and drugs. In one story they are persuaded to smuggle a shipment of hashish from Morocco, which involves them in a series of comic misadventures. (It is also the occasion for some gratuitous stereotypes of corrupt officials and Arab bandits that would not have seemed out of place in *Carry On Follow That Camel*: for all their radical politics, underground comix were just as prone to stereotyping as their mainstream counterparts.) The strip includes what amounts to a do-it-yourself guide to manufacturing hash from harvesting cannabis plants to processing the oil. Drug-use is presented as a harmless activity with no social consequences. It also enhances sexual pleasure. At one point the two engage in

Ogoth and Ugly Boot (H. Bunch Associates, 1973).

intercourse on a bed of hash resin: 'Tell me, Suzie, have you ever screwed lying on a couple [of] hundred weights?'[11]

The counterculture itself was also the target of satire. Chris Welch's *Ogoth and Ugly Boot* (1973) follows the adventures of two Hell's Angels in a postapocalyptic future London where social order has collapsed and rival gangs of 'coons' and 'faggots' battle for control. It is a satire of the tribalism within the counterculture and the hostility between different groups. The story is based on the premise that a nerve agent developed by the Israelis and released following an attack by the Palestinian Liberation Front has 'proliferated beyond expectation to the extent that almost the entire human race suffered massive and prolonged psychedelic experiences'. Ninety per cent of the population is 'either dead or mindless', while the only survivors are 'those already experienced in the use of psychedelics'.[12]

Two of the major concerns of the counterculture – the liberalization of drug laws and harassment by the police – are recurring themes of the British underground. *Cozmic Comics* actively promoted the decriminalization of soft drugs. In 1973 it published a spoof of public information films entitled 'Parental Drug Abuse: What Every Child Should Know'. The twist is that it is children who are being warned of the tell-tale signs of drug-taking by adults ('Most responsible children are familiar with the much publicized trend toward parental drug abuse and addiction, but in too many cases not enough is known to enable children to spot their own grownups part in these tragic habits') and that all the drugs in question (caffeine, tobacco, tranquilizers, alcohol) are in fact legal.[13] And in 1974 *Dope Fiend Funnies* included 'How to Spot a Dope Fiend', explaining that an addict can be identified by 'long matted hair, unshaven face, dazed expression, dirty feet, sandals and Ban the Bomb badges, usually carrying copies of "underground literature", e.g. *International Times, Oz, The Guardian.*'[14]

The institution that British comix disliked most was the police. The police (often drawn as pigs) are caricatured either as buffoons or as thugs whose role in society is to oppress the counterculture. The cover of *Zip Comics*, for example, shows goose-stepping policemen confiscating comics from a long-haired youth while declaring: 'Achtung decadent hippies . . . Laughter is against the law! No more laffink undt no more geshtunkener funny books!'[15] (This appeared shortly after the Obscene Publications Squad had raided the offices of *Nasty Tales.*) And *Edward's Heave* featured a recruiting advertisement for 'a disgruntled viscious [sic] malconent' to join 'The Mets'.[16] Jonnie the hippie frequently found himself the victim of police persecution. One episode of *The Laid-Back Adventures of Suzie and Jonnie* features a gang of ape-like policemen beating up hippies ('Longhaired faggots!') with one urging his colleague to 'Give him the ol' Blair Peach special'.

Zip Comics (H. Bunch Associates, 1973).

This was a reference to the death of a protestor at a demonstration in Southall during the general election campaign in 1979 that was blamed on members of the Metropolitan Police Special Patrol Group.

British comix offered their readers a mixture of social commentary, satire and sex. Mike Weller's *The Firm* exposed the casual sexism and racism of the workplace with its pre-David Brent caricature of the boss from hell. J. C. Moody's 'Holy Joe Funnies' (*Cozmic Comics*) satirized television evangelists such as the controversial American preacher Billy Graham. The excesses of rock'n'roll behaviour were a frequent target, including Greg Irons's *Rock'n'Roll Madness* and Geoff Rowley and Chris Welch's '2002: A Rock Oddity' (*Streetcomix*). A favourite device was to subvert classic cartoons and comics through the insertion of more explicit content. Malcolm Livingstone's 'Lil' Red Rider' (*Cozmic Comics*) parodies the style of Tex Avery's cartoons for MGM. It features a drooling Big Wolf fondling Red's breasts and concludes with an implied act of bestiality as a passing woodcutter 'looked thro' the open door and had to wait his turn'.[17] Even Denis Gifford's *Ally Sloper* – a newsstand comic that combined nostalgic tributes to the golden age of British comics with material by underground creators – got in on the act. Gifford drew a strip entitled 'T.V. Filth', a spoof of The Sex Pistols' notoriously foul-mouthed appearance on *The Bill Grundy Show*. Grundy welcomes back 'our old pals the Sex Pistols', remains urbanely unperturbed by their constant swearing and gleefully tells Johnny Rotten to 'eff off'.[18] With his accurate spoof of the style of traditional British humour comics, Gifford anticipated *Viz* by nearly three years.

While British comix rarely demonstrated the pornographic extremes of some of their American counterparts, they nevertheless exhibited some of the same misogyny. The humour is often crude and women are usually its butt. There was a peculiar vogue for cartoons of male 'flashers' such as 'Charles Flaccid – The Phantom Flasher' (*Zip Comics*) and 'Whip It Out Yet Again' (*Edward's Heave*), while 'The World Breast Boxing Championships' (*Edward's Heave*) was a lame satire of the craze for televised wrestling in the 1970s. These strips, and many others in a similar vein, can be seen as cruder versions of the slapstick of television programmes like *The Benny Hill Show*. They exemplify what Leon Hunt, in his study of British low culture of the 1970s, describes as 'permissive populism': the permeation of the values of the permissive society into residual forms of popular culture.[19]

Yet comix were not all about flashers or women having bananas thrust up their anus. Some artists were interested in exploring the formal properties and story-telling conventions of the comic-strip medium rather than indulging in bad taste simply for the sake of it. This is best demonstrated by *Streetcomix*, which largely eschewed the vulgar humour of the *Cozmic* line in favour of more experimental and self-reflexive work by artists such as Kevin O'Neill, Steve Bell and Suzy Varty (one of the few female comix artists). In particular *Streetcomix* provided a showcase for the distinctive talents of Hunt Emerson, whose delightful, if bizarre, funnies combined the anthropomorphic surrealism of the American underground artists with the anarchic energy of British children's comics such as *Beano* and *Dandy*. Shaun Johnson's 'The Man Who Was Stuck in a Comic' is an existentialist meditation featuring an ordinary man who thinks he is the hero of a comic strip but is unable to reconcile this with his mundane everyday life: 'OK, so I'm a comic-strip hero, but, I mean, where's the punchline? This fuckin' comic doesn't even have a plot. It just drags on, panel after panel.'[20] And Bryan Talbot's 'Komix Comics' – a satire of the production and marketing of underground comix – can be seen as a precursor to Scott McCloud's self-reflexive *Understanding Comics* (1993) as an exploration of the medium told in comic-strip form.[21]

Roger Sabin contends that the British underground comix movement was 'a vibrant complement to its American counterpart' and 'represented both an alternative to the comics establishment and a ribald satirical challenge to the political and cultural status quo'.[22] It is difficult to estimate the size of the underground market. *Brainstorm Comix* is reckoned to have been the most successful, with sales of around 12,000, though this was still insufficient to sustain it beyond six issues.[23] There was enough interest in the underground scene, however, for two 'Konventions of Alternative Komix' (KAKs) to be held in Birmingham in 1976 and 1977. Perhaps the most significant outcome of the British underground, though, was not so much the content of the comix themselves but the possibility they suggested for an alternative method of production. Most comix were co-operatively owned, and allowed creators to maintain copyright in their work and even to receive a royalty on sales. The issue of creators' rights and royalties would gain momentum over the next decade, influencing the editorial policies of mainstream titles such as *Warrior*, *Crisis*, *Deadline* and *Revolver*.

All that said, the historical moment of the British underground was brief. There are several reasons for its decline from the mid-1970s. One is that the moral and legal backlash had impacted upon them: *Nasty Tales* had been acquitted of obscenity but still published only one more issue before it folded. Other comix creators and publishers, either consciously or unconsciously, toned down their content in the wake of the obscenity trials. Another reason is that many comix creators were not sufficiently business-minded to exploit their work fully. In particular they neglected the distribution side of the business. A revealing fact is that the Birmingham Arts Lab would print 10,000 copies of *Streetcomix* but that only 2,000 would be sold. Hunt Emerson put his finger on the problem when he told David Huxley:

> We weren't into distribution. We were into producing the things. We were hopeless – we were involved with a distribution co-op towards the end of our existence... and we had a lot of problems with them because they didn't like what we did, basically. We never got the distribution together at all.[24]

More generally, like all genres closely associated with a particular cultural movement, comix were vulnerable to social and cultural change, which in the 1970s was rapid and in constant flux. The end of the Vietnam War, which had provided a focal point for protest movements, was a watershed for the counterculture which never found another such potent cause. And in the late 1970s a new, anarchic, violently oppositional subculture exploded onto the scene: punk. Punk was spontaneous, aggressive and emphasized working-class 'street cred' rather than the laid-back hedonistic idealism of the hippie movement. And its favoured mode of expression was not comics but music, particularly heavy metal.

* * *

The decline of the underground overlapped with the emergence of a new type of alternative comic that was a product of the burgeoning fan culture. The late 1970s and early 1980s saw a proliferation of independent small press comics in Britain – a genre that came to be known as 'Fast Fiction'. The context for much 'Fast Fiction' was the growth of the comics fan culture, particularly the emergence of a specialized fan press ('fanzines'). There was a significant cross-over between the fan cultures for music and for comics. Most early fanzines were very basic, consisting of little more than xeroxed sheets of reviews and commentary that had expanded from mail-order lists, but titles such as *Fantasy Advertiser, Comic Media News,* BEM (*Bug-Eyed Magazine*) and *Speakeasy* marked the origins of what would in time become the specialist comic press. The rise of organized fandom coincided with the opening of specialist shops including Nostalgia Comics in Birmingham (1977) and Forbidden Planet in London (1978). The growth of fandom allowed small publishers to bypass conventional distribution by selling direct to their readers.

The emergence of small press comics was made possible by access to new production technologies. The advent of photocopy shops enabled the production of copies quickly and at low cost. There was also a sense of immediacy to the process. As Eddie Campbell, one of the foremost new talents to emerge from the small press, put it in 1983: 'This is what I like about the current situation . . . Not for me the old style of leaving the job with a printer for two weeks and crossing fingers. Making the books has become an immediate physical process.'[25] Most small press comics were xeroxed A4 pages folded in half to A5 and stapled together. Accordingly their style was to a very large degree technologically determined, as this method of production favoured clear-line drawing without washes or shading. However, it also meant they could experiment with uncommercial material. Small press comics were produced by and for enthusiasts: they were not expected to make money (and for the most part did not). Lew Stringer, one of the most prolific small press artists, characterized them as 'amateur, non-profit comics produced by people who (usually) were not yet ready for professional work but who wanted to test their creative muscles and receive feedback'.[26] *Silicon Fish*, for example, was produced to showcase the work of students at the Portobello Projects Comic Workshop, a voluntary organization set up in 1984 (David Lloyd was the first tutor) which 'positively bloomed with an air of optimism from the young artists involved.'[27]

The rise of small press comics saw the emergence of alternative forms of distribution. They were sold at comic 'marts', in record shops and through mail order via classified ads in fanzines such as *Fantasy Advertiser*. Print runs were small: Gerald Midgley, who founded *The Alternative Headmaster's Bulletin* in 1979, claimed that its sales of 250 copies was 'the biggest first issue ever of a small-press comic'.[28] Andrew Muir printed only 50 A4 copies of the first issue of *Zero Order* in 1984 but reprinted it 'umpteen' times reduced to A5 'to keep the price reasonable'.[29] In 1980 Paul Gravett set up his 'Fast Fiction' stall at the Westminster Comics Mart which became the unofficial hub of the alternative comics scene in London and led to the establishment of a mail order service, newsletter and anthology of the same title. *Fast Fiction* published the work of, among others, Eddie Campbell, Phil Elliott, Ed Pinsent and Ian Wieczorek, and gave a name to this new wave of comic publishing.

While there was some continuity with the underground comix of the 1970s – creators such as Hunt Emerson were common to both movements – the small press comics were rather different in form and content. They eschewed the psychedelic trappings and LSD-influenced 'trips' of the underground in favour of a more personal and low-key style. The humour strips were zany rather than vulgar – examples included Lew Stringer's hapless costumed crime-fighter 'Brickman' and John Jackson's James Bond spoof 'Agent Adam x3' – while the more socially realistic strips treated sex within the context of relationships rather than as spectacle for its own sake. 'Fast Fiction' was also influenced by imported comics, particularly *Love and Rockets* by the Mexican-American brothers Jaime and Gilbert Hernandez, whose stories were notable for their empathetic writing, especially regarding women and ethnic minorities, and which first appeared in Britain in the early 1980s.

Many artists used the medium as a form of social observation. The best examples are the work of Eddie Campbell and Myra Hancock. Campbell's strips 'Booboo' and 'Georgette' document the everyday lives of ordinary young people: episodes are built around going to the pub or chatting on the phone. 'Alec' is a semi-autobiographical strip that records friendships, lovers and incidental events in the life of a bedsit philosopher: it is particularly notable for its wry observation of social behaviour and the fleeting nature of friendship. Hancock's 'Sharon & Maureen' features two flat-sharing punkettes whose lives revolve around drinking vodka, cat fights and trying to pull men in nightclubs. The works of Campbell and Hancock are rites of passage dramas for older teenagers and young adults – the assumed readership for these comics. Hancock's *Myra*, for example, which she sold on Camden Lock Market, advertised itself as being 'for femmes with vigour and boys with a hint of machismo'.[30]

'A Tale from Gimbley', *Fast Fiction* (September 1985).

Other 'Fast Fiction' creators were more inclined towards whimsy. Phil Elliott's 'Tales from Gimbley' are a series of reminiscences by the eponymous Gimbley ranging from the ordinary to the absurd. Over the course of the series, which appeared first in *Fast Fiction* and then in *Escape*, Elliott's style developed from rough sketches to a clear line form reminiscent of European artists. Ed Pinsent specialized in bizarre fairytales such as 'Mysterioso' and 'Henrietta' characterized by their nonsensical stories. Pinsent's 'The Adventures of Windy Wilberforce' and 'Geoffrey Unsworth and His Dog' have been seen as visual equivalents of the nonsense verse of Edward Lear.[31] He also created 'Primitif', about an ancient warrior's battles with gods and nature, drawn in a stylized pastiche of cave paintings.

It would be fair to say that the quality of artwork and the originality of ideas in these comics were variable, to say the least, though the best of them possessed a certain rough and ready charm. What they lacked in professional production values they more than made up for in energy and enthusiasm. Some small presses even made a virtue of their own limitations and amateurish production in order to assert their difference from professionally produced comics. *Weird Fun*, for example, advertised itself as an 'amazing, overpriced, undersexed, thrill-filled spectacular piece of junk, just for you, the discerning consumer!!'[32] They would also parody mainstream comics. *Captain Crab's Tales of Horrific Terror* ('Not for sale to Dr Frederick [*sic*] Wertham') was a crudely drawn though accurate spoof of EC horror comics that promised its readers 'tales of hideous corpses, screaming virgins, crawling flesh, and a recipe for almond and raisin cake using only two to three ounces of sugared almonds'.[33]

The nature of independent publishing – cheaply produced, not for profit and therefore not dependent on sales or advertising – meant that small press comics were more able to take risks than mainstream titles. They often featured subversive parodies of popular culture. *Weird Fun*, for example, turned the cartoon character Wile E. Coyote into a gun-toting Red Brigade revolutionary ('Fuck yew copper') and featured a cruel parody of the sitcom *On the Buses* in which the unpopular inspector Blakey is crucified in front of a No. 72 bus. This was a more extreme example of the satirical popular culture references in *2000AD*, but small press comics were so far under the critical radar that they evidently did not fear lawsuits.

For some creators, small press comics provided an opportunity to address issues that the mainstream media largely avoided. Crispin Green's 'Hey Whitey!', for example, which appeared in *Fast Fiction* in 1985, satirized the homophobic nature of black street culture in its panels of young black males – provocatively drawn to resemble the 'gollywog' stereotype – taunting a homosexual white man cruising their neighbourhood. The captions are in rhyming couplets: 'Hey, Whitey, walkin' down the street / You and my black ass will never meet! Hey, Whitey, you nigger lovin' boy / You ain't gonna share my black assed joy! Hey, Whitey, just cos you's queer / Doesn't mean the black man gonna kiss your ear! Hey, Whitey, why you so 'fraid / Of lovin' the white boys who've got ass to trade.'[34] This provocative mix of racism, homosexuality and male prostitution demonstrates that comics were prepared to confront head-on some of the social issues that even in the 1980s remained taboo in the mass media.

Escape, an anthology title created by Paul Gravett and Peter Stanbury in 1983, was an attempt to provide a wider audience for small press artists. It published the work of creators who had started out producing their own comics, including Glenn Dakin, Phil Elliott, Myra Hancock, Phil Laskey, Ed Pinsent and Edwin Pouncey (better known under his pen name of 'Savage Pencil'). *Escape* was, essentially, a more professionally produced version of the *Fast Fiction* anthology, which Gravett had relinquished to Phil Elliott and Ian Wieczorek. But *Escape*, which advertised itself as a 'comics magazine of style and vision', was also inspired, partly at least, by the American avant-garde

Weird Fun was an example of the small press comics of the early 1980s known as 'Fast Fiction' (1985).

anthology *Raw*, edited by Art Spiegelman and Françoise Mouly, which adopted the slogan 'the graphix magazine for damned intellectuals'. Indeed, *Escape* also featured the work of contemporary European artists, including Javier Mariscal, Joost Swarte and Jacques Tardi, who had also been published in *Raw*.

Escape was nothing if not diverse in its content. It ranged from autobiographical stories such as Jonathan Bagnall's 'Punk Memories' to experimental strips such as 'Johnny Tomorrow' (a superhero story printed in 3D credited to 'Shaky Kane' – pen name of Michael Coulthard). It provided an early outlet for Rian Hughes, whose 'Norm' is a lonely, existential cartoon philosopher. *Escape* also published work by former underground artists, notably Hunt Emerson, whose 'Calculus Cat' is one of his most sublime creations. 'Calculus Cat' is a bad-tempered, manic depressive cartoon cat who is driven to distraction (often violently so) by his television, which bombards him with advertisements and inane light entertainment. Emerson subverts the conventions of cartoon favourites such as George Herriman's 'Krazy Kat' and the *Dandy*'s 'Korky the Cat' to create a character whose smiling public persona conceals his grumpy true self.

Escape was committed to promoting the idea of comics as 'a vital form of personal expression'. It took its inspiration from France, and coined the term 'United Kingdom Bande Dessinée', or 'UKBD', promising 'Story-Strips presenting UKBD artists and writers to an International audience. New British Strips, New British Styles.'[35] Its second issue declared:

> *Escape* is a Story-Strip Magazine. Today's *Escape* Artists, in this issue and the new ones in issues to come, are in general young and in their early stages of story-telling. We're interested in their drawing, but not for its own sake, rather for its narrative qualities. And their stories don't always have to be conventional with a beginning, middle and end. We're keen to encourage their own ideas, individual and inspired. We don't need any more impersonators of the American mainstream giants of the last twenty years – there are too many of those already and their massive output has inundated Britain. For comics to have a future here – as they already have in Europe and elsewhere – the people drawing them must bring in new ideas and influences to draw about.[36]

This was perhaps the nearest thing to a manifesto for 'Fast Fiction', which was committed to the notion that comic strips were an art form in their own right and that comic artists should not be constrained by formulae and conventions.

The grumpy 'Calculus Cat' is perhaps Hunt Emerson's most sublime creation. *Escape* (Escape Publishing, 1983).

Escape was an undoubted landmark for British alternative comics. Dave Roach, for example, feels that 'its sheer diversity and quality have yet to be surpassed'.[37] And for Roger Sabin it was 'the most progressive British comic to be seen since the underground'.[38] It lasted from 1983 until 1990, growing from A5 to a larger glossy magazine format and even finding a degree of high-street distribution. It developed from a comic into an independent publisher, also producing a number of stand-alone graphic novels. These included Phil Laskey's *Night of the Busted Nose* (1984), an account of life in a rough northern town; Dave Thorpe and Phil Elliott's delirious political thriller *Doc Chaos* (1985); and Neil Gaiman and Dave McKeen's *Violent Cases* (1988), a disturbing reflection on childhood and memory. *Escape* should be seen as a genuine attempt both to promote an indigenous British comics culture and to raise the cultural status of comics to the same level they enjoyed in Europe. That it never reached the readership it deserved was due in large measure to the prevalent view of most high-street retailers that comics were essentially a medium for children and who declined to stock alternative publications. As *Escape* itself observed in one editorial: 'If you must point the finger anywhere, it should be at the unimaginative publishers and retailers in this country who fail to appreciate the potential of strip magazines for wider audiences.'[39]

* * *

There was one alternative comic, however, that did succeed in reaching a mass audience. *Viz* is the undoubted success story of the alternative comics scene in Britain: what started out as a small press comic for a local readership, with bargain-basement production values and a print run of 150, grew to a national institution that at one point had sales in excess of 1 million and was one of the best-selling magazines (let alone comics) in Britain. It did so, however, not through the sophisticated story-telling or philosophical reflection that had characterized *Escape* but rather through a combination of toilet humour and bawdy satire.

The origin of *Viz* is to be found not in the rise of comic fandom – Chris Donald, the founder of *Viz*, has said that the only comics he read as a child were the Tintin books[40] – but rather in the alternative music scene in the north-east of England in the late 1970s. *Viz* was originally conceived as a music fanzine focusing on the Newcastle-based independent record label Anti-Pop and its two principal acts, Arthur 2 Stroke and the Chart Commandos (a two-tone/ska revival band) and punk rockers the Noise Toys. The first issue, in December 1979, included music reviews and humorous cartoons drawn by Donald, a nineteen-year-old DHSS clerk, and his schoolfriend Jim Brownlow. According to Donald's 'inside story' of *Viz*:

> I assembled the artwork on a card table in my bedroom. It was a bit like doing a jigsaw, trying to slot everything together neatly. There were still a few gaps to fill, so I asked my brother Simon if he fancied doing a cartoon. Simon had recently formed his own noisy youth club band, Johnny Shiloe's Movement Machine, but he took time out from his budding acting and pop career to do a three-frame cartoon containing sex, cake and vomiting. It was a terrific combination.[41]

Viz was printed by the Tyneside Free Press, a not-for-profit publishing collective, and was sold in pubs and record shops. Encouraged by the response, Donald printed 500 copies of the second issue. This brought a review in the *Newcastle Evening Chronicle* describing *Viz* as '*Sparky* for grown-ups' and praising it for 'taking a wry look at society in the form of cartoon strips'.[42] This was the first indication that *Viz* was understood as something more than just an exercise in vulgar humour: that it also provided an insight into social mores and behaviour.

In the early 1980s *Viz* was very much a local phenomenon specific to the north-east. It relied heavily on word-of-mouth for its sales and catered for its readers with a heavy dose of Geordie street slang. It became something of a cult among university students, despite its reputation as an 'anti-student' magazine. ('Jim and I hated students', Donald confessed. 'We were envious of their cushy, low-price accommodation, their cheap booze, cheap food, cheap and exclusive live entertainment, and the fact that they were surrounded by young women.'[43]) As Anti-Pop waned, the fanzine element of *Viz* was dropped in favour of more cartoon strips and spoof articles. Its production was irregular, but its circulation gradually increased: by 1982 it was selling 2,500 copies and by 1985 it had reached 7,000.[44]

It was in the later 1980s that *Viz* developed from a regional to a national publication. In 1985 the Virgin chain agreed to put it on sale in their record stores, which guaranteed nationwide distribution. In 1987 the managing director of Virgin Books, John Brown, left to set up his own company specifically to publish *Viz*. In 1988 the high street newsagent W. H. Smith agreed to stock the comic: within a year its sales rose from 60,000 to 500,000.[45] In 1989 it passed 1 million copies. At its peak in the early 1990s *Viz* was selling 1.2 million copies and was the fourth biggest-circulation periodical in Britain (after *Radio Times*, *TV Times* and *Woman's Weekly*). It also branched out into branded merchandizing and spin-off publications such as *The Viz Book of Crap Jokes* and *Roger's Profanisaurus*. 'In commercial terms it was a staggering achievement', writes Sabin. 'Very few comics in history can be said to have tapped into the national *zeitgeist* in such a way.'[46]

Why was *Viz* so successful? The obvious and straightforward explanation – that it was simply very funny – is insufficient in itself. *Viz* exhibited a particular brand of humour that was not to everyone's taste. Where it succeeded was in appealing to a specific demographic. According to its own market research the readership of *Viz* was 85 per cent male and 82 per cent under 25.[47] And it appealed to readers who did not usually buy comics: *Viz* was seen as much as a humorous magazine (a downmarket *Private Eye*) than as a comic per se.

The humorous strategy of *Viz* was twofold: to parody (and subvert) the style of British children's comics (the *Beano* especially) and to spoof the sensationalist nature of the tabloid press. Most of its strips have always been one- or two-page funnies drawn in a pastiche of the *Beano* style with the addition of a large dose of swearing and scatological humour. Examples include 'Johnny Fartpants', 'Captain Incontinent', 'Billy Bottom and his Zany Toilet Pranks', 'Felix and his Amazing Underpants', 'Buster Gonad and his

From fanzine to phenomenon: the anarchic *Viz* is the most successful of all British alternative comics.

Unfeasibly Large Testicles' and 'Nobby's Piles'. Donald suggested that the appeal of such strips was that they broke the taboo around finding bodily functions funny: 'Twelve-year-old kids all find farts and toilets and willies very funny, but because they're told not to laugh at them they never grow out of it. What we've done is provide a joke for people who never realised others think these sort of thoughts as well.'[48] *Viz* also drew upon the shock value of transgressing social norms. The humour of 'Roger Mellie – The Man on the Telly', a regular favourite, arises from his highly inappropriate behaviour: Roger is an egotistical television presenter who is unable to control his language. When the strip first appeared in 1981 it was still very much a taboo to swear on television, but Roger can turn even *Songs of Praise* into a tirade of four-letter words.

Other characters were extreme parodies of particular social types. These include 'Biffa Bacon' (a bully from a violently dysfunctional working-class family), 'Norman the Doorman' (a psychotic nightclub bouncer), 'Norbert Colon' (a miserable old miser), 'Mrs Brady Old Lady' (an absent-minded granny who causes havoc with her shopping trolley), and 'Spoilt Bastard' (an insufferable middle-class child with a pathetically doting mother). As Donald explained: 'This was a standard formula for us – taking a recognizable stereotype and exaggerating it – and we used it over and over again with varying degrees of success.'[49] Perhaps the definitive *Viz* characters, both arising from Geordie stereotypes, were the outrageous 'Sid the Sexist' (a chauvinistic working-class male whose catchphrase is 'tits oot for the lads') and 'The Fat Slags' (a pair of grotesquely obese, over-sexed secretaries who crawl the night spots of Newcastle in search of 'a quick shag an' a bag o' chips').

Included with the cartoon strips were spoof articles, letters and advertisements. *Viz* sent up the sensational style of tabloid journalism with cover headlines such as 'Cabinet minister had sex with dolphin' and 'Shag and tell revelations of Hollywood sex stuntman'. It ran competitions with silly prizes ('Win 500 toilet rolls!') and spoof advertisements ('Learn to swear in just three weeks with Swear-Aid'). The letters page – originally made up by the editors but later including genuine examples – became a favourite feature. Letters included mock-profound observations, highly unlikely anecdotes and pointless advice such as: 'Save money on expensive earrings by sticking Mint Imperials and Sugared Almonds to your ears with blu-tac.' *Viz* mercilessly poked fun at celebrity culture and mounted sustained assaults against those it regarded as 'annoying twats' such as Radio 1 DJ Danny Baker, *Sun* journalist Garry Bushell and the pop singer Morrissey.

It has been suggested that *Viz* can be aligned with the rise of what became known as 'alternative comedy' during the 1980s.[50] Alternative comedy was a new brand of politically aware comedy that originated in London comedy clubs like the Comedy Store and Jongleurs, associated with stand-up performers such as Ben Elton and Alexei Sayle and with television series such as BBC2's *The Young Ones* and Channel 4's *The Comic Strip Presents*. However, *Viz* differed from alternative comedy in two key respects. First, while alternative comedy was often explicitly political – jokes directed against 'Maggie Thatcher' were a favourite device for performers like Ben Elton – *Viz* was entirely apolitical. It would happily satirize both the left and the right. And second, whereas alternative comedy embraced political correctness by emphasizing its non-sexist, non-racist and non-discriminatory credentials, *Viz* could never be described as politically correct when its strips included 'Terry Fuckwitt' ('the stupidest boy in comics'), 'Tubby Tucker' ('the big fat person') and 'Specky Twat' (self-explanatory). *Viz* sent up the extremes of political correctness with 'Millie Tant' (Beryl the Peril reinvented as a fearsome feminist) and 'The Modern Parents' (a satire of trendy left-liberal views of child-raising). It even satirized the 'right on' nature of alternative comedy with 'Lenny Left' (an unfunny comedian). But lest it be accused of political bias it also directed broadsides against conservative institutions such as the church ('Paul Whicker the Tall Vicar' – a sadistic cleric with a penchant for corporal punishment) and satirized the Tory-inspired 'back to basics' campaign of the early 1990s with 'Victorian Dad' (a stern disciplinarian).

What *Viz* represented, rather, was a throwback to an older tradition of humour. It should be seen as part of the lineage of British low comedy that includes the earthy humour of northern stand-up comedians such as Max Miller, Frank Randle, Les Dawson, Bernard Manning, Roy 'Chubby' Brown and Peter Kay, and the critically despised but popular *Carry On* films that traded on stereotypes and double entendres.[51] Indeed, an early *Viz* strip, 'Finbarr Saunders and his Double Entendres', employed a similar strategy to the *Carry On* films in that Finbarr's every line can be read as a sexual innuendo ('Ho! Ho! It sounds like Mr Gimlet and Mum are inflating the lilo!'). Characters such as Sid the Sexist and the Fat Slags, furthermore, can be seen as modern equivalents of the caricatures on the saucy postcards of Donald McGill with their sexually frustrated husbands and their large-bosomed women with lascivious appetites. The key point about Sid the Sexist, for example, is that his unwavering belief in his ability to 'pull' is utterly misplaced: the strips invariably end in his humiliation. George Orwell's essay on 'The Art of Donald McGill' also seems entirely applicable to *Viz*:

> It will not do to condemn them [seaside postcards] on the ground that they are vulgar and ugly. That is exactly what they are meant to be. Their whole meaning and virtue is in their unredeemed lowness, not only in the sense of obscenity, but lowness of outlook in every direction whatever. The slightest hint of 'higher' influences would ruin them utterly . . . Their existence, the fact that people want them, is symptomatically important. Like the music halls, they are a sort of saturnalia, a harmless rebellion against virtue.[52]

Viz is vulgar in both senses of the word: it is lowbrow and it speaks a vernacular language. It too would be ruined if it aspired to a higher tone of humour.

It might be expected that *Viz* would have drawn howls of outraged protest from the politically correct lobby. The comic itself anticipated as much, even including spoof articles supporting 'the campaign to have *Viz* banned from Student Union shops throughout Britain'.[53] In fact, however, *Viz* was treated with amused tolerance by most of the left-liberal media, who were keen to show they were in on the joke. Andy Medhurst, for example, wrote that '*Viz* is a joke about comics as well as a comic with jokes . . . *Viz* has an extremely shrewd grasp of popular culture.'[54] Even the women's page of the *Guardian* was inclined to suggest that 'the Fat Slags stand out as the most appalling and the funniest strip, perhaps because they contain a hint of truth and tragedy'.[55] From the other side of the spectrum, the *Sun* – seemingly oblivious to the fact that it was the target of much of the comic's tabloid satire – championed it as an example of the Thatcherite ethos of private enterprise: '*Viz* magazine is the comic sweeping Britain and its readers are in stitches. The biggest joke of all is that the startled Geordie creators are laughing all the way to the bank.'[56]

This is not to say that *Viz* was without its detractors. At the height of its popularity, indeed, the comic went out of its way to provoke controversy. A strip entitled 'The Thieving Gypsy Bastards' would seem to have been calculated to cause offence. Donald later admitted that 'I knew we were batting on a sticky wicket'.[57] 'The Thieving Gypsy Bastards' features a family of travellers, the somewhat improbably named McO'Dougles, who travel from town to town camping in people's gardens, picking pockets, stealing property and putting curses on those who refuse to buy their lucky heather. The strip is a satire of political correctness: an aggrieved home-owner who reports the gypsies to the police is arrested 'for the harassment of these friendly, harmless, traditional Romany travelling folk'.[58] The inevitable complaints followed, including one from a lecturer in Romany Studies accusing the strip of 'exciting the same kind of outrage among Gypsies as *The Satanic Verses* have among Muslims'.[59]

Donald recognized the value of such controversies for publicity: 'The Thieving Gypsy Bastards' coincided with sales of *Viz* passing 1 million. This marked the high point of *Viz* as a cultural phenomenon. Its sales peaked in 1992, whereafter there was a steady (though far from precipitous) decline. *Viz* responded with the slogan 'not as funny as it used to be' and with new characters including 'Student Grant' (a privileged university student) and 'Cockney Wanker' (an East End wide boy). The early 1990s saw a short-lived cycle of *Viz* imitators – including *Zit*, *Smut*, *Spit*, *Gas* and *Poot!* – none of which succeeded in matching its distinctive style of humour. What the copyists failed to understand was that, while *Viz* was outrageous, its humour was not cruel. In contrast, the characters in *Zit* – 'Angus McBastard' and 'Terry the Twat', for example – were nasty without being funny. In any event they were jumping on a bandwagon that had passed. By the mid-1990s *Viz* was generally regarded as having run out of steam. It had also lost its ability to shock. Donald was disappointed in 1998 when 'Diana and Hopkirk Deceased' – a spoof of *Randall and Hopkirk (Deceased)* featuring the ghost of Princess Diana and her police bodyguard – failed to provoke the outrage he had expected.[60] In 2001 *Viz* was sold to IFG Entertainment, a company belonging to James Brown, founder of *Loaded* magazine. It continues to be published, though, like that other great survivor of the 1970s, *2000AD*, its sales are a fraction of what they had been at the height of its success.

* * *

This has been a necessarily brief survey of the history of alternative comics in Britain. It is an uneven and fragmented history: other than *Viz* and, to a lesser extent, *Escape*, few alternative comics have ever achieved any degree of stability or longevity. They have been handicapped by their sporadic production and limited distribution. And the quality of alternative comics, to be fair, has been very mixed: while some have been genuinely innovative, others are crude and derivative. Yet, in the long term, the influence of alternative comics has been significant. Since the late 1970s the underground has permeated the mainstream both in Britain and in America. A number of artists who came to prominence through the underground movement – including Brian Bolland, Dave Gibbons, Kevin O'Neill and Bryan Talbot – all contributed to *2000AD* and have since worked for major US comic publishers. Steve Bell, who started his career with *Streetcomix*, later became political cartoonist for the *Guardian*. Eddie Campbell graduated from self-publishing to collaborating with Alan Moore on the graphic novel *From Hell*. And Hunt Emerson, perhaps the most distinctive talent to emerge from the British underground, was happy to draw the adventures of 'Little Plumb' for the *Beano*.

The legacy of small press comics, however, persists. The ethos of *Fast Fiction* and *Escape* can be seen in independent distributors such as Small Zone, Future Quake and Solar Wind and in collectives such as London Underground Comics, which, even in the age of the Internet, maintains a stall on Camden Lock Market. A new model of distribution has emerged in the form of print-to-order and subscription-only comics, though the most high profile of these, DFC (*David Fickling Comic*), a new children's comic launched in 2008, which grew out of the children's pages of the *Guardian*, still failed to dent the market dominance of *Beano* and *Dandy*. It was a bold experiment, but folded after 43 issues. Since the late 1990s, furthermore, the expansion of the World Wide Web has opened up new possibilities for comic publishing and distribution. The field of 'webcomics' is continually expanding and is constantly in flux, though it might tentatively be suggested that while these have been innovatory in their adoption of new formal conventions they have mostly clung to traditional genres. Notable examples of British webcomics include John Allison's *Scary Go Round* (which describes itself as 'postmodern British horror') and Huw Davy's *Bunny* (anthropomorphic humour). However, this is clearly an area for further research.

CHAPTER NINE

The Growing Pains of British Comics

> For a period, comics in the UK almost became the new rock'n'roll, regularly reviewed in music papers or hip fashion rags like *The Face* and *ID* . . . This was something of a boom time for the British comics industry, with even Marvel UK commissioning new material both for its superhero comics, and creating new titles like *Strip*, which published more alternative work. IPC launched *Revolver* and *Crisis*, which featured work with a more 'mature', less fantasy or SF outlook . . . However, we all know how the market went belly up in a short time.
> Phil Elliott.[1]

While the 1970s had been a period of instability for British comic publishing, the 1980s saw the industry in crisis. The decade witnessed the collapse of the juvenile comic market – total sales dropped from around 10 million a week in the mid-1970s to barely 3 million a decade later – and marked the end of the road for many old favourites including *Hotspur, Tiger, Warlord, Battle, Jinty, Debbie* and *Tammy*.[2] As there had been for the growth of the comics market after the Second World War, there were several reasons for its severe contraction in the 1980s. One factor was a sharp decline in the birth rate in the mid-1970s, which meant that by the end of the 1980s there were half a million fewer seven- to fourteen-year-olds than at the start of the decade.[3] Another explanation was the emergence of rival forms of visual entertainment, especially the video cassette rental market and the advent of home computers such as the ZX Spectrum. The 1980s saw the birth of the video-gaming culture that has since largely displaced comics as the foremost leisure activity of many adolescents. So terminal was the decline that the two publishing giants which had dominated the industry for the past half century all but withdrew from the field. In 1987 IPC sold off most of its juvenile comics line – including *2000AD*, *Eagle* and *Roy of the*

Near Myths (Galaxy Media, 1979).

Rovers – to Robert Maxwell's Mirror Group, while D. C. Thomson launched no new titles after *Nikki* in 1985.

As the juvenile market declined, the industry responded by attempting to attract new readers through the publication of different types of comics. There was a boom in comics for 'mature' readers (generally meaning the over-sixteens), who, it was supposed, would have more disposable income than children. This meant more sophisticated and adult content and a trend away from newsprint comics to more glossy magazine-style publications that could justify higher prices. The trend was led by smaller independent publishers who were quick to recognize the changing nature of British comics culture, especially the rise of fandom. There were two distinct waves. The first, between 1978 and 1982, comprised mostly SF and fantasy themed comics, 'grown up' alternatives to *2000AD* such as *Graphixus* (1978–9), *Near Myths* (1978–9), *Psst!* (1982) and *Warrior* (1982–5), while a second wave, between 1988 and 1991, centred around so-called 'style comics' such as *Heartbreak Hotel* (1988), *Crisis* (1988–91), *Deadline* (1988–95), *Revolver* (1990), *Strip* (1990), *Meltdown* (1991), *Xpresso* (1991), *Blast!* (1991) and *Toxic!* (1991).

Although few of these titles lasted beyond a handful of issues – the most successful were *Warrior* (26 issues), *Crisis* (63) and *Deadline* (69) – collectively they represented an important landmark in British comics publishing in that they demonstrated the cultural and intellectual ambitions of the medium beyond traditional juvenile fare.[4]

* * *

The first wave of new comics in the late 1970s and early 1980s coincided with the revival of SF and fantasy cinema heralded by the success of films like *Star Wars, Superman, Star Trek – The Motion Picture, Alien* and *Blade Runner*.[5] There has always been significant cross-over between comic fandom and SF and fantasy: Forbidden Planet, the specialist shop opened by former *2000AD* editor Nick Landau in London in 1978, catered for both markets. *Graphixus* and *Near Myths*, which ran for six and five issues respectively, were the first adult British SF and fantasy comics. *Graphixus*, edited by Mal Burns, featured work by underground creators Hunt Emerson and Brian Bolland. It was inspired to some extent by European erotica: 'Succuba', for example, was an 'erotik space fantasy' whose comely heroine was a clone of Jean-Claude Forest's *Barbarella*. *Near Myths*, edited by Rob King, included two notable firsts: the early instalments of Bryan Talbot's SF epic 'The Adventures of Luther Arkwright' and Grant Morrison's first published strip 'Gideon Stargrave'. The reference points for *Near Myths* were the French adult comic *Métal Hurlant* (which translates literally as 'Screaming Metal') and the 'new wave' SF of British writer Michael Moorcock.

It is significant that the first attempts to create British adult comics looked to Europe for inspiration: comic strips had long been regarded as an adult medium, especially in France. The most ambitious attempt to emulate the intellectual sophistication and artistic ambition of European comics was *Pssst!*, launched in 1982 by French entrepreneur and comics enthusiast Serge Bossevain. *Pssst!* was a glossy magazine resembling *Métal Hurlant*. It advertised itself as 'the cartoon and strip monthly for mature readers' and combined adventure, humour and experimental strips. It continued to serialize Talbot's 'The Adventures of Luther Arkwright', but otherwise preferred stand-alone stories rather than serials. *Psst!* offered creators rights in their own work – an innovation of the underground that would also be taken up by *Warrior* and other independent comics – but it failed to find a readership and folded after ten issues. It has been suggested that *Pssst!* failed because it was 'too experimental'.[6] Its high cover price (at £1.25 it was considerably more expensive than other comics of the time) and the fact that it looked more like an art magazine than a comic are also likely to have been deterrents.

The failure of these adult SF comics notwithstanding, however, they did produce one undoubted classic. Bryan Talbot's 'The Adventures of Luther Arkwright' is a landmark of extended narrative that has some claim to being the first graphic novel.[7] It is an intellectually ambitious parallel worlds adventure told on an epic scale. Talbot acknowledged the influence of Michael Moorcock's Jerry Cornelius books (compiled in *The Cornelius Chronicles*, 1977) in creating the character of Luther Arkwright, an intra-dimensional agent who combats the forces of chaos across alternate worlds where historical events have taken a different course. The disruptors seek to spread chaos throughout the multiverse: they create wars, disasters and disease. Arkwright is sent to alternate world 00-72-87 – in which Britain is ruled by a fascist Puritan dictatorship that has ruled since the end of the civil war – to 'cause an imbalance too great for the disruptors to handle'.[8] Here he makes contact with the royalist underground to overthrow the brutal regime of Lord Protector Nathaniel Cromwell. Queen Anne's royalists are aided by the Prussian and Russian empires who plan to destroy the Commonwealth and rule Britain as a satellite state. In the final cataclysmic battle (Ragnarok) the Puritan armies are overwhelmed and the Prussian plot foiled. Queen Anne assumes the throne, in effect an absolute monarch, and pledges to 'build an Empire on which the sun will never set'.[9]

'The Adventures of Luther Arkwright' can be read as an extended commentary on the issue of historical determinism. In drawing parallels between Puritan Britain and Nazi Germany – Cromwell speaks of 'one people, one Commonweal, one leader' and prepares for the 'Final Solution' against the Roman Catholics – the strip suggests that the potential for Fascism existed in Britain.[10] It can also be seen as a commentary on contemporary politics. Queen Anne projects herself as 'the Iron Lady' and her address to the nation upon assuming the throne echoes the words attributed to St Francis of Assisi that incoming Conservative Prime Minister Margaret Thatcher quoted outside 10 Downing Street in 1979: 'Where there is discord, may we bring harmony . . . Where there is despair, may we bring hope.'[11] Talbot's alternate history of the British Empire and his adoption of 'steampunk' motifs established a template for other alternate histories including Alan Moore and Kevin O'Neill's *The League of Extraordinary Gentlemen* and Ian Edginton and D'Israeli's *Scarlet Traces*.

'The Adventures of Luther Arkwright' stood out among the content of *Near Myths* and *Psst!* through its British subject-matter. The failure of these comics to find a readership might be explained by their 'European' style. The success, in relative terms, of *Warrior*, which lasted for nearly three years and ran for a total of 25 issues, would seem to corroborate this thesis. *Warrior* was welcomed as a bastion of indigenous British talent and creativity in a comic

Bryan Talbot's 'The Adventures of Luther Arkwright' was a brilliant experiment in extended narrative and alternate history. *Psst!* (Artpool/Never Ltd, August 1982).

industry that was increasingly becoming dominated by the US giants DC and Marvel. 'I must say it is very enjoyable to be able to read what could be called "pure" British comic strips', said one reader, who also felt that *Warrior* 'reflects a national character by its overt lack of superheroic exaggeration'.[12] Others agreed: 'At last here is something British to challenge the American comic' and '*Warrior* is uniquely British, no matter where else it is sold or what influences it might come under.'[13] *Warrior* adopted the slogan 'The Best of British' and set out 'to show the world a range of strips which would hopefully have international appeal, but would still remain intrinsically British'.[14]

Warrior was the brainchild of Dez Skinn, the former editorial director of Marvel UK, editor of the British edition of *Mad* magazine and founder of the fanzines *House of Hammer* and *Starburst*. Skinn was committed to a policy of editorial and creative independence. In his first editorial – entitled 'Freedom's Road' after a speech by John F. Kennedy – Skinn claimed that the British comic industry was suffering 'a period of creative regression' and the aim of *Warrior* was to 'spark off enough interest to get things moving again'.[15] *Warrior* exhibited a progressive editorial policy in that creators maintained control over their strips. Skinn equated autonomy with innovation. He explained: '*Warrior*'s somewhat idealistic, perhaps naively so. We try experiments and take risks because we want to. All of us. With *Warrior* the creators are able to take their ideas *further*. In fact they want to because they are their *own* ideas. I don't grab the copyright.'[16]

Warrior was nothing if not ambitious. It was 'dedicated to the long-term effects [sic] of attempting to elevate British comics, and providing a portfolio of top British talent'.[17] Skinn recruited a group of emerging comic writers and artists who represented the cream of British talent. Writers included Alan Moore, Steve Moore, Steve Dillon and Paul Neary, and artists included John Bolton, Dave Gibbons, Garry Leach, David Lloyd, Steve Parkhouse and John Ridgway. Alan Moore's two strips – 'Marvelman' (drawn first by Garry Leach, later by Alan Davis) and 'V for Vendetta' (drawn by David Lloyd) – soon established themselves as the readers' favourites. It was his work for *Warrior* that established Moore as the pre-eminent British comic writer and where he was able for the first time to develop longer 'story arcs' in contrast to the stand-alone stories he had written for *Doctor Who Weekly* and *2000AD*. The other debut stories included a sword-and-sorcery fantasy epic ('The Spiral Path'), historical myth ('The Legend of Prester John'), SF action-adventure ('Laser Eraser and Pressbutton') and a supernatural horror strip inherited from *House of Hammer* ('Father Shandor – Demon Stalker').[18] Steve Moore's 'A True Story' was a humorous stand-alone story reminiscent of the underground: a comic-strip writer is dragged into an alternate dimension by an alien tyrant who needs help to crush a slave revolt, telling him that 'a long range brain-scan of all the people on Earth shows there are none so brilliant or inventive as comic-strip writers!'[19]

At its best *Warrior* did indeed highlight the inventiveness of the medium. The most ambitious strip was 'V for Vendetta'. This dark tale of a masked anarchist conducting a one-man 'terrorist' campaign against a fascist government in the near-future Britain of 1997 is characterized by a degree of psychological complexity and moral ambiguity unprecedented in British comics. Its protagonist is a ruthless avenger who sets out to assassinate leading members of the regime – all of whom transpire to be associated with a concentration camp where 'V' was once incarcerated and tortured. It is formally innovative: Moore and Lloyd dispense with thought bubbles and sound effect captions (such as inserting 'Bang!' when a firearm is discharged) and often include pages with no text at all. There had been other 'silent' strips, especially in alternative comics, but this was the first time the technique had been applied to a continuing serial. And its content was very different from traditional comic fare. As Lew Stringer put it: 'I can't really envisage the Houses of Parliament being blown up or a young girl attempting prostitution in the pages of *The Victor* somehow.'[20]

'V for Vendetta' demonstrates how *Warrior* associated itself with British subjects and themes. Skinn had originally asked David Lloyd to provide a

'V for Vendetta', *Warrior* (Quality Communications Ltd, October 1983).

film noir-styled vigilante story in the American pulp tradition similar to the 'Night Raven' strip he had drawn for Marvel UK's *Hulk Weekly*. However, this developed, through collaboration with Alan Moore, into a futuristic parable with a distinctively British flavour. According to Moore: 'Dave and I both wanted to do something that would be uniquely British rather than emulate the vast amount of American material on the market.'[21] While 'V for Vendetta' draws upon an eclectic range of cultural references – The Shadow, Batman, Robin Hood, *Fahrenheit 451*, *The Abominable Dr Phibes* and Shakespeare among them – its cultural roots are firmly in the tradition of British dystopian fiction represented by George Orwell and Aldous Huxley. The influence of Orwell's *Nineteen Eighty-Four* is to be found in the grim urban landscapes, ever-present surveillance cameras and the prevalence of propaganda posters declaring 'Strength Through Purity, Purity Through Faith', while from Huxley's *Brave New World* comes the challenge to an authoritarian state from an individual versed in political philosophy. 'V for Vendetta'

229

is perhaps Moore's most profound work: certainly it is the strip that most fully explores his own views about the relationship between anarchy and personal freedom.[22]

The social politics of *Warrior* are broadly progressive – it is racially inclusive and preaches tolerance towards outsiders – except in the area of gender. Here it demonstrates one of the charges frequently levelled against SF and fantasy comics: that their female characters are stereotypes of male fantasy such as Amazonian warriors and sexy Barbarella clones. For a while, at least, *Warrior* avoided gratuitous sexism, even spoofing this tendency in a one-off story called 'The All-Girl Amazon Attack Battalion', but as sales declined it resorted to more examples of 'bad girl art' painted covers that can be seen as a means of selling the comic to its core (male) readership. One reader even wrote in to complain: 'Please, no more "Tits and Ass" covers. You don't really need them to sell such high quality stories as "V".'[23]

The letter pages of *Warrior* provide revealing evidence about the nature of British comic fandom in the 1980s. Skinn adopted the Marvel policy of encouraging debate and printed as many letters as space would allow: often up to three pages of very small print. It is clear that the readership was overwhelmingly male and consisted predominantly of teenagers and young adults. There was evidently cross-over with other comics, particularly *2000AD*, though there is also a sense of brand loyalty to *Warrior*. The readership of *Warrior* extended to North America (Skinn reported that 10,000 copies – a quarter of the total print run – went to America) where there is some evidence that it was welcomed as a more serious variation on the familiar superhero and fantasy genres. And fandom was very creator-focused: it was in the letter pages of *Warrior* that the cult of Alan Moore really began to take shape. It also demonstrates the excesses of 'fanboy' obsession in the highly opinionated nature of much commentary and the inability of some fans to see points of view other than their own. This came to a head in 1983 when one reader's violent reaction to Paul Neary's strip 'Madman' ('Paul Neary's stories are always too stupid to be believed and the art is pathetic . . . Do not continue this rubbish!') provoked an outraged reply from artist Steve Parkhouse, who found it 'disturbing than an individual can express such acid feelings for a colleague of mine merely on the grounds of disliking his work'. Parkhouse then vented 'some of my own feelings about comics today':

> Since my initial involvement in comics about fifteen years ago, I have noted with some dismay that the medium tends to attract the intellectually stunted and the emotionally warped, both inside and outside the professional ranks . . . Do comics wrap people in a cloak of fantasy that prevents them from thinking clearly? Do

they bring out the lurking child in us all, providing an easy escape from the harsher world of reality? . . . *Warrior* magazine has ventured a tiny way towards encouraging an attitude of liberalism. But judging from some of the letters in 'Dispatches', it still has a long way to go.[24]

Another reader was moved to complain about the 'frighteningly immature and rasping letters page'.[25] The highly introspective and extremely opinionated nature of many letters did little to dispel the perception that comic fandom was immature and obsessive.

That said, *Warrior* was recognized by the comic industry as a force to be reckoned with. In 1983 it won nine Eagle Awards, including best British comic, best new comic and best story ('Marvelman'), while Alan Moore was voted best writer largely on the basis of his contributions to *Warrior*. Its success prompted Marvel UK to relaunch *The Mighty World of Marvel* in 1983, featuring work by several *Warrior* creators including Moore and Alan Davis. Ironically this recognition for *Warrior* came just as a perceptible decline in quality had begun to set in. Several creators, including Garry Leach and Steve Dillon, drifted away, while its star writer Alan Moore was lured by DC to write *Swamp Thing* and his contributions to *Warrior* became fewer. In 1984 'Marvelman', one of the two outstanding strips, was dropped following a protracted legal correspondence with lawyers acting for Marvel Comics who had taken exception to the publication of a *Marvelman Special*.[26] It would probably be fair to say that replacement strips such as 'Big Ben' ('The man with no time for crime') and 'Bogey' were from the second division. What really killed *Warrior*, however, was its failure to secure consistent distribution. The letters page provides much anecdotal evidence of the poor distribution, while editorials complained of the lack of interest from retailers. Skinn lambasted 'the archaic and hypocritical attitude of much of the British trade' but to little effect.[27] *Warrior* ceased publication, without prior warning, in February 1985.[28] Nevertheless its contribution to the history of British comics had been very important. It demonstrated for the first time that mainstream comics for mature readers were credible; it marked a major step forward in the campaign for creators' rights; and it provided a showcase for a generation of writers and artists whose work would transform not just British but American comics too.

* * *

Warrior was to some extent ahead of its time: the real boom in adult comics in Britain came half a decade later. *Crisis, Deadline, Heartbreak Hotel, Revolver, Strip, Meltdown, Xpresso, Blast!* and *Toxic!* all came – and, with the exception of *Deadline*, went – within three years between 1988 and 1991. How can we explain this moment of critical mass at the end of the 1980s? It is impossible to exaggerate the importance for the comic industry of the impact created by the publication of three graphic novels in the mid-1980s – Art Spiegelman's *Maus* (1987), Frank Miller's *The Dark Knight Returns* (1986) and Alan Moore and Dave Gibbons's *Watchmen* (1987) – that brought an unprecedented degree of critical attention to the medium. These publications were reviewed in the broadsheet press and alerted the mass media to the notion that comics could be taken seriously.[29] There was a sense that comics were shifting away from adolescent fantasy and were looking to address social and political issues more directly. As Nick Landau observed: 'Comics are focusing on issues that people relate to. They're not dealing with the fantasy world they were previously. They now show the reality, the dirt – not the clean, healthy world of barbarians and superheroes.'[30]

The adult comics of the late 1980s and early 1990s demonstrate a range of strategies for appealing to mature readers. *Crisis*, for example, was the most overtly political. *Crisis*, launched in September 1988 by the newly renamed Fleetway Publications (as IPC's Youth Group became following its sale to Robert Maxwell in 1987), was conceived as a companion paper to *2000AD* and was intended to cater for readers who had outgrown juvenile SF. The fact that *2000AD* was itself moving in a more adult direction by the late 1980s seems to have been overlooked: this was probably due to a degree of uncertainty within Fleetway under its new ownership regime. New editorial director John Davidge later observed: 'No-one knew what was going on, no-one was in control. They were completely rudderless. I think the Maxwells had completely forgotten they owned Fleetway.'[31] Yet, as so often in the media industries, institutional instability created conditions that allowed a large degree of editorial autonomy. *Crisis* promoted itself as a comic with a radical agenda. It saw itself as performing an agit-prop role: editorials urged its readers to become involved in political activism. It also argued that to buy the comic was to support its politics: 'Every time you fork out 65p for *Crisis* you are, in effect, approving the paper's editorial policy. The moment you stop buying the paper, sales fall and disaster looms.'[32] The disaster was averted for over two years: sales settled around 20,000, insufficient to sustain the comic in the long term, but it was kept alive by Fleetway who welcomed the critical kudos it brought.

The lead strip of *Crisis* was 'Third World War', written by Pat Mills and drawn by Carlos Ezquerra with occasional issues by 'guest artists' including Angie Mills and D'Israeli (Matt Brooker). 'Third World War' is a Marxist critique of global capitalism thinly disguised as an adventure strip. It posits the scenario that in the year 2000 multinational corporations have taken over responsibility for policing the trouble spots of the Third World. One such organization is MultiFoods, which has set up FreeAid (Free World Agency for International Development) 'to restore economic and political stability to the Third World'.[33] The strip follows a group of (mostly unwilling) recruits to FreeAid's Psychological Warfare Battalion who are sent to an unnamed Central American country to win the 'hearts and minds' of the local population. The story is told mostly from the perspective of Eve Collins, a young black British woman who is shocked by what she witnesses: demonstrators are gassed and clubbed, villages are destroyed and the people sent to internment camps, and dissidents are murdered by secret death squads and their bodies dumped on rubbish tips. Eve's conscience causes her to question the ideological conditioning of FreeAid: 'I know we shouldn't be here giving these people so much grief. They've every right to live the way they want.'[34]

'Third World War' is a powerful if heavily didactic commentary on the exploitation of the Third World by the West. It asserts that the West has been

'Third World War', *Crisis* (Fleetway Publications, 1–14 October 1988).

fighting a continuous war to pacify the Third World for decades: 'Vietnam in the 60s . . . El Salvador and Eritrea in the 80s . . . Here in 2000 . . . The war in the Third World has been going on for over fifty years.'[35] It is explicitly Marxist in its examination of the strategies adopted by multinationals to maximize food production in the Third World (even if this means spraying farmers with pesticides) and to coerce producers into a dependent relationship that leaves them with massive debts. The hypocrisy of MultiFoods is exposed when Eve discovers a secret policy document revealing their 'corporate objectives' are 'to impose our commercial philosophy on the country . . . in such a way as not to expose its ambitions for dominance'.[36] The story concludes, however, with MultiFoods driven out by an uprising by the Guerrilla Army of the Poor: the scenes of evacuation by helicopter bring to mind the US evacuation of Saigon in 1975.

Crisis originally comprised two long strips (fourteen pages each) with the ambition of repackaging them as comic books for the US market. 'Third World War' was complemented by John Smith and Jim Blaikie's 'New Statesmen', a *Watchmen*-inspired cautionary tale of superheroes in which televangelist Pheonix, former member of superhero team the Statesmen and now leader of the evangelical League of Light, stands in the US presidential election on a neo-conservative platform: 'The prospect of one of them playing God in the White House is something I think we should all be extremely wary of.'[37] The two-strip format was dropped after fourteen issues, however, and 'New Statesmen' was replaced by 'Sticky Fingers' (Myra Hancock's sitcom of life in Camden Town) and 'Troubled Souls' (the first published work by Belfast-born writer Garth Ennis set against the background of sectarian violence in Northern Ireland). 'Third World War' continued with Eve returning to a trouble-torn Britain where the economy has collapsed and social order is breaking down.

The politics of *Crisis* need to be understood in the historical context of the late 1980s. Its publication history coincided with a period of mounting popular dissent against the Conservative government of Margaret Thatcher – exemplified by the 'Poll Tax' riots of 1989 – and with such epoch-defining events as the fall of the Berlin Wall (November 1989) and the release of Nelson Mandela from long-term imprisonment in South Africa (February 1990). *Crisis* responded to events such as the Tiananmen Square massacre ('China in Crisis') and the oppression of the ANC in South Africa ('The Student Konstabel'). It aligned itself with progressive causes: in March 1990, for example, it published a special issue in collaboration with Amnesty International that highlighted true cases of imprisonment and torture in Israel ('A Kind of Madness') and South Africa ('The Death Factory'). *Crisis* was as radical in political terms as anything seen since the underground movement:

it was without question the most left-leaning of any mainstream title in British comic history.

While *Crisis* adhered to its particular blend of radical politics and social commentary, other adult-themed comics adopted different strategies. The late 1980s saw the emergence of so-called 'style comics' which combined strips with aspects drawn from lifestyle magazines, particularly features on 'indie' pop music. *Heartbreak Hotel* was the first, advertising itself as 'The Lifestyle Comic Magazine', but it was *Deadline* that proved the most successful of the new style comics. *Deadline* was privately funded by Tom Astor, grandson of Britain's first woman MP Nancy Astor, and edited by *2000AD* regulars Steve Dillon and Brett Ewins. In contrast to the didactic politics of *Crisis*, *Deadline* had no agenda other than to embrace 'cool' and 'street cred'. To this extent it combined interviews and feature articles with an eclectic range of strips including continuing serials and stand-alone stories. The regular strips included 'Beryl the Bitch' (a spiky-haired man-eater), 'Sharp' (the unlikely adventures of a local television reporter: 'What!? Are you saying there's a CIA agent smuggling monster recipes to Earth through a British TV station?') and 'Johnny Nemo' (a futuristic hard-boiled private-eye spoof). However, the undoubted star of *Deadline* was a bizarre punk-influenced radical feminist skinhead with a talking kangaroo boyfriend called Booga.

'Tank Girl', by Jamie Hewlett and Alan Martin, had cult written all over it from the start: 'What's bald, and smelly, snogs kangaroos, wears shoes that don't fit and a bra that's too tight (and knickers that need a good wash), smokes, drinks, and fights too much for her own good, and at this moment in time has a mega hangover?'[38] Tank Girl (so called because she drives a tank around the Australian outback) is perhaps best described as a cross between

'Tank Girl', *Deadline* (Deadline Publications Ltd, April 1989).

Madonna and Mad Max: the character combines rock-chick popular feminism with an anti-authoritarian attitude and a penchant for extreme violence. This helps to explain why the character seems to have appealed to both men and women: readers' letters would suggest that *Deadline* attracted a larger following among women than most comics. Tank Girl is sexy without being sexist: an antidote to characters such as Judge Anderson of *2000AD*.

'Tank Girl' can be understood as a deconstruction of the comic-strip medium – to this extent it owes something to the underground comix of the 1970s – and particularly of the sexist gender politics of mainstream adolescent comics. Tank Girl herself is aware of her own fictionality and frequently engages in a dialogue with readers and her creators. So, for example, when she is rudely awoken by the arrival of ninja assassins, she starts to dress for action only to discover that someone has been interfering with her clothes: 'Very funny I don't think! Wonder which pervoid cut holes in all my bras so I'd have to spend the whole issue topless?!'[39] Tank Girl's answer is to place 'harassment stickers' over her nipples. The episode ends with Tank Girl addressing the reader: 'Just think, if we'd had enough time to collect together another three pages you could of [sic] seen me slap these ninja geezers all over the outback completely topless!! I guess you tight-fisted heterosexuals will have to buy the next issue to see the outcome!'[40] In another episode Tank Girl reprimands her creators for toning down her outrageous behaviour: 'Ah, Hewlett and Martin, you old bastards! What's going on with this strip? What happened to all the violence and grog supping promised at the end of the last story? Are we gonna do this bloody comic or what?'[41]

In the early 1990s Tank Girl briefly became something of a cultural icon: her 'look' (Doc Martens, jeans, body piercings) influenced 'grunge' and rock bands like the Riot Grrrls. A range of meanings, sometimes contradictory, became attached to the character, who on the one hand was claimed by the lesbian community in protests against the controversial Clause 28 of the Local Government Act and on the other became the face of Wrangler jeans in a multi-million pound advertising campaign.[42] While some commentators claimed Tank Girl as a symbol of female empowerment, however, others were not convinced. Charlotte Raven in the *Guardian* was sceptical: 'I can't help thinking that the "empowerment of women" could and should mean something more than the freedom (elusive though it still is) to fight, fart and pick your nose in public.'[43] Tank Girl was popular enough to attract the attention of Hollywood, though the film, starring Lori Petty and released in 1995, was indescribably awful and deservedly disappeared into video rental oblivion. In any event the moment of Tank Girl had passed: her appearances in *Deadline* had become less frequent since the early 1990s and the anarchic energy that characterized the early strips was proving increasingly elusive. The failure of the movie also marked the end of the road for *Deadline*, which folded in 1995.

None of the other adult comics of the late 1980s and early 1990s matched the relative longevity of *Crisis* or *Deadline*. Marvel's *Strip*, for example, a fortnightly comic launched for the British market in February 1990, lasted for less than a year. Its one strip of any note was Pat Mills and Kevin O'Neill's 'Marshal Law', an anti-superhero narrative that shares similar ground with *Watchmen*.[44] Fleetway's *Revolver*, a glossy monthly launched in July 1990, was even shorter lived, lasting for only seven issues, though it maintained a consistently high quality. *Revolver* took its title from The Beatles' album of the same name, and according to its editor Peter Hogan was an attempt to recapture something of the spirit of the 1960s: 'Why *Revolver?* Because what goes around comes around, and looking out my window it appears to be 1966 again . . . Because maybe – just *maybe* – comics might occupy that slot that rock music used to.'[45] The comic featured an eclectic range of strips including 'Purple Days' (an account of the early life of Jimi Hendrix written by his biographer Charles Shaar Murray), 'Dire Streets' (a flatshare sitcom) and 'Rogan Gosh' (a surreal mixture of Eastern mysticism and gay sex set around an Indian restaurant in Stoke Newington). The flagship strip of *Revolver*, however, was Grant Morrison and Rian Hughes's reimagining of Dan Dare.

Roger Sabin was sceptical about this latest revival of the old *Eagle* favourite:

> In 'Dare', this quintessential 50s hero is given the Dark Knight revisionist treatment, with a partially paralysed Dare hobbling around the countryside after one space battle too many. It's all very 'adult' and clever, but the fact is that Dan Dare isn't Batman. People knew about Batman from the TV series and elsewhere, and so the whole Dark Knight idea had at least some chance of mainstream success. Dare, however, is an icon of a much lesser order, and however desperate things look for Dan in the new strip, I can't see the 16–25 target-readership getting too excited about a star who was already old hat when their parents were reading comics.[46]

However, despite these reservations, 'Dare' is a brilliantly rendered revisionist strip that pays homage to the original while reinterpreting its ideological values for the present.

'Dare' features an ageing Dan Dare, retired, crippled, estranged from his old friend Digby and longing for a purpose in life. He is persuaded to become

Revolver (Fleetway Publications, July 1990).

a figurehead for the governing Unity Party, a neo-Fascist party whose poll ratings are declining in the face of rising unemployment and social unrest. That this is intended as an anti-Thatcherite allegory is made explicit when Dare meets Prime Minister Gloria Monday, who is drawn as an exaggerated caricature of Margaret Thatcher: 'The Unity Party has been in power for ten years now – but the rot cannot be allowed to continue. I simply *must* have these next five years to bring my policies to fruition. I *must* win this election.' She sees Dare as 'a personification of the values that we represent. Patriotism. The strength of the individual. An optimistic, enterprising spirit.'[47] It transpires, of course, that Dare is being used for political ends. In the course of time he learns that the Unity Party have concluded a secret alliance with his old foe the Mekon and that they were responsible for the murder of Professor Peabody when she discovered that a government scheme to reduce youth unemployment was really a cover for a programme of mass murder. Dare is left disillusioned, though he has the final word in the form of his last diary entry: 'Once upon a time I believed in an England that was fair and honourable. I'm almost glad you taught me that England only ever existed in my head. It means it can never really be destroyed.'[48]

The last (and least) of the major adult comics was *Toxic!*, a weekly title that ran from March until October 1991. *Toxic!* eschewed both the polemic of *Crisis* and the trendiness of *Deadline* and *Revolver*: its aim instead was to embrace bad taste and excess for all they were worth. The tone was set in the first editorial from 'Doc Tox': 'I come to pollute your mind! I bring you stories to fry your brain – artwork to explode your eyeballs! A collection of corruption so corrosive it makes projectile vomiting seem like kids' stuff!'[49] Quite. *Toxic!* drew upon the talents of *2000AD alumni* Pat Mills, Alan Grant, John Wagner, Kevin O'Neill and Mike McMahon: the aim seems to have been to produce a more explicit, violent and sexed-up alternative to *2000AD*. As well as continuing 'Marshal Law', early strips included 'Accident Man' (an assassin whose speciality is making deaths look like accidents), 'The Bogie Man' ('Scotland's most famous lunatic'), 'Makabre' (a religious maniac serial killer), 'Sex Warrior' (an army of sexually aggressive women fighting an 'age war' against a puritannical elite) and 'Detritus Rex' (post-apocalyptic ecological warrior). There were few redeeming qualities about *Toxic!*: its gender politics were reactionary to say the least and its content was largely derivative. This would certainly seem to have been the verdict of readers: *Toxic!* folded after 31 issues when its publisher, Apolcalypse Ltd, went bankrupt.

The failure of the adult comics of the late 1980s and early 1990s to achieve any level of sustained popularity would suggest either that there was not a large enough market for adult comics in Britain or that whatever market there was had become saturated. The comics were all keen to differentiate themselves from one another while acknowledging that they shared a particular slice of the market. Or, as one editorial rather bizarrely put it: '*Crisis* and *Strip* may well have an overlap of readership, but they cater for (and *set out* to cater for) very different tastes and métiers. You don't write up calculus problems on a blackboard with Gruyère and you don't spread pineapple and chive flavour chalk on your crisp bread.'[50] The launch of several relatively expensive comics (*Deadline* cost £1.50, *Revolver* £1.65) during a time of economic downturn cannot have helped. And, perhaps, the failure to reach a general readership beyond diehard comic fans simply reflected public scepticism about the whole project of adult comics. The fact that *Beano* and *Dandy* significantly outsold *Crisis* and *Deadline* would suggest that, for most readers, comics remained the preserve of children.

* * *

The failure of the British adult comics of the 1980s had the effect of driving many creators into the arms of American publishers. The US market was more open to adult comics: DC, for example, developed a line of comics for older readers through its Vertigo imprint. Among those who crossed the Atlantic (metaphorically if not always physically) were Alan Moore, who wrote *Swamp Thing*, *Watchmen* and *Batman: The Killing Joke* for DC; Grant Morrison, who took over *The Doom Patrol* and *The Invisibles* for DC as well as writing the Batman story *Arkham Asylum*; and Garth Ennis, who has written *Hitman* and *The Preacher*, again for DC. Other British writers to work in US comics include Jamie Delano (*Hellblazer*), Neil Gaiman (*Sandman*) and Peter Milligan (*The Odyssey* – a spin-off from the *Tank Girl* film). British artists Brian Bolland (*The Killing Joke*), Dave Gibbons (*Watchmen*), Sean Philips (*The Invisibles*) and Simon Bisley (*The Doom Patrol*) have also worked extensively in US comics. Such was the exodus that by the late 1980s commentators were speaking of a 'British invasion' of the American comics scene – another comparison between comics in the 1980s and pop music in the 1960s.

There were several reasons for the exodus of British talent to the USA in the 1980s. At a time when the British market was contracting, the American market remained large enough to sustain comics for mature readers. Writers, especially, were attracted by the opportunity to develop longer narratives and to see them through to their natural conclusion. In contrast serials in British comics were all too often left incomplete. Furthermore, American publishers by this time were offering not only superior remuneration but also better contractual conditions, especially regarding creators' rights. As a DC talent scout in charge of recruiting British creators remarked in 1987: 'We found that the British bring a level of maturity and sophistication not otherwise available in the United States, where comic readers are often in their mid-twenties. Quite honestly, conditions in Britain are so backward, securing their services was no problem.'[51]

What conclusions can be drawn from the history of British adult comics in the 1980s? While the short life of titles like *Warrior*, *Crisis*, *Deadline* and *Revolver* would seem to suggest that the market for adult comics in Britain was limited, this does not mean they are of no significance. Quite the contrary in fact: at a time when the market overall was shrinking these comics marked a bold if ultimately unsuccessful attempt to create a new market. They were characterized by their broadly progressive outlook and by their willingness to take both cultural and economic risks. Strips such as 'V for Vendetta' and 'Third World War' can be seen as genuinely radical, while 'Tank Girl' was attuned to a particular pop-cultural zeitgeist. Collectively what these comics represented – alongside the impact of graphic novels like *The Dark Knight Returns* and *Watchmen* – was an increasing critical recognition of the role of the comic creator. It was in the 1980s that writers such as Alan Moore emerged as the equivalent of auteurs in the film industry or cult authors in literature. It is to the work of contemporary British comic writers since the 1980s that we now turn.

CHAPTER TEN

The British Comics Renaissance

> It's almost as if a large section of America's populace don't seem to really understand that there are countries in the world other than America, and that there was ever a historical event that Americans didn't play . . . But the response to *The League*, which is all set in Britain, and where there's hardly an American influence to be seen – the response to that, like I say, is really reassuring, really encouraging . . . It was very gratifying to think that I could do something that was so personal in some ways, so perversely English, and to have it go down so well in America is tremendous.
>
> Alan Moore.[1]

The decline of the comic market and the exodus of British writers and artists to America has fundamentally altered the landscape of comics in Britain. The British comic market is now dominated by imports – principally American superhero titles and Japanese *manga* comics – while the only British comics still in continuous publication are *Dandy, Beano, Commando, 2000AD* and *Judge Dredd Megazine*. While the market has contracted, however, the medium itself has enjoyed something of a renaissance over the last two decades. This assessment is based not so much on the volume of comics produced as on their quality. In particular the work of a group of British writers – including, but not limited to, Alan Moore, Neil Gaiman, Grant Morrison, Ian Edginton, Warren Ellis and Garth Ennis – has brought a new level of critical acclaim and even cultural respectability to the comic industry. While these writers have undertaken much of their work for American publishers, their work has also maintained a sense of British identity. A recent academic study of Alan Moore, for example, maintains that although much of his work, including the seminal *Watchmen*, has focused on American subject-matter, nevertheless 'it is important to remember that his graphic novels also retain a very tight bond with distinctively English cultural, social and aesthetic subjects.'[2] It is an indication of the status of British writers in the industry, moreover, that American publishers have been prepared to back comics focusing on British subjects such as Moore's *The League of Extraordinary Gentleman*, Edginton's *Scarlet Traces* and Ellis's *Ministry of Space*. This would suggest that the Britishness of contemporary comics is not just an indicator of cultural prestige but also carries some economic weight. This chapter considers the work of modern British comic writers and their engagement with British subjects and themes.

* * *

Alan Moore is by common consent among fans and critics the most important contemporary comic writer. He is the one British creator whose influence on the medium can be compared to such legendary figures as Marvel's Stan Lee, Jack Kirby and Steve Ditko.[3] Since the early 1980s Moore has produced a body of work – including *V for Vendetta, Watchmen, From Hell, Lost Girls, Promethea* and *The League of Extraordinary Gentlemen* – that has redefined the nature of the comic medium. Moore's is a diverse and varied oeuvre that includes work across several genres including superheroes (*Watchmen*), horror (*From Hell*), fantasy (*Promethea*), pornography (*Lost Girls*) and steampunk (*The League of Extraordinary Gentlemen*). Working with various artists (including David Lloyd, Dave Gibbons, Eddie Campbell, Melinda Gebbie and Kevin O'Neill), Moore has created comics distinguished by their formal innovation, narrative complexity and psychological depth. Much of his work has been for independent publishers: Moore's relations with the US giants DC and Marvel have been problematic, to say the least. He has also maintained a critical distance from several film adaptations of his work, even to the extent of insisting that his name be removed from the credits.[4]

Moore had started out as an artist, selling cartoons to the music press, but found his métier as a writer in the early 1980s. He wrote numerous standalone stories for *2000AD* and *Doctor Who Weekly* before *Warrior* provided the opportunity to develop continuing serials in 'Marvelman' and 'V for Vendetta'. He also took over writing 'Captain Britain' for Marvel in 1982, the strips appearing in *Marvel Superheroes, The Daredevils* and *The Mighty World of Marvel*. In 1984 he took over DC's *Swamp Thing* and revamped a minor horror comic into an examination of contemporary social issues including environmentalism and racial prejudice. He wrote the seminal Batman/Joker graphic novel *The Killing Joke* for DC and the two-part Superman story 'Whatever Happened to the Man of Tomorrow?'. *Watchmen*, published first as a twelve-part series and collected into a trade paperback in 1987, secured his reputation as a master of the comic medium. Moore used his new-found status in the industry to undertake more personal projects outside the mainstream. He wrote in support of political causes such as the campaign against the controversial Clause 28 of the Local Government Act (*AARGH!*) and undertook a number of small-scale projects such as *A Small Killing*.[5] Moore spent much of the 1990s working on two ambitious projects, *From Hell* and *Lost Girls*, that would not be completed until 1999 and 2006 respectively. Critic Roz Kaveney contends that 'both of these are monuments to just how fine non-superhero comics can be as serious works of art'.[6] Moore returned to the mainstream with *Spawn*, *WildCATS* and *Supreme* for Image Comics, before joining Jim Lee of Wildstorm in 1999 to set up a new imprint, America's Best Comics (ABC), writing *The League of Extraordinary Gentlemen*, *Tom Strong* and *Promethea*.

For all the variety of subject-matter, there are certain recurring themes and motifs that run throughout Moore's work. Three in particular stand out. The first is the use of the comic as a vehicle of social and political comment. Sometimes this may be explicit, such as *V for Vendetta* and *AARGH!* (which stands for 'Artists Against Rampant Government Homophobia'), while elsewhere it may be more oblique. Moore has said that he believes in telling 'stories that actually have some sort of meaning in relation to the world about us, stories that reflect the nature and texture of life in the closing years of the 20th century'.[7] The second characteristic of Moore's work is its formal innovation. His early work, especially, is notable for devices – developed in association with various artists – such as abandoning sound effect captions (*V for Vendetta*) and thought balloons ('The Ballad of Halo Jones'). *Watchmen* is a self-consciously formalist work characterized by its multiple lines of narrative, symmetrical page layouts and self-reflexivity. It has been described as 'the *Citizen Kane* of comics'.[8] The third particular feature of Moore's work is that it is steeped in the history not just of comics but of literature more generally. *The League of Extraordinary Gentlemen* and *Lost Girls* are both posited on the notion that characters from popular literature inhabit the same fictional universe. *Albion* turns on the idea that the world of the British fantasy and adventure comics is real. And *Watchmen* was originally to have featured the 'Charlton superheroes' until DC insisted that Moore create an entirely new set of characters for the story.[9]

We have already considered 'Marvelman' and 'V for Vendetta' in the context of the trend towards comics for mature readers in the 1980s. *Swamp Thing*, *Watchmen* and Moore's other American work are outside the scope of this book, but *From Hell* and *The League of Extraordinary Gentlemen* are key works by dint of their British subject-matter. *From Hell*, which he developed over eleven years in collaboration with artist Eddie Campbell, has been described as 'an authentic masterpiece'.[10] It can be located in a tradition of British fictions and pseudo-histories about Jack the Ripper, the serial killer who murdered five prostitutes in the East End of London in 1888. Indeed, *From Hell* locates itself in that tradition through an appendix in which Moore and Campbell trace the history of 'Ripperology' over the ensuing century. Moore explained that his interest in the subject was not from the perspective of a conventional 'whodunit' but rather as a historical and psychological enquiry:

> At first, I dismissed the idea of Jack the Ripper as having been done to death and being too played out. Later, I took another look at the case and realized that, yeah, there was a way that I could write about the Jack the Ripper story in such a way that hadn't been done before, and which would enable me to explore the things I wanted to explore about a murder. Sometimes it will be an abstract idea like that, where I've not got any particular story that I want to tell, but where it will strike me that, if I was going to write a murder story, say, I wouldn't do it in the style of a whodunit. So, how would I do it? And that kind of thought leads to *From Hell*.[11]

From Hell develops the thesis of Stephen Knight's book *Jack the Ripper: The Final Solution* (1977) that the Ripper was Sir William Gull, the royal surgeon, and that the murders of five women were carried out to silence those who knew of an illegitimate baby and secret marriage between Prince Albert, grandson of Queen Victoria, and shop-girl Annie Crook. This was hardly a new idea – Knight's book had informed the film *Murder By Decree*[12] – but what distinguishes Moore's narrative is how he uses the Ripper case to explore the social and intellectual landscape of late Victorian London. Gull is a Freemason and a zealot who invests the murders with a ritualistic significance (hence the abominal mutilations performed upon his victims) and who believes that he has a moral duty to protect civilization from corrupting influences and new ideas. He is characterized as an extreme misogynist for whom murdering women becomes a counter to the rise of Victorian feminism:

> Could you, for instance, tolerate a world where females ruled? With men bound to their whims and governed by their scorn? . . . Then offer up a prayer of thanks to these black tenements, these soot encrusted walls . . . 'Twas here that womankind's last hopes and dreams were put to the sword.[13]

Like many of the best thrillers, *From Hell* uses the genre to examine the nature of power and corruption. It is made emphatically clear that the British establishment is not only aware of the Ripper's identity but is complicit in the

From Hell (Knockabout Comics, 2000).

murders and in covering up the truth. Gull is instructed to undertake his gruesome task by Queen Victoria herself: 'The woman, one "Annie Crook", has been taken to Guy's Hospital to await your attentions. We have promised our grandson that she shall not feel the fullest extent of our displeasure, but if this scandal is not to rock the throne she must be SILENCED.'[14] And when Inspector Abberline of Scotland Yard finally unmasks Gull as the Ripper, he is instructed to keep quiet by his superiors: 'Think what the Socialist Press would make of it, him bein' Her Majesty's doctor 'an all. Ye'd not want them turnin' this tragedy into an uprisin' would ye? . . . Sir William will be dealt with privately, but it's best for Queen and Country if the matter's quietly dropped.'[15] Abberline is a likeable but compromised figure: his silence is bought by a generous pension.

From Hell is a perfect illustration of Moore's approach to story-telling. It draws upon a range of devices, including pastiches of contemporary newspapers and photographs. The device of opening each chapter with a quotation from a contemporary figure – including James Hinton, W. B. Yeats, Oscar Wilde and Sir Arthur Conan Doyle – and references to the paintings of Walter Sickert and the satirical cartoons of John Tenniel serve to locate the narrative within a particular historical and social context. It is as if Moore and Campbell are suggesting that to understand the Ripper we must understand the society that gave rise to him. There is a sense in which Jack the Ripper was an invention of the Victorians to justify their own moral and social order. Moore and Campbell are also concerned to explore the mythology of the Ripper. The appendix documents the development of 'Ripperology' and examines the many theories surrounding the identity of the Ripper. Moore writes into this sequence his own experiences in researching *From Hell*, concluding that there is probably no entirely satisfactory explanation of the events:

Slowly it dawns on me that despite the Gull theory's obvious attractions, the idea of a solution, any solution, is inane. Murder isn't like books. Murder, a human event located in both space and time, has an imaginary field completely unrestrained by either. It holds meaning, and shape, but no solution.[16]

The League of Extraordinary Gentlemen may also be understood as an exploration of popular mythology: in this case the world of Victorian fiction. *League* is essentially a period variation on the superhero team-up narrative: a sort of Justice League of Victorian Britain. Its premise is that in 1898 the British government assembles a team of adventurers drawn from the world of Victorian popular literature: Allan Quatermain, Captain Nemo, Dr Henry Jekyll (and Mr Edward Hyde), Hawley Griffin (the Invisible Man) and Wilhelmina Murray (Mina Harker of *Dracula*). The role of the League, who turn out to be one of many such groups over the centuries, is to defend the British Empire from the threats posed by the fiendish oriental mastermind Dr Fu Manchu (*League Volume I*) and from Martian invaders (*League Volume II* is the 'true' story of the events of *The War of the Worlds*). *League* is a veritable cornucopia of literary allusions and intertextual references, both verbal and visual, which range from the highbrow to the world of underground erotica. Among the many sources quoted, directly or indirectly, are the novels of H. Rider Haggard (*King Solomon's Mines, She*), Jules Verne (*Twenty Thousand Leagues Under the Sea, Robur the Conqueror*), Robert Louis Stevenson (*The Strange Case of Dr Jekyll and Mr Hyde*), H. G. Wells (*The Invisible Man, The Island of Dr Moreau, The War of the Worlds, The First Men in the Moon*), Bram Stoker (*Dracula*), Oscar Wilde (*The Picture of Dorian Gray*), Anthony Hope (*The Prisoner of Zenda*), Herman Melville (*Moby Dick*), the Sherlock Holmes stories of Arthur Conan Doyle, the Fu Manchu stories of Sax Rohmer and the John Carter of Mars stories by Edgar Rice Burroughs.[17]

Moore has described *The League of Extraordinary Gentlemen* as a 'literary connect-the-dots puzzle'.[18] There is some evidence to suggest that the success of the series prompted some readers to revisit the original sources.[19] Yet the *League* should be understood as more than just a clever pastiche of the world of Victorian fiction: Moore and artist Kevin O'Neill examine the ideologies of the source texts even to the point of deconstructing them. Thus, for example, the characterization of Captain Nemo as a Sikh and the presence of the 'Yellow Peril' in the person of Fu Manchu are used to comment on the racial politics of the originals. Moore said that he wanted to explore 'the absurdity of the Victorian vision, this idea of a supremacist Britain that ruled the entire world'.[20] *League* can be understood as a critique of late Victorian imperial hubris. It presents a *fin de siècle* Britain that finds its assumptions of cultural and racial superiority challenged by both internal and external threats. To this extent it is consistent with some of the original sources: *The War of the Worlds*, for example, has been read as a Victorian nightmare in which the world's greatest imperial power experiences colonialism from the other side as it is invaded by a technologically superior alien 'other'.

The League of Extraordinary Gentlemen is a sophisticated parody of adventure story, steampunk science fiction and comics. It draws attention to its own fictionality through its exaggerated caricatures and a splendid parody of the prose style of contemporary boys' story papers: 'The next edition of our new Boys' Picture Monthly will continue this arresting yarn, in which the Empire's finest are brought into conflict with the sly Chinee, accompanied by a variety of coloured illustrations from our artist that are sure to prove exciting to the manly, outwardgoing youngster of today.'[21] The collected editions of the *League* also include a wide range of appendices and supporting materials including a complete prose story in the style of the Aldine Press ('Allan and the Sundered Veil' in *League Volume I*) and a 'New Traveller's Almanac' (*League Volume II*) documenting the field reports of other British agents. In short the *League* is nothing less than a tour de force of narrative and visual imagination. Moore has suggested that the narrative possibilities for the series are endless: 'I've got the whole of the geographic cosmos of fiction as our stamping ground . . . I can imagine no end of stories.'[22]

The League of Extraordinary Gentlemen: Black Dossier demonstrates that the series need not be confined to the Victorian period. This extends the concept to an alternate 1950s Britain after the fall of the IngSoc government of Big Brother and where a later incarnation of the League – including an ageing Bulldog Drummond, his goddaughter Emma Knight (the future Emma Peel of *The Avengers*) and a womanizing secret agent known as Jimmy – are on the trail of a secret dossier documenting members of the many Leagues throughout history. In *Black Dossier* the range of intertextual allusions extends beyond literary fiction – including George Orwell's *Nineteen Eighty-Four*, Evelyn Waugh's *Scoop*, the James Bond novels of Ian Fleming and the Greyfriars stories of Charles Hamilton – to include film and television: *The Third Man*, *Dixon of Dock Green*, *Coronation Street*, *Danger Man*, *The Avengers*, *The Prisoner* and many other incidental references. As in previous volumes Moore reinterprets the source materials: the James Bond figure is portrayed as a violent would-be rapist ('You like it rough occasionally, girls like you') and Greyfriars turns out to have been a recruiting school for secret agents. This brilliant idea demonstrates Moore's familiarity not just with the originals but with the critical debate around them: it develops Orwell's argument that public-school fiction was a vehicle of propaganda for conservatism and the establishment. Thus it turns out that all the Greyfriars boys became members of the political elite or the intelligence services: Harry Wharton became Big Brother, Frank Nugent became Francis Waverly (*The Man From U.N.C.L.E.*) and Bob Cherry became Harry Lime and later, following Lime's apparent death in the sewers of Vienna, assumed the position of 'M'.[23]

Moore was also responsible for the concept of *Albion*, written by his daughter Leah Moore and John Reppion and drawn by Shane Oakley. *Albion* was conceived 'as a vehicle for resurrecting IPC's library of iconic British adventure heroes'.[24] It combines the premise of the *League* (a shared fictional universe of comic characters) with the theme of *Watchmen* (political and social anxieties around the activities of unregulated costumed adventurers). It is based on the premise that the protagonists of IPC adventure and fantasy comics – including Robot Archie, Mytek the Mighty, Captain Hurricane, The Steel Claw, Adam Eterno, Cursitor Doom and Grimly Fiendish – were hunted down by The Spider, acting on the orders of the Thatcher government, and incarcerated in a high-security establishment. The Spider was promised a pardon – 'if I turned on my own, on people England wanted out of the way' – but the government reneged on the deal ('Nobody does treachery like the English') and imprisoned him too.[25] *Albion* turns The Spider into a sinister Hannibal Lecter figure: when FBI agent Zachary Nolan visits him in his cell to solicit his knowledge it recalls a similar scene from *The Silence of the Lambs*.[26] The reason for the incarceration of costumed heroes was to control them and to appropriate their powers for the state: Margaret Thatcher survived the IRA bomb at the Grand Hotel in Brighton in 1984 because she was protected by the Eye of Zoltec! *Albion* was followed by a volume of reprints (*Albion: Origins*) and a new version of *Thunderbolt Jaxon* by Dave Gibbons and John Higgins, while Leah Moore has gone on to script *Doctor Who* and *The Trial of Sherlock Holmes* for Avatar Press.

* * *

While no other contemporary comic writers have achieved the cult status of Alan Moore, the important contributions made to the field by a range of other writers must not be overlooked. We have already considered Grant Morrison's 'Zenith' for *2000AD* and 'Dare' for *Revolver*: both strips are notable for their explicitly anti-Thatcherite politics. Morrison enjoyed a brief moment of public notoriety when *Crisis* published his controversial 'The New Adventures of Hitler' in 1990. There was also a minor tabloid storm over *St Swithin's Day*, which he wrote for the independent publisher Trident Comics: the story of a disillusioned young unemployed man who fantasizes about shooting Margaret Thatcher. Morrison's last major contribution to the British comics scene came when he and Mark Millar were given free reign over *2000AD* for its so-called 'summer offensive' in 1993. Their 'Big Dave' is a vicious satire of tabloid culture and popular nationalism in which Britain's self-styled 'hardest man' is sent to Iraq to 'sort out' Saddam Hussein. Later episodes see Dave sleeping with Princess Diana and leading an army of football hooligans to lay waste to Majorca.[27] This would be Morrison's farewell to British comics: subsequently he has written extensively for US superhero lines, including *Justice League of America, The Invisibles, The Doom Patrol, New X-Men* and *Batman*.

The path from British comics to the American mainstream was also followed by Neil Gaiman and Jamie Delano. Gaiman, who succeeded Alan Moore on *Miracleman*, combines writing for comics, notably the much admired *Sandman*, with prose fiction and screenplays, while Delano, who succeeded Moore on *Captain Britain*, enjoyed his biggest success with *Hellblazer*, itself a spin-off from Moore's *Swamp Thing*. Ian Edginton, who has formed a highly successful partnership with the artist D'Israeli (Matt Brooker), represents a different trajectory from most of his contemporaries in that he made his name in America, largely through film and television spin-offs for Dark Horse Comics (*The Terminator, Aliens, Predator, Planet of the Apes, Xena: Warrior Princess*), before joining the ranks of *2000AD* with 'Leviathan' (a science fiction *Titanic*) and 'Stickleback' (a grotesque nineteenth-century villain in the style of *Gormenghast*). Edginton and D'Israeli's graphic novel *Scarlet Traces* was published first on the Internet before a print volume followed in 2003. It is a sequel to *The War of the Worlds* which posits that following the invasion of 1898 Britain has assimilated the Martians' technology and has become the strongest military and industrial power in the world. However, it transpires that this technological advancement is dependent upon a surviving Martian who feeds on human blood: the government conspires to provide a fresh supply by luring girls from poor families to London with the promise of a job.

Scarlet Traces ends with the British Empire launching a retaliatory war against the Martians:

> We shall take the battle back to their homes and hearths, where we will deliver such a crushing blow as to prevent them from ever threatening our world again! Britain alone bore the brunt of the conflict without the succour of our neighbours and we ask no one to fight our battles for us now.[28]

It is difficult not to read this as an indirect comment on the British decision to join the invasion of Iraq in 2003 where military intervention was justified in terms of the apparent threat posed by Saddam Hussein's regime. This interpretation is lent further credence by the sequel, *The Great Game*, which followed in 2006 and which depicts the British army fighting a bloody campaign against Martian counter-insurgents. A weakened Britain is unable to resist demands for independence from the colonies but turns its attention to social reform: 'Life isn't perfect, but on the whole we've become a kinder, gentler country . . . For all its faults and foibles, this is a new world now. A new England.'[29] While Edginton's alternate history of Britain may be less well known to the general readership than Moore's, it shares similar themes around British history and identity. And it also deploys intertextuality as a narrative strategy: there are cameo appearances from Tintin and Captain Haddock, while Danny Dravott of Kipling's *The Man Who Would Be King* turns up as a government enforcer.

It is in the work of the near-contemporaries Warren Ellis and Garth Ennis, however, that we find perhaps the most sustained engagement with British subject-matter and themes. Ellis and Ennis are both significant for the way in which they have negotiated (rather more successfully than Alan Moore, for example) the competing demands of the US-dominated commercial mainstream with a distinctive if idiosyncratic engagement with British history. Ellis, in particular, has acknowledged the influence of Moore: his first publications were fan letters to *Warrior* in the early 1980s and he nominated *From Hell* as his 'all-time favourite graphic novel'. Ellis published his first comic strips in *Deadline* and *Blast!* in the early 1990s and was then recruited by Marvel for whom he contributed to *Hellstorm* and British-themed superhero series *Excalibur*. His best-known mainstream work is probably *Transmetropolitan*, which he wrote for DC's mature imprint Vertigo, but Ellis has also written for independent publishers such as Wildstorm and Avatar Press. In recent years he has shifted away from the long-running superhero sagas such as *The Fantastic Four* and *Iron Man* and has preferred to write stand-alone mini-series including *Desolation Jones* (an ex-MI6 agent now working as a private eye in Los Angeles), *Anna Mercury* (a British equivalent of Sydney Bristow of the television series *Alias*), *Ignition City* (alternate history adventure in the 1950s) and *Captain Swing and the Electrical Pirates of Cindery Island* (nineteenth-century steampunk).

Ellis returns consistently to British subjects in his work. *Ministry of Space*, a three-part series published in 2001, is an alternate history in which Britain takes the lead in the space race following the acquisition of German rocket technology at the end of the Second World War. It explores the relationship between space exploration and discourses of national power: 'We could have men on the moon itself by nineteen sixty. It's all out there waiting for us and we can get it first and claim it all for King and Country and the British Empire.'[30] Britain does indeed launch the first man into space (1950) and sends manned expeditions to the Moon (1959) and Mars (1969). However,

Crécy (Avatar Press, 2007).

Ellis subverts the progressive ideology of *Dan Dare* through the revelation that the British space programme was secretly funded by gold stolen from victims of the Holocaust. *Ministry of Space* is drawn by Chris Weston in what is best described as a 'retro futuristic' style: a modern take on a 1950s vision of the future. The five-part *Ignition City* from 2009 is to some extent the reverse of *Ministry of Space*: Britain in the 1950s is about to decommission its space programme as it cannot afford it. Commander Crabb (based on real-life naval frogman 'Buster' Crabb) remarks: 'My country's not a power anymore, y'see. It'd like to be, but it's not. And having rocket ships swooping around – it attracts unwanted attention in a country still trying to pay for a war.'[31]

Crécy, a short graphic novel published in 2007, is not one of Ellis's better known works but it is among the most distinctive of recent examinations of nationhood. *Crécy* is an account of 'England's greatest battle' during the Hundred Years War drawn by Raulo Caceres in the style of medieval woodcuts. It is 'a story about the English and the French and why the English hate the French'. It is narrated by William of Stonham, an English archer, whose dialogue is full of modern colloquialisms: 'We pissed off the locals good and proper'; 'Their king Philip is frankly a bit of a knobend'; 'It'll kick off soon'. Ellis uses the story to suggest that Crécy marked the origin of modern warfare as the English army inflicted carnage upon the French with its superior weapon: the longbow. That *Crécy* is intended as a statement about the Iraq War is left in no doubt by the cover blurb: 'A highly trained but under equipped army invades another country due to that country's perceived threat to home security. The army conducts shock-and-awe raids designed to terrify the populace.'[32]

The career of Garth Ennis mirrors that of Ellis. Ennis was another of the new writers to emerge from the British adult comic boom of the late 1980s. He started with the acclaimed 'Troubled Souls' for *Crisis* in 1989 and in the early 1990s was entrusted with replacing John Wagner as chief writer of 'Judge Dredd'. Ennis was hired by DC to take over *Hellblazer* and for whom he also wrote *The Preacher*. In 2001 he began *The Punisher* for Marvel and also contributed to several superhero lines including *Spider-Man* and *Hulk*. His other works include a future war story centred on a tough female mercenary (*Bloody Mary*), a violent series about a group of enforcers tasked with curbing the excesses of superheroes (*The Boys*), and an ex-government assassin trying to escape his past (*A Man Called Kev*). Ennis's work is characterized by its emphasis on masculinity, its hostility towards organized religion, its irreverent attitude towards superheroes and often by its extreme violence.

In recent years, however, Ennis has also been almost single-handedly responsible for a revival of one of the favourite subjects of British comics: the Second World War. The British war comic had been largely defunct since the demise of *Battle* and *Victor*: only *Commando* kept the tradition alive and even it had diversified into other conflicts including the Falklands and Gulf Wars. In 2000, however, Ennis wrote *Adventures in the Rifle Brigade*, which he dedicated 'to the writers, artists and editorial staff of *Battle Picture Weekly*, *Battle*, *Battle Picture Library*, *War Picture Library* and *Commando*'.[33] *Adventures in the Rifle Brigade* is an irreverent spoof of men-on-a-mission narratives like *The Dirty Dozen* drawn by *Battle* artist Carlos Ezquerra in an exaggerated parody of his own 'The Rat Pack' and 'Major Eazy'. In 2006, with artist Colin Wilson, Ennis resurrected an old favourite in the form of a five-part *Battler Britton*. However, this is a different Battler Britton from the character who had starred in *Air Ace Picture Library* in the 1960s. Again it is difficult not to interpret the series as an indirect comment on the Iraq War. It is set in the Western Desert in 1942 where Squadron-Leader Robert Britton is assigned to a joint Anglo-American squadron. The series explores Anglo-American tension and deals with difficult subjects such as deaths by 'friendly fire'. When an American pilot is killed in 'a stupid goddamn accident', Britton advises his CO to disguise the truth for the sake of the boy's parents: 'You tell them what a magnificent contribution he made to the squadron. How all your men looked up to him. How he died in combat against the enemy.' Reminded by his colleague that 'that ain't quite the whole truth', Britton replies: 'For Mr and Mrs Plowman – the whole truth is unthinkable.'[34]

Ennis has also written stand-alone stories collected together under the banner of *War Stories* (DC) and a series of three-parters called *Battlefields* (Dynamite). These have been illustrated by different artists – including Dave Gibbons, Gary Erskine, Carlos Ezquerra, Cam Kennedy, David Lloyd and

Chris Weston – and are characterized by their broadly revisionist treatment of aspects of the Second World War. While the subject-matter of *War Stories* may be familiar – including the Arctic convoys ('Nightingale'), strategic bombing ('J for Jenny'), the Special Air Service ('The Reivers') and the Italian campaign ('D-Day Dodgers') – Ennis's approach avoids the gung-ho heroics of comics like *Warlord* and *Battle* and focuses instead on the effects of war on ordinary combatants. *Battlefields* examines some of the less familiar aspects of the Second World War, including two stories that, unusually for the genre, place women at the centre of the narrative, 'The Night Witches' (the role of Russian women pilots) and 'Dear Billy' (the psychological trauma of nurses captured by the Japanese), though the favourite seems to have been 'The Tankies' (the crew of a British Cromwell facing German Tiger tanks in the *bocage* country of Normandy). *War Stories* and *Battlefields* are notable for their unflinching realism, including a harrowing account of the rape and murder of prisoners ('Dear Billy') and the terror of being burned alive when a tank 'brews up' ('The Tankies').

The Second World War is also a major reference point for Ennis and Gary Erskine's *Dan Dare*, published as a seven-part series by Virgin Comics in 2008. This is the fifth revival of the old *Eagle* favourite, following *2000AD*, *Eagle* Mk II, *Revolver* and a CGI television series in 2001. It is also the most satisfying overall: Ennis succeeds in combining something of the ethos of the original Dan Dare with the revisionism of Grant Morrison's 'Dare'. Ennis explained how he had drawn upon the different versions of the character:

> I loved the *2000AD* stories as a kid, though you don't have to read too much of the Hampson stuff to see that *2000AD*'s version wasn't really Dan Dare. Having looked at the Titan Books reprints, I can definitely see the charm of the original . . . Essentially I'm more interested in the idea of Dan Dare than the specifics of what we've seen in previous stories; he's the quintessential Englishman, honour and decency personified. An idealised hero of the kind we like to imagine at Waterloo or Trafalgar, or piloting a Spitfire in the summer of 1940.[35]

Dan Dare is replete with references to the Second World War, from the ships of the Royal Space Navy to Dan's pet dogs Stuffy and Bomber.[36] Ennis has recognized the reference points of the original strip and has remained faithful to it.

Dan Dare is a beautifully rendered, elegiac narrative that follows a familiar formula: the old hero recalled to save the world one last time. It is set some twenty years or so after Hampson's *Dan Dare – Pilot of the Future*. The

Dan Dare (Virgin Comics, November 2007).

World Government has collapsed following an atomic war between the USA and China: Britain, protected by a missile shield developed by chief scientific officer Professor Peabody, has emerged as 'the strongest nation on Earth'. Peabody is now Home Secretary in a government clearly modelled on New Labour (the Prime Minister's office is now in Millbank Tower) but Dan has become a recluse, living alone in the asteroid belt in an idealized English village created by computer hologram. Dan is characterized as having a sentimental attachment to the past – old cricket bats, Spitfires, sailing ships – and feels that modern Britain has lost touch with its traditional values: 'These are the things that I think we've lost, Prime Minister, that Britain has lost.'[37] Dan is recalled to service when the Mekon reappears with an enormous Treen battlefleet and a portable black hole. The Prime Minister, fearing that Earth will be annihilated, favours appeasement and concludes a secret deal with the Mekon that will see him installed as head of a puppet government. Dan, however, rallies the fleet, and although the Royal Navy suffers heavy losses, including Digby, the Mekon is defeated at the Battle of Neptune.

Dan Dare is an examination of Britishness and what it means today. It asserts that the values Dan represents – patriotism, duty, loyalty, honour, courage, tolerance, compassion – are as relevant to the modern world as they were in the past. Dan's old-fashioned values and his sense of history are contrasted with the Prime Minister, who has never heard of the Battle of Britain ('Small matter of saving the country, and western civilisation along with it') and to whom the notion of patriotism is entirely alien ('I simply don't understand why you're still so willing to fight for it'). Yet *Dan Dare* is also at pains to emphasize that patriotism is not the same thing as nationalism. In one key scene, as they wait for news of the space battle that will decide their fate, Peabody tells one of her colleagues how Dan was once approached by the National Front. Unlike Grant Morrison's 'Dare', however, where he had unwittingly become a figurehead for a neo-Fascist party, this Dan has no truck with the Far Right:

> They contacted him under false pretences. It was at the decomissioning of the *Anastasia*, we were still together at that stage. They wanted Dan to be a figurehead for their movement into mainstream politics. Keeping Britain British, that sort of thing, although you knew immediately that what they meant was *white*. Digby wanted to give them the trashing of their lives, but Dan was simply polite to them. He said we'd enjoyed the fruits of the British Empire, and now we owed its children a debt of care. And then he asked them to leave. He was heartbroken that night . . . But it wasn't that these thugs would think he'd want anything to do with them, that wasn't what was so awful for him. It was what the rise of these monsters *meant*. Because once they began identifying their cause with men like Dan, they'd taint the very notion of being British. They'd wrap themselves in the flag, and an entire generation of immigrant people would look at the Union Jack and see a swastika.[38]

It is impossible to read this as anything other than a commentary on the resurgence of the Far Right in early twenty-first-century Britain. The British National Party enjoyed some popular support in local council elections, especially in areas where anxieties around immigration fuelled its racist policies, and during the general election campaign of 2010 outraged many by associating itself with iconic British figures such as Winston Churchill. In distancing Dan from the politics of the Far Right, Ennis is stating his view of organizations like the British National Party and how they have appropriated national symbols for their own ideological ends. It is yet another example of how contemporary comic writers have used the medium to respond to the cultural and ideological climate of their times.

* * *

Dan Dare is an appropriate point on which to conclude this history of British comics. It can be seen both as a summary of the maturity of the medium today and as a link to its historic traditions. While comics are no longer the mass medium they once were, there are signs that, finally, they are being taken more seriously both as an art form and as a social practice. There is still a long way to go before the British comic enjoys the prestige of the *bande dessinée* or the cult appeal of *manga*, but the work of contemporary British writers and artists, working both in Britain and in the American comic industry, has shown what the medium at its best can achieve. It is my contention that the work of comic writers such as Alan Moore, Garth Ennis and Warren Ellis is the equal of any modern literary fiction, that graphic novels like *From Hell* and *The League of Extraordinary Gentlemen* are just as significant postmodern texts as Umberto Eco's *The Name of the Rose* and *Foucault's Pendulum*, that *Battlefields* is as vivid a representation of the Second World War as Steven Spielberg's *Saving Private Ryan*, and that *Ministry of Space* deserves to be afforded as much cultural currency as Tom Wolfe's *The Right Stuff*. It is ironic that it is not until the comic has ceased to be a mass medium that it has been recognized as a legitimate subject for critical and historical analysis.

References

INTRODUCTION

1 Paul Dawson, 'The comics come of age', *The Times Higher Educational Supplement* (23 December 1988), p. 14.
2 Ann Miller, *Reading Bande Dessinée: Critical Approaches to French-language Comic Strip* (Bristol, 2007), p. 66. Miller includes a full bibliography of the critical literature on the *bande dessinée* in both French and English. See also Bart Beaty, *Unpopular Culture: Transforming the European Comic Book in the 1990s* (Toronto, 2007).
3 The best and most comprehensive study of American comics is Bradford W. Wright, *Comic Book Nation: The Transformation of Youth Culture in America* (Baltimore, MA, 2001). Other useful histories include Mike Benton, *The Comic Book in America: An Illustrated History* (Dallas, TX, 1989); Les Daniels, *Comix: A History of Comic Books in America* (New York, 1971); and William W. Savage Jr, *Commies, Cowboys, and Jungle Queens: Comic Books and America, 1945–1954* (Middletown, CT, 1990).
4 The popular historiography of comics is extensive. The preference for American comics is exemplified by Reinhold Reitberger and Wolfgang Fuchs, *Comics: Anatomy of a Mass Medium* (London, 1972). Denis Gifford's *The International Book of Comics* (London, 1984), despite its title, focuses largely on America and Britain. See also George Perry and Alan Aldridge, *The Penguin Book of Comics* (Harmondsworth, 1967).
5 Lindsay Anderson, 'Alfred Hitchcock', *Sequence*, 9 (1949), p. 113.
6 Quoted in Alastair Crompton, *The Man Who Drew Tomorrow* (Bournemouth, 1985), p. 209.
7 Quoted in Chad Boudreau, 'Phil Elliott: The past and present of the UK comic industry', n.d., www.comicreaders.com/modules (accessed 15 January 2010).
8 *Warrior*, 12 (August 1983), p. 50.
9 On the publication history of the Tintin albums in Britain, see Anon., 'The Initial Hergé', *Escape*, 2 (Summer 1983), pp. 24–8. See also Pierre Assouline, *Hergé: The Man Who Created Tintin*, trans. Charles Ruas (Oxford, 2009).
10 Brian Walker, *Comic Cuts: An Exhibition of Comic Papers and Christmas Periodicals from 1850 to the Present Day*, exh. cat., Bath Reference Library (1971), n.p.

11 Quoted in 'AARGH lives – but the blood is printed red', *Evening Standard* (23 February 1976), p. 3.
12 Julie Burchill, 'Grin and Bear It', *20/20*, 5 (September 1989), p. 20.
13 Richard Hoggart, *The Uses of Literacy* (Harmondsworth, 1958), pp. 164–5.
14 See Martin Barker, *A Haunt of Fears: The Strange History of the British Horror Comics Campaign* (London, 1984).
15 'Melchester hero answers soccer fans' pleas to return', *Guardian* (12 August 1993), p. 1.
16 George Orwell, 'Boys' Weeklies', in *The Collected Essays, Journalism and Letters of George Orwell. Volume I: An Age Like This, 1920–1940*, ed. Sonia Orwell and Ian Angus (Harmondsworth, 1970), p. 528.
17 For a historical overview of juvenile periodicals and their readers, see Kirsten Drotner, *English Children and Their Magazines, 1751–1945* (New Haven, CT, 1988). On the story papers see Kelly Boyd, *Manliness and the Boys' Story Paper in Britain: A Cultural History, 1855–1940* (Basingstoke, 2003), and Mary Cadogan and Patricia Craig, *You're A Brick Angela! A New Look at Girls' Fiction from 1839 to 1975* (London, 1976). The themes of imperialism and militarism are discussed in Jeffrey Richards, ed., *Imperialism and Juvenile Literature* (Manchester, 1989), and Michael Paris, *Warrior Nation: Images of War in British Popular Culture, 1850–2000* (London, 2000).
18 Owen Dudley Edwards, 'The Famous Five', in *The D. C. Thomson Bumper Fun Book*, ed. Paul Harris (Edinburgh, 1977), p. 66. It is a particular quirk of Edwards's that he refers to picture papers as 'tabloids': tabloid in fact refers to the size of the paper.
19 *The Times Literary Supplement* (8 January 1971), p. 38.
20 Martin Barker, *Comics: Ideology, Power and the Critics* (Manchester, 1989).
21 Roger Sabin, *Adult Comics: An Introduction* (London, 1993), p. 1.
22 On the girls' comics, see especially Melanie Elizabeth Gibson, 'Remembered Reading: Memory, Comics and Post-War Construction of British Girlhood', unpublished PhD thesis, University of Sunderland, 2001.
23 The only work to date is, characteristically, by Denis Gifford, *Stap Me! The British Newspaper Strip* (Aylesbury, 1971), essentially an annotated collection of selected strips. I particularly regret the absence from this study of Peter O'Donnell and Jim Holdaway's 'Modesty Blaise' and the work of Posy Simmonds: these remain subjects for further research.
24 The semiotic approach is best exemplified by Thierry Groensteen, *The System of Comics*, trans. Bart Beaty and Nick Nguyen (Jackson, MI, 2007). A range of critical approaches are employed in both Ann Magnussen and Hans-Christian Christiansen, eds, *Comics and Culture: Analytical and Theoretical Approaches to Comics* (Copenhagen, 2000), and Robin Varnum and Christina T. Gibbons, eds, *The Language of Comics: Word and Image* (Jackson, MI, 2001). For a more traditional art-historical approach, see David Carrier, *The Aesthetics of Comics* (University Park, PA, 2000).

1 COMIC CUTS AND SAUCY STRIPS

1. Max Pemberton, *Lord Northcliffe: A Memoir* (London, 1922), p. 40.
2. Roberto Bartual, 'William Hogarth's *A Harlot's Progress*: The Beginnings of a Purely Pictorial Sequential Language', *Studies in Comics*, I/1 (2010), pp. 83–105. The historical development of the form is expertly mapped by David Kunzle, *History of the Comic Strip Volume I. The Early Comic Strip: Narrative Strips and Picture Stories in the European Broadsheet from c. 1450 to 1825* (Berkeley, CA, 1973).
3. Quoted in Kevin Carpenter, *Penny Dreadfuls and Comics: English Periodicals for Children from Victorian Times to the Present Day*, exh. cat., Bethnal Green Museum of Childhood (London, 1983), p. 68.
4. Denis Gifford, *The Complete Catalogue of British Comics* (Exeter, 1985), p. 6. See also Gifford's 'The Evolution of the British Comic', *Historical Journal* (1971), pp. 349–58.
5. The best historical overview is Alan J. Lee, *The Origins of the Popular Press in England 1855–1914* (London, 1976). On the political economy of the press, see James Curran and Jean Seaton, *Power Without Responsibility: The Press and Broadcasting in Britain* (London, 1981).
6. The phrase was coined by Gareth Stedman Jones, 'Working Class Culture and Working Class Politics in London, 1870–1900: Notes on the Remaking of the Working Class', *Journal of Social History*, 7 (1974), pp. 460–509. The historiography is now extensive, albeit focusing largely on the metropolitan experience. See, for example, Peter Bailey, *Leisure and Class in Victorian England: Rational Recreation and the Contest for Control 1830–1885* (London, 1978); Andrew Horrall, *Popular Culture in London c.1890–1918: The Transformation of Entertainment* (Manchester, 2001); and James Walvin, *Leisure and Society, 1830–1950* (London, 1978). On the response of the left, see Chris Waters, *British Socialists and the Politics of Popular Culture, 1884–1914* (Manchester, 1990).
7. Quoted in Pemberton, *Lord Northcliffe*, pp. 29–30.
8. The 'penny dreadfuls' of the 1860s and 1870s were part-works issued as weekly serials, often dramatizing the lives of notorious criminals such as Dick Turpin, Sweeney Todd and Charles Peace. They provoked a moral panic that has some similarities (though also important differences) with the campaign against horror comics in the early 1950s. See Patrick A. Dunae, 'New Grub Street for Boys', in *Imperialism and Juvenile Literature*, ed. Jeffrey Richards (Manchester, 1989), pp. 12–33; W.O.G. Lofts, 'Success and Failure: A Short History of English "Penny Dreadfuls" and Publishers', *The Round-Up*, V/3 (February 1977), pp. 9–12; and John Springhall, 'Disseminating Impure Literature: The "Penny Dreadful" Publishing Business Since 1860', *Economic History Review*, XCVII/3 (1994), pp. 567–84. The penny dreadfuls' place in the history of moral panics is discussed in Geoffrey Pearson, *Hooligan: A History of Respectable Fears* (Basingstoke, 1983).
9. Quoted in Victor Neuberg, *Popular Literature: A History and a Guide* (Harmondsworth, 1977), p. 231.
10. *Funny Folks*, 1 (12 December 1874).
11. Roger Sabin, *Adult Comics: An Introduction* (London, 1993), p. 17.
12. H. G. Wells, *Tono-Bungay and A Modern Utopia* (London, n.d.), p. 39. (*Tono-Bungay* was first published in 1909.)

13 E. R. Pennell, 'The Modern Comic Newspaper: The Evolution of a Popular Type', *Contemporary Review*, 50 (October 1886), p. 514.
14 David Kunzle, 'The First Ally Sloper: The Earliest Popular Cartoon Character as a Satire on the Victorian Work Ethic', *Oxford Art Journal*, VIII/1 (1985), pp. 40–48.
15 The publisher declared that anyone found dead at the scene of a railway accident with a copy of *Ally Sloper's Half-Holiday* on their person would be entitled to life insurance up to £150. This was evidently more than just a gimmick: three claims had been paid according to the issue of 30 April 1892 (no. 418).
16 Peter Bailey, 'Ally Sloper's Half-Holiday: Comic Art in the 1880s', *History Workshop*, 16 (1981), pp. 4–31.
17 'A. Sloper, The Hot Member', *Ally Sloper's Half-Holiday*, 82 (21 November 1885).
18 Bailey, 'Ally Sloper's Half-Holiday', p. 23.
19 Ibid., p. 9.
20 J. M. Golby and A. W. Purdue, *The Civilisation of the Crowd: Popular Culture in England 1750–1900*, 2nd edn (Stroud, 1999), pp. 201–2.
21 This remains an under-researched period of British comic history. See Carpenter, *Penny Dreadfuls and Comics*, pp. 73–9; Gifford, 'The Evolution of the British Comic', pp. 349–58; and Gifford, *Victorian Comics* (London, 1976). A short contemporary history can be found in J. F. Wilson, 'Comic Papers of the Victorian Era', *Sell's Dictionary of the World's Press* (London, 1902), pp. 67–8.
22 Kelly Boyd, *Manliness and the Boys' Story Paper in Britain: A Cultural History, 1855–1940* (Basingstoke, 2003), p. 36.
23 Alfred Harmsworth was ennobled as Lord Northcliffe in 1905, and Harold became Lord Rothermere in 1914. Harmsworth wrote no memoir, though there are several accounts by close confidantes, including Hamilton Fyfe, *Northcliffe: An Intimate Biography* (London, 1930), and Pemberton, *Lord Northcliffe*. More recent studies include S. J. Taylor, *The Great Outsiders: Northcliffe, Rothermere and the 'Daily Mail'* (London, 1996), and J. Lee Thompson, *Northcliffe: Press Baron in Politics, 1865–1922* (London, 2000).
24 *Comic Cuts*, 1 (17 May 1890).
25 Alan Clark, *Dictionary of British Comic Artists, Writers and Editors* (London, 1998), pp. 30–31.
26 Simon Popple, '"But the Khaki-Covered Camera is the *Latest* Thing": The Boer War Cinema and Visual Culture in Britain', in *Young and Innocent? The Cinema in Britain 1896–1930*, ed. Andrew Higson (Exeter, 2002), p. 13.
27 Walter Benjamin, 'The Work of Art in the Age of Mechanical Reproduction' [1935], trans. Andy Blunden, at www.marxists.org/reference/subject/philosophy/works/ge/ benjamin.htm (accessed 2 July 2010). See also Gerry Beegan, *The Mass Image: A Social History of Photomechanical Reproduction in Victorian London* (Basingstoke, 2008).
28 Paul Gravett includes an unreferenced quotation from Charlie Chaplin: 'I started the little tramp simply to make people laugh and because those other old tramps, Weary Willie and Tired Tim, had always made me laugh.' Paul Gravett and Peter Stanbury, *Great British Comics: Celebrating a Century of Ripping Yarns and Wizard Wheezes* (London, 2006), p. 19.

29 Michael Chanan, *The Dream That Kicks: The Prehistory and Early Years of Cinema in Britain* (London, 1980); Higson, ed., *Young and Innocent? The Cinema in Britain 1896–1930*; Rachael Low and Roger Manvell, *The History of the British Film 1896–1906* (London, 1948); Rachael Low, *The History of the British Film 1906–1914* (London, 1949). On the early history of British film comedy, see Alan Burton and Laraine Porter, eds, *Pimple, Pranks and Pratfalls: British Film Comedy Before 1930* (Trowbridge, 2000).
30 Quoted in Boyd, *Manliness and the Boys' Story Paper in Britain*, p. 32.
31 Although the phrase is widely quoted I have been unable to identify the original source. The Harmsworth papers are discussed in John Springhall, '"Healthy Papers for Manly Boys": Imperialism and Race in the Harmsworths' Halfpenny Boys' Papers of the 1890s and 1900s', in *Imperialism and Juvenile Literature*, ed. Jeffrey Richards (Manchester, 1989), pp. 107–25.
32 *Funny Wonder*, 191 (26 September 1896).
33 *Illustrated Chips*, 486 (23 December 1899); *Illustrated Chips*, 503 (21 April 1900).
34 The front page of *World's Comic*, 1 (6 July 1892), for example, features stereotypes of a North American Indian ('Makes poor Indian look like rum and molasses'), a Chinaman ('Makee hi-tiddlee-hi-ti laughee tillee crackee sidee') and a black African ('Golly! Dis am a gum-tickler') reading the paper.
35 *Big Budget*, 30 (8 January 1898); *Big Budget*, 37 (26 February 1898); *Big Budget*, 55 (2 July 1898); *Big Budget*, 106 (24 June 1899).
36 As 'Martin Clifford' Hamilton wrote the St Jim's stories in *Gem* (1907–39), and as 'Frank Richards' he wrote the Greyfriars stories in *Magnet* (1908–40). It has been estimated that during his lifetime he wrote over 60 million words under at least 25 pseudonyms. See W.O.G. Lofts and Derek Adley, *The World of Frank Richards* (London, 1975). On the Greyfriars stories, see especially Jeffrey Richards, *Happiest Days: The Public Schools in English Fiction* (Manchester, 1988), pp. 266–97.
37 A.J.P. Taylor, *English History 1914–1945* (Oxford, 1965), p. 313. See also Jeffrey Richards, *The Age of the Dream Palace: Cinema and Society in Britain, 1930–1939* (London, 1984).
38 On D. C. Thomson's juvenile periodicals, see Joseph McAleer, *Popular Reading and Publishing in Britain, 1914–1950* (Oxford, 1992), pp. 162–205. For an insider's history, see George Rosie, 'The Warlocks of British Publishing', in *The D. C. Thomson Bumper Fun Book*, ed. Paul Harris (Edinburgh, 1977), pp. 9–49.
39 The full titles were originally *The Dandy Comic* and *The Beano Comic*. A third title, *The Magic Comic*, was launched in 1939 but discontinued during the Second World War.
40 Clark, *Dictionary of British Comic Artists*, pp. 178–9.
41 Roger Sabin, *Comics, Comix and Graphic Novels* (London, 1996), p. 28.
42 Most commentary on *Dandy* and *Beano* focuses on the period between the 1950s and the 1980s. See, for example, Leo Baxendale, *On Comedy: The Beano and Ideology* (Stroud, 1989); and Owen Dudley Edwards, 'Cow Pie and All That', in *The D. C. Thomson Bumper Fun Book*, ed. Paul Harris (Edinburgh, 1977), pp. 82–104.
43 Mass-Observation Archive, University of Sussex, File Report 2545: Article for *Penguin World*, December 1947.

44 'Those Dandy days when life was a Beano', *Daily Mail* (11 September 2006), p. 16.
45 'The time we could bank on Bank Holiday', *Daily Mail* (25 August 2008), p. 16.
46 'Rules of the comic world of swopsies', *Daily Mail* (4 March 1999), p. 14.
47 A. J. Jenkinson, *What Do Boys and Girls Read? An Investigation into Reading Habits with Some Suggestions about the Teaching of Literature in Secondary and Senior Schools* (London, 1940), p. 64.
48 George Orwell, 'Boys' Weeklies', in *The Collected Essays, Journalism and Letters of George Orwell. Volume 1: An Age Like This 1920–1940*, ed. Sonia Orwell and Ian Angus (Harmondsworth, 1970), p. 512.
49 Jenkinson, *What Do Boys and Girls Read?*, pp. 72–3.
50 Ibid., pp. 214–15.
51 Ibid., p. 64.
52 Ibid., p. 217.
53 Denis Gifford, *The International Book of Comics* (London, 1984), p. 7.
54 This item can be found in Box 83 of the Denis Gifford Collection held by the Special Collections Unit of the British Film Institute: *Scrapbooks/Comics*. It includes a self-coloured 'Jane' strip from the *Daily Mirror*. Gifford's other homemade comics in this collection include *Well-Known Comics*, *Merry Moments* and *Mirror Comics*.
55 Some American comic books did find their way into Britain during the war: they were often used as ballast in cargo ships. Children living near US camps in Britain would also have access to comics through GIs: comics were ideal reading matter for troops in transit.
56 Clark, *Dictionary of British Comic Artists*, p. 8.
57 For a comprehensive survey, see Owen Dudley Edwards, *British Children's Fiction in the Second World War* (Edinburgh, 2007).
58 Taylor, *English History 1914–1945*, p. 548.
59 Denis Gifford, *Stap Me! The British Newspaper Strip* (Aylesbury, 1971), p. 8.
60 Mass-Observation FR 3009: 'The Press and its Readers', June 1948. The report was published as *The Press and its Readers: A Report Prepared by Mass-Observation for the Advertising Service Guild* (London, 1949).
61 Ibid.
62 'Secret life of the soldiers' pin-up', *Daily Mail* (8 December 2003), p. 36; 'Jane's Gang', *The Stage* (3 November 2005), p. 12. See also the obituary for Chrystabel Leighton-Porter in the *Guardian* (16 December 2000), p. 24.
63 Quoted in 'Jane takes off into the sunset', *Guardian* (12 October 1959), p. 5.
64 Mass-Observation FR 2427: 'Famous People', 8 October 1946.
65 Leslie Thomas, 'Introduction', *Jane* (London, 1983), p. 5.
66 'What is a Pin-Up Girl?', *Picture Post* (23 September 1944), p. 15.
67 The 'Jane' strips have been reprinted several times. The most complete collection is *Jane at War* (London, 1976), which includes all the daily strips from 4 September 1939 to 14 August 1945. *Jane* (London, 1983) – published to tie in with the BBC series *Jane* starring Glynis Barber – reprints 'Hush Hush House' and the post-war 'Nature in the Raw', while another volume entitled *Jane at War* (Exeter, 1995) includes 'The Day War Broke Out', 'Land Girl', 'Married By

Proxy' and 'Summer Idle'. *The Misadventures of Jane* (London, 2009) is a handsomely produced volume including the stories 'N.A.A.F.I. Say Die!' and 'Behind the Front' along with supporting material including illustrations from *Jane's Journal* and an article from the Canadian forces newspaper *Maple Leaf* (July 1945).
68 See Antonia Lant, *Blackout: Reinventing Women for Wartime British Cinema* (Princeton, 1991), and Penny Summerfield, *Reconstructing Women's Wartime Lives: Discourse and Subjectivity in Oral Histories of the Second World War* (Manchester, 1998).
69 Steve Chibnall and Brian McFarlane, *The British 'B' Film* (London, 2009), pp. 124–5.
70 *Kinematograph Weekly* (24 November 1949), p. 24D.
71 *The Adventures of Jane* was not the last attempt to film the comic strip. In the early 1980s BBC2 broadcast *Jane* (1983) and *Jane in the Desert* (1984), featuring live actors against a cartoon background. Each series consisted of five ten-minute episodes and starred Glynis Barber as Jane. *Jane and the Lost City* (dir. Terry Marcel, 1988) was a sub-Indiana Jones romp with Kirsten Hughes as Jane and comedian Jasper Carrott as a camp German villain: it manages the not inconsiderable feat of being even worse than the 1949 film.

2 ON THE WINGS OF EAGLES

1 Marcus Morris, '"Comics" that take horror into the nursery', *Sunday Dispatch* (13 February 1949), p. 4.
2 Quoted in Sally Morris and Jan Hallwood, *Living With Eagles: Priest to Publisher – The Life and Times of Marcus Morris* (Cambridge, 1988), p. 88.
3 Martin Barker, *A Haunt of Fears: The Strange History of the British Horror Comics Campaign* (London, 1984). See also Barker's revisiting of the subject following the release of Cabinet Office papers relating to the Children and Young Person's (Harmful Publications) Bill in 'Getting a Conviction: Or, How the British Horror Comics Campaign Only *Just* Succeeded', in *Pulp Demons: International Dimensions of the Postwar Anti-Comics Campaign*, ed. John A. Lent (Madison, WI, 1999), pp. 69–92.
4 Morris does not name any comics in the article, but Denis Gifford has identified the Arab pirate story as 'The Golden Scarab' in *Comet* and the brassièred girl detective as 'Cat Girl' in *Topical Funnies: The International Book of Comics* (London, 1984), p. 186.
5 The *Daily Worker* was the mouthpiece of the Communist Party of Great Britain and a leading voice in its campaign against Americanization. See William Rust, *The Story of the 'Daily Worker'* (London, 1949).
6 Peter Mauger, 'Should US "comics" be banned?', *Picture Post* (17 May 1952), p. 35.
7 Peter Mauger [uncredited], *The Lure of the 'Comics'* (London, 1952), pp. 4–5.
8 The National Archives, Kew, London (hereafter TNA) LO 2/387: Sir Theobald Matthew (Office of the DPP) to Alistair Macdonald (Royal Courts of Justice), 4 August 1955.
9 'The sales of children's comics', *Financial Times* (17 February 1954).

10 It would seem there was only one British issue of *Haunt of Fear*, one *Vault of Horror* and two *Tales from the Crypt*: these were all reprints by the Arnold Book Company from the EC originals. The other comics cited by the campaign include: *Black Magic* (Arnold, 16 issues), *Crime Detective* (Streamline, 3 issues), *Crime Does Not Pay* (Arnold, 2 issues; Pemberton, 6 issues), *Down With Crime* (Miller, 7 issues), *Eerie* (Thorpe & Porter, 2 issues), *Frankenstein Comics* (Arnold, 5 issues) and *Ghostly Weird Stories* (Arnold, 1 issue). See Barker, *A Haunt of Fears*, pp. 233–6; and Denis Gifford, *The Complete Catalogue of British Comics* (Exeter, 1985).

11 'Imported "comics" criticized', *The Times* (3 January 1952), p. 2.

12 George Pumphrey, *Comics and Your Children* (London, 1954), pp. 4–19.

13 *Parliamentary Debates: House of Commons*, 5th series, vol. 503, col. 2332, 17 July 1952.

14 TNA BT 230/313: R.H.S. Crossman to Sir David Maxwell Fyfe, 3 July 1952. Crossman himself did not advocate an outright ban: 'This matter came up when I was doing "Any Questions" on the BBC the other day and I found myself agreeing with Lord Elton (!) in throwing doubt on the desirability or practicability of censorship, though I did say that one should not spend dollars importing them.'

15 Ibid.: Fyfe to Crossman, n.d.

16 Ibid.: Memorandum by V. I. Chapman (Board of Trade), 12 July 1952.

17 TNA PREM 11/858: P. G. Oates to R. J. Guppy, 20 February 1954.

18 Ibid.: Memorandum entitled 'American Type Comics', n.d. (*c.* February 1954).

19 Ibid.: Oates to Prime Minister, 17 February 1954.

20 Ibid. This is inferred from a memo from Churchill's private secretary 'Jock' Colville to Brendan Bracken, 6 March 1954: 'You were talking to the Prime Minister the other day about American comics and the amount sold by the notorious Mr Thompson [*sic*] . . .'

21 Martin Gilbert, *World in Torment: Winston S. Churchill 1916–1922* (London, 1975), pp. 885–7.

22 TNA PREM 11/858: 'American Type Comics', n.d..

23 Ibid.: Sir Norman Brook (Cabinet Secretary) to Churchill, 1 December 1954.

24 '"Horror comics" campaign', *The Times* (12 November 1954), p. 2.

25 'Action against "evil" comics', *The Times* (17 November 1954), p. 6.

26 'Most say ban horror comics', *News Chronicle* (29 November 1954).

27 TNA PREM 11/858: 'Horror Comics'. Memorandum by the Home Secretary, Secretary of State for Scotland and the Minister of Education, 25 November 1954.

28 Ibid.: 'Horror comics'. Memorandum by the Home Secretary, 22 January 1955.

29 TNA FO 371/114437: M. A. Wenner to S. Burley, 23 February 1954.

30 Ibid.: Burley to Wenner, 19 February 1955.

31 *Parliamentary Debates: House of Commons*, 5th series, vol. 537, cols 1074–1186, 22 February 1954.

32 Letter from A. P. Herbert, 'Horror Comics', *The Times* (21 February 1955), p. 9.

33 Children and Young Persons (Harmful Publications) Act 1955 (*c.* 28), *The UK Statute Law Database*, at www.statutelaw.gov.uk/content.aspx (accessed 28 Oct. 2008).

34 The first publisher reported to the police under the Act was L. Miller & Son in relation to *Batman*, *Whiz Comics* and *Monster Comics* in August 1955. The

Director of Public Prosecutions felt that 'these publications do not come within the Act' and the Attorney General agreed (TNA LO 2/387). The first prosecution was brought against L. Miller & Co. in 1970 in relation to the imported comics *Terror Tales, Tales from the Tomb, Weird, Tales of Voodoo* and *Witches Tales* (TNA DPP 2/4800).

35 Marcus Morris, 'Introduction', *The Best of Eagle* (London, 1977), p. 3.
36 Quoted in Morris and Hallwood, *Living With Eagles*, p. 110.
37 Ibid., p. 110.
38 Tom Hopkinson, *Of This Our Time: A Journalist's Story, 1905–50* (London, 1982), p. 274.
39 'New Hulton Press weekly "on sale or return" for a month', *Newspaper World* (30 March 1950), p. 443.
40 'Trade orders for the Eagle had to be cut', *Newspaper World* (20 April 1950), p. 542.
41 Quoted in Morris and Hallwood, *Living With Eagles*, p. 117.
42 'Profile – Comics Editor', *Observer* (21 March 1954), p. 3.
43 The names of the first 100 readers to join the Eagle Club were published in the paper: there were 86 boys and fourteen girls: *Eagle*, 5 (12 May 1950), p. 11. It seems reasonable to assume that this broadly reflected the readership of the comic until the launch of its sister paper *Girl* in 1951.
44 'The New Children's Paper', *Picture Post* (15 April 1950), pp. 40–41.
45 *Eagle*, II/4 (4 May 1951), p. 11.
46 Arthur Marwick, *British Society Since 1945*, 3rd edn (Harmondsworth, 1996), p. 114.
47 *Eagle*, IX/43 (25 October 1958), p. 15.
48 *Eagle*, 1 (14 April 1950), p. 15.
49 Ibid.
50 *Eagle*, 22 (8 September 1950), p. 13.
51 *Eagle*, 43 (2 February 1951), p. 11; *Eagle*, 48 (9 March 1951), p. 11.
52 *Eagle*, III/23 (12 September 1952), p. 11.
53 *Eagle*, II/49 (14 March 1952), p. 11.
54 Marwick, *British Society Since 1945*, p. 106.
55 Chad Varah, *Before I Die Again* (London, 1992), p. 141.
56 'The Case of the Terrible Twins', *Eagle*, II/20 (24 August 1951), p. 3.
57 *Fort Apache* (dir. John Ford, 1948); *She Wore A Yellow Ribbon* (dir. John Ford, 1949). The Monument Valley image is in 'Riders of the Range', *Eagle*, II/3 (27 April 1951), p. 7.
58 *Eagle*, IX/43 (25 October 1958), p. 15.
59 *The Times Literary Supplement*, Children's Literature Supplement (16 June 1950), p. 16.
60 Letter from G. Greening, 'Children's Pleasures', *Observer* (28 March 1954), p. 2.
61 *Jew Süss/Jud Süss* (dir. Veit Harlan, 1940); *The Eternal Jew/Der Ewige Jude* (dir. Fritz Hippler, 1940).
62 Hampson was the sole artist for the first adventure – originally untitled but subsequently known as 'Voyage to Venus' – which ran from 14 April 1950 until 28 September 1951. Thereafter he concentrated on sketching the story boards and

shared the inking and colouring with other artists, including Don Harley, Harold Johns, Greta Tomlinson and Keith Watson. Ill-health meant that Hampson was unable to contribute to the third Dan Dare adventure, 'Marooned on Mercury', or the fifth, 'Prisoners of Space'. Hampson also wrote or co-wrote all the early adventures except for 'Marooned on Mercury', which was the work of Chad Varah. His regular collaborator, from the start of 'Prisoners of Space' until the end of 'Safari in Space', was Alan Stranks.

63 Frank Hampson, 'Foreword', *Dan Dare's Spacebook* (London, n.d.), p. 3.
64 Quoted in Alastair Crompton, *The Man Who Drew Tomorrow* (Bournemouth, 1985), p. 51.
65 David Pringle, ed., *The Ultimate Encyclopedia of Science Fiction* (London, 1996), p. 188.
66 For a discussion of the visual style of the strip, see Alastair Crompton, 'Frank Hampson's Dan Dare', at www.frankhampson.co.uk/dandare.php (accessed 23 October 2008).
67 'Wonderman' (23 November 1950), the second of a series of six talks on *Heroes* written and presented by 'Henry Gibson' (Wolf Mankowitz) for the BBC Light Programme. I am grateful to Tony Dunn for providing a copy of the broadcast script for this programme.
68 *Just Imagine* (dir. David Butler, 1930); *Things to Come* (dir. William Cameron Menzies, 1936).
69 Kenneth O. Morgan, *The People's Peace: Britain 1945–1990* (Oxford, 1990), p. 110. On the Festival of Britain, see Mary Banham and Bevis Hillier, eds, *A Tonic to the Nation: The Festival of Britain* (London, 1976).
70 Edward James, 'The Future Viewed from Mid-Century Britain: Clarke, Hampson and the Festival of Britain', *Foundation: The Review of Science Fiction*, 41 (1987), pp. 42–51.
71 'Wonderman', BBC Light Programme, 23 November 1950.
72 'Dan Dare – Pilot of the Future', *Eagle*, II/18 (10 August 1951), p. 1; 'Reign of the Robots', *Eagle*, VIII/9 (1 March 1957), p. 1.
73 'The Red Moon Mystery', *Eagle*, III/1 (10 April 1952), p. 2; 'The Red Moon Mystery', *Eagle*, III/2 (18 April 1952), p. 1.
74 'The man who draws Dan Dare gives us his thoughts on the future of space travel', *Eagle*, IX/9 (28 February 1958), p. 8.
75 On the idea of the 'new woman' and its representation, see Christine Geraghty, *British Cinema in the Fifties: Gender, Genre and the 'New Look'* (London, 2000), pp. 155–74.
76 'Dan Dare – Pilot of the Future', *Eagle*, 5 (12 May 1950), p. 2.
77 'Dan Dare – Pilot of the Future', *Eagle*, 19 (18 August 1950), p. 2.
78 'The Red Moon Mystery', *Eagle*, II/49 (14 March 1952), p. 2.
79 Umbopa, an archetype of the 'noble savage', appears in Sir Henry Rider Haggard's *King Solomon's Mines* (London, 1885). Ostensibly a bearer for white hunter Allan Quatermain, he turns out to be the exiled king of the Kikuyu people.
80 For further discussion of Dan Dare and ideologies of Britishness, see James Chapman, 'Onward Christian Spaceman: *Dan Dare – Pilot of the Future* as British Cultural History', *Visual Culture in Britain*, IX/1 (2008), pp. 55–79; and Tony

Watkins, 'Piloting the Nation: Dan Dare and the 1950s', in *A Necessary Fantasy? The Heroic Figure in Children's Popular Culture*, ed. Dudley Jones and Tony Watkins (New York, 2000), pp. 153–75.
81 'Prisoners of Space', *Eagle*, v/29 (16 July 1954), p. 2.
82 'Prisoners of Space', *Eagle*, v/31 (30 July 1954), p. 1.
83 David Cannadine, 'James Bond and the Decline of England', *Encounter*, l/3 (November 1979), p. 46.
84 *Parliamentary Debates: House of Lords*, 5th series, vol. 236, col. 157, 6 December 1961.
85 Alan Vince, 'An Interview with Frank Hampson' [1974], in *Dan Dare: The Red Moon Mystery* (London, 2004), p. xii.
86 Quoted in Martin Gilbert, *Finest Hour: Winston S. Churchill 1939–1941* (London, 1983), pp. 570–71.
87 'Dan Dare – Pilot of the Future', *Eagle*, 21 (1 September 1950), p. 2.
88 'Operation Saturn', *Eagle*, iv/28 (16 October 1953), p. 2.
89 'Reign of the Robots', *Eagle*, viii/14 (5 April 1957), p. 1.
90 Quoted in Anthony Aldgate and Jeffrey Richards, *Britain Can Take It: The British Cinema in the Second World War* (Oxford, 1986), p. 141.
91 *This England* (dir. David Macdonald, 1941); *The Prime Minister* (dir. Thorold Dickinson, 1941); *The Young Mr Pitt* (dir. Carol Reed, 1942); *Henry V* (dir. Laurence Olivier, 1944).
92 'Dan Dare – Pilot of the Future', *Eagle*, ii/20 (24 August 1951), p. 2.
93 'Dan Dare – Pilot of the Future', *Eagle*, ii/25 (28 September 1951), p. 2.
94 Crompton, *The Man Who Drew Tomorrow*, p. 157.
95 Ibid., p. 125.
96 Frank Bellamy took over from Hampson mid-way through 'Terra Nova' in 1959 and continued with 'Trip to Trouble' and 'Project Nimbus' from scripts by Eric Eden. Don Harley drew 'Mission of the Earthmen' and 'The Solid Space Mystery', again from scripts by Eden. Keith Watson took over drawing the strip, and David Motton scripting it, from 'The Platinum Planet' until 'The Menace from Jupiter'.
97 Crompton, *The Man Who Drew Tomorrow*, pp. 118–22.
98 Gifford, *The International Book of Comics*, pp. 212–13.
99 Jan Johnson, 'The French Dan Dare', *Eagle Times: The Quarterly Journal of the Eagle Society*, xii/2 (1999), pp. 24–7.
100 Zvonimir Freivogel, 'Croatian Dan Dare', *Spaceship Away*, 7 (2005), p. 22.
101 Michael Anglo, *Nostalgia Spotlight on the Fifties* (London, 1985), p. 113.
102 Letter from Steve Holland, *Eagle Times: The Quarterly Journal of the Eagle Society*, xi/1 (1998), pp. 52–3.
103 Douglas Bader, 'Why I am editing *Rocket*', *Rocket* 1 (21 April 1956), p. 5.
104 *Rick Random – Space Detective: 10 Classic Interplanetary Comic Book Adventures*, ed. Steve Holland (London, 2008), p. 261.
105 Sydney Jordan, 'Introduction', *Jeff Hawke: The Ambassadors* (London, 2008), p. 4.
106 Marwick, *British Society Since 1945*, p. 11; Morgan, *The People's Peace*, p. 158.
107 Quoted in Morris and Hallwood, *Living With Eagles*, p. 210.

108 Dan Lloyd, 'Those Were the Days', *Eagle Times: The Quarterly Journal of the Eagle Society*, XII/2 (1999), p. 9.
109 *Eagle and Boys' World* (10 April 1965), p. 4.

3   RIPPING YARNS

1   P. M. Pickard, *British Comics: An Appraisal* (London, 1955), p. 7.
2   It is difficult to find any sales figures for this period, but the *Financial Times* offers these weekly circulation figures for the first six months of 1953: *Beano* (approx. 1,000,000), *Dandy* (approx. 1,000,000), *School Friend* (945,768), *Eagle* (approx. 750,000), *Mickey Mouse Weekly* (523,497), *Lion* ('well in excess of half a million'), *Girl* (approx. 500,000), *TV Comic* (268,391), *Children's Newspaper* (205,052) and *Robin* (approx. 200,000). A combined circulation of 1,300,000 is cited for *Knockout*, *Radio Fun* and *Film Fun*, and 435,000 for *Comet*, *Sun*, *Tip Top* and *Jingles*. The circulations for story papers are: *Rover* (394,301), *Wizard* (386,534), *Hotspur* (343,079), *Adventure* (339,715) and *Champion* (133,000). 'The sales of children's comics', *Financial Times* (17 February 1954).
3   Asa Briggs, *The History of Broadcasting in the United Kingdom. Volume V: Competition 1955–1974* (Oxford, 1995), p. 1005.
4   Arthur Marwick, *British Society Since 1945*, 3rd edn (Harmondsworth, 1996), p. 110.
5   This format emerged largely by chance. *Cowboy Comics* were reprints of Kit Carson and Buck Jones strips previously published in Australia. Edward Holmes of Amalgamated Press wanted to issue them in Britain, but when no presses were available he turned to the printers of the *Sexton Blake Library*, a 64-page small-format story paper. The 'library' format happened to fit easily into a blazer pocket and so were ideal for schoolchildren.
6   In the first six months of 1953 combined sales of *Rover*, *Wizard*, *Hotspur* and *Adventure* were 1,463,629, but over the next six months this shrunk by nearly a third to 1,051,415. The National Archives, Kew, London PREM 11/858: Gordon Newton to Lord Bracken, 11 March 1954.
7   Quoted in Andrew Fyall, 'Gone are the heroes who taught us to read', unidentified press clipping, 27 March 1973. British Film Institute Special Collections Unit: Denis Gifford Collection Box 90: *Scrapbooks – British and American Cuttings*.
8   Owen Dudley Edwards, 'The Famous Five', in *The D. C. Thomson Bumper Fun Book*, ed. Paul Harris (Edinburgh, 1976), p. 65.
9   Quoted in Alastair Crompton, *The Man Who Drew Tomorrow* (Bournemouth, 1985), p. 209.
10 See Norman Wright and David Ashford, *Masters of Fun and Frolics: The British Comic Artists*, vol. 1 (Swanage, 2008). Wright and Ashford have also contributed occasional essays on 'The Great British Comic Artists' to *Book and Magazine Collector* since 2000. Bellamy, Embleton and Lawrence are discussed in George Khoury, ed., *True Brit: A Celebration of the Great Comic Book Artists of the UK* (Raleigh, NC, 2004), and Bellamy is included in P. R. Garriock, *Masters of Comic Book Art* (London, 1978).

11 David Roach, 'The History of British Comic Art', in *True Brit*, p. 12.
12 *Archive Adventures No. 12: The Chronicles of Captain Flame* (Oxford, n.d.), p. 2. *Archive Adventures* is a series of privately published, limited-edition reprints of classic comic strips from the late 1940s and '50s.
13 See Steve Holland and David Roach, *The Fleetway Picture Library Index Volume I: The War Libraries* (London, 2007), pp. 7–11. Biographical details for many of these artists are elusive: see 'The Agency Artists' at www.dandare.info/artists/studio_artists.htm (accessed 29 January 2010).
14 Michael Anglo, *Nostalgia Spotlight on the Fifties* (London, 1977), pp. 115–6.
15 Malcolm Mullen, 'Leading a comic life for a living is most profound', unidentified newspaper article *c.* 1973. BFI Denis Gifford Collection Box 87: *Scrapbooks – Cuttings*.
16 'Horror comics "could lead to murder"', *The Times* (23 October 1970), p. 5.
17 George Orwell, 'Boys' Weeklies', in *The Collected Essays, Journalism and Letters of George Orwell. Volume I: An Age Like This, 1920–1940*, ed. Sonia Orwell and Ian Angus (Harmondsworth, 1970), p. 528.
18 The historiography of British society during the Second World War is extensive. See in particular Paul Addison, *The Road to 1945: British Politics and the Second World War* (London, 1975); Corelli Barnett, *The Audit of War: The Illusion and Reality of Britain as a Great Nation* (London, 1986); Angus Calder, *The People's War: Britain 1939–45* (London, 1969); Mark Connelly, *We Can Take It! Britain and the Memory of the Second World War* (Harlow, 2004); Nick Hayes and Jeff Hill, eds, *Millions Like Us? British Culture in the Second World War* (Liverpool, 1999); and Robert Kee, *1945: The World We Fought For* (London, 1985). A summary of the debate can be found in Bill Purdue and James Chapman, *The People's War?: A Study Guide* (Milton Keynes, 2004).
19 Edwards, 'The Famous Five', p. 76.
20 Arthur Hopcraft, 'The Legion of Tall Heroes', unidentified press clipping (from internal evidence published in 1961). BFI Denis Gifford Collection Box 90: *Scrapbooks – British and American Cuttings*.
21 Keith Dewhurst, 'Boy, myth and magic', *Guardian* (22 July 1970), p. 8.
22 Raymond Williams, *Problems in Materialism and Culture* (London, 1980), pp. 40–41.
23 David Ashford and Steve Holland, *Thriller Picture Library: An Illustrated Guide* (Rotherham, 1991).
24 *The Flame and the Arrow* (dir. Jacques Tourneur, 1950); *The Crimson Pirate* (dir. Robert Siodmak, 1952); *Ivanhoe* (dir. Richard Thorpe, 1952); *The Story of Robin Hood and His Merrie Men* (dir. Ken Annakin, 1952); *Rob Roy, the Highland Rogue* (dir. Harold French, 1953); *Knights of the Round Table* (dir. Richard Thorpe, 1953); *Prince Valiant* (dir. Henry Hathaway, 1954); *The Black Knight* (dir. Tay Garnett, 1954); *The Adventures of Quentin Durward* (dir. Richard Thorpe, 1955); *The Black Shield of Falworth* (dir. Rudolph Maté, 1954). For commentary see Jeffrey Richards, *Swordsmen of the Screen: From Douglas Fairbanks to Michael York* (London, 1977).
25 Marwick, *British Society Since 1945*, pp. 105–6.

26 *Archive Adventures No. 10: Spies of Spain* (Oxford, n.d.), p. 20. 'Spies of Spain' ran in *Knock-Out*, 16 February–12 April 1952.
27 'Hunters of the Tower of London Traitors', *Lion*, 86 (10 October 1953).
28 *Frank Bellamy's Robin Hood: The Complete Adventures*, ed. Steve Holland (London, 2008), p. 16. 'Robin Hood and his Merry Men' and 'Robin Hood and Maid Marian' ran in *Swift*, 12 May 1956–17 August 1957.
29 Jeffrey Richards, 'Robin Hood on Film and Television since 1945', *Visual Culture in Britain*, II/1 (2001), pp. 65–80.
30 'Claude Duval – The Laughing Cavalier', *Comet*, 401 (24 March 1956), p. 16.
31 *The Gay Cavalier* was produced by George King for Associated-Rediffusion in 1957 and ran for thirteen episodes. It starred French actor Christian Marquand as Claude Duval. No episodes are available in the National Film and Television Archive. *Comet* changed the title of its strip to 'The Gay Cavalier' in 1958.
32 See James Sharpe, *Dick Turpin: The Myth of the English Highwayman* (London, 2004).
33 Letter from Ross Crawford, *The Round-Up*, IV/3 (February 1976), p. 28.
34 Dewhurst, 'Boy, myth and magic', p. 8.
35 Quoted in Colin Morgan, *The Rover Index* (Rotherham, n.d.), p. 52.
36 'Alan Moore: In a league of his own', *Cinefantastique*, XXXV/3 (2003), p. 21.
37 'Rafferty's Own', *Victor*, 285 (6 August 1966).
38 *Kim* (dir. Victor Saville, 1950); *Soldiers Three* (dir. Tay Garnett, 1951); *King of the Kyber Rifles* (dir. Henry King, 1953); *Khyber Patrol* (dir. Seymour Friedman, 1954); *The Bandit of Zhobe* (dir. John Gilling, 1959); *North West Frontier* (dir. J. Lee Thompson, 1959). For commentary see Jeffrey Richards, *Visions of Yesterday* (London, 1973).
39 'Action in the Khyber', *Battle*, 2 (December 1960).
40 'The Gun on Four Legs', *Victor*, 265 (19 March 1966).
41 'The Mystery Man at Inside Left', *Victor*, 311 (4 February 1967).
42 Dave Russell, *Football and the English: A Social History of Association Football in England, 1863–1995* (Preston, 1997), p. 139.
43 Brendan Gallagher, *Sporting Supermen: The True Stories of Our Childhood Comic Heroes* (London, 2006), pp. 110–12.
44 'Chained to his Bat', *Hotspur*, 244 (20 June 1964).
45 Gallagher, *Sporting Supermen*, pp. 44–5.
46 Richard Holt, *Sport and the British: A Modern History* (Oxford, 1989), p. 279.
47 Gallagher, *Sporting Supermen*, p. 72.
48 'The Tough of the Track', *Victor*, 184 (29 August 1964).
49 'The Tough of the Track', *Victor*, 500 (19 September 1970).
50 Russell, *Football and the English*, pp. 144–5.
51 Quoted in 'Behind the Scenes – The Writers', *The Official Roy of the Rovers Website*: www.royoftherovers.com/behindthescenes/writers.aspx (accessed 17 August 2009).
52 *The Bumper Book of Roy of the Rovers* (London, 2008), p. 107.
53 Alan Tomlinson and Christopher Young, 'Golden Boys and Golden Memories: Fiction, Ideology, and Reality in *Roy of the Rovers* and the Death of the Hero', in

A Necessary Fantasy? The Heroic Figure in Children's Popular Culture, ed. Dudley Jones and Tony Watkins (New York, 2000), pp. 177–205.
54 Mike Conroy, *War Comics: A Graphic History* (Lewes, 2009), p. 108.
55 John Sutherland, 'The comic side of war', *Financial Times*, 13 December 2008: www.ft.com/cms/s/0/26a3e370-c8b7.html (accessed 31 March 2009).
56 Brian Edwards, 'The Popularisation of War in Comic Strips 1958–1988', *History Workshop Journal*, 42 (1996), pp. 181–9.
57 Harry Pearson, *Achtung Schweinehund! A Boy's Own Story of Imaginary Combat* (London, 2007), p. 28.
58 *The Wooden Horse* (dir. Jack Lee, 1950); *Angels One Five* (dir. George More O'Ferrall, 1952); *The Cruel Sea* (dir. Charles Frend, 1953); *The Colditz Story* (dir. Guy Hamilton, 1954); *Above Us the Waves* (dir. Ralph Thomas, 1955); *The Dam Busters* (dir. Michael Anderson, 1955); *The Battle of the River Plate* (dir. Michael Powell, 1956); *Reach for the Sky* (dir. Lewis Gilbert, 1956); *Ill Met By Moonlight* (dir. Michael Powell, 1957); *Carve Her Name With Pride* (dir. Lewis Gilbert, 1958); *Dunkirk* (dir. Leslie Norman, 1958); *Sink the Bismarck!* (dir. Lewis Gilbert, 1960).
59 Michael Paris, *Warrior Nation: The Representation of War in British Popular Culture, 1850–2000* (London, 2000), pp. 222–61.
60 See Jonathan Bignell, 'The Meanings of War-Toys and War-Games', in *War, Culture and the Media: Representations of the Military in 20th Century Britain*, ed. Ian Stewart and Susan L. Carruthers (Trowbridge, 1996), pp. 165–84.
61 There are of course exceptions: 'Captain Hurricane' of *Valiant* is a fantasy superhero, capable of bending gun barrels with his bare hands and often bashing dozens of 'sausage guzzlers' or 'macaroni munchers' at a time.
62 Quoted in Steve Holland, 'Introduction', *Let 'Em Have It: 12 of the Best Battle Picture Library Comic Books Ever!* (London, 2008), p. 5.
63 Nicholas Johnson, 'What do children learn from war comics?', *New Society* (7 July 1966), p. 10.
64 Martin Gilbert, *Finest Hour: Winston S. Churchill 1939–1941* (London, 1983), pp. 570–71.
65 'Action Stations', *War Picture Library*, 3 (October 1958).
66 'Devil's Island', *War Picture Library*, 227 (January 1964).
67 'Secret of the Sands', *Air Ace Picture Library*, 494 (March 1970).
68 Edwards, 'The Popularisation of War', p. 185.
69 Sutherland, 'The comic side of war'.
70 'Abdul Hafiz vc', *Victor*, 299 (12 November 1966); 'The Enemy at Cassino', *Victor* 294 (8 October 1966).
71 'The Battle Line', *Victor*, 337 (5 August 1967).
72 'The Battle Line', *Victor*, 327 (27 May 1967).
73 'Pride of Lions', *Battle Picture Library*, 313 (September 1967).
74 'The Broken Line', *Battle Picture Library*, 221 (October 1965).
75 Johnson, 'What do children learn from war comics?', pp. 7–13.
76 'Sound the Alarm', *War Picture Library*, 212 (October 1963).
77 *The One That Got Away* (dir. Roy Baker, 1957); *Ice Cold in Alex* (dir. J. Lee Thompson, 1958). See John Ramsden, *Don't Mention the War: The British and the*

Germans Since 1890 (London, 2006), pp. 294–324.
78 John Ramsden, 'Refocusing the People's War: British War Films of the 1950s', *Journal of Contemporary History*, XXXIII/1 (1998), pp. 35–63; Neil Rattigan, 'The Last Gasp of the Middle Class: British War Films of the 1950s', in *Re-Viewing British Cinema, 1900–1992: Essays and Interviews*, ed. Wheeler Winston Dixon (Albany, NY, 1994), pp. 143–53.
79 'Hogan's Patrol', *Victor*, 272 (7 May 1966).
80 Edwards, 'The Famous Five', p. 76. See also Paris, *Warrior Nation*, pp. 234–5.
81 Paris, *Warrior Nation*, p. 292.
82 Denis Butts, 'Biggles – Hero of the Air', in *A Necessary Fantasy? The Heroic Figure in Children's Popular Culture*, ed. Dudley Jones and Tony Watkins (New York, 2000), pp. 137–52.
83 'Born to Fly', *Victor*, 176 (4 July 1964).
84 Hopcraft, 'The Legion of Tall Heroes'.
85 *Room at the Top* (dir. Jack Clayton, 1959); *Saturday Night and Sunday Morning* (dir. Karel Reisz, 1960).
86 'Braddock of the Bombers', *Victor*, 487 (20 June 1970).
87 'Braddock of the Rocket Squadron', *Victor*, 359 (6 January 1968).
88 'The Secret War of Sergeant Braddock', *Victor*, 464 (10 January 1970).
89 'Crumbs! It's all still jolly D', *Observer* (2 June 1971), p. 13.
90 Dewhurst, 'Boy, myth and magic', p. 8.
91 'IPC magazine division is reorganised', *Guardian* (13 August 1968), p. 12.
92 'Wham! What's *your* son reading?', *Evening News* (11 January 1967), p. 8.
93 *Doctor Who* (BBC, 1963–89); *The Avengers* (ABC [UK], 1961–9); *The Champions* (ATV, 1967–8); *The Man From U.N.C.L.E.* (NBC, 1964–7); *Voyage to the Bottom of the Sea* (ABC [USA], 1964–8); *Batman* (ABC [USA], 1966–8); *The Time Tunnel* (ABC [USA], 1966–7); *Star Trek* (NBC, 1966–9).
94 For example, Frank Bellamy wrote 'The Winged Avenger', an episode of *The Avengers* in which the villain turns out to be a comic-strip artist: the climax features a stylized fight scene with 'Bang!' and 'Pow!' captions in the style of *Batman*.
95 *Supercar* (ATV, 1961–2); *Fireball XL5* (ATV, 1963); *Stingray* (ATV, 1964–5); *Thunderbirds* (ATV, 1965–6); *Captain Scarlet and the Mysterons* (ATV, 1968); *Joe 90* (ATV, 1968).
96 Graham Bleatham and Sam Denham, eds, *Thunderbirds: Classic Comic Strips from TV Century 21* (London, 2001), p. 10.
97 See Nicholas J. Cull, 'Was Captain Black really Red? The TV Science Fiction of Gerry Anderson in its Cold War Context', *Media History*, XII/2 (2006), pp. 193–207.
98 Arthur Marwick, *The Sixties: Cultural Revolution in Britain, France, Italy and the United States, c. 1958–c. 1974* (Oxford, 1998), p. 248.

4 GIRLS ON TOP

1 Quoted in Sally Morris and Jan Hallwood, *Living With Eagles: Priest to Publisher – The Life and Times of Marcus Morris* (Cambridge, 1988), p. 164.
2 L. Fenwick, 'Periodicals and Adolescent Girls', *Studies in Education*, II/1 (1953), p. 31.

3   'The sales of children's comics', *Financial Times* (17 February 1954).
4   Kirsten Drotner, *English Children and Their Magazines, 1751–1945* (New Haven, CT, 1988), p. 239.
5   Ibid., p. 215.
6   A. J. Jenkinson, *What Do Boys and Girls Read? An Investigation into Reading Habits with Some Suggestions about the Teaching of Literature in Secondary and Senior Schools* (London, 1940), p. 217.
7   *Eagle*, II/29 (26 October 1951), p. 11.
8   Fenwick, 'Periodicals and Adolescent Girls', p. 30.
9   *Girl*, III/5 (3 February 1954), p. 11.
10 *Deadline*, 2 (November 1988), p. 50.
11 Quoted in Paul Gravett and Peter Stanbury, *Great British Comics: Celebrating a Century of Ripping Yarns and Wizard Wheezes* (London, 2006), p. 135.
12 'Elsie Probyn' was a pseudonym for John McKibbin, 'Ida Melbourne' for Eric Rosman. See Alan Clark, *Dictionary of British Comic Artists, Writers and Editors* (London, 1998).
13 Morris and Hallwood, *Living With Eagles*, p. 164.
14 Quoted in Hilary Young, 'Representation and Reception: An Oral History of Gender in British Children's Story Papers, Comics and Magazines in the 1940s and 1950s', unpublished PhD thesis, University of Strathclyde, 2006, p. 209.
15 Ibid., p. 85.
16 'The Silent Three', *School Friend* (3 September 1960).
17 Arthur Hopcraft, 'The Legion of Tall Heroes', unidentified press clipping (from internal evidence published in 1961). BFI Denis Gifford Collection Box 90: *Scrapbooks – British and American Cuttings*.
18 'Rivals of the Fourth Form', *Girl*, III/12 (24 March 1954), p. 1.
19 Quoted in Young, 'Representation and Reception', p. 211.
20 'Kitty Hawke', *Girl*, 1 (2 November 1951), p. 1.
21 Ben Singer, 'Female Power in the Serial-Queen Melodrama: The Etiology of an Anomaly', *Camera Obscura: A Journal of Feminism and Film Theory*, 22 (1990), pp. 91–129.
22 'Angela – Air Hostess', *Girl*, VIII/36 (24 October 1957).
23 'Tracy – Teenage Fashion Model', *School Friend* (6 August 1960).
24 Mel Gibson, 'What became of *Bunty*?': The Emergence, Evolution and Disappearance of the Girls' Comic in Post-War Britain', in *Art, Narrative and Childhood*, ed. Morag Styles and Eve Bearne (Stoke on Trent, 2003), p. 88.
25 *Girl*, II/50 (7 October 1953), p. 5; *Girl*, III/20 (19 May 1954), p. 5.
26 *Girl*, III/15 (14 April 1954), p. 11.
27 *Girl*, III/51 (22 December 1954), p. 11
28 *Girl*, III/19 (12 May 1954), p. 11.
29 Gibson, 'What became of *Bunty*?', p. 91.
30 Ibid., p. 92.
31 'The Dancing Life of Moira Kent', *Bunty*, 5 (15 February 1958).
32 'The Four Marys', *Bunty*, 8 (8 March 1958).
33 Mary Cadogan and Patricia Craig, *You're A Brick, Angela! A New Look at Girls' Fiction from 1839 to 1975* (London, 1976), p. 251.

34 'Lonesome Lucy', *Bunty*, 37 (27 September 1958).
35 'Comic cuts – "mergers make economic sense"', *Newsagent and Bookshop* (20 December 1974), p. 14.
36 Gibson, 'What became of *Bunty*?', p. 90.
37 *Jackie* has been the focus of some critical interest. See, for example, Elizabeth Frazer, 'Teenage Girls Reading *Jackie*', *Media, Culture and Society*, 9 (1987), pp. 407–25; and Angela McRobbie, '*Jackie*: An Ideology of Adolescent Femininity', Centre for Contemporary Cultural Studies Occasional Paper (University of Birmingham, 1978).
38 Flann and Mary Campbell, 'Comic love', *New Society*, 14 (3 January 1963), p. 25.
39 Len Miller had published British editions of US romance comics in the early 1950s, such as *I Love You*, *Love Affair* and *My Own Romance*.
40 Gibson, 'What became of *Bunty*?', p. 89.
41 Arthur Marwick, *The Sixties: Cultural Revolution in Britain, France, Italy and the United States, c. 1958–c. 1974* (Oxford, 1998), p. 19.
42 Cynthia L. White, *The Women's Periodical Press in Britain 1946–1976* (London, 1977), p. 39.
43 Campbell, 'Comic love', p. 24.
44 'Through Spanish eyes', *Daily Mirror* (21 September 1973), p. 15.
45 White, *The Women's Periodical Press*, p. 11.
46 'Comic cuts', p. 14.
47 Quoted in Martin Barker, *Comics: Ideology, Power, and the Critics* (Manchester, 1989), p. 17.
48 Gibson, 'What became of *Bunty*?', p. 94.
49 'Slaves of War Orphan Farm', *Tammy* (6 February 1971).
50 'Bella at the Bar', *Tammy* (17 May 1975).
51 'Lill Waters Run Deep', *Tammy* (10 May 1975).
52 'Bella's Ballet Boat', *Tammy* (21 June 1975).
53 'The IPC Magazine Division', *IPC News*, 3 (September 1971), p. 13; 'ABC Guide – latest figures', *IPC News*, 9 (March 1972), p. 2.
54 *Tammy* (17 May 1975).
55 See, for example, Tom Sweetman, 'Play Misty for Me', *Crikey! The Great British Comics Magazine!*, 1 (2007), pp. 30–34.
56 *Carrie* (dir. Brian de Palma, 1976).

5 THE VIOLENT YEARS

1 *Action* (14 February 1976), p. 2.
2 'Wham! What's *your* son reading?', *Evening News* (11 January 1967), p. 8.
3 'Crumbs! It's all still jolly D', *Observer* (2 June 1971), p. 13.
4 Royal Commission on the Press, *Periodicals and the Alternative Press: Research Series 6* Cmnd. 6810-6 (London, 1977), p. 10.
5 'Most children read about four comics a week', *The Times* (16 December 1974), p. 3.
6 Quoted in 'Comic cuts – "mergers make economic sense"', *Newsagent and Bookshop* (20 December 1974), p. 14.

7   Ibid.
8   'Vital facts for the funny men', *IPC News*, v/10 (May 1976), p. 16.
9   *Periodicals and the Alternative Press*, p. 34.
10 Quoted in 'Comic cuts', p. 14.
11 IPC's first new boys' comic of the decade, *Thunder*, lasted only five months before merging with *Lion* in 1971, which in turn merged with *Valiant* in 1974, itself swallowed by *Battle* in 1976. The success of *2000AD* in 1977 spawned two further SF papers, *Starlord* (1978) and *Tornado* (1979), which both merged with their stablemate after only 22 issues. In the field of girls' comics, *Tammy*, launched in 1970, became something of a predator that swallowed a succession of other titles: *Sally* in 1971, *Sandie* in 1973, *June* in 1974, *Misty* in 1980 and *Jinty* in 1981. At D. C. Thomson, *Victor* absorbed *Wizard* in 1978, *Hotspur* and *Scoop* in 1981, *Buddy* in 1983, *Champ* in 1985 and *Warlord* in 1986.
12 George Rosie, 'The Warlocks of British Publishing', in *The D. C. Thomson Bumper Fun Book*, ed. Paul Harris (Edinburgh, 1977), p. 34.
13 See, for example, 'Doyle of E-Boat Alley' (1966), the first of a series in *Victor* following the adventures of Midshipman Bill Doyle and Lieutenant 'Killer' Kennedy.
14 Quoted in Mike Conroy, *War Comics: A Graphic History* (Lewes, 2009), p. 113.
15 Gerry Finley-Day was probably the most prolific writer for *Battle*, with 'D-Day Dawson', 'The Bootneck Boy', 'Rat Pack', 'The Sarge', 'The General Dies at Dawn' and 'Panzer G-Man'. Eric Hebden wrote 'Day of the Eagle', Alan Hebden (Eric's son) wrote 'Major Eazy', 'Crazy Keller' and 'Fighting Mann', John Wagner wrote 'Darkie's Mob' and 'Joe Two Beans', and Tom Tully wrote 'Johnny Red'.
16 *The Dirty Dozen* (dir. Robert Aldrich, 1967); *Where Eagles Dare* (dir. Brian G. Hutton, 1969); *Play Dirty* (dir. André de Toth, 1969); *Kelly's Heroes* (dir. Brian G. Hutton, 1970).
17 *The Day of the Jackal* (dir. Fred Zinnemann, 1973). The story also bears some similarity to Geoffrey Household's novel *Rogue Male*, filmed as *Man Hunt* (dir. Fritz Lang, 1941).
18 *Battle Picture Weekly* (6 November 1976).
19 *Battle* (5 March 1977).
20 'Darkie's Mob', *Battle Picture Weekly* (14 August 1976).
21 *Battle Picture Weekly* (13 November 1976).
22 *Stalingrad* (dir. Frank Wisbar, 1958); *The Star of Africa* (dir. Alfred Weidenmann, 1957); *Punishment Battalion 999* (dir. Harald Philipp, 1959).
23 *Battle-Action* (14 January 1978).
24 *Battle and Valiant* (26 December 1976); *Battle-Action* (14 January 1978).
25 'How four in ten adults relax today', *Daily Mail* (12 December 1975), p. 6.
26 Rosie, 'The Warlocks of British Publishing', pp. 36–7.
27 John Heeley, 'Boys' Comics: Violence rules', *Sunday Times* (27 February 1983), p. 13.
28 *Battle-Action* (28 July 1979).
29 Ibid.
30 'Major Eazy', *Battle-Action* (7 January 1978).

31 Conroy, *War Comics*, p. 48.
32 Colquhoun's art for 'Charley's War' is a sophisticated pastiche of the style of contemporary painting. See E. MacCallum-Stewart, 'The First World War and British Comics', *University of Sussex Journal of Contemporary History*, 6 (2003), pp. 5–18.
33 Quoted in Alan Burton, 'Death or Glory? The Great War in British Film', in *British Historical Cinema*, ed. Claire Monk and Amy Sargeant (London, 2002), p. 31.
34 'Charley's War', *Battle-Action* (6 January 1979).
35 Pat Mills, 'Introduction', *Charley's War: 2 June 1916–1 August 1916* (London, 2004), p. 4.
36 'Charley's War', *Battle-Action* (14 July 1980).
37 'Charley's War', *Battle-Action* (28 July 1979).
38 *All Quiet on the Western Front* (dir. Lewis Milestone, 1930); *Paths of Glory* (dir. Stanley Kubrick, 1957); *King and Country* (dir. Joseph Losey, 1964); *Oh! What A Lovely War* (dir. Richard Attenborough, 1969).
39 Martin Barker, *Comics: Ideology, Power and the Critics* (Manchester, 1989), p. 25.
40 Quoted in Martin Barker, *Action: The Story of a Violent Comic* (London, 1990), p. 5.
41 Gerry Finley-Day wrote 'Hellman of Hammer Force', Tom Tully wrote 'Death Game 1999', Ron Carpenter wrote 'The Coffin Sub', John Wagner wrote 'Black Jack', Pat Mills and Ken Armstrong wrote 'Hookjaw', Steve MacManus wrote 'The Running Man', Chris Lowder wrote 'Hell's Highway' and 'Kids Rule OK'. 'Dredger', a series rather than a serial, featured stories by Mills, MacManus, Lowder, Kelvin Gosnell and Geoff Kemp.
42 *Jaws* (dir. Steven Spielberg, 1975).
43 *Dirty Harry* (dir. Don Siegel, 1971).
44 *Rollerball* (dir. Norman Jewison, 1975).
45 *The Fugitive* (ABC, 1963–7).
46 The Gunnar (Gunner) Asch series was about a German tank gunner: the novels included *Gunner Asch* (1957), *The Revolt of Gunner Asch* (1958) and *What Became of Gunner Asch?* (1964).
47 *Action* (13 March 1976).
48 *Action* (10 April 1976).
49 *Action* (3 April 1976).
50 'Dredger', *Action* (14 February 1976).
51 Brian Jackson, 'An all-white world: Look!', *Sunday Times* (11 February 1973), p. 11. For a study of ethnic characterization in comics (though not including *Action*) see Pat Bidmead, 'Differences in Presentation of White, Black, Asian and Oriental Ethnic Groups in British Comic and Magazine Publications for Children', unpublished PhD thesis, University of Warwick, 1998.
52 'Black Jack', *Action* (20 March 1976).
53 Where it went was that Jack became a kung-fu popstar!
54 *King Kong* (dir. Merian C. Cooper, 1933).
55 'AARGH lives – but the blood is printed red', *Evening Standard* (23 February 1976), p. 5.

56 'The sevenpenny nightmare', *Sun* (30 April 1976), p. 7.
57 'Comic strip hooligans', *Daily Mail* (17 September 1976), p. 27.
58 'Comic is withdrawn', *Guardian* (7 October 1976), p. 20.
59 Barker, *Action*, p. 8.
60 'Guardian Diary', *Guardian* (19 August 1977), p. 11.
61 Barker, *Action*, p. 8.
62 'Death Game 1999', *Action* (26 June 1976).
63 'Hellman of Hammer Force', *Action* (14 February 1976).
64 'Hookjaw', *Action* (21 February 1976).
65 Barker, *Comics: Ideology, Power and the Critics*, p. 49.

6 I AM THE LAW!

1 The original memorandum is quoted in Colin M. Jarman and Peter Acton, *Judge Dredd: The Mega-History* (Harpenden, 1995), p. 15. Gosnell said that his memo was prompted by reading an article by *Evening Standard* film critic Alexander Walker. The most complete version of the 'official' history of *2000AD* is by its former editor David Bishop, *Thrill-Power Overload: Thirty Years of 2000AD, The Galaxy's Greatest Comic* (Oxford, 2007).
2 *Rollerball* (dir. Norman Jewison, 1975); *Death Race 2000* (dir. Paul Bartel, 1975); *The Ultimate Warrior* (dir. Robert Clouse, 1975); *The Man Who Fell to Earth* (dir. Nicolas Roeg, 1976); *Logan's Run* (dir. Michael Anderson, 1976); *Futureworld* (dir. Richard T. Heffron, 1976); *Star Wars* (dir. George Lucas, 1977); *Close Encounters of the Third Kind* (dir. Steven Spielberg, 1977).
3 Quoted in Bishop, *Thrill-Power Overload*, p. 8.
4 Ibid., pp. 12–13.
5 'Dan Dare flies Eagle-high again', *Guardian* (6 November 1975), p. 5; 'London Letter', *Guardian* (7 November 1975), p. 11.
6 Bishop, *Thrill-Power Overload*, pp. 11–12.
7 Quoted in Jarman and Acton, *Judge Dredd: The Mega-History*, p. 18.
8 Quoted in Bishop, *Thrill-Power Overload*, p. 21.
9 *2000AD*, 12 (14 May 1977).
10 Norman Wright, *The Dan Dare Dossier* (London, 1990), p. 78.
11 'Cold war takes a comic turn', *Guardian* (21 February 1977), p. 1.
12 'Comic with a thermonuclear impact', *Guardian* (23 February 1977), p. 10.
13 'Dare they zap our hero Dan?', *Daily Mirror* (18 July 1977).
14 'Invasion!', *2000AD*, 6 (2 April 1977).
15 *The Six Million Dollar Man* (ABC, 1973–8).
16 *The Valley of the Gwangi* (dir. James O'Connelly, 1968).
17 *Ice Station Zebra* (dir. John Sturges, 1968).
18 *Them!* (dir. Gordon Douglas, 1954).
19 *Have Gun, Will Travel* (CBS, 1957–63).
20 Quoted in Daniel O'Brien, *SF: UK – How British Science Fiction Changed the World* (London, 2000), p. 119.
21 *Survivors* (BBC, 1975–7); *Blake's 7* (BBC, 1978–81); *Quatermass* (Thames, 1979).

See John R. Cook and Peter Wright, eds, *British Science Fiction Television: A Hitch Hiker's Guide* (London, 2005), pp. 21–51, 131–53, 174–91.
22 *2000AD*, 13 (21 May 1977).
23 *2000AD*, 278 (21 August 1982).
24 *2000AD*, 66 (27 May 1978); *2000AD*, 78 (19 August 1978).
25 'Penny Dreddful', *Time Out* (20–26 August 1982), p. 10.
26 'Strontium Dog' is credited to T. P. Grover: this is one of several pseudonyms used by the prolific John Wagner.
27 Bishop, *Thrill-Power Overload*, p. 51.
28 *Starlord*, 22 (7 October 1978).
29 *2000 AD and Starlord*, 93 (30 December 1978); *2000 AD and Starlord*, 95 (13 January 1979).
30 Marvel's *Star Wars* strip is notable for the fact that it includes the 'missing' scenes from the film: Luke Skywalker's farewell to his friend Biggs who leaves Tatooine to join the Rebellion and Han Solo's meeting with Jabba the Hut in the Mos Eisley spaceport.
31 See James Chapman, *Inside the Tardis: The Worlds of 'Doctor Who' – A Cultural History* (London, 2006), pp. 118–33.
32 'Doctor Who and the Iron Legion', *Doctor Who*, 2 (24 October 1979).
33 'Comic strip heroes storm the screen', *Readers' Digest* (March 1981), p. 79.
34 'Punk, and pop, goes the Eagle', *Guardian* (8 January 1982), p. 2.
35 *Rocky* (dir. John G. Avildsen, 1976); *Tron* (dir. Steven Lisberger, 1982); *The Professionals* (London Weekend Television, 1977–83).
36 'Comics: A battle for survival', *Observer* (21 July 1985), p. 29.
37 *Damnation Alley* (dir. Jack Smight, 1977).
38 *Soylent Green* (dir. Richard Fleischer, 1973); *A Clockwork Orange* (dir. Stanley Kubrick, 1971); *Escape from New York* (dir. John Carpenter, 1981); *The Omega Man* (dir. Boris Segal, 1971).
39 'Judge Dredd', *2000AD*, 2 (5 March 1977).
40 *2001: A Space Odyssey* (dir. Stanley Kubrick, 1968); *The Forbin Project* (dir. Joseph Sargent, 1969); *Demon Seed* (dir. Donald Cammell, 1977).
41 John Tulloch and Manuel Alvarado, *Doctor Who: The Unfolding Text* (London, 1983).
42 Wagner has written the vast majority of the Judge Dredd stories either as sole author (under his own name and as T. P. Grover or John Howard) or jointly with Alan Grant. Other writers in the formative years of the strip included Pat Mills (24 episodes), Kelvin Gosnell (2 episodes), Malcolm Shaw (2 episodes), Chris Lowder (2 episodes) and Gerry Finley-Day (1 episode). Garth Ennis wrote the strip in the early 1990s when Wagner was concentrating on *Judge Dredd Megazine*.
43 'Judge Dredd', *2000AD*, 3 (12 March 1977).
44 'Judge Dredd', *2000AD*, 6 (2 April 1977).
45 'Judge Dredd', *2000AD*, 20 (9 July 1977).
46 'Judge Dredd', *2000AD*, 7 (9 April 1977).
47 'Diary of a Mad Citizen', *2000AD*, 229 (12 September 1981).

48 John Newsinger, *The Dredd Phenomenon: Comics and Contemporary Society* (Bristol, 1999), p. 20.
49 'The Graveyard Shift', *2000AD*, 335–341 (24 September 1983–5 November 1983).
50 'Otto Sump's Ugly Clinic', *2000AD*, 189 (6 December 1980).
51 'What if the Judges Did the Ads?', *2000AD*, 521 (9 May 1987).
52 'Bum Rap!', *2000AD*, 1070 (25 November 1997).
53 'Whole New Judge Dredd', *2000AD*, 1620 (29 October 2008).
54 'The Last Meal', *2000AD*, 84 (30 September 1978).
55 'Burger Law!', *2000AD*, 72 (8 July 1978).
56 'Judge Dredd', *2000AD*, 14 (28 May 1977).
57 'The Apocalypse War', *2000 AD*, 245–270 (2 January 1982–26 June 1982).
58 'Mega-City', *2000AD*, 272 (10 July 1982).
59 *Octopussy* (dir. John Glen, 1983); *Red Dawn* (dir. John Milius, 1984).
60 *2000 AD*, 263 (8 May 1982).
61 'The Graveyard Shift', *2000AD*, 336 (2 October 1983).
62 'Letter From A Democrat', *2000AD*, 460 (8 March 1986).
63 'Politics', *2000AD*, 656 (9 December 1989).
64 'Revolution', *2000AD*, 531 (18 July 1987).
65 'Nightmare', *2000AD*, 706 (24 November 1990).
66 'Twilight's Last Gleaming', *2000AD*, 756 (9 November 1991).
67 Quoted in Jarman and Acton, *Judge Dredd: The Mega-History*, p. 122.
68 'America', *Judge Dredd Megazine*, 1 (October 1990).
69 'America', *Judge Dredd Megazine*, 7 (April 1991).
70 *2000AD*, 689 (28 July 1990).
71 *2000AD*, 768 (1 February 1992).
72 *2000AD*, 110 (28 April 1979).
73 Bishop, *Thrill-Power Overload*, p. 107.
74 Pat Mills wrote 'Invasion', 'Ro-Busters', 'The ABC Warriors', 'Nemesis the Warlock' and 'Sláine'; John Wagner wrote 'Robo-Hunter' and 'Strontium Dog'; Wagner and Alan Grant wrote 'Ace Trucking Co.' and 'Anderson, Psi Division' (under various pseudonyms including Grant Grover); Tom Tully wrote 'Harlem Heroes' and 'The Mean Arena'; and Gerry Finley-Day wrote 'The VCs' and 'Rogue Trooper'.
75 *Platoon* (dir. Oliver Stone, 1986); *Full Metal Jacket* (dir. Stanley Kubrick, 1987).
76 'Bad Company', *2000AD*, 501 (20 December 1986).
77 *2000AD*, 687 (14 July 1990).
78 'Strontium Dog', *Starlord*, 3 (27 May 1978).
79 'Nemesis the Warlock', *2000AD*, 223 (1 August 1981).
80 *2000AD*, 696 (15 September 1990).
81 Newsinger, *The Dredd Phenomenon*, p. 72.
82 *2000AD*, 395 (8 December 1984).
83 *2000AD*, 675 (21 April 1990).
84 *2000AD*, 691 (11 August 1990).
85 'Engram', *2000AD*, 761 (14 December 1991).

86 *Alien* (dir. Ridley Scott, 1979); *Star Trek – The Motion Picture* (dir. Robert Wise, 1979).
87 *Rambo: First Blood Part II* (dir. George Pan Cosmatos, 1985); *Total Recall* (dir. Paul Verhoeven, 1990).
88 Prog 534 (8 August 1987) includes a sketch of a poster for a film of *Judge Dredd* sent in by a young Danny Cannon. It is clearly influenced by *Blade Runner*: to be directed by Ridley Scott and starring Harrison Ford as Dredd, with Darryl Hannah as Judge Anderson and Christopher Walken as Rico. It is tempting to speculate that this would have turned out a more interesting Dredd film.
89 'Judged and found wanting', *Daily Telegraph* (9 January 1995), p. 16.
90 'Dredd nought', *The Independent* (30 July 1995), S2, p. 11; 'Dredd boring', *Financial Times* (20 July 1995), p. 17; 'A slice of stale Dredd', *Guardian* (20 July 1995), S2, pp. 8–9.
91 Martin Barker and Kate Brooks, *Knowing Audiences: Judge Dredd, Its Fans, Friends and Foes* (Luton, 1998).
92 '"Judge Dredd": Production Information', p. 2. A copy of this publicity release is on the microfiche for *Judge Dredd* held by the National Library of the British Film Institute.
93 Ibid., p. 4.
94 'I was a teenage Dredd head', *Independent on Sunday* (16 July 1995), p. 23.
95 Ibid.
96 'Beyond the Call of Duty', *2000AD*, 1106 (29 August 1998).
97 *Judge Dredd: Origins* (Oxford, 2007).

7 THE STRANGE WORLD OF THE BRITISH SUPERHERO

1 *Captain Britain Monthly*, 5 (May 1985), p. 24.
2 See Les Daniels, *Comix: A History of Comic Books in America* (New York, 1971); Gerard Jones, *Men of Tomorrow: Geeks, Gangsters and the Birth of the Comic Book* (London, 2005); and Bradford W. Wright, *Comic Book Nation: The Transformation of Youth Culture in America* (London, 2001).
3 Roz Kaveney, *Superheroes! Capes and Crusaders in Comics and Films* (London, 2008), p. 4.
4 Fredric Wertham, *The Seduction of the Innocent: The Influence of the Comic Book on Today's Youth* (New York, 1954), pp. 234–5. Wertham's work has been the subject of extensive commentary: the most recent analysis is Bart Beaty, *Fredric Wertham and the Critique of Mass Culture* (Jackson, MI, 2005).
5 See Robert Genter, '"With Great Power Comes Great Responsibility": Cold War Culture and the Birth of Marvel Comics', *Journal of Popular Culture*, xxxx/6 (2007), pp. 953–78.
6 'Marvel Continues to Captivate Kids', Marvel Entertainment Group News Release, n.d. [c. 1983]. BFI Denis Gifford Collection Box 113: *Comics Research*.
7 Michael Anglo, *Nostalgia Spotlight on the Fifties* (London, 1977), p. 116.
8 Ibid., p. 118.
9 Ibid., p. 120.

10 *The Marvelman Annual* (London, 1959), p. 4.
11 'Marvelman and King Canute', *Marvelman*, 346 (n.d.); 'Marvelman and the Spanish Armada', *Marvelman*, 344 (n.d.).
12 'Marvelman and the Magic Tinder Box', *Marvelman*, 346 (n.d.).
13 'Marvelman and the Land of Make-Believe', *Marvelman*, 345 (n.d.).
14 'Horror comics "could lead to murder"', *The Times* (23 October 1970), p. 5.
15 Ken Bulmer and Jésus Blasco, *The Steel Claw: The Vanishing Man* (London, 2005).
16 Jerry Siegel, Ted Cowan and Reg Bunn, *The Spider: King of Crooks* (London, 2005).
17 *Captain Britain*, 1 (13 October 1976).
18 'Captain Britain', *Captain Britain* (13 October 1976); 'From the Holocaust – A Hero', *Captain Britain* 2 (20 October 1976).
19 *Gawain and the Green Knight* (dir. Stephen Weeks, 1973); *Excalibur* (dir. John Boorman, 1981).
20 Chris Claremont, 'Introduction', *Captain Britain* (London, 1989), p. 5.
21 'Riot on Regent Street', *Captain Britain*, 8 (1 December 1976).
22 'Captain Britain', *Captain Britain*, 1 (13 October 1976).
23 *The Man With the Golden Gun* (dir. Guy Hamilton, 1974). See also the *Doctor Who* serials 'Inferno' (1970) and 'Invasion of the Dinosaurs' (1974).
24 'A Throne Threatened', *Captain Britain*, 39 (6 July 1977).
25 'Giving 'em stick', *Guardian* (14 October 1976), p. 13.
26 James Chapman, *Saints and Avengers: British Adventure Series of the 1960s* (London, 2002), pp. 52–99.
27 *Captain Britain*, 32 (18 May 1977).
28 'Only the Strong Survive', *Captain Britain*, 32 (18 May 1977).
29 'Demon-Fire', *Captain Britain*, 9 (8 December 1976).
30 *Captain Britain*, 37 (22 June 1977).
31 *Captain Britain*, 12 (29 December 1976).
32 Quoted in *Captain Britain Volume 2: A Hero Reborn* (Tunbridge Wells, 2007), p. 9.
33 'Mayhem on a Monday Morning', *Captain Britain*, 3 (27 October 1976).
34 'Captain Britain Has Been Beaten!', *Captain Britain*, 5 (20 November 1976).
35 'Call for Captain Britain', *Evening News* (27 September 1976), p. 9.
36 *Super Spider-Man and Captain Britain*, 240 (14 September 1977).
37 *Super Spider-Man and Captain Britain*, 253 (14 December 1977).
38 *Mighty World of Marvel*, 9 (February 1984).
39 *Mighty World of Marvel*, 10 (March 1984).
40 *Mighty World of Marvel*, 15 (August 1984).
41 'Flotsam and Jetsam', *Captain Britain*, 3 (March 1985), p. 5.
42 *Captain Britain*, 7 (July 1985), p. 35.
43 *Captain Britain*, 5 (May 1985), p. 24.
44 'Myth, Memory and Legend', *Captain Britain*, 1 (January 1985), pp. 4–11.
45 *Captain Britain*, 5 (May 1985), p. 24.
46 *Captain Britain*, 3 (March 1985), p. 27.
47 'Marvelman', *Warrior*, 2 (April 1982), p. 7.
48 'Marvelman – When Johnny comes marching home', *Warrior*, 3 (July 1982), p. 8.

49 'Marvelman – Blue Murder', *Warrior*, 8 (December 1982), p. 7.
50 *Warrior*, 8 (December 1982), p. 49.
51 *Warrior*, 7 (November 1982), p. 50.
52 *Warrior*, 25 (December 1984), p. 4. For a full account of the Marvel controversy and subsequent disputes over the copyright of Marvelman/Miracleman, see George Khoury, ed., *Kimota! The Miracleman Companion* (Raleigh, NC, 2001).
53 *Miracleman*, 15 (November 1988).
54 Robert Eaglestone, 'Madness or Modernity?: The Holocaust in Two Anglo-American Comics', *Rethinking History*, VI/3 (2002), pp. 319–30.
55 Quoted on the inside cover of David Thorpe, Lawrence Gray and Phil Elliott, *Doc Chaos* (1985).
56 Grant Morrison, 'Introduction', *Zenith: Book One* (London, 1988), p. 1.
57 'Zenith', *2000AD*, 552 (28 November 1987).
58 'Zenith', *2000AD*, 560 (6 February 1988).
59 'Zenith: Phase II/14: Zero Hour', *2000AD*, 603 (3 December 1988).
60 'Paul Grist: The Comicology Interview', *Comicology*, II/2 (2000), p. 20.
61 *Jack Staff Volume 2: Soldiers* (August 2004), p. 146.
62 *Comics Reporter* (17 June 2005), at www.comicsreporter.com/index/cr_reviews/1916 (accessed 31 March 2009).
63 'Flag Waving', *The Weird World of Jack Staff*, 1 (July 2007).
64 *Jack Staff Volume 2*, p. 57.
65 'The Guns of Avalon', *Captain Britain and MI13*, 4 (October 2008).
66 'The Guns of Avalon', *Captain Britain and MI13*, 1 (July 2008).
67 'Gordon Brown left red-faced in Commons after world saviour gaffe', *Times Online*, 10 December 2008, at www.timesonline.co.uk/tol/news/politics/article5319124.ece (accessed 31 March 2009).

8 THE RISE AND FALL OF ALTERNATIVE COMICS

1 Quoted in George Khoury, ed., *True Brit: A Celebration of the Great Comic Book Artists of the UK* (Raleigh, NC, 2004), p. 186.
2 There are several useful studies of underground comics, mostly focusing on the United States. See in particular Mark Estren, *A History of Underground Comics* (San Francisco, 1974); Charles Hatfield, *Alternative Comics: An Emerging Literature* (Jackson, MS, 2005); Patrick Rosenkranz, *Rebel Visions: The Underground Comix Revolution, 1963–1975* (Seattle, WA, 2002); and Dez Skinn, *Comix: The Underground Revolution* (London, 2004). To date, however, the only study of the British context is David Huxley, 'The Growth and Development of British Underground and Alternative Comics 1966–1986', unpublished PhD thesis, University of Loughborough, 1990.
3 Arthur Marwick, *The Sixties: Cultural Revolution in Britain, France, Italy and the United States, c. 1958–c. 1974* (Oxford, 1998), p. 17.
4 Roger Sabin, 'The Last Laugh: Larfing All the Way to the Dock', *Index on Censorship*, 6 (2000), pp. 121–5.
5 Jonathon Green, *All Dressed Up: The Sixties and the Counterculture* (London, 1998), p. 375.

6 Marwick, *The Sixties*, p. 13.
7 Huxley, 'The Growth and Development of British Underground and Alternative Comics 1966–1986', p. 59.
8 Ibid., p. 29.
9 Quoted in George Khoury, ed., *The Extraordinary Works of Alan Moore: Indispensable Edition* (Raleigh, NC, 2008), p. 34.
10 Quoted in Roger Sabin, *Adult Comics: An Introduction* (London, 1993), p. 43.
11 *The Laid-Back Adventures of Suzie and Jonnie* (London, 1981).
12 *Ogoth and Ugly Boot* (London, 1973).
13 'Parental Drug Abuse: What Every Child Should Know', *Cozmic Comics*, 5 (February 1973).
14 'How to Spot a Dope Fiend', *Dope Fiend Funnies*, 1 (1974).
15 *Zip Comics*, 1 (1973).
16 *Edward's Heave*, 1 (April 1973).
17 'Lil' Red Rider', *Cozmic Comics*, 5 (1972).
18 'T.V. Filth', *Ally Sloper*, 4 (January 1977).
19 Leon Hunt, *British Low Culture: From Safari Suits to Sexploitation* (London, 1998), p. 34.
20 'The Man Who Was Stuck in a Comic', *Streetcomix*, 3 (May 1977), pp. 26–7.
21 'Komix Comics', *Streetcomix*, 3 (May 1977), pp. 24–5.
22 Sabin, *Adult Comics*, p. 45.
23 Skinn, *Comix*, p. 190.
24 Quoted in Huxley, 'The Growth and Development of British Underground and Alternative Comics 1966–1986', p. 33.
25 Quoted in 'The Virtues of Xerography', *Escape*, 3 (Autumn 1983), p. 55.
26 Lew Stringer, 'We called them Stripzines', 29 December 2006, at http://lewstringer. blogspot. com/2006/12/we_called_them_stripzines.html (accessed 15 January 2010).
27 *Silicon Fish*, 1 (1985), p. 29.
28 *The Alternative Headmaster's Bulletin*, 6 (1985).
29 *Zero Order*, 1 (Winter 1984/85).
30 *Myra*, 4 (1983).
31 *Escape*, 2 (Summer 1983), p. 52.
32 *Weird Fun*, 1 (Spring 1985).
33 *Captain Crab's Horrific Tales of Terror*, 1 (July–August 1985).
34 'Hey Whitey!', *Fast Fiction*, 16 (September 1985).
35 'Setting the Tone', *Escape*, 1 (Spring 1983), p. 2.
36 'A New Way of Talking', *Escape*, 2 (Summer 1983), p. 2.
37 Dave Roach, 'The History of British Comic Art', in Khoury, ed., *True Brit*, p. 25.
38 Roger Sabin, *Comics, Comix and Graphic Novels: A History of Comic Art* (London, 1996), p. 193.
39 *Escape*, 4 (Winter 1983/84), p. 2.
40 Chris Donald, *Rude Kids: The Inside Story of 'Viz'* (London, 2004), p. 7.
41 Ibid., pp. 28–9.
42 Ibid., p. 37.
43 Ibid., p. 30.

44 Ibid., p. 85
45 Ibid., p. 119.
46 Sabin, *Adult Comics*, p. 124.
47 Ibid., p. 122.
48 Quoted in 'The Viz vision', *Guardian* (29 November 1988), pp. 37.
49 Donald, *Rude Kids*, p. 130.
50 Sabin, *Adult Comics*, pp. 120–21.
51 See Andy Medhurst, *A National Joke: Popular Comedy and English Cultural Identities* (London, 2007).
52 George Orwell, 'The Art of Donald McGill' [1941], *Decline of the English Murder and Other Essays* (Harmondsworth, 1965), pp. 153–4.
53 'Ban this filth!', *Viz*, 44 (October/November 1990), p. 5.
54 'Comic uncut', *Listener* (3 November 1988), p. 89.
55 'Comic strippers', *Guardian* (7 November 1989), p. 21.
56 'There's no biz like show Viz', *Sun* (11 August 1989), p. 9.
57 Donald, *Rude Kids*, p. 156.
58 'The Thieving Gypsy Bastards', *Viz*, 44 (October/November 1990), p. 3.
59 Donald, *Rude Kids*, p. 157.
60 Ibid., p. 348.

9 THE GROWING PAINS OF BRITISH COMICS

1 Quoted in Chad Boudreau, 'Phil Elliott: The past and present of the UK comic industry', n.d., at www.comicreaders.com/modules (accessed 15 January 2010).
2 *Hotspur* and *Jinty* both folded in 1981, *Debbie* in 1983, *Tammy* in 1984, *Tiger* in 1985, *Warlord* in 1986 and *Battle* in 1988.
3 'Comics: A battle for survival', *Observer* (21 July 1985), p. 29.
4 *Escape* (1983–1990) spans the period from *Warrior* in 1982 until *Crisis* and *Deadline* in 1988. However, I see *Escape* as emerging from the self-published 'Fast Fiction' of the early 1980s: it is discussed in this context in Chapter 8.
5 *Star Wars* (dir. George Lucas, 1977); *Superman* (dir. Richard Donner, 1978); *Star Trek – The Motion Picture* (dir. Robert Wise, 1979); *Alien* (dir. Ridley Scott, 1979); *Blade Runner* (dir. Ridley Scott, 1982).
6 Dez Skinn, *Comix: The Underground Revolution* (London, 2004), p. 198.
7 The publication history of 'Luther Arkwright' is complex. The character first appeared in a one-off story ('The Papist Affair') in the underground comic *Mixed Bunch* in 1977. The continuing serial began in *Near Myths* in 1978 and was repeated and extended in *Psst!* in 1982. The collected strips were published in one volume in 1982, though at this stage the narrative was incomplete. Talbot finished the story in 1988 and it was issued as a nine-part mini-series by Valkyrie Press. The complete series (minus 'The Papist Affair') was published in one volume by Dark Horse Comics in 1991 with a second edition in 2007.
8 Bryan Talbot, *The Adventures of Luther Arkwright* (London, 2007), p. 23.
9 Ibid., p. 209.
10 Ibid., p. 109.
11 Ibid., p. 208.

12 *Warrior*, 5 (September 1982), p. 33.
13 *Warrior*, 7 (November 1982), p. 48; *Warrior*, 15 (November 1983), p. 49.
14 *Warrior*, 8 (December 1982), p. 48.
15 'Freedom's Road', *Warrior*, 1 (March 1982), p. 4.
16 'Sweat Shop Talk II', *Warrior*, 16 (December 1983), p. 14.
17 *Warrior*, 13 (September 1983), p. 50.
18 'Father Shandor' was a character from the Hammer horror *Dracula – Prince of Darkness* (dir. Terence Fisher, 1966), where he was played by Andrew Keir.
19 'A True Story', *Warrior* 1 (March 1982), pp. 22–3.
20 *Warrior*, 5 (September 1982), p. 33.
21 'Behind the Painted Smile', *Warrior*, 17 (March 1984), p. 19.
22 Annalisa Di Liddo, *Alan Moore: Comics as Performance, Fiction as Scalpel* (Jackson, MS, 2009), pp. 111–5.
23 *Warrior*, 23 (October 1984), p. 4.
24 *Warrior*, 12 (August 1983), p. 50.
25 *Warrior*, 13 (September 1983), p. 50.
26 The correspondence with Marvel Comics was published in *Warrior*, 26 (February 1985), pp. 4–5.
27 *Warrior*, 23 (October 1984), p. 4.
28 The demise of *Warrior* left stories unfinished. 'Marvelman' became *Miracleman* and was published by Eclipse Comics from 1985: Moore's run on the story ended in 1989. *V for Vendetta* was published as a ten-part series by DC in 1988–9.
29 The impact of the 'big three' is discussed in Roger Sabin, *Adult Comics: An Introduction* (London, 1993), pp. 87–95.
30 Quoted in Gilly Filsner, 'Alternative comics', *Evening Standard* (25 March 1988), p. 21.
31 Quoted in David Bishop, *Thrill-Power Overload: Thirty Years of 2000AD, The Galaxy's Greatest Comic* (Oxford, 2007), p. 129.
32 *Crisis*, 19 (27 May–9 June 1989).
33 'Third World War', *Crisis*, 1 (17–30 September 1988).
34 'Third World War', *Crisis*, 5 (12–25 November 1988).
35 'Third World War', *Crisis*, 2 (1–14 October 1988).
36 'Third World War', *Crisis*, 14 (18–31 March 1989).
37 'New Statesmen', *Crisis*, 1 (17–30 September 1988).
38 'Tank Girl', *Deadline*, 2 (November 1988), p. 5.
39 'Tank Girl', *Deadline*, 5 (March 1989), p. 7.
40 Ibid., p. 9.
41 'Tank Girl', *Deadline*, 17 (April 1990), p. 5.
42 'Tales of the unexpected', *Guardian* (17 June 1991), p. 32.
43 'Girl Crazy', *Guardian* (25 May 1995), p. 28.
44 'Marshal Law' is another strip with a complex publication history. It had first appeared in 1987 in a US series published by Marvel's mature imprint Epic. After the demise of *Strip* it would have a run in *Toxic!* Titan Books published *Marshal Law: Fear and Loathing* as a graphic novel in 2002.
45 *Revolver*, 1 (July 1990), p. 48.
46 Roger Sabin, 'Revolver', *Guardian* (17 July 1990), p. 35.

47 'Dare', *Revolver*, 2 (August 1990), p. 7.
48 'Dare', *Crisis*, 56 (March 1991). The last episode of 'Dare' was published in *Crisis* following the closure of *Revolver*.
49 *Toxic*, 1 (25 March 1991), p. 2.
50 *Strip*, 11 (7 July 1990), p. 38.
51 Quoted in 'A twist in the comic book story line', *Guardian* (30 November 1987), p. 13.

10 THE BRITISH COMICS RENAISSANCE

1 Quoted in George Khoury, ed., *The Extraordinary Works of Alan Moore: Indispensable Edition* (Raleigh, NC, 2008), p. 181.
2 Annalisa Di Liddo, *Alan Moore: Comics as Performance, Fiction as Scalpel* (Jackson, MI, 2009) p. 102.
3 Stan Lee was editor-in-chief of Marvel Comics and devised its line of superhero comics in the early 1960s, while Jack Kirby (*The Fantastic Four*) and Steve Ditko (*The Amazing Spider-Man*) were the artists who came to define the Marvel style.
4 *From Hell* (dir. Albert and Allen Hughes, 2001); *The League of Extraordinary Gentlemen* (dir. Stephen Norrington, 2003); *V for Vendetta* (dir. James McTeigue, 2005); *Watchmen* (dir. Zack Snyder, 2009).
5 *A Small Killing* (1991) was published by Victor Gollancz and was only Moore's second true graphic novel after *Batman: The Killing Joke* (1988). Most of his works, including *Watchmen*, *From Hell* and *The League of Extraordinary Gentlemen*, are mini-series collected into trade paperbacks.
6 Roz Kaveney, *Superheroes! Capes and Crusaders in Comics and Films* (London, 2008), p. 60.
7 *Alan Moore's Writing for Comics* [1985] (Rantoul, IL, 2008), p. 2.
8 Lance Parkin, *Alan Moore*, 2nd edn (London, 2009), p. 52.
9 Khoury, *The Extraordinary Works*, p. 109.
10 John Newsinger, *The Dredd Phenomenon: Comics and Contemporary Society* (Bristol, 1999), p. 77.
11 *Alan Moore: On His Work and Career – A Conversation with Bill Baker* (New York, 2008), p. 40.
12 *Murder by Decree* (dir. Bob Clark, 1979)
13 Alan Moore and Eddie Campbell, *From Hell: Being a Melodrama in Sixteen Parts* (London, 2000), ch. 4, p. 6.
14 Ibid., ch. 2, p. 28.
15 Ibid., ch. 12, p. 15.
16 Ibid., Appendix, p. 16.
17 Jess Nevins, *Heroes and Monsters: The Unofficial Companion to 'The League of Extraordinary Gentlemen'* (Austin, TX, 2003); Jess Nevins, *A Blazing World: The Unofficial Companion to 'The League of Extraordinary Gentlemen, Volume Two'* (Austin, TX, 2004); Jess Nevins, *Impossible Territories: The Unofficial Companion to 'The League of Extraordinary Gentlemen, The Black Dossier'* (Austin, TX, 2008).
18 Quoted in Khoury, *The Extraordinary Works*, p. 180.
19 Maryanne Rhett, 'The Graphic Novel and the World History Classroom', *World*

      History Connected, IV/2 (2007), at www.historycooperative.org/journals/whc/4.2/rhett.html (accessed 29 January 2010).
20 Quoted in Nevins, *Heroes and Monsters*, p. 58.
21 Alan Moore and Kevin O'Neill, *The League of Extraordinary Gentlemen*, vol. 1 (La Jolla, CA, 2000), Book 5.
22 Quoted in Nevins, *A Blazing World*, pp. 278–9.
23 Alan Moore and Kevin O'Neill, *The League of Extraordinary Gentlemen: Black Dossier* (La Jolla, CA, 2007).
24 'IPC Media and DC Comics resurrect legendary U.K. comic book characters', IPC Press Release, 22 November 2004, at www.ipcmedia.com/press/article/59630 (accessed 27 March 2009).
25 Alan Moore, Leah Moore, John Reppion, Shane Oakley, George Freeman, *Albion* (La Jolla, CA, 2007).
26 *The Silence of the Lambs* (dir. Jonathan Demme, 1990).
27 'Big Dave', *2000AD*, 842–845 (3 July–24 July 1993); 'Monarchy in the UK', *2000AD*, 846–849 (31 July–21 August 1993); 'Costa del Chaos', *2000AD*, 869–872 (8 January–28 January 1994).
28 Ian Edginton and D'Israeli, *Scarlet Traces* (Milwaukie, OR, 2003), p. 70.
29 Ian Edginton and D'Israeli, *Scarlet Traces: The Great Game* (Milwaukie, OR, 2007), p. 100.
30 Warren Ellis, Chris Weston and Laura Martin, *Ministry of Space*, 1 (May 2001).
31 Warren Ellis and Gianluca Pagliarani, *Ignition City*, 1 (April 2009).
32 Warren Ellis and Raulo Caceres, *Crécy* (Rantoul, IL, 2007).
33 Garth Ennis and Carlos Ezquerra, *Adventures in the Rifle Brigade* (New York, 2004).
34 Garth Ennis and Colin Wilson, *Battler Britton*, 2 (October 2006).
35 Quoted in 'Where Ennis Dares', *Comics International*, 205 (March 2008), p. 34.
36 These were nicknames of the heads of Fighter and Bomber Command: Air Chief Marshal Sir Hugh 'Stuffy' Dowding and Air Chief Marshal Sir Arthur 'Bomber' Harris.
37 Garth Ennis and Gary Erskine, 'Under an English Heaven', *Dan Dare*, 1 (November 2007).
38 Garth Ennis and Gary Erskine, 'The Price of Admiralty', *Dan Dare*, 7 (July 2008).

Sources

The principal primary sources for this book are the comics themselves: where I have referred to specific strips and issues these can be traced through the endnotes. The field of comics scholarship is still in its infancy: as yet there are no universal scholarly conventions for citing comics. I have endeavoured to provide as full references as possible so that interested readers may consult the originals. Many comics are unpaginated: if no page references are included this is why. Most of the comics referred to in the text are either from my own collection or from comics loaned to me by others. The fullest publicly accessible collection of comics in Britain is held by the British Library: see the 'British Comics Collection' guide on the British Library website (www.bl.uk/reshelp/britcomics.index.html). Even the British Library collection is not complete: the rare first issue of the *Beano*, for example, is missing.

Other primary sources are patchy. The Northcliffe papers (British Library Additional Manuscripts) include Alfred Harmsworth's diaries and some correspondence from the 1890s that list circulation figures for *Comic Cuts* and other papers. The National Archives contain some documents relating to the horror comics campaign of the 1950s: these can be found in the PREM (Premier), BT (Board of Trade), FO (Foreign Office) and DPP (Director of Public Prosecutions) series. The company archives of D. C. Thomson and Amalgamated Press/IPC are not open to researchers, though the internal newsletter *IPC News* is held by the British Library and was useful for the 1970s as it published audited circulation figures and included articles about the Juvenile Periodicals Division. The Denis Gifford papers held by the Special Collections Unit of the British Film Institute include numerous files of newspaper cuttings, articles, interviews and Gifford's own research notes, including an unpublished manuscript entitled 'History of British Strips' from the mid-1970s.

There are two indispensable reference works on British comics: Denis Gifford's *The Complete Catalogue of British Comics* (Exeter, 1985) and Alan Clark's *Dictionary of British Comic Artists, Writers and Editors* (London, 1998). Guides to particular titles and publishers include David Ashord and Steve Holland's independently published *Thriller Picture Library: An Illustrated Guide* (Rotherham, 1991), Holland's *The Fleetway Companion* (Rotherham, 2002) and Holland and David Roach's *The War Libraries: The Fleetway Picture Library Index* (London, 2007). A somewhat partial history of the world of D. C. Thomson can be found in Paul Harris, ed., *The D. C. Thomson Bumper*

Fun Book (Edinburgh, 1977). Much of the research to establish the identity of writers and artists and the provenance of particular strips has been undertaken by fans and enthusiasts, appearing in magazines such as *Comic Cuts: Newsletter of the Association of Comic Enthusiasts, Illustrators: The Newsletter of the Association of Illustrators* and *Eagle Times: The Quarterly Journal of the Eagle Society*. The World Wide Web is an ever-changing landscape and new websites come and go with the frequency of British comics in the 1970s and '80s. The information here is often incomplete: perhaps the most useful is *British Comics* (www.britishcomics.com, active as at June 2010). Internet forums, message boards and blogs must be treated with caution, though the UK Comics Scholar Listserve (www.jiscmail.ac.uk/lists/UKCOMICSCHOLARS.html) is a useful academic forum for both teachers and researchers.

There is an extensive popular historiography of comics. The best general history is Roger Sabin's handsomely illustrated *Comics, Comix and Graphic Novels* (London, 1996). See also George Perry and Alan Aldridge, *The Penguin Book of Comics* (Harmondsworth, 1967). All comic fans and historians in Britain are indebted to the pioneering work of Denis Gifford, including *Discovering Comics* (Tring, 1971), *Stap Me! The British Newspaper Strip* (Aylesbury, 1971), *Victorian Comics* (London, 1976) – still the only significant work on the formative period of the medium – and *The International Book of Comics* (London, 1984). The best popular histories of British comics are Paul Gravett and Peter Stanbury, *Great British Comics: Celebrating A Century of Ripping Yarns and Wizard Wheezes* (London, 2006), and George Khoury, ed., *True Brit: A Celebration of the Great Comic Book Artists of the UK* (Raleigh, NC, 2004). On the 1950s and '60s, especially, see Norman Wright and David Ashford, *Masters of Fun and Thrills: The British Comic Artists* (Swanage, 2008). There are two very useful 'inside' histories of major titles: David Bishop, *Thrill-Power Overload: Thirty Years of 2000AD, The Galaxy's Greatest Comic* (Oxford, 2007), and Chris Donald, *Rude Kids: The Inside Story of 'Viz'* (London, 2005). Leo Baxendale's *A Very Funny Business: 40 Years of Comics* (London, 1978) is one of the few autobiographies by a major British artist. Sally Morris and Jan Hallwood, *Living With Eagles: Priest to Publisher – The Life and Times of Marcus Morris* (Cambridge, 1998) is a candid biography of the editor of *Eagle* and *Girl*.

Academic work on the British comic has been much less extensive. Martin Barker's *Comics: Ideology, Power and the Critics* (Manchester, 1989) and Roger Sabin's *Adult Comics: An Introduction* (London, 1993) are the two books from which it has been difficult to maintain a respectable distance. Barker's *A Haunt of Fears: The Strange History of the British Horror Comics Campaign* (London, 1984) was the first academic study of British comics: it remains indispensable. Similarly, Barker's *Action: The Story of a Violent Comic* (London, 1990) is to date the only in-depth study of a particular title. John Newsinger, *The Dredd Phenomenon: Comics and Contemporary Society* (Bristol, 1999) is a polemical study of *2000AD, Crisis* and the work of various writers including Pat Mills, Alan Moore, Grant Morrison, Warren Ellis and Garth Ennis. Chapter 4 draws upon Melanie Elizabeth Gibson, 'Remembered Reading: Memory, Comics and Post-War Construction of British Girlhood', unpublished PhD thesis (University of Sunderland, 2001). Similarly, chapter 8 is informed by David Huxley, 'The Growth and Development of British Underground and Alternative Comics 1966–1988', unpublished PhD thesis (University of Loughborough, 1990). To date the only scholarly monograph on the work of a British comic writer is Annalisa Di Liddo, *Alan Moore:*

Comics as Performance, Fiction as Scalpel (Jackson, MI, 2009). Journals such as the *International Journal of Comic Art, Studies in Comics* and *Visual Culture in Britain* have published articles on British comics.

The dearth of scholarly work on British comics further reflects the neglect of the medium in contrast to American comic books and other national traditions such as the *bande dessinée* and *manga*. *The Great British Comic* has been the first attempt to map a history of British comics as social practice: its many gaps and omissions demonstrate that this is a subject in need of further research.

Acknowledgements

This book was a long time in the making. My thanks are due (in no particular order) to: the staff of the British Library (St Pancras), the British Newspaper Library (Colindale) and the National Library of the British Film Institute for their unfailing courtesy and assistance; Professor Martin Barker, Professor Nicholas J. Cull, Professor Krista Cowman, Dr Ann Miller, Professor Michael Paris and Professor Jeffrey Richards for their encouragement and support; Philip Chaston, Tony Dunn, Mark Murphy and Oliver Redmayne for various suggestions and sources; colleagues and students in the Department of History of Art and Film at the University of Leicester for tolerating my homilies about comics; Vivian Constantinopoulos at Reaktion Books for her faith in this book and her patience in awaiting delivery of the manuscript; and to my parents for letting me take *Victor* as a boy. The book is immeasurably better due to all these individuals: it goes without saying, however, that I alone bear responsibility for any errors, lacunae and flights of interpretational fancy. Kimota!

Index

2000AD 10, 79, 107, 109, 125, 126, 129, 143, 144–171, *147*, *153*, *155*, *162*, *164*, 193, 212, 222, 223, 232, 236, 242, 249–50, 254
2001: A Space Odyssey 144, 154

AARGH! 244
'ABC Warriors, The' 162
'Abslom Daak – Dalek Killer' 150–51
'Accident Man' 239
Ace Malloy 95
'Ace Trucking Co.' 162
Action 9, 79, 107, 123, 125, 129, 131, 135–43, *137*, *138*, *142*, 145–6, 148
Action Comics 11, 37, 172
'Action in the Khyber' 89, *90*
'Action Stations' 99
'Addie and Hermy – the Nasty Nazis' 37
Adrian, Jack 136
Adventure 12, 30, 78
Adventures in the Rifle Brigade 253
Adventures of Dan Dare: Pilot of the Future, The 69
Adventures of Jane, The 43, 44
'Adventures of Luther Arkwright, The' 225–7, *227*
Adventures of Mr Spoonbiscuit, The 202
'Adventures of P.C. 49, The' 59, *59*
'Adventures of Peggy, The' 43
'Adventures of Penny Wise, The' 110
Adventures of Robin Hood, The (film) 86
Adventures of Robin Hood, The (TV series) 86
Adventures of Tintin in the Land of the Soviets, The 8
'Adventures of Windy Wilberforce, The' 211
'Agent Adam x3' 210
Agnew, Stephen 87
Ainsworth, William 87
Air Ace Picture Library 78, 95, 253
Air War Picture Stories 95
Albion 182, 244, 249
Aldine Press 79, 87, 248
Aldis, Brian 149
'Alec' 210
Alien 167, 225
'All-Girl Amazon Attack Battalion, The' 230
All Quiet on the Western Front 133, 135
'Allan and the Sundered Veil' 248
Allen, J. B. 78, 81
Allison, John 222
Ally Sloper 206–7
Ally Sloper's Half-Holiday 11, 19–22, *21*, 28
Alternative Headmaster's Bulletin, The 210
Alvorado, Manuel 154
Amalgamated Press 24, 29, 33, 54, 55, 70, 77–81, 95, 104, 108
Amazing Spider-Man, The 174
'America' 160
America's Best Comics 244
'Anderson of Psi Division' 165–6
Anderson, Gerry 105–7, 117
Anderson, Lindsay 2, 69
'Andy Capp' 20
'Angela – Air Hostess' 114
Anglo, Michael 70, 81–2, 89, 175–6, 178
'Angus McBastard' 221
Animal Weirdness 202
Anna Mercury 251
'Anne Mullion' 110
Answers to Correspondents 18, 24
'Ant Wars' 148
Anvil, The 45, 53, 61
Apocalypse Ltd 239
'Apocalypse War, The' 158
Arnold Book Company 47, 70, 81
'Arry's Budget 23
Arts Labs 202
Ashford, David 79
Assante, Armand 169
Association of Assistant Mistresses 48
Astor, Tom 235
Avatar Press 249, 251
Avengers, The 105, 117, 180, 185
Avery, Tex 206

293

'Bad Company' 162–3
Bader, Douglas 70
Bagnall, Jonathan 214
Bailey, Peter 22
Bailey, Ray 114
Baker, Charles 176
Baker, Danny 219
'Ballad of Halo Jones, The' 165, 244
Ballard, J. G. 149
bande dessinée 7, 14, 257
Banger, Harry 37
Bannister, Roger 91, 92
Barb Wire 168
Barbarella 225
Barbie 124
Barker, Dennis 185
Barker, Edward 202
Barker, Martin 7, 13, 46, 131, 136, 141–3
'Bash Street Kids, The' 33
Batman 167, 169
Battle (Michael Anglo) 89, 90
Battle (IPC Magazines) 79, 107, 123, 125, 127–35, *131*, *134*, 145, 148, 150, 162, 223, 253
'Battle Line, The' 100
'Battle of the Burger Barons' 157
Battle Picture Library 78, 95–6, 100
Battle Picture Weekly see Battle
Battlefields 253–4
Battler Britton (Garth Ennis) 253
'Battler Britton – Air Ace' 95, *96*
Baxendale, Leo 33
Baxter, W. G. 20
Beano 9, 10, 31–3, *32*, 37, 77, 108, 126, 207, 217, 222, 239, 242
Beaumont, Reg 37
Beckum, Chuck 192
Beeton, Samuel 18
Beezer 9, 77
'Beezlebub Jones' 38
Belardinelli, Massimo 136, 149
Bell, Ronald 52

Bell, Steve 207, 222
'Bella at the Bar' 122
Bellamy, Frank 69, 75, 79, 86, 105–7
'Belle of the Ballet' 111, 116
BEM (*Bug-Eyed Magazine*) 209
Ben-Hur 170
Benjamin, Walter 26
Benny Hill Show, The 207
Bensberg, Ted 98
'Beryl the Bitch' 235
Bewes, Rodney 151
'Biffa Bacon' 218
'Biffo the Bear' 31
'Big Ben' 231
Big Budget 23, 25
'Big Dave' 249–50
Bill Grundy Show, The 207
'Billy Bottom and his Zany Toilet Pranks' 217
'Billy Bunter of Greyfriars' 84
Birnage, Derek 95
Bishop, David 149, 170–71
Bisley, Simon 240
'Black Jack' 136, 139
Black Magic 47, 50
Black, Frank 70
Black, Jock 89
'Blackbow the Cheyenne' 75
Blackhawk 81
Blade Runner 168, 225
Blaikie, Jim 234
Blake's 7 149
Blasco, Jesús 81, 149, 178–9
Blast! 224, 231, 251
'Blitz Kids, The' 37–8
'Blondie' 31
Bloody Mary 253
Blue Jeans 123
Boardman, T. V. 81
Bogarde, Dirk 101
'Bogey' 231
'Bogie Man, The' 239
Bolland, Brian 149, 165, 202, 222, 235, 240
Bolton, John 228
'Bomber Braddock' 129
Bombs Go Down, The 102
'Booboo' 210
'Bootneck Boy, The' 130
Bossevain, Serge 225

Boswell, Hilda 110
Boyfriend 118
Boy's Comic Journal 18
Boy's Own Paper 12, 18, 35, 46, 54, 58–9, 79
Boys, The 253
Boys' Cinema 29, *31*, 35
Boys' Friend 24
Boys of England 18, 87
Boys' World 74
Bracken, Brendan 50
Bradbury, Eric 129
Bradbury, Ray 148
Braddock and the Flying Tigers 102
'Braddock of the Bombers' 102
'Braddock of the Rocket Squadron' 102
Brainstorm Comix 203, 208
Branson, Richard 195
Brasher, Chris 92
Brazil, Angela 12
Brereton, F. S. 13
Brett, Edwin J. 18
'Brickman' 210
British Board of Film Censors 44
British Board of Film Classification 167
British Comics: An Appraisal 76
British National Council of Teachers for Peace 46
British National Party 256–7
Brock, H. M. 79
'Broken Line, The' 100
Brooker, Matt: see D'Israeli
'Broons, The', 33
Brown, Gordon 199
Brown, James 222
Brown, John 217
Brown, Roy 'Chubby' 220
Browne, Tom 25–6
Brownlow, Jim 216
Bryce-Hamilton, William 86, 110
Bubbles 33
'Buck Ryan' 38
Budiansky, Bob 186
Bulldog Brittain Commando 82, *83*, 95
Bullet 135

Buffalo Bill 81
Bulmer, Ken 98, 178
Bunn, Reg 79, 180
Bunny 222
Bunty 9, 10, 108, 110, 114, 115–17, *117*, 120, 122, 125
Burchill, Julie 9
'Burger Law!' 157
Burns, Mal 225
Burton, Tim 167
Buscema, John 187
Bushell, Gary 219
'Buster Gonad and his Unfeasibly Large Testicles' 217–18
Butterfly 28, 33, 35

C. H. Ross's Variety Paper 23
Cacares, Raulo 252
Cadogan, Mary 116
Caesar, Kurt 98
'Calculus Cat' 214, *215*
Callaghan, James 185
Camelot 183
Campbell, Eddie 209, 210, 222, 243, 244
Campion, Geoff 79, 86, 87, 129, 136
Cannon, Danny 167, 170
Captain 79, 87
Captain Britain 182–9, *184*, *189*
Captain Britain and MI13 198–9
'Captain Clyde' 193
Captain Crab's Tales of Horrific Terror 212
'Captain Flame – Pirate Hunter' 79
'Captain Incontinent' 217
Captain Marvel 50, 81, 104, 175–6
Captain Marvel Jr 175
Captain Midnight 175
Captain Miracle 178
'Captain Starling' 110
Captain Swing and the Electrical Pirates of Cindery Island 251
Captain Valiant 81
Captain Video 81
Carolco 167
Carpenter, Ron 136

Carrie 123
Casey Ruggles Western Comic 50
Casson, Hugh 63
'Chained to his Bat' 91
Champion 29, 34
Chaplin, Charlie 26
'Charley's War' 133–5, *134*
Charlton, Bobby 95
Chattaway, Christopher 92
Chaykin, Howard 150
'Chester P. Hackenbush, Psychedelic Alchemist' 203–4
Chicks' Own 29
Children and Young Persons (Harmful Publications) Act (1955) 10, 52–3, 82, 178
Children's Newspaper 35
Chilton, Charles 69
'China in Crisis' 234
Christopher, John 149
'Chubblock Holmes' 25
Chuckles 28
Chums 79
Church, Doug 145
Churchill, Winston S. 49–51, 67, 95, 97, 98, 257
City Magazines 105, 118
Claremont, Chris, 182, 184, 186, 189
Clarke, Arthur C. 61
'Claude Duval – The Laughing Cavalier' 87
Close Encounters of the Third Kind 144
Cocking, Percy 26
'Cockney Wanker' 221
'Code-Name Warlord' 129
'Coffin Sub, The' 136
Coloured Comic 23
Colquhon, Joe 79, 129, 133, 134
Combat Picture Library 95–6
Comet 76, 77, 78, 81, 84, 85, 87
Comic Cuts 11, 23–5, 29, 33, 35
Comic Home Journal 23, 25
Comic Life 23, 28
Comic Media News 209
Comic News 17

Comic Strip Presents, The 219
Comics and Your Children 48–9, *49*
Comics Campaign Council 46, 48
Comics Code Authority (US) 200
Comics Reporter 196
'comix' 11, 200–9
Commando 10, 78, 95–6, 104, 127, 129, 148, 242, 253
Communist Party of Great Britain 46, 47
'Computer Warrior, The' 152
Cornell, Paul 198
Coulthard, Michael 214
Countdown 107
Cowan, E. George 86
Cowan, Ted, 95, 180
Cowboy Comics Library 78
Cozmic Comics 202, 205
Cracker 29, 33
Craig, Patricia 116
Crécy 252, *252*
Crime Detective 47
Crime Does Not Pay 47, 49
Crisis 11, 166, 223, 224, 231–5, *233*, 239, 240, 249, 253
Crossman, Richard 49
Cruikshank, George 16
Crumb, R. 200, 201
Cunningham, Jack 119
'Cursed Earth, The' 152–3, 157
Cyclone 37
Cyclops 201

DC Comics 198, 231, 240, 243
D. C. Thomson 29–35, 50–51, 78, 88, 95, 104, 108, 115, 117–8, 120, 125–6, 135, 182, 195, 224
D'Antonio, Gino 81
D'Israeli (Matt Brooker) 226, 232, 250
'D-Day Dawson' 130
'D-Day Dodgers' 254
Daily Express 72
Daily Mail 24, 79, 131, 140
Daily Mirror 20, 24, 32, 38–9, 107

295

Daily Sketch 31, 43
Dakin, Glenn 212
Dalyell, Tam 195
Dalziel, Gilbert 18–20, 23
Damnation Alley 153
'Dan Dare' (*2000AD*) 146
Dan Dare (Garth Ennis) 254–7, *255*
Dan Dare on Mars 69
'Dan Dare – Pilot of the Future' 10, 53, 60–70, *62, 64,* 105, 151, 254
Dandy 9, 10, 31–3, 37, 77, 108, 126, 207, 214, 222, 239, 242
'Dancing Life of Moira Kent, The' 116
Daniels, Frank 176
'Dare' 237–9, 249, 254
Daredevils, The 187, 243
Dark Horse Comics 250
Dark Knight Returns, The 232, 240
'Darkie's Mob' 130
Davidge, John 232
Davis, Alan 187, 188
Davy, Huw 222
Dawson, Basil 69
Dawson, Gilbert 92, 102
Dawson, Les 220
Dawson, Paul 7
'Day of the Eagle' 129
Day of the Jackal, The 129
De Laurentiis, Dino 169
De Savary, Paul 145
De Seta, Enrico 81
De Souza, Steven E. 167
Deadline 11, 166, 224–5, 231, 235–7, *237,* 239, 240, 251
'Dear Billy' 254
'Death Factory, The' 234
'Death Game 1999' 136, 141
Death Race 2000 144
'Death Squad' 130–31
Death Wish 141
Debbie 117, 120, 123, 223
Del Orco, Pino 81
Delano, Jamie 188, 240, 250
Demon Seed 154
'Dennis the Menace' 33
Desolation Jones 251
Detective Comics 10, 11, 37, 172

'Detritus Rex' 239
'Devil's Island' 99
Dewhurst, Keith 84, 104
Di Gaspari, Giorgio 81
Diana 108, 117
'Diana and Hopkirk Deceased'
Dick Barton – Special Agent 69
'Dick Turpin's Ride to York' 87
Dillon, Steve 228, 231, 235
'Dire Streets' 237
Dirty Dozen, The 129, 253
Dirty Harry 136
Ditko, Steve 243
Dix, Otto 133
Doc Chaos 193, *194,* 215
Doctor Who 105, 150, 185
'Doctor Who and the Iron Legion' 150, *151*
Doctor Who Weekly 150–51, *151,* 182, 228, 243
Don Winslow of the Navy 81, 175
Donald, Chris 216–8
Dooley, Derek 94
Doom Patrol, The 194, 240, 250
Dope Fiend Funnies 202, 205
Down With Crime 47
Doyle, Richard 17
'Drake of E-Boat Alley' 129
'Dredger' 131, 136, 138–9, 141
Drum, The 88
Duval, Marie (Emilie de Tessier) 19
Dynamic Thrills 81

Eagle (Hulton Press) 9, 10, 11, 45, 53–69, *56, 59, 62, 64,* 73–5, 76, 78, 81, 84, 95, 105, 109, 111, 115, 145, 152, 254
Eagle (IPC) 151–2, 223, 254
Earheart, Amelia 114
Eastwood, Clint 136
Eccles, David 51
Eclipse Comics 192
Eco, Umberto 257
Ede, P. M. 110
Edelman, Maurice 49
Eden, Eric 105, 107

Edginton, Ian 226, 242, 250–51
Education Act (1870) 18
Education Act (1944) 83
Edward's Heave 202, 205
Edwards, Brian 100
Edwards, Owen Dudley 13, 78, 84, 102
Eerie 47
Egmont 166–7
Elliott, Phil 8, 193, 210, 211, 212, 215, 223
Ellis, Warren 11, 242, 251–2, 257
Elton, Ben 219
Embleton, Jerry 151
Embleton, Ron 79, 107
Emerson, Hunt 202, 207, 208, 210, 214, *215,* 222, 225
Emma 120
Ennis, Garth 11, 154, 234, 240, 242, 251, 253–7
Eros Pictures 44
Erskine, Gary 253
Escape 211, 212–16, *215,* 222
Eternal Jew, The 60
Evening Standard 139–40
Ewins, Brett 235
Excalibur 189, 251
Express Newspapers 70
Eyles, Derek 79
Ezquerra, Carlos 129, 145, 149, 232, 253

Fabulous Furry Freak Brothers, The 201
Famous Funnies 11, 37
Fantastic Four, The 251
Fantasy Advertiser 209
Fast Fiction 211, 212, 222
'Fast Fiction' (small press comics) 8, 209–14, *211, 213*
'Fat Slags, The' 219
'Father Shandor – Demon Stalker' 228
Fawcett Publications 81, 175
'Felix and his Amazing Underpants' 217
Fennell, Alan 105
Festival of Britain 58, 63
'Fiends of the Eastern Front' 162

'Fighter for Truth' 55
Film Fun 29, 33–4, 36
Film Picture Stories 29, 87
'Finbarr Saunders and his Double Entendres' 220
Finley-Day, Gerry 129, 136, 162
Finney, Albert 103
Fireball XL5 105
Firm, The 202
'Fists of Danny Pyke, The' 152
'Flash Gordon' 63, 72
Flash Gordon (film) 169
Fleetway Publications 74, 79, 104, 112, 166, 232, 237
'Flesh' 148
Flinders, Evelyn 110
Flynn, Errol 86
Foot, Michael 52
Forbidden Planet 209, 225
Forbin Project, The 154
Ford, John 59
Ford, Murray 23
Fort Apache 59
Foster, Hal 63
'Four Marys, The' 116–17, *117*
Fox, Charles 18
Fox, James 151
Foxwell, Herbert 28
Frankenstein Comic 50
'Fraser of Africa' 75
Friedrich, Gary 187
Fritz the Cat 201
'Frogmen Are Tough' 95
From Hell 10, 222, 243, 244–7, *246*, 251
Frost, Conrad 70
Fuente, Victor 81
Fugitive, The 136
Full Metal Jacket 162
Fun 17
Funnies Album 81
Funny Cuts 23, 25
Funny Folks 17
Funny Wonder 23, 28
Fury 128, 182
Future Quake 222
Futureworld 144

G. I. Joe 82
Gaiman, Neil 11, 162, 192, 215, 240, 242, 250

Galvez, Jorde Badia 119
Garcia, Luis 119
'Garth' 38, 107
Gas 221
Gaskell, Valerie 110
Gawain and the Green Knight 183
Gay Cavalier, The 87
Gebbie, Melinda 243
Gem 12, 29, 34, 35
'General Dies at Dawn, The' 130
'Geoffrey Unsworth and His Dog' 211
'Georgette' 210
Ghostly Weird Stories 47
Ghura, Antonio 204–5
Gibbons, Dave 149, 150, 162, 202, 222, 228, 232, 240, 243, 249, 253
Gibson, Ian 149
Gibson, Melanie 115, 118
'Gideon Stargrave' 225
Gifford, Denis 9, 17, 36, 82, 140, 176, 195, 206–7
Gillray, James 16
Girl 73, 75, 81, 108–15, *113*, 117, 123
Girl's Own Paper 12, 54, 109
Girls' Cinema 29, 35
Girls' Crystal 29, 78, 108, 109, 111
Girls' Weekly 115
Gladstone, William E. 26
Golby, J. M. 22
'Gorgeous Gus' 91
Gosnell, Kelvin 144–5, 150
Grace, W. G. 19, 28
Grand Adventure Comics 37
'Grand Opening of the Intercontinental Fuck-In and Orgy Riot' 202
Grant, Alan 11, 109, 110, 154, 171, 239
Graphixus 224, 225
Gravett, Paul 210, 212
'Graveyard Shift, The' 155
Gray, Lawrence 193
'Great Adventurer, The' 55, 56
Great Game, The 250–51
Green, Crispin 212
Green, Jonathon 201–2
Greene, Richard 86

Grist, Paul 195–7
'Growing-Up of Emma Peel, The' 117
'Guns of Avalon, The' 199
Guardian 146, 221, 236
'Gypsy Granny' 202

Hailsham, Viscount 67
Half Assed Funnies 202
Halfpenny Comic 23
Hamilton, Charles 29, 248
Hampson, Frank 10, 53, 55, 60–69, 74, 254
Hancock, Myra 210, 212, 234
Happy Days 9, 29
'Happy Warrior, The' 57, 95
'Hard Men, The' 152
Hardaker, Alan 140
Harding, Tony 136
'Harlem Heroes' 148, 163
Harley, Don 69
Harmsworth, Alfred (Lord Northcliffe) 11, 18, 23–5, 26, 28
Harmsworth, Harold (Lord Rothermere) 24
'Harris Tweed' 75
Harrison, Harry 72
Harry, Debbie 165
Harvey, Laurence 103
Haunt of Fear 47
Haunt of Fears, A 13, 46
Have Gun, Will Travel 148
Hawkins, Jack 101
Heartbreak Hotel 224, 231, 235
Hebden, Alan 129
Heeley, John 132
'Hell Comes to Birmingham' 199
Hellblazer 250, 253
'Hellman of Hammer Force' 136–7, 141
Hellstorm 251
Henderson, James 18, 19, 23
'Henrietta' 211
Henry V 68
Henty, G. A. 13, 101
Hergé 8, 193
'Heros the Spartan' 75
Herriman, George 214
Hewlett, Jamie 235–6
'Hey Whitey!' 212

Higgins, John 249
Hill Street Blues 195
Hill, Graham 91
Hitman, The 240
Hoe, Richard 17
Hogan, Peter 237
'Hogan's Patrol' 102
Hogarth, William 16
Hoggart, Richard 9–10
Holding, Val 98
Holmes, Edward 70
Holmes, Fred 87
Holt, Richard 92
'Holy Joe Funnies' 206
Home, Earl of, 51
Home-Gall, Edward R. 79
'Hookjaw' 136, 139, 141–3, *142*, 148
Hopcraft, Arthur 84, 102
Hope, Anthony 85
Hopkinson, Tom 54
Hornet 78
'horror comics' 10, 45–53
Horsburgh, Florence 49
Hotspur 12, 30, 78, 104, 107, 125, 127, 182, 223
'House of Dolmann, The' 182
House of Hammer 227, 228
'How to Spot a Dope Fiend' 205
Hubbard, Michael 43
Hughes, Rian 214, 237
Hulk Weekly 229
Hulton Press 54, 73–4, 81, 104, 108
Hunt, Gareth 151
Hunt, Leon 207
Hunter, Jeffrey 72
'Hunters of the Tower of London Traitors' 86
Hurricane 78, 104
Hussein, Saddam 250
Hutchinson, George A. 59
Huxley, Aldous 229
Huxley, David 202, 208

'I Flew with Braddock' 102
Ice Cold in Alex 101
Ice Station Zebra 148
IFG Entertainment 221–2
Ignition City 251, 252
Illustrated Chips 11, 23, *23*, *24–5*

Illustrated London News 16
Image Comics 196, 244
'In Battle with Braddock' 103, *103*
'Inferno' 163
Institute of Contemporary Arts 13
International Times see IT
'Invasion!' 146–8, *147*
Invisibles, The 194, 240, 250
IPC (International Publishing Corporation) 104, 107, 120, 125–7, 135, 140–41, 144–5, 151, 166, 182, 223
Iron Man 251
IT (*International Times* 201
'It's Goals That Count' 91
It's Only Rock'n'Roll Comix 202
'Ivanhoe' 85

'J for Jenny' 254
'Jack O'Lantern' 59
Jack Staff 197–8, *197*
Jackie 110, 117–8
Jackson, John 210
Jag 104
'Jane' 31, *39*, *40*, *41*, 38–44
Jane's Journal 41, 43–4
'Jaspers' Warp' 187
Jaws 136, 139
'Jeff Hawke' 72–3
Jenkins, Roy 52
Jenkinson, Augustus 34–5, 109
Jesse James 50
Jester 29, 35
Jew Süss 60
Jingles 33
Jinty 120, 223
Joe 90 104
'Joe Two Beans' 130
'Johnny Fartpants' 217
'Johnny Nemo' 235
'Johnny Red' 130
'Johnny Tomorrow' 214
Johns, W. E. 63, 102
Johnson, Amy 114
Johnson, Johnny 140
Johnson, Noel 69
Johnson, Shaun 207
Joker 23, 33, 35
Jordan, Sydney 72

'Judge Dredd' 145, 150, 152–60, *153*, *155*, *164*, 171, 253
Judge Dredd (film) 167–71, *168*
Judge Dredd Megazine 160, 170, 242
'Judge Dredd: Origins' 171
Judy (C. H. Ross) 17, 19–20
Judy (D. C. Thomson) 10, 108, 114, 117, 122, 125
June 108, 117
Just Imagine 63
Justice League of America 194, 250

Kane 195
Kaveney, Roz 244
'Kay of the "Courier"' 114
Kay, Peter 220
Kelly's Heroes 129
Kemp, Geoff 136
Kennedy, Cam 129, 253
Keston, Bob 72
Keystone New World Productions 44
Khoury, George 202
'Kids Rule OK' *137*, 140
Killing Joke, The 240, 243
Kim 88
'Kind of Madness, A' 234
Kinema Comic 29
Kinematograph Weekly 44
King and Country 135
'King Cobra' 182
King, Rex 79
King, Rob 225
Kipling, Rudyard 88
Kirby, Jack 243
Kirst, Hans Hellmut 137
'Kitty Hawke' 110, 114
Knight, Stephen 245
Knock-Out 37, 79, *80*, 86
'Komix Comics' 207
'Korky the Cat' 31, 214
'Krazy Kat' 11, 214

Lady Chatterley's Lover 201
Lady Penelope 105, 117
Laid-Back Adventures of Suzie and Jonnie, The 203–5, *203*
Landau, Nick 150, 225, 232
Lane, Diana 168

298

'Lanky Larry and Bloated Bill' 25
Large Cow Comix 202
Larks! 23
'Laser Eraser and Pressbutton' 228
Laskey, Phil 212, 215
Lawrence, Don 79, 176
Le Grand, Jack 140–41, 178
Lea, Charlton 87
Leach, Garry 189, 228, 231
Lear, Edward 211
League of Extraordinary Gentlemen, The 190, 226, 243, 244, 247–9, 257
League of Extraordinary Gentlemen: The Black Dossier, The 248–9
League of Gentlemen, The 196
Lee, Jim 244
Lee, Stan 174–5, 182–3, 243
Leech, John 17
'Legend of Prester John, The' 228
Leighton-Porter, Chrystabel 38, 40, 43–4
'Lenny Left' 219
'Letter from a Democrat' 159
'Leviathan' 250
'Li'l Abner' 31
'Li'l Red Rider' 206
'Limpalong Leslie' 91
Lion 55, 76, 78, 79, 84, 86, 95, 112, 178, *181*, 198
Lippincott, Charles 167
Little Britain 196
'Little Plumb' 222
'Little Willy and Tiny Tim' 28
Livingstone, Malcolm 202, 206
Lloyd, Dan 74
Lloyd, David 209, 228–9, 243, 253
Lloyd, Edward 17
Lloyd George, Gwilym 51
Local Government Act (1988) 236, 244
Lofthouse, Nat 94
Logan's Run 144
London Underground Comics 222
'Lone Commandos, The' 95

Lone Star Magazine 72
Loneliness of the Long Distance Runner, The 93
'Lonesome Lucy' 116–17, 120
'Look out for Lefty!' 140
'Lord Haw-Haw – The Broadcasting Humbug from Hamburg' 37
Lord of the Flies 137
'Lord Snooty' 33
Lost Girls 243, 244
'Lost Pals of 9 Platoon' 95
Love and Rockets 210
Lowder, Chris 136
'Luck of the Legion' 59
Lure of the 'Comics', The 47
Lutterworth Press 54

McCloud, Scott 207
McKeen, Dave 215
McLaglen, Victor 87
McMahon, Mike 145, 239
MacArthur, Douglas 68
Maclean, Catherine 73
MacManus, Steve 150, 162, 166
'M.A.C.H. 1' 146, 148
'Madman' 230
Magnet 12, 29, 34, 35
'Major Eazy' 129, 133, 253
'Makabre' 239
Man Called Kev, A 253
'Man from Nowhere, The' 68–9
Man from U.N.C.L.E., The 105, 180
Man Who Fell to Earth, The 144
'Man Who Was Stuck in a Comic, The' 207
Mandy 108, 117
manga 14, 242, 257
Mankowitz, Wolf 63
Manning, Bernard 220
Marchant, Leslie 43
Marilyn, 118–9
Marks, Beau 167
Mariscal, Javier 214
'Marooned on Mercury' 67
'Marshal Law' 237, 239
Martin, Alan 235–6
Marvel 24, 26
Marvel Comics 128, 150,
174–5, 182–9, 192, 198, 223, 237, 243
Marvel Super-Heroes 187, 243
Marvelman (L. Miller & Co) 176–8
'Marvelman' (Alan Moore) 189–92, *191*, 228, 231, 243
'Marvelman and King Canute' 177
'Marvelman and the Magic Tinder Box' 177
'Marvelman and the Land of Make-Believe' 177–8
'Marvelman and the Spanish Armada' 177, *177*
Marwick, Arthur 77, 118, 201, 202
Mary Marvel 175
'Masked Ballerina, The' *112*
Mason, A.E.W. 88
Mass-Observation 33, 38–40, 111, 114
Matthews, Leonard 79, 87
Matthews, Stanley 91
Mauger, Peter 47
Maus 232
Maxwell, Robert 166, 224, 232
'Mean Arena, The' 163
Medhurst, Andy 220–1
Meltdown 224, 231
Mendoza, Philip 86
Métal Hurlant 225
Metropolis 72
Mickey Mouse Weekly 34
Micron Publishing 95
Midgley, Gerald 210
Mighty World of Marvel, The 151, 182, 187, 231, 243
Millar, Mark 249–50
Miller, Frank 232
Miller, Len 47, 81, 82, 95, 175–6
Miller, Max 220
'Millie Tant' 219
Milligan, Peter 11, 162, 240
Mills, Angie 232
Mills, John 101
Mills, Pat 11, 110, 120, 127, 133–4, 135, 144–5, 150, 153, 154, 162, 232, 237, 239

Milne, A. A. 26
Ministry of Space 251–2
Mirabelle 118–9
Miracleman 10, 192–3
Mirror Group 74, 104, 224
Misty 120, 123
Modern Boy 29, 35
'Modern Parents, The' 219
Monster of Frankenstein 47
Montserrat, Nicholas 97
Moody, J. C. 206
'Moonstone' 123
Moorcock, Michael 225, 226
Moore, Alan 10, 11, 88, 162, 165, 182, 187–8, 189–93, 202, 222, 226, 228–31, 227, 232, 240–41, 242–9, 246, 257
Moore, Bobby 95
Moore, Leah 249
Moore, Roger 145
Moore, Steve 11, 150, 228
More, Kenneth 101
Morris, Marcus 45–6, 53–8, 61, 65, 73–4, 108–11, 115
Morrison, Grant 11, 162, 193–5, 225, 237–9, 240, 242, 249–50, 254
Morrisey 219
Mouly, Françoise 214
'Mrs Brady Old Lady' 218
Muir, Andrew 210
'Musso the Wop' 37
My Guy 123
Myra 210
Myskow, Nina 110
'Mysterioso' 211
'Mystery Man at Inside-Left, The' 91

Nasty Tales 202, 205, 208
National Magazine Company 74
National Periodical Publications 175
National Union of Teachers 46, 51
National Viewers' and Listeners' Association 141
Nationwide 140
Near Myths 224, 224, 225
Neary, Paul 228, 230
'Nemesis' 192–3

'Nemesis the Warlock' 162, 164
Neville, Richard 201
Nevinson, Richard 133
'New Adventures of Adolf Hitler, The' 249
'New Statesmen' 234
New X-Men 194
Newnes, George 18, 23, 79, 87
News of the World 43
Newsinger, John 155, 165
Newton, Trevor 98
Nicolle, Patrick 79, 85, 86, 87
Night of the Busted Nose 215
'Night Raven' 229
'Night Witches, The' 254
'Nightingale' 254
'Nightmare' 159–60
Nikki 224
'Nobbler and Jerry' 25
'Nobby's Piles' 218
Noble, Mike 107
'Norbert Colon' 218
'Norman the Doorman' 218
Nostalgia Comics 209
Nuggets 23
Nyoka the Jungle Girl 81, 175

O'Neill, Kevin 146, 207, 222, 226, 237, 239, 243, 247
Oakley, Shane 249
Odhams Press 74, 104
Ogoth and Ugly Boot 202, 204, 205
Oh Boy 123
Oh! What a Lovely War 135
'One-Eyed Jack' 131
One That Got Away, The 101
Only Fools and Horses 20
'Oor Wullie' 33
'Operation Saturn' 67
'Orphan of the Circus' 115
Ortiz, José 81
Orwell, George 12, 34, 60, 82–3, 220, 229
'Our Ernie' 37
'Our Janie' 122
Oz 201

'Paddy Payne – Warrior of the Skies' 95

'Panzer G-Man' 130
'Parental Drug Abuse: What Every Child Should Know' 205
Paris, Michael 97
Parker, Roy 176
Parkhouse, Steve 150, 228, 230–31
Parlett, George 176
'Pat of Paradise Isle' 111
Paths of Glory 135
Patterson, Willie 72
'Paul Whicker the Tall Vicar' 220
Pavlow, Muriel 65
Pearson, C. A. 19, 23, 95, 118
Pearson, Harry 97
Peg's Paper 115
Pemberton, Max 16
Penalva, Jordi 81, 119
Pennell, Elizabeth 19
Penny 120
'penny dreadfuls' 18
Pepper, Frank S. 8, 10, 79, 93, 95
Periodical Publishers Association 54
Perrier, Arthur 43
Petagno, Joe 202
Pett, Norman, 39–40, 43
Petty, Lori 236
Philips, Sean 240
Pictorial Times 16
Picture Post 47, 54, 55
'picture libraries' 78
Picture Romance Library 118
Picture Stories of World War II 95
Pictures Don't Lie 73
Pinsent, Ed 210, 211, 212
Platoon 162
Play Dirty 129
'Play Till You Drop' 136
Playbox 28
Playhour 75
Pluck 24, 87
'Politics' 159
Poot! 221
'Pop' 31
'Popeye' 31
Popple, Simon 26
Portobello Projects Comic Workshop 209

Pouncey, Edwin 212
Pratt, Hugo 81
Preacher, The 240, 253
'Pride of Lions' 100
'Primitif' 211
'Prince Valiant' 63
Princess 75, 108, 117
'Prisoner of Zenda, The' 85
'Prisoners of Space' 66
Prochnow, Jürgen 169
Promethea 243, 244
Psst! 224, 225, 227
Puck 28, 35
Pumphrey, George 48–9
Punch 16, 17, 20
Punisher, The 253
'Punk Memories' 214
Purdie, John 110
Purdue, A. W. 22
'Purple Days' 237

Quality Comics 81
Quatermass 149

Radio Fun 36, 37
'Rafferty's Own' 88
'Ragamuffin Queen' 115
Rainbow 28, 35
Rambo 167
Randle, Frank 220
'Rat Pack, The' 129, 253
Raven, Charlotte 236
Raw 214
Rawlings, Leo 176
Raymond, Alex 62–3, 72, 79
Rebellion (publisher) 167
'Red Moon Mystery, The' 65, 66
Reed International 141
'Reign of the Robots' 64, 67
'Reivers, The' 254
Religious Tract Society 18, 58–9
Rémi, Georges 8
Reppion, John 249
Responsible Society 141
'Return of the Claw, The' 180
'Return of the Spider, The' 181
'Revolution' 159
Revolver 11, 166, 223, 224, 237–9, *238*, 240, 249, 254

'Rex King' 37
Richards, Frank (Charles Hamilton) 12
'Rick Random and the Space Pirates' 71–2
'Rick Random and the Terror from Space' *73*
'Rick Random and the Threat from Space' 70–71
'Riders of the Range' 59, 75
Ridgway, John 228
'Rip Kirby' 79
Roach, Dave 215
'Road of Courage, The' 60, 74
'Robbie of Red Hall' 111
Robin 73, 75, 81
'Robin Hood and His Merry Men' 86
'Robin Hood and Maid Marian' 86
Robocop 170
'Robot Wars' 158
Rocket 70, 71
Rod Cameron Western 50
Rodriguez, Mañuel 201
'Rogan Gosh' 237
'Roger Mellie – The Man on the Telly' 218
'Rogue Planet' 62, 69
'Rogue Trooper' *162*
Rollerball 136, 144, 148
'romance' comics 118–20
Romantic Confessions Picture Library 118
Romeo 118–19
Rookwood 87
Rosie, George 132
Ross, Charles 19
Rover 12, 30, 37–8, 78, 84, 88, 92–3, 102
Rowley, Geoff 206
Roxy 118–9
'Roy of the Rovers' 10, 93–5, 94
Roy of the Rovers 79, 126, 223
Royal Commission on the Press (1977) 120, 126–7
'Ruggles' 38
'Running Man, The' 136

Sabin, Roger 7, 13–14, 19, 33, 215, 237

'Safari in Space' 69
St Swithin's Day 249
Sally 108
'Sally of Studio Seven' 114
San Francisco Comic Book Company 200
Sanders, John 126–7, 135–6, 140, 145, 146, 166
Sandie 120
Sandman 192, 240
'Sarah in the Shadows' 122
Saturday Night and Sunday Morning 103
Savage, William W. 14
Sayle, Alexei 219
Scarlet Traces 226, 250
Scary Go Round 222
School Friend 12, 35, 78, 108, 109, 111–12, *112*, 114–15, 117, 123
Schoolgirls' Own 29
Schoolgirls' Weekly 29
Schwarzenegger, Arnold 167
Scorcher 126
Scott, Septimus E. 79–80
Scott, Walter 85
Scraps 19
'Second-Hand Sue' 115
'Secret Invasion' 199
'Secret Tunnellers of Calitz Camp, The' 95
'Secret War of Sergeant Braddock, The' 102
Seduction of the Innocent, The 49
Sergeant Fury and His Howling Commandos 97
Sergeant Rock 82, 97
'Sex Warrior' 239
'Shako' 148
'Sharon & Maureen' 210
'Sharp' 235
She Wore A Yellow Ribbon 59
Shelton, Gilbert 201
'Shepherd Boy, The' 57
Sheridan, Dinah 65
Shrubb, Alf 92
'Sid the Sexist' 219
Siegel, Jerry 181
'Silent Three, The' 111–12
Silicon Fish 209
Six-Gun Heroes 81
Six Million Dollar Man, The 148

Sketch 26
'Skid Solo' 91
Skinn, Dez 8, 227–8, 230, 231
Skipper 30, 35, *36*, 78
'Sláine' 162
'Slaughterbowl' 163
'Slaves of the Hot Stove' 121
'Slaves of War Orphan Farm' 117, 120–21, *121*
Slick Fun 37
'Slick Steele of the Secret Service' 37
Small Killing, A 244
Small Zone 222
Smith, John 234
Smut 221
Snap Shots 23
Society for Christian Publicity 45
Sola, Ramon 136
Solar Wind 222
Soskice, Frank 52
'Sound the Alarm' 101
'Space Ace' 72
Space Comics 70
Space Commander Kerry 81
Space Commando 70
Space Hero 70
Spawn 244
Speakeasy 209
'Specky Twat' 219
Spellbound 120, 123
'Spinball Warriors, The' 131
'Spider, The' 178, 180–82, *181*
Spiegelman, Art 214, 232
Spielberg, Steven 257
'Spies of Spain' 86
'Spiral Path, The' 228
Spirit, The 81
Spit 221
'Spoilt Bastard' 218
'Spotlight on Sally' 43
Spy Smasher 81, 175
Stallone, Sylvester 167–8
Stanbury, Peter 212
Star-Rocket 70
Star Trek – The Motion Picture 167, 235
Star Wars 144, 149, 150, 167, 235
Star Wars Weekly 150, 182
Starburst 227

Starlord 148, 150, 162
Starship Troopers 170
'Steel Claw, The' 178–80, *179*
Stewart, Jackie 91
'Stickleback' 250
'Sticky Fingers' 234
'Storm Nelson' 59
'Strange Story, The' 122–3
Streetcomix 202, 208, 222
Stringer, Lew 209, 210, 228
Strip 223, 224, 231, 237
'Strontium Dog' 148, 162–4
'Student Konstabel, The' 234
'Student Grant' 221
'Succuba' 225
Sun (comic) 78, 84, 85
Sun (newspaper) 140, 221
Sunbeam 29, 35
Sunday Dispatch 43, 45–6, 53
Sunday Post 29, 33
Super Detective Picture Library 70, 73, 78
Super-Heroes, The 182
Super-Sonic 70
Super Spider-Man 187
Superman (comic) 175
Superman (film) 225
Supreme 244
Survivors 149
'Susan of St Bride's' 114
'Susie' 43
Sutherland, John 96, 100
Sutherland, Peter 86
Swamp Thing 192, 231, 240, 243
Swan, Gerald G. 37, 81
Swarte, Joost 214
Sweeney, The 141
Swift 73–4, 81, 86

Tacconi, Ferdinando 69, 81
Talbot, Bryan 203–4, 207, 222, 225, 226–7, 227
'Tales from Gimbley' 211, *211*
Tales from the Crypt 47
Tales of the Unexpected 122, 162
Tammy 110, 116, 120–23, *121*, 223
'Tank Girl' 235–7, *235*, 240
Tank Girl (film) 168, 236, 240

'Tankies, The' 254
Tardi, Jacques 214
Target 107
Taylor, A.J.P. 29, 38
Taylor, John 78
Tenniel, John 17
'Terra Nova' 69
'Terry Fuckwitt' 219
'Terry the Twat' 221
'Tess and the Mystery Journey' 111
'Tessa of Television' 114
Thatcher, Margaret 158–9, 219, 226, 234, 249
'Tharg's Future Shocks' 162
Them! 148
'Thieving Gypsy Bastards, The' 221
Things to Come 63
'Third World War' 232–4, *233*, 240
Thomas, Colin 98
Thomas, Leslie 40
Thomas, W. F. 20
Thorpe, David 187, 193, 215
Thrill Comics 37
Thriller Picture Library 78, 79, 81, 85, 87, 95, *96*
Thunderbirds 105, 115
Thunderbolt Jaxon 249
Tiger 10, 78, 79, 91, 93, 112, 162, 223
Tiger Tim's Weekly 29, 35
'Tijuana Bibles' 200
Times, The 24
Times Literary Supplement, The 13, 60
Tiny Tots 29, *30*
Tip Top 29
Tit-Bits 18, 24
Titans, The 182
Todd, Richard 86, 101
Tom Strong 244
Tomlinson, Barry 151
Topical Funnies 37
Topper 9, 10, 77
Total Recall 167, 170
Totleben, John 192
'Tough of the Track, The' 79, 92, *93*
Toxic! 224, 231, 239
'Tracy – Teenage Fashion Model' 114
'Tracy of Tobruk' 99, *99*

Trapps, Holmes & Co. 23
Trashman 201
Trial of Sherlock Holmes, The 249
Trials of Nasty Tales, The 202
Trident Comics 249
Trimpe, Herb 182, 186
'Troubled Souls' 234, 253
Triumph 29, 35
True Crime 47
'Tubby Tucker' 219
Tulloch, John 154
Tully, Tom 79, 95, 162
Turner, Ron 72, 79
TV Action 107
TV Century 21 104–7, *106*
TV Comic 104
TV Express 104
'TV Filth' 207
TV Fun 104
TV Tornado 104
TV Toyland 104
'Twilight's Last Gleaming' 159–60
Tyneside Free Press 216

Ultimate Warrior, The 144
Underground Press Syndicate 200
Understanding Comics 207
Union Jack 24, 87

'V for Vendetta' 10, 228–30, *229*, 240, 243, 244
Vajna, Andrew 167
Valentine 118–9
Valiant 78, 79, 96, 104, 107, 131, 178, *179*, 198
Valley of the Gwangi, The 148
'Vampire State' 199
Varah, Chad 55, 59, 110, 114
Varty, Suzy 207
Vault of Horror 47, 52
Verhoeven, Paul 170
Verne, Jules 61, 72, 247
Vertigo Comics 240
Victor 10, 76, 78, 84, 88, 92–3, *93*, 96, 100, 102–3, 107, 125, 127, 129, 253

'Victorian Dad' 220
View from the Void 202
Violent Cases 215
Virgin Books 217
Virgin Comics 254
Viz 207, 216–22, *218*
Von Sydow, Max 169
'Voyage to Venus' 63–4, 67, 68

W. H. Smith 17, 141, 217
Wagner, John 110, 120, 127, 145, 150, 154, 160, 171, 239
'Waifs of the Wig Maker' 121
Walker, Norman 98
Wallace, Edgar 181
War at Sea Picture Library 95
War Comic 37
War Picture Library 78, 81, 95–6, 98–100, *99*, 127
War Stories 253–4
War of the Worlds, The 248, 250
Warlord 125, 127–9, *128*, 132, 148, 223
Warrior 8, 11, 189, *191*, 192, 224, 226–31, *227*, 251
Watchmen 10, 190, 232, 234, 240, 242, 243, 244, 249
Waterhouse, Keith 33–4
Watkins, Dudley D. 33
Watson, Keith 69
'Weary Willie and Tired Tim' 23–6, *24–5*
Weekly Budget 19
Weird Fun 212, *213*
Welch, Chris 202, 205, 206
Weller, Mike 202, 205
Wells, H. G. 19, 179, 247
'Wendy and Jinx' 112–14, *113*
Wenn, Lennox 110
Wertham, Fredric 7, 49, 174
Western War Comic 81
Western, Mike 79
Weston, Chris 252, 254
Where Eagles Dare 129
'Whip It Out Yet Again' 207

White, Mike 136
Whitford, Joan 110
Whiting, Edward G. 44
Whitlock, John 176
Whiz Comics 81
Wieczorek, Ian 210, 212
WildCATS 244
Wildstorm Comics 251
Williams, Raymond 84
Wilson, Colin 253
Wilson, Harold 105
Wilson, Ron 187
Wilson, S. Clay 201
Wisher, William 167
Wizard 12, 30, 34, 78, 88
'Wolf of Kabul, The' 79, 88
Wolfe, Tom 257
Woman 114
Woman's Own 114
Wonder 29
Wordsworth, William 16–17
World at War, The 128
'World Breast Boxing Championships, The' 207
World's Comic 23, 27
Wright, Bradford W. 14
Wyndham, John 149

X Men 174, 182
Xpresso 224

Yates, Jack Butler 25
'Yellow Kid, The' 11
Young Americans, The 167
Young Marvelman 176, 178
Young Men of Great Britain 18
Young Ones, The 219
Young Romance 118
'Young Wolf' 129
'Youngest Disciple, The' 57

Zap Comix 200
Zeccara, Nevio 81
Zelazney, Roger 153
'Zenith' 193–5, 249
Zero Order 210
Zip Comics 202, 205, *206*
Zit 221
Zomik Comix 202